SUNDAY MISSAL

2010-2011

with Prayers and Hymns

Approved for use in Canada

NOVALIS

©2010 Novalis Publishing Inc.

Novalis Publishing Inc.
10 Lower Spadina Ave., Suite 400
Toronto, ON M5V 2Z2
Canada

Telephone: 1-800-387-7164
Fax: 1-800-204-4140
Email: books@novalis.ca

www.novalis.ca

NOVALIS

Novalis has dedicated itself since 1936 to the development of pastoral resources which assist the People of God in preparing for and participating in the liturgy.

Please write, phone, or visit us for further information on our publications, or visit our website at www.novalis.ca.

For more suggested intentions for the Prayer of the Faithful or to hear the Sunday Psalm, please visit: www.livingwithchrist.ca

Editor-in-chief: Louise Pambrun, email: LWC@novalis.ca

Associate editor: Nancy Keyes

Music editor: Bernadette Gasslein

Psalm settings: © Gordon Johnston/Novalis

Music: All credits accompany the music texts.

Cover design: Blair Turner Communication Design Inc.

Layout: Francine Petitclerc

Photos & illustrations: Benedictine Nuns of Turvey Abbey and McCrimmon Publishing Co. Ltd., 10-12 High Street, Great Wakering, Essex SS3 0EQ www.mccrimmon.com; Crestock; Eugene Kral; Alejandro Ochoa; PhotoDisc; Gene Plaisted; Renaud Thomas

ISBN: 978 289646 281 0

ISSN: 0832-5324

Printed in Canada

We acknowledge the financial support of the Government of Canada through the Book Publishing Industry Development Program (BPIDP) for our publishing activities.

Contents

Dear Readers,

This year 2011 is a time of great celebration for all of us at Novalis, publisher of this Sunday Missal. We are marking the 75th anniversary of our service to Christians in Canada.

You will be able to read more about our history in the following pages. For the moment, I would just like to highlight the most important people involved in our long ministry — you. If not for your own expressed desire to follow the Eucharist more closely, delve more deeply into Scripture and love our God more dearly (my apologies to Saint Richard of Chichester), our Sunday Missal and its many related publications would not exist.

It is because of you — in particular lay Catholics across the country — that the Catholic Centre was founded in Ottawa and that the organization that eventually became Novalis found creative and yet authoritative ways to engage the laity in the sacramental life of the Church. It is because of you that this Sunday Missal began publication 25 years ago. And it is because of you that we continue to bring fresh and thoughtful Christian reflections on Scripture to our readers every year.

In the years ahead, we will continue to ensure that this missal reflects solid scholarship and the direction of our Church in our efforts to deepen our love for and understanding of the Eucharist.

A profound thank you to you, our readers, from all of us at Novalis Publishing. And God bless.

Joseph Sinasac
Publishing Director
Novalis

***Dear Friends of* Living with Christ,**

Seventy-five years ago, in December 1935, Father André Guay, OMI, founded The Catholic Centre at the University of Ottawa. Established during the Depression, the Centre sought to respond to the social and spiritual needs of ordinary, working-class Catholics of the Ottawa Diocese.

Within six months, with the help of professors and students, the Centre launched its first liturgical project: to provide leaflets at church doors on Sunday mornings. In the leaflet was the Mass of the day in English or French, depending on the parish, so that church-goers could more readily participate in the Latin liturgy. At 1¢ each, these pamphlets 'sold like hot-cakes'!

Almost thirty years later, the Second Vatican Council opened in October 1962, and the Constitution on the Sacred Liturgy (*Sacrosanctum Concilium*) followed in 1963. The resulting liturgical reform was grounded in a key phrase from the Constitution on the Sacred Liturgy: "all the faithful should be led to take that full, conscious, and active part in liturgical celebrations which is demanded by the very nature of the liturgy" (*CSL* §14). This echoed Father Guay's vision and confirmed the importance of The Catholic Centre's mission to help Catholics participate more fully in the Mass.

In September 1969, in keeping with the spirit of the Second Vatican Council and inspired by the New Testament image of Christ sowing seed in the good soil, the Centre changed its name to *Novalis,* a Latin word referring to a ploughed field ready for sowing.

Today, these immensely popular Mass booklets are known as *Living with Christ* and *Prions en Église*. In addition to the Canadian editions, the missalettes are available in the United States and in French-speaking Europe.

The *Living with Christ Sunday Missal* that you are holding is an annual edition, launched in 1986, and celebrating its 25th anniversary. It has become a perennial best-seller, produced cover-to-cover in Canada, by Canadians, for Canadians.

Besides the well-known monthly missalettes, in regular and large-print editions, other *Living with Christ* products include: the *Living with Christ Sunday Missal for Young Catholics;* the three-volume *Living with Christ Psalms for the Liturgical Year;* as well as special occasion issues such as World Youth Day (Toronto, 2002), the International Eucharistic Congress (Quebec City, 2008), and the Celebration of the Canonization of Brother André (Montreal, 2010).

In 2008, the Oblates of Mary Immaculate and Saint Paul University entrusted Novalis to Bayard Press Canada, an apostolic work of the Augustinian Fathers of the Assumption. As we celebrate 75 years of publishing and 25 years of the *Living with Christ Sunday Missal*, we at Novalis remain committed to the goals of Father Guay, our founder: "To create and publish material which allows people to better understand their faith and integrate it into daily life."

Louise Pambrun, Editor
www.livingwithchrist.ca

INTRODUCTORY RITES

ENTRANCE ANTIPHON

(Turn to the appropriate day)

GREETING

In the name of the Father, and of the Son, and of the Holy Spirit. **Amen**.

1   The grace of our Lord Jesus Christ and the love of God and the fellowship of the Holy Spirit be with you all. **And also with you.**

2   The grace and peace of God our Father and the Lord Jesus Christ be with you. **And also with you.**

3   The Lord be with you. **And also with you.**

RITE OF BLESSING AND SPRINKLING HOLY WATER (*or* PENITENTIAL RITE, *p. 9*)

Dear friends, this water will be used to remind us of our baptism. Ask God to bless it, and to keep us faithful to the Spirit he has given us.

1   God our Father, your gift of water brings life and freshness to the earth; it washes away our sins and brings us eternal life.

We ask you now to bless this water, and to give us your protection on this day which you have made your own. Renew the living spring of your life within us and protect us in spirit and body, that we may be free from sin and come into your presence to receive your gift of salvation. We ask this through Christ our Lord.

2   Lord God almighty, creator of all life, of body and soul, we ask you to bless this water: as we use it in faith, forgive our sins and save us from all illness and the power of evil.

Lord, in your mercy give us living water, always springing up as a fountain of salvation: free us, body and soul, from every danger, and admit us to your presence in purity of heart. Grant this through Christ our Lord.

3   *During the Easter season:*
Lord God almighty, hear the prayers of your people: we celebrate our creation and redemption. Hear our prayers and bless this water which gives fruitfulness to the fields, and refreshment and cleansing to us. You chose water to show your goodness when you led your people to freedom through the Red Sea and satisfied their thirst in the desert with water from the rock. Water was the symbol used by the prophets to foretell your new covenant with us. You made the water of baptism holy by Christ's baptism in the Jordan: by it you give us a new birth and renew us in holiness. May this water remind us of our baptism and let us share the joy of all who have been baptized at Easter. We ask this through Christ our Lord.

Where it is customary to bless salt also, add:

Almighty God, we ask you to bless this salt as once you blessed the salt scattered over the water by the prophet Elisha. Wherever this salt and water are sprinkled, drive away the power of evil, and protect us always by the presence of your Holy Spirit. Grant this through Christ our Lord.

During the sprinkling, an appropriate song may be sung.

May almighty God cleanse us of our sins, and through the eucharist we celebrate make us worthy to sit at his table in his heavenly kingdom. **Amen.**

(Turn to the GLORY TO GOD, *p. 12)*

PENITENTIAL RITE

My brothers and sisters, to prepare ourselves to celebrate the sacred mysteries, let us call to mind our sins.

1 **I confess to almighty God, and to you, my brothers and sisters, that I have sinned through my own fault, in my thoughts and in my words, in what I have done, and in what I have failed to do; and I ask blessed Mary, ever virgin, all the angels and saints, and you, my brothers and sisters, to pray for me to the Lord our God.**

May almighty God have mercy on us, forgive us our sins, and bring us to everlasting life. **Amen.**

Lord, have mercy. **Lord, have mercy.**

Christ, have mercy. **Christ, have mercy.**

Lord, have mercy. **Lord, have mercy.**

2 Lord, we have sinned against you: Lord, have mercy. **Lord, have mercy.**

Lord, show us your mercy and love. **And grant us your salvation.**

May almighty God have mercy on us, forgive us our sins, and bring us to everlasting life. **Amen.**

3a You were sent to heal the contrite: Lord, have mercy. **Lord, have mercy.**

You came to call sinners: Christ, have mercy. **Christ, have mercy.**

You plead for us at the right hand of the Father: Lord, have mercy. **Lord, have mercy.**

May almighty God have mercy on us, forgive us our sins, and bring us to everlasting life. **Amen.**

3b Lord Jesus, you came to reconcile us to one another and to the Father: Lord, have mercy. **Lord, have mercy.**

Lord Jesus, you heal the wounds of sin and division: Christ, have mercy. **Christ, have mercy.**

Lord Jesus, you intercede for us with your Father: Lord, have mercy. **Lord, have mercy.**

May almighty God have mercy on us, forgive us our sins, and bring us to everlasting life. **Amen.**

3c You raise the dead to life in the Spirit: Lord, have mercy. **Lord, have mercy.**

You bring pardon and peace to the sinner: Christ, have mercy. **Christ, have mercy.**

You bring light to those in darkness: Lord, have mercy. **Lord, have mercy.**

May almighty God have mercy on us, forgive us our sins, and bring us to everlasting life. **Amen.**

3d Lord Jesus, you raise us to new life: Lord, have mercy. **Lord, have mercy.**

Lord Jesus, you forgive us our sins: Christ, have mercy. **Christ, have mercy.**

Lord Jesus, you feed us with your body and blood: Lord, have mercy. **Lord, have mercy.**

May almighty God have mercy on us, forgive us our sins, and bring us to everlasting life. **Amen.**

3e Lord Jesus, you healed the sick: Lord, have mercy. **Lord, have mercy.**

Lord Jesus, you forgave sinners: Christ, have mercy. **Christ, have mercy.**

Lord Jesus, you give us yourself to heal us and bring us strength: Lord, have mercy. **Lord, have mercy.**

May almighty God have mercy on us, forgive us our sins, and bring us to everlasting life. **Amen.**

GLORY TO GOD

Omitted during Advent and Lent.

Glory to God in the highest, and peace to his people on earth.

Lord God, heavenly King, almighty God and Father, we worship you, we give you thanks, we praise you for your glory.

Lord Jesus Christ, only Son of the Father, Lord God, Lamb of God, you take away the sin of the world: have mercy on us; you are seated at the right hand of the Father: receive our prayer.

For you alone are the Holy One, you alone are the Lord, you alone are the Most High, Jesus Christ, with the Holy Spirit, in the glory of God the Father. Amen.

OPENING PRAYER   *(Turn to the appropriate day)*

LITURGY OF THE WORD

READINGS *(Turn to the appropriate day)*

HOMILY

PROFESSION OF FAITH: APOSTLES' CREED

I believe in God, the Father almighty, creator of heaven and earth.

I believe in Jesus Christ, his only Son, our Lord. He was conceived by the power of the Holy Spirit and born of the Virgin Mary.

He suffered under Pontius Pilate, was crucified, died, and was buried. He descended to the dead. On the third day he rose again. He ascended into heaven, and is seated at the right hand of the Father. He will come again to judge the living and the dead.

I believe in the Holy Spirit, the holy catholic Church, the communion of saints, the forgiveness of sins, the resurrection of the body, and the life everlasting. Amen.

PROFESSION OF FAITH: NICENE CREED

We believe in one God, the Father, the almighty, maker of heaven and earth, of all that is seen and unseen.

We believe in one Lord, Jesus Christ, the only Son of God, eternally begotten of the Father, God from God, Light from Light, true God from true God, begotten, not made, one in Being with the Father. Through him all things were made. For us men and for our salvation he came down from heaven: by the power of the Holy Spirit he was born of the Virgin Mary, and became man. For our sake he was crucified under Pontius Pilate; he suffered, died, and was buried. On the third day he rose again in fulfillment of the Scriptures; he ascended into heaven and is seated at the right hand of the Father. He will come again in glory to judge the living and the dead, and his kingdom will have no end.

We believe in the Holy Spirit, the Lord, the giver of life, who proceeds from the Father and the Son. With the Father and the Son he is worshipped and glorified. He has spoken through the Prophets.

We believe in one holy catholic and apostolic Church. We acknowledge one baptism for the forgiveness of sins. We look for the resurrection of the dead, and the life of the world to come. Amen.

PRAYER OF THE FAITHFUL

(Turn to the appropriate day)

Liturgy of the Eucharist

PREPARATION OF THE GIFTS

Blessed are you, Lord, God of all creation. Through your goodness we have this bread to offer, which earth has given and human hands have made. It will become for us the bread of life.

Blessed be God for ever.

> By the mystery of this water and wine may we come to share in the divinity of Christ, who humbled himself to share in our humanity.

Blessed are you, Lord, God of all creation. Through your goodness we have this wine to offer, fruit of the vine and work of human hands. It will become our spiritual drink.

Blessed be God for ever.

> Lord God, we ask you to receive us and be pleased with the sacrifice we offer you with humble and contrite hearts. Lord, wash away my iniquity; cleanse me from my sin.

Pray, friends, that our sacrifice may be acceptable to God, the almighty Father.

May the Lord accept the sacrifice at your hands for the praise and glory of his name, for our good, and the good of all his Church.

PRAYER OVER THE GIFTS

(Turn to the appropriate day)

EUCHARISTIC PRAYER

The Lord be with you. **And also with you.**

Lift up your hearts. **We lift them up to the Lord.**

Let us give thanks to the Lord our God. **It is right to give him thanks and praise.**

PREFACES

The priest selects an appropriate preface. Masses of Reconciliation, Children's Masses and Masses for Various Needs and Occasions incorporate specific prefaces.

ADVENT I

Father, all-powerful and ever-living God, we do well always and everywhere to give you thanks through Jesus Christ our Lord.

When he humbled himself to come among us as a human being, he fulfilled the plan you formed long ago and opened for us the way to salvation. Now we watch for the day, hoping that the salvation promised us will be ours when Christ our Lord will come again in his glory.

And so, with all the choirs of angels in heaven we proclaim your glory and join in their unending hymn of praise: **Holy, Holy** *(p. 33)*

ADVENT II

Father, all-powerful and ever-living God, we do well always and everywhere to give you thanks through Jesus Christ our Lord.

His future coming was proclaimed by all the prophets. The virgin mother bore him in her womb with love beyond all telling. John the Baptist was his herald and made him known when at last he came. In his love Christ has filled us with joy as we prepare to celebrate his birth, so that when he comes he may find us watching in prayer, our hearts filled with wonder and praise.

And so, with all the choirs of angels in heaven, we proclaim your glory and join in their unending hymn of praise: **Holy, Holy** *(p. 33)*

CHRISTMAS I

Father, all-powerful and ever-living God, we do well always and everywhere to give you thanks through Jesus Christ our Lord.

In the wonder of the incarnation your eternal Word has brought to the eyes of faith a new and radiant vision of your glory. In him we see our God made visible and so are caught up in love of the God we cannot see.

And so, with all the choirs of angels in heaven, we proclaim your glory and join in their unending hymn of praise: **Holy, Holy** *(p. 33)*

CHRISTMAS II

Father, all-powerful and ever-living God, we do well always and everywhere to give you thanks through Jesus Christ our Lord.

Today you fill our hearts with joy as we recognize in Christ the revelation of your love. No eye can see his glory as our God, yet now he is seen as one like us. Christ is your Son before all ages, yet now he is born in time. He has come to lift up all things to himself, to restore unity to creation, and to lead us from exile into your heavenly kingdom.

With all the angels of heaven we sing our joyful hymn of praise: **Holy, Holy** *(p. 33)*

CHRISTMAS III

Father, all-powerful and ever-living God, we do well always and everywhere to give you thanks through Jesus Christ our Lord.

Today in him a new light has dawned upon the world: God has become one with humanity, and we have become one again with God. Your Eternal Word has taken upon himself our human weakness, giving our mortal nature immortal value. So marvellous is this oneness between God and humanity that Christ our brother restores the gift of everlasting life to his brothers and sisters.

In our joy we sing to your glory with all the choirs of angels: **Holy, Holy** *(p. 33)*

BLESSED VIRGIN MARY I

Father, all-powerful and ever-living God, we do well always and everywhere to give you thanks as we celebrate the motherhood of the Blessed Virgin Mary.

Through the power of the Holy Spirit, she became the virgin mother of your only Son, our Lord Jesus Christ, who is for ever the light of the world.

Through him the choirs of angels and all the powers of heaven, praise and worship your glory. May our voices blend with theirs as we join in their unending hymn: **Holy, Holy** *(p. 33)*

EPIPHANY

Father, all-powerful and ever-living God, we do well always and everywhere to give you thanks.

Today you revealed in Christ your eternal plan of salvation and showed him as the light of all peoples. Now that his glory has shone among us you have renewed humanity in his immortal image.

Now, with angels and archangels, and the whole company of heaven, we sing the unending hymn of your praise: **Holy, Holy** *(p. 33)*

BAPTISM OF THE LORD

Father, all-powerful and ever-living God, we do well always and everywhere to give you thanks.

You celebrated your new gift of baptism by signs and wonders at the Jordan. Your voice was heard from heaven to awaken faith in the presence among us of the Word made flesh. Your Spirit was seen as a dove, revealing Jesus as your servant, and anointing him with joy as the Christ, sent to bring to the poor the good news of salvation.

In our unending joy we echo on earth the song of the angels in heaven as they praise your glory for ever: **Holy, Holy** *(p. 33)*

SUNDAYS IN ORDINARY TIME I

Father, all-powerful and ever-living God, we do well always and everywhere to give you thanks through Jesus Christ our Lord.

Through his cross and resurrection he freed us from sin and death and called us to the glory that has made us a chosen race, a royal priesthood, a holy nation, a people set apart.

Everywhere we proclaim your mighty works, for you have called us out of darkness into your own wonderful light.

And so, with all the choirs of angels in heaven, we proclaim your glory and join in their unending hymn of praise: **Holy, Holy** *(p. 33)*

SUNDAYS IN ORDINARY TIME II

Father, all-powerful and ever-living God, we do well always and everywhere to give you thanks through Jesus Christ our Lord.

Out of love for sinners, he humbled himself to be born of the Virgin. By suffering on the cross he freed us from unending death, and by rising from the dead he gave us eternal life.

And so, with all the choirs of angels in heaven, we proclaim your glory and join in their unending hymn of praise: **Holy, Holy** *(p. 33)*

SUNDAYS IN ORDINARY TIME III

Father, all-powerful and ever-living God, we do well always and everywhere to give you thanks.

We see your infinite power in your loving plan of salvation. You came to our rescue by your power as

God, but you wanted us to be saved by one like us. The human family refused your friendship, but it was restored by our Lord and brother Jesus Christ.

Through him the angels of heaven offer their prayer of adoration as they rejoice in your presence for ever. May our voices be one with theirs in their triumphant hymn of praise: **Holy, Holy** *(p. 33)*

SUNDAYS IN ORDINARY TIME IV

Father, all-powerful and ever-living God, we do well always and everywhere to give you thanks through Jesus Christ our Lord.

By his birth we are reborn. In his suffering we are freed from sin. By his rising from the dead we rise to everlasting life. In his return to you in glory we enter into your heavenly kingdom.

And so, we join the angels and the saints as they sing their unending hymn of praise: **Holy, Holy** *(p. 33)*

SUNDAYS IN ORDINARY TIME V

Father, all-powerful and ever-living God, we do well always and everywhere to give you thanks.

All things are of your making, all times and seasons obey your laws, but you chose to create us in your own image, setting us over the whole world in all its wonder. You made us the stewards of creation, to praise you day by day for the marvels of your wisdom and power, through Jesus Christ our Lord.

We praise you, Lord, with all the angels in their song of joy: **Holy, Holy** *(p. 33)*

SUNDAYS IN ORDINARY TIME VI

Father, all-powerful and ever-living God, we do well always and everywhere to give you thanks.

In you we live and move and have our being. Each day you show us a Father's love; your Holy Spirit, dwelling within us, gives us on earth the hope of unending joy. Your gift of the Spirit, who raised Jesus from the dead, is the foretaste and promise of the paschal feast of heaven.

With thankful praise, in company with the angels, we glorify the wonders of your power: **Holy, Holy** *(p. 33)*

SUNDAYS IN ORDINARY TIME VII

Father, all-powerful and ever-living God, we do well always and everywhere to give you thanks.

So great was your love that you gave us your Son as our redeemer. You sent him as one like ourselves, though free from sin, that you might see and love in us what you see and love in Christ. Your gifts of grace, lost by disobedience, are now restored by the obedience of your Son.

We praise you, Lord, with all the angels and saints in their song of joy: **Holy, Holy** *(p. 33)*

SUNDAYS IN ORDINARY TIME VIII

Father, all-powerful and ever-living God, we do well always and everywhere to give you thanks.

When your children sinned and wandered far from your friendship, you reunited them with yourself through the blood of your Son and the power of the Holy Spirit. You gather them into your Church, to be one as you, Father, are one with your Son and the Holy Spirit. You call them to be your people, to praise your wisdom in all your works. You make them the body of Christ and the dwelling-place of the Holy Spirit.

In our joy we sing to your glory with all the choirs of angels: **Holy, Holy** *(p. 33)*

CHRISTIAN UNITY

Father, all-powerful and ever-living God, we do well always and everywhere to give you thanks through Jesus Christ our Lord.

Through Christ you bring us to the knowledge of your truth, that we may be united by one faith and one baptism to become his body. Through Christ you have given the Holy Spirit to all peoples.

How wonderful are the works of the Spirit, revealed in so many gifts! Yet how marvellous is the unity the Spirit creates from their diversity, as he dwells in the hearts of your children, filling the whole Church with his presence and guiding it with his wisdom!

In our joy we sing to your glory with all the choirs of angels: **Holy, Holy** *(p. 33)*

LENT I

Father, all-powerful and ever-living God, we do well always and everywhere to give you thanks through Jesus Christ our Lord.

Each year you give us this joyful season when we prepare to celebrate the paschal mystery with mind and heart renewed. You give us a spirit of loving reverence for you, our Father, and of willing service to our neighbour. As we recall the great events that gave us new life in Christ, you bring the image of your Son to perfection within us.

Now, with angels and archangels, and the whole company of heaven, we sing the unending hymn of your praise: **Holy, Holy** *(p. 33)*

LENT II

Father, all-powerful and ever-living God, we do well always and everywhere to give you thanks.

This great season of grace is your gift to your family to renew us in spirit. You give us strength to purify our hearts, to control our desires, and so to serve you in freedom. You teach us how to live in this passing world, with our heart set on the world that will never end.

Now, with all the saints and angels, we praise you for ever: **Holy, Holy** *(p. 33)*

LENT IV

Father, all-powerful and ever-living God, we do well always and everywhere to give you thanks.

Through our observance of Lent you correct our faults and raise our minds to you, you help us grow in holiness and offer us the reward of everlasting life through Jesus Christ our Lord.

Through him the angels and all the choirs of heaven worship in awe before your presence. May our voices be one with theirs as they sing with joy the hymn of your glory: **Holy, Holy** *(p. 33)*

FIRST SUNDAY OF LENT

Father, all-powerful and ever-living God, we do well always and everywhere to give you thanks through Jesus Christ our Lord.

His fast of forty days makes this a holy season of self-denial. By rejecting the devil's temptations he has taught us to rid ourselves of the hidden corruption of evil, and so to share his paschal meal in purity of heart, until we come to its fulfillment in the promised land of heaven.

Now we join the angels and the saints as they sing their unending hymn of praise: **Holy, Holy** *(p. 33)*

SECOND SUNDAY OF LENT

Father, all-powerful and ever-living God, we do well always and everywhere to give you thanks through Jesus Christ our Lord.

On your holy mountain he revealed himself in glory in the presence of his disciples. He had already prepared them for his approaching death. He wanted to teach them through the Law and the Prophets that the promised Christ had first to suffer and so come to the glory of his resurrection.

In our unending joy we echo on earth the song of the angels in heaven as they praise your glory for ever: **Holy, Holy** *(p. 33)*

THIRD SUNDAY OF LENT

Father, all-powerful and ever-living God, we do well always and everywhere to give you thanks, through Jesus Christ our Lord.

When he asked the woman of Samaria for water to drink, Christ had already prepared for her the gift of faith. In his thirst to receive her faith he awakened in her heart the fire of your love.

With thankful praise, in company with the angels, we glorify the wonders of your power: **Holy, Holy** *(p. 33)*

FOURTH SUNDAY OF LENT

Father, all-powerful and ever-living God, we do well always and everywhere to give you thanks, through Jesus Christ our Lord.

He came among us as a man, to lead us from darkness into the light of faith. Through Adam's fall we were born as slaves of sin, but now through baptism in Christ we are reborn as your adopted children.

Earth unites with heaven to sing the new song of creation, as we adore and praise you for ever: **Holy, Holy** *(p. 33)*

FIFTH SUNDAY OF LENT

Father, all-powerful and ever-living God, we do well always and everywhere to give you thanks, through Jesus Christ our Lord.

As a man like us, Jesus wept for Lazarus his friend. As the eternal God, he raised Lazarus from the dead. In his love for us all, Christ gives us the sacraments to lift us up to everlasting life.

Through him the angels of heaven offer their prayer of adoration as they rejoice in your presence for ever. May our voices be one with theirs in their triumphant hymn of praise: **Holy, Holy** *(p. 33)*

PASSION SUNDAY

Father, all-powerful and ever-living God, we do well always and everywhere to give you thanks through Jesus Christ our Lord.

Though he was sinless, he suffered willingly for sinners. Though innocent, he accepted death to save the guilty. By his dying he has destroyed our sins. By his rising he has raised us up to holiness of life.

We praise you, Lord, with all the angels in their song of joy: **Holy, Holy** *(p. 33)*

EASTER I

Father, all-powerful and ever-living God, we do well always and everywhere to give you thanks through Jesus Christ our Lord.

We praise you with greater joy than ever on this Easter night (day), when Christ became our paschal sacrifice. He is the true Lamb who took away the sins of the world. By dying he destroyed our death; by rising he restored our life.

And so, with all the choirs of angels in heaven we proclaim your glory and join in their unending hymn of praise: **Holy, Holy** *(p. 33)*

EASTER II

Father, all-powerful and ever-living God, we do well always and everywhere to give you thanks through Jesus Christ our Lord.

We praise you with greater joy than ever in this Easter season, when Christ became our paschal sacrifice. He has made us children of the light, rising to new and everlasting life. He has opened the gates of heaven to receive his faithful people. His death is our ransom from death; his resurrection is our rising to life.

The joy of the resurrection renews the whole world, while the choirs of heaven sing for ever to your glory: **Holy, Holy** *(p. 33)*

EASTER III

Father, all-powerful and ever-living God, we do well always and everywhere to give you thanks through Jesus Christ our Lord.

We praise you with greater joy than ever in this Easter season, when Christ became our paschal sacrifice. He is still our priest, our advocate who always pleads our cause. Christ is the victim who dies no more, the Lamb, once slain, who lives for ever.

The joy of the resurrection renews the whole world, while the choirs of heaven sing for ever to your glory: **Holy, Holy** *(p. 33)*

EASTER IV

Father, all-powerful and ever-living God, we do well always and everywhere to give you thanks through Jesus Christ our Lord.

We praise you with greater joy than ever in this Easter season, when Christ became our paschal sacrifice. In him a new age has dawned, the long reign of sin is ended, a broken world has been renewed, and we are once again made whole.

The joy of the resurrection renews the whole world, while the choirs of heaven sing for ever to your glory: **Holy, Holy** *(p. 33)*

EASTER V

Father, all-powerful and ever-living God, we do well always and everywhere to give you thanks through Jesus Christ our Lord.

We praise you with greater joy than ever in this Easter season, when Christ became our paschal sacrifice. As he offered his body on the cross, his perfect sacrifice fulfilled all others. As he gave himself into your hands for our salvation, he showed himself to be the priest, the altar, and the lamb of sacrifice.

The joy of the resurrection renews the whole world, while the choirs of heaven sing for ever to your glory: **Holy, Holy** *(p. 33)*

ASCENSION I

Father, all-powerful and ever-living God, we do well always and everywhere to give you thanks.

Today the Lord Jesus, the king of glory, the conqueror of sin and death, ascended to heaven while the angels sang his praises. Christ, the mediator between God and man, judge of the world and Lord of all, has passed beyond our sight, not to abandon us but to be our hope. Christ is the beginning, the head of the Church; where he has gone, we hope to follow.

The joy of the resurrection and ascension renews the whole world, while the choirs of heaven sing for ever to your glory: **Holy, Holy** *(p. 33)*

ASCENSION II

Father, all-powerful and ever-living God, we do well always and everywhere to give you thanks through Jesus Christ our Lord.

In his risen body he plainly showed himself to his disciples and was taken up to heaven in their sight to claim for us a share in his divine life.

And so, with all the choirs of angels in heaven, we proclaim your glory and join in their unending hymn of praise: **Holy, Holy** *(p. 33)*

PENTECOST

Father, all-powerful and ever-living God, we do well always and everywhere to give you thanks.

Today you sent the Holy Spirit on those marked out to be your children by sharing the life of your only Son, and so you brought the paschal mystery to its completion.

Today we celebrate the great beginnings of your Church when the Holy Spirit made known to all peoples the one true God, and created from the many languages of earth one voice to profess one faith.

The joy of the resurrection renews the whole world, while the choirs of heaven sing for ever to your glory: **Holy, Holy** *(p. 33)*

TRINITY

Father, all-powerful and ever-living God, we do well always and everywhere to give you thanks.

We joyfully proclaim our faith in the mystery of your Godhead. You have revealed your glory as the glory also of your Son and of the Holy Spirit: three Persons equal in majesty, undivided in splendour, yet one Lord, one God, ever to be adored in your everlasting glory.

And so, with all the choirs of angels in heaven, we proclaim your glory and join in their unending hymn of praise: **Holy, Holy** *(p. 33)*

HOLY EUCHARIST I

Father, all-powerful and ever-living God, we do well always and everywhere to give you thanks through Jesus Christ our Lord.

He is the true and eternal priest who established this unending sacrifice. He offered himself as a victim for our deliverance and taught us to make this offering in his memory. As we eat his body which he gave for us, we grow in strength. As we drink his blood which he poured out for us, we are washed clean.

Now, with angels and archangels, and the whole company of heaven, we sing the unending hymn of your praise: **Holy, Holy** *(p. 33)*

HOLY EUCHARIST II

Father, all-powerful and ever-living God, we do well always and everywhere to give you thanks through Jesus Christ our Lord.

At the last supper, as he sat at table with his apostles, he offered himself to you as the spotless lamb, the acceptable gift that gives you perfect praise. Christ has given us this memorial of his passion to bring us its saving power until the end of time. In this great sacrament you feed your people and strengthen them in holiness, so that the human family may come to walk in the light of one faith, in one communion of love. We come then to this wonderful sacrament to be fed at your table and grow into the likeness of the risen Christ.

Earth unites with heaven to sing the new song of creation as we adore and praise you for ever: **Holy, Holy** *(p. 33)*

CHRIST THE KING

Father, all-powerful and ever-living God, we do well always and everywhere to give you thanks.

You anointed Jesus Christ, your only Son, with the oil of gladness, as the eternal priest and universal king. As priest he offered his life on the altar of the cross and redeemed the human race by this one perfect sacrifice of peace.

As king he claims dominion over all creation, that he may present to you, his almighty Father, an eternal and universal kingdom: a kingdom of truth and life, a kingdom of holiness and grace, a kingdom of justice, love, and peace.

And so, with all the choirs of angels in heaven we proclaim your glory and join in their unending hymn of praise: **Holy, Holy** *(p. 33)*

EUCHARISTIC PRAYER II

Father, it is our duty and our salvation, always and everywhere to give you thanks through your beloved Son, Jesus Christ.

He is the Word through whom you made the universe, the Saviour you sent to redeem us. By the power of the Holy Spirit he took flesh and was born of the Virgin Mary. For our sake he opened his arms on the cross; he put an end to death and revealed the resurrection. In this he fulfilled your will and won for you a holy people.

And so we join the angels and the saints in proclaiming your glory as we say: **Holy, Holy** *(p. 33)*

EUCHARISTIC PRAYER IV

Father in heaven, it is right that we should give you thanks and glory: you are the one God, living and true.

Through all eternity you live in unapproachable light. Source of life and goodness, you have created all things, to fill your creatures with every blessing and lead all men to the joyful vision of your light. Countless hosts of angels stand before you to do your will; they look upon your splendour and praise you, night and day.

United with them, and in the name of every creature under heaven, we too praise your glory as we say:

HOLY, HOLY

Holy, holy, holy Lord, God of power and might, heaven and earth are full of your glory. Hosanna in the highest. Blessed is he who comes in the name of the Lord. Hosanna in the highest.

Praise to the Father

We come to you, Father, with praise and thanksgiving, through Jesus Christ your Son. Through him we ask you to accept and bless these gifts we offer you in sacrifice.

For the Church

We offer them for your holy catholic Church. Watch over it, Lord, and guide it; grant it peace and unity throughout the world. We offer them for N., our pope, for N., our bishop, and for all who hold and teach the catholic faith that comes to us from the apostles.

For the living

Remember, Lord, your people, especially those for whom we now pray, N. and N.

> *Christian Initiation (Scrutinies and Baptism):*
> Remember, Lord, these godparents who (will) present your chosen men and women for baptism, N. and N.

Remember all of us gathered here before you. You know how firmly we believe in you and dedicate ourselves to you. We offer you this sacrifice of praise for ourselves and those who are dear to us. We pray to you, our living and true God, for our well-being and redemption.

To honour the saints

In union with the whole Church, we

Christmas and Octave of Christmas:
celebrate that day (night) when Mary without loss of her virginity gave the world its Saviour. We

Epiphany:
celebrate that day when your only Son, sharing your eternal glory, showed himself in a human body. We

Holy Thursday:
celebrate that day when Jesus Christ, our Lord, was betrayed for us. We

Easter Vigil to Second Sunday of Easter:
celebrate that day (night) when Jesus Christ, our Lord, rose from the dead in his human body. We

Ascension:
celebrate that day when your only Son, our Lord, took his place with you and raised our frail human nature to glory. We

Pentecost:
celebrate the day of Pentecost when the Holy Spirit appeared to the apostles in the form of countless tongues. We

honour Mary, the ever-virgin mother of Jesus Christ our Lord and God. We honour Joseph, her husband, the apostles and martyrs Peter and Paul, Andrew,

James, John, Thomas, James, Philip, Bartholomew, Matthew, Simon and Jude; we honour Linus, Cletus, Clement, Sixtus, Cornelius, Cyprian, Lawrence, Chrysogonus, John and Paul, Cosmas and Damian and all the saints. May their merits and prayers gain us your constant help and protection.

Invocation of the Holy Spirit

Father, accept this offering from your whole family.

> *Christian Initiation (Scrutinies):*
> We offer it especially for the men and women you call to share your life through the living waters of baptism.

> *Christian Initiation (Baptism):*
> and from those born into new life by water and the Holy Spirit with all their sins forgiven. Keep them one in Christ Jesus the Lord, and may their names be written in the book of life.

> *Holy Thursday:*
> in memory of the day when Jesus Christ, our Lord, gave the mysteries of his body and blood for his disciples to celebrate.

> *Easter Vigil to Second Sunday of Easter:.*
> and from those born into the new life of water and the Holy Spirit, with all their sins forgiven.

Grant us your peace in this life, save us from final damnation, and count us among those you have chosen.

Bless and approve our offering; make it acceptable to you, an offering in spirit and in truth. Let it become for us the body and blood of Jesus Christ, your only Son, our Lord.

The Lord's Supper

The day before he suffered

Holy Thursday:
to save us and all people, that is today,

he took bread in his sacred hands and looking up
to heaven, to you, his almighty Father, he gave
you thanks and praise. He broke the bread, gave
it to his disciples, and said:

Take this, all of you, and eat it:
this is my body which will be given up for you.

When supper was ended, he took the cup. Again
he gave you thanks and praise, gave the cup to his
disciples, and said:

Take this, all of you, and drink from it:
this is the cup of my blood,
the blood of the new and everlasting covenant.
It will be shed for you and for all
so that sins may be forgiven.
Do this in memory of me.

Memorial Acclamation

1 Let us proclaim the mystery of faith: **Christ has died, Christ is risen, Christ will come again.**

2 Praise to you, Lord Jesus, firstborn from the dead! **Dying you destroyed our death, rising you restored our life. Lord Jesus, come in glory.**

3 We are faithful, Lord, to your command: **When we eat this bread and drink this cup, we proclaim your death, Lord Jesus, until you come in glory.**

4 Christ is Lord of all ages! **Lord, by your cross and resurrection, you have set us free. You are the Saviour of the world.**

Memorial Prayer

Father, we celebrate the memory of Christ, your Son. We, your people and your ministers, recall his passion, his resurrection from the dead, and his ascension into glory; and from the many gifts you have given us we offer to you, God of glory and majesty, this holy and perfect sacrifice: the bread of life and the cup of eternal salvation.

Look with favour on these offerings and accept them as once you accepted the gifts of your servant Abel, the sacrifice of Abraham, our father in faith, and the bread and wine offered by your priest Melchisedech.

Almighty God, we pray that your angel may take this sacrifice to your altar in heaven. Then, as we receive from this altar the sacred body and blood of your Son, let us be filled with every grace and blessing.

For the dead

Remember, Lord, those who have died and have gone before us marked with the sign of faith, especially those for whom we now pray, N. and N.

May these, and all who sleep in Christ, find in your presence light, happiness, and peace.

In communion with the saints

For ourselves, too, we ask some share in the fellowship of your apostles and martyrs, with John the Baptist, Stephen, Matthias, Barnabas,

Ignatius, Alexander, Marcellinus, Peter, Felicity, Perpetua, Agatha, Lucy, Agnes, Cecilia, Anastasia and all the saints. Though we are sinners, we trust in your mercy and love. Do not consider what we truly deserve, but grant us your forgiveness.

Through Christ our Lord you give us all these gifts, you fill them with life and goodness, you bless them and make them holy.

In praise of God

Through him, with him, in him, in the unity of the Holy Spirit, all glory and honour is yours, almighty Father, for ever and ever. **Amen.**

(Turn to the LORD'S PRAYER, *p. 65)*

EUCHARISTIC PRAYER II

Invocation of the Holy Spirit

Lord, you are holy indeed, the fountain of all holiness. Let your Spirit come upon these gifts to make them holy, so that they may become for us the body and blood of our Lord, Jesus Christ.

The Lord's Supper

Before he was given up to death, a death he freely accepted, he took bread and gave you thanks. He broke the bread, gave it to his disciples, and said:

Take this, all of you, and eat it:
this is my body which will be given up for you.

When supper was ended, he took the cup. Again he gave you thanks and praise, gave the cup to his disciples, and said:

Take this, all of you, and drink from it:
this is the cup of my blood,
the blood of the new and everlasting covenant.
It will be shed for you and for all
so that sins may be forgiven.
Do this in memory of me.

Memorial Acclamation

1 Let us proclaim the mystery of faith: **Christ has died, Christ is risen, Christ will come again.**

2 Praise to you, Lord Jesus, firstborn from the dead! **Dying you destroyed our death, rising you restored our life. Lord Jesus, come in glory.**

3 We are faithful, Lord, to your command: **When we eat this bread and drink this cup, we proclaim your death, Lord Jesus, until you come in glory.**

4 Christ is Lord of all ages! **Lord, by your cross and resurrection, you have set us free. You are the Saviour of the world.**

Memorial Prayer

In memory of his death and resurrection, we offer you, Father, this life-giving bread, this saving cup. We thank you for counting us worthy to stand in your presence and serve you. May all of us who share in the body and blood of Christ be brought together in unity by the Holy Spirit.

For the Church

Lord, remember your Church throughout the world; make us grow in love, together with N., our pope, N., our bishop, and all the clergy.

> *Christian Initiation (Baptism):*
> Remember all those who have been baptized (and confirmed) today as members of your family. Help them to follow Christ your Son with loving hearts.

For the dead

Remember our brothers and sisters who have gone to their rest in the hope of rising again; bring them and all the departed into the light of your presence.

In communion with the saints

Have mercy on us all; make us worthy to share eternal life with Mary, the virgin Mother of God, with the apostles, and with all the saints who have done your will throughout the ages. May we praise you in union with them, and give you glory through your Son, Jesus Christ.

In praise of God

Through him, with him, in him, in the unity of the Holy Spirit, all glory and honour is yours, almighty Father, for ever and ever. **Amen.**

(Turn to the LORD'S PRAYER, p. 65)

Praise to the Father

Father, you are holy indeed, and all creation rightly gives you praise. All life, all holiness comes from you through your Son, Jesus Christ our Lord, by the working of the Holy Spirit. From age to age you gather a people to yourself, so that from east to west a perfect offering may be made to the glory of your name.

Invocation of the Holy Spirit

And so, Father, we bring you these gifts. We ask you to make them holy by the power of your Spirit, that they may become the body and blood of your Son, our Lord Jesus Christ, at whose command we celebrate this eucharist.

The Lord's Supper

On the night he was betrayed, he took bread and gave you thanks and praise. He broke the bread, gave it to his disciples, and said:

> Take this, all of you, and eat it:
> this is my body which will be given up for you.

When supper was ended, he took the cup. Again he gave you thanks and praise, gave the cup to his disciples, and said:

> Take this, all of you, and drink from it:
> this is the cup of my blood,
> the blood of the new and everlasting covenant.
> It will be shed for you and for all
> so that sins may be forgiven.
> Do this in memory of me.

Memorial Acclamation

1 Let us proclaim the mystery of faith: **Christ has died, Christ is risen, Christ will come again.**

2 Praise to you, Lord Jesus, firstborn from the dead! **Dying you destroyed our death, rising you restored our life. Lord Jesus, come in glory.**

3 We are faithful, Lord, to your command: **When we eat this bread and drink this cup, we proclaim your death, Lord Jesus, until you come in glory.**

4 Christ is Lord of all ages! **Lord, by your cross and resurrection, you have set us free. You are the Saviour of the world.**

Memorial Prayer

Father, calling to mind the death your Son endured for our salvation, his glorious resurrection and ascension into heaven, and ready to greet him when he comes again, we offer you in thanksgiving this holy and living sacrifice.

Look with favour on your Church's offering, and see the Victim whose death has reconciled us to yourself. Grant that we, who are nourished by his body and blood, may be filled with his Holy Spirit, and become one body, one spirit in Christ.

May he make us an everlasting gift to you and enable us to share in the inheritance of your saints, with Mary, the virgin Mother of God; with the apostles, the martyrs, (Saint N.) and all your saints, on whose constant intercession we rely for help.

For the Church

Lord, may this sacrifice, which has made our peace with you, advance the peace and salvation of all the world. Strengthen in faith and love your pilgrim Church on earth; your servant, Pope N., our bishop N., and all the bishops, with the clergy and the entire people your Son has gained for you. Father, hear the prayers of the family you have gathered here before you.

> *Christian Initiation (Baptism):*
> Strengthen those who have now become your people by the waters of rebirth (and the gift of the Holy Spirit). Help them to walk in newness of life.

In mercy and love unite all your children wherever they may be.

For the dead

Welcome into your kingdom our departed brothers and sisters, and all who have left this world in your friendship. We hope to enjoy for ever the vision of your glory, through Christ our Lord, from whom all good things come.

In praise of God

Through him, with him, in him, in the unity of the Holy Spirit, all glory and honour is yours, almighty Father, for ever and ever. **Amen.**

(Turn to the LORD'S PRAYER, *p. 65)*

Praise to the Father

Father, we acknowledge your greatness: all your actions show your wisdom and love. You formed man in your own likeness and set him over the whole world to serve you, his creator, and to rule over all creatures.

Even when he disobeyed you and lost your friendship you did not abandon him to the power of death, but helped all men to seek and find you. Again and again you offered a covenant to man, and through the prophets taught him to hope for salvation.

Father, you so loved the world that in the fullness of time you sent your only Son to be our Saviour. He was conceived through the power of the Holy Spirit and born of the Virgin Mary, a man like us in all things but sin.

To the poor he proclaimed the good news of salvation, to prisoners, freedom, and to those in sorrow, joy. In fulfillment of your will he gave himself up to death; but by rising from the dead, he destroyed death and restored life.

And that we might live no longer for ourselves but for him, he sent the Holy Spirit from you, Father, as his first gift to those who believe, to complete his work on earth and bring us the fullness of grace.

Invocation of the Holy Spirit

Father, may this Holy Spirit sanctify these offerings. Let them become the body and blood of Jesus Christ our Lord as we celebrate the great mystery which he left us as an everlasting covenant.

The Lord's Supper

He always loved those who were his own in the world. When the time came for him to be glorified by you, his heavenly Father, he showed the depth of his love.

While they were at supper, he took bread, said the blessing, broke the bread, and gave it to his disciples, saying:

Take this, all of you, and eat it:
this is my body which will be given up for you.

In the same way, he took the cup, filled with wine. He gave you thanks, and giving the cup to his disciples, said:

Take this, all of you, and drink from it:
this is the cup of my blood,
the blood of the new and everlasting covenant.
It will be shed for you and for all
so that sins may be forgiven.
Do this in memory of me.

Memorial Acclamation

1   Let us proclaim the mystery of faith: **Christ has died, Christ is risen, Christ will come again.**

2   Praise to you, Lord Jesus, firstborn from the dead! **Dying you destroyed our death, rising you restored our life. Lord Jesus, come in glory.**

3 We are faithful, Lord, to your command: **When we eat this bread and drink this cup, we proclaim your death, Lord Jesus, until you come in glory.**

4 Christ is Lord of all ages! **Lord, by your cross and resurrection, you have set us free. You are the Saviour of the world.**

Memorial Prayer

Father, we now celebrate this memorial of our redemption. We recall Christ's death, his descent among the dead, his resurrection, and his ascension to your right hand; and, looking forward to his coming in glory, we offer you his body and blood, the acceptable sacrifice which brings salvation to the whole world.

For the Church

Lord, look upon this sacrifice which you have given to your Church; and by your Holy Spirit, gather all who share this one bread and one cup into the one body of Christ, a living sacrifice of praise.

Lord, remember those for whom we offer this sacrifice, especially N. our pope, N. our bishop, and bishops and clergy everywhere. Remember those who take part in this offering, those here present,

> *Christian Initiation (Baptism):*
> those born again today by water and the Holy Spirit,

and all your people, and all who seek you with a sincere heart.

For the dead

Remember those who have died in the peace of Christ and all the dead whose faith is known to you alone.

In communion with the saints

Father, in your mercy grant also to us, your children, to enter into our heavenly inheritance in the company of the Virgin Mary, the Mother of God, and your apostles and saints. Then, in your kingdom, freed from the corruption of sin and death, we shall sing your glory with every creature through Christ our Lord, through whom you give us everything that is good.

In praise of God

Through him, with him, in him, in the unity of the Holy Spirit, all glory and honour is yours, almighty Father, for ever and ever. **Amen.**

(Turn to the LORD'S PRAYER, *p. 65)*

EUCHARISTIC PRAYER FOR MASS OF
RECONCILIATION I

Preface

Father, all-powerful and ever-living God, we do well always and everywhere to give you thanks and praise. You never cease to call us to a new and more abundant life.

God of love and mercy, you are always ready to forgive; we are sinners, and you invite us to trust in your mercy. Time and time again we broke your covenant, but you did not abandon us. Instead, through your Son, Jesus our Lord, you bound yourself even more closely to the human family by a bond that can never be broken.

Now is the time for your people to turn back to you and be renewed in Christ your Son, a time of grace and reconciliation. You invite us to serve the family of mankind by opening our hearts to the fullness of your Holy Spirit.

In wonder and gratitude, we join our voices with the choirs of heaven to proclaim the power of your love and to sing of our salvation in Christ: **Holy, Holy** *(p. 33)*

Praise to the Father

Father, from the beginning of time you have always done what is good for man so that we may be holy as you are holy.

Look with kindness on your people gathered here before you: send forth the power of your Spirit so that these gifts may become for us the

49

body and blood of your beloved Son, Jesus the Christ, in whom we have become your sons and daughters.

When we were lost and could not find the way to you, you loved us more than ever: Jesus, your Son, innocent and without sin, gave himself into our hands and was nailed to a cross. Yet before he stretched out his arms between heaven and earth in the everlasting sign of your covenant, he desired to celebrate the Paschal feast in the company of his disciples.

The Lord's Supper

While they were at supper, he took bread and gave you thanks and praise. He broke the bread, gave it to his disciples, and said:

> Take this, all of you, and eat it:
> this is my body which will be given up for you.

At the end of the meal, knowing that he was to reconcile all things in himself by the blood of his cross, he took the cup, filled with wine. Again he gave you thanks, handed the cup to his friends, and said:

> Take this, all of you, and drink from it:
> this is the cup of my blood,
> the blood of the new and everlasting covenant.
> It will be shed for you and for all
> so that sins may be forgiven.
> Do this in memory of me.

Memorial Acclamation

1 Let us proclaim the mystery of faith: **Christ has died, Christ is risen, Christ will come again.**

2 Praise to you, Lord Jesus, firstborn from the dead! **Dying you destroyed our death, rising you restored our life. Lord Jesus, come in glory.**

3 We are faithful, Lord, to your command: **When we eat this bread and drink this cup, we proclaim your death, Lord Jesus, until you come in glory.**

4 Christ is Lord of all ages! **Lord, by your cross and resurrection, you have set us free. You are the Saviour of the world.**

Memorial Prayer

We do this in memory of Jesus Christ, our Passover and our lasting peace. We celebrate his death and resurrection and look for the coming of that day when he will return to give us the fullness of joy. Therefore we offer you, God ever faithful and true, the sacrifice which restores man to your friendship.

For the Church

Father, look with love on those you have called to share in the one sacrifice of Christ. By the power of your Holy Spirit make them one body, healed of all division.

Keep us all in communion of mind and heart with N., our pope, and N., our bishop. Help us to work together for the coming of your kingdom, until at last we stand in your presence to share the life of the saints, in the company of the Virgin Mary and the apostles, and of our departed brothers and sisters whom we commend to your mercy.

Then, freed from every shadow of death, we shall take our place in the new creation and give you thanks with Christ, our risen Lord.

In praise of God

Through him, with him, in him, in the unity of the Holy Spirit, all glory and honour is yours, almighty Father, for ever and ever. **Amen.**

(Turn to the LORD'S PRAYER, *p. 65)*

EUCHARISTIC PRAYER FOR MASS OF RECONCILIATION II

Preface

Father, all-powerful and ever-living God, we praise and thank you through Jesus Christ our Lord for your presence and action in the world.

In the midst of conflict and division, we know it is you who turn our minds to thoughts of peace. Your Spirit changes our hearts: enemies begin to speak to one another, those who were estranged join hands in friendship, and nations seek the way of peace together. Your Spirit is at work when understanding puts an end to strife, when hatred is quenched by mercy, and vengeance gives way to forgiveness.

For this we should never cease to thank and praise you. We join with all the choirs of heaven as they sing for ever to your glory! **Holy, Holy** *(p. 33)*

Praise to the Father

God of power and might, we praise you through your Son, Jesus Christ, who comes in your name.

He is the Word that brings salvation. He is the hand you stretch out to sinners. He is the way that leads to your peace.

God our Father, we had wandered far from you, but through your Son you have brought us back. You gave him up to death so that we might turn again to you and find our way to one another.

Therefore we celebrate the reconciliation Christ has gained for us. We ask you to sanctify these gifts by the power of your Spirit, as we now fulfill your Son's command.

The Lord's Supper

While he was at supper on the night before he died for us, he took bread in his hands, and gave you thanks and praise. He broke the bread, gave it to his disciples, and said:

> Take this, all of you, and eat it:
> this is my body which will be given up for you.

At the end of the meal he took the cup. Again he praised you for your goodness, gave the cup to his disciples, and said:

> Take this, all of you, and drink from it:
> this is the cup of my blood,
> the blood of the new and everlasting covenant.
> It will be shed for you and for all
> so that sins may be forgiven.
> Do this in memory of me.

Memorial Acclamation

1   Let us proclaim the mystery of faith: **Christ has died, Christ is risen, Christ will come again.**

2   Praise to you, Lord Jesus, firstborn from the dead! **Dying you destroyed our death, rising**

you restored our life. **Lord Jesus, come in glory.**

3 We are faithful, Lord, to your command: **When we eat this bread and drink this cup, we proclaim your death, Lord Jesus, until you come in glory.**

4 Christ is Lord of all ages! **Lord, by your cross and resurrection, you have set us free. You are the Saviour of the world.**

Memorial Prayer

Lord our God, your Son has entrusted to us this pledge of his love. We celebrate the memory of his death and resurrection and bring you the gift you have given us, the sacrifice of reconciliation. Therefore, we ask you, Father, to accept us, together with your Son. Fill us with his Spirit through our sharing in this meal. May he take away all that divides us.

For the Church

May this Spirit keep us always in communion with N., our pope, N., our bishop, with all the bishops and all your people. Father, make your Church throughout the world a sign of unity and an instrument of your peace.

In communion with the saints

You have gathered us here around the table of your Son, in fellowship with the Virgin Mary, Mother of God, and all the saints. In that new world where the fullness of your peace will be revealed, gather people of every race, language, and way of life to share in the one eternal banquet with Jesus Christ the Lord.

In praise of God

Through him, with him, in him, in the unity of the Holy Spirit, all glory and honour is yours, almighty Father, for ever and ever. **Amen.**

(Turn to the LORD'S PRAYER, *p. 65)*

EUCHARISTIC PRAYER FOR MASS WITH CHILDREN I

Preface

God our Father, you have brought us here together so that we can give you thanks and praise for all the wonderful things you have done.

We thank you for all that is beautiful in the world and for the happiness you have given us. We praise you for daylight and for your word which lights up our minds. We praise you for the earth, and all the people who live on it, and for our life which comes from you.

We know that you are good. You love us and do great things for us. So we all sing together:

Holy, holy, holy Lord, God of power and might, heaven and earth are full of your glory. Hosanna in the highest.

Father, you are always thinking about your people; you never forget us. You sent us your Son Jesus, who gave his life for us and who came to save us. He cured sick people; he cared for those who were poor and wept with those who were sad. He forgave sinners and taught us to forgive each other. He loved everyone and showed us how to be kind. He took children in his arms and blessed them. So we all sing together:

Blessed is he who comes in the name of the Lord. Hosanna in the highest.

God our Father, all over the world your people praise you. So now we pray with the whole Church: with N., our pope, and N., our bishop. In heaven the blessed Virgin Mary, the apostles and all the saints always sing your praise. Now we join with them and with the angels to adore you as we sing:

Holy, holy, holy Lord, God of power and might, heaven and earth are full of your glory. Hosanna in the highest. Blessed is he who comes in the name of the Lord. Hosanna in the highest.

God our Father, you are most holy and we want to show you that we are grateful.

We bring you bread and wine and ask you to send your Holy Spirit to make these gifts the body and blood of Jesus your Son. Then we can offer to you what you have given to us.

On the night before he died, Jesus was having supper with his apostles. He took bread from the table. He gave you thanks and praise. Then he broke the bread, gave it to his friends, and said:

> Take this, all of you, and eat it:
> this is my body which will be given up for you.

When supper was ended, Jesus took the cup that was filled with wine. He thanked you, gave it to his friends, and said:

Take this, all of you, and drink from it:
this is the cup of my blood,
the blood of the new and everlasting covenant.
It will be shed for you and for all
so that sins may be forgiven.

Then he said to them:

Do this in memory of me.

We do now what Jesus told us to do. We remember his death and his resurrection and we offer you, Father, the bread that gives us life, and the cup that saves us. Jesus brings us to you; welcome us as you welcome him.

1 Let us proclaim the mystery of faith: **Christ has died, Christ is risen, Christ will come again.**

2 Praise to you, Lord Jesus, firstborn from the dead! **Dying you destroyed our death, rising you restored our life. Lord Jesus, come in glory.**

3 We are faithful, Lord, to your command: **When we eat this bread and drink this cup, we proclaim your death, Lord Jesus, until you come in glory.**

4 Christ is Lord of all ages! **Lord, by your cross and resurrection, you have set us free. You are the Saviour of the world.**

Father, because you love us, you invite us to come to your table. Fill us with the joy of the Holy Spirit as we receive the body and blood of your Son.

Lord, you never forget any of your children. We ask you to take care of those we love, especially of N. and N.; and we pray for those who have died.

Remember everyone who is suffering from pain or sorrow. Remember Christians everywhere and all other people in the world.

We are filled with wonder and praise when we see what you do for us through Jesus your Son, and so we sing:

Through him, with him, in him, in the unity of the Holy Spirit, all glory and honour is yours, almighty Father, for ever and ever. **Amen.**

(Turn to the LORD'S PRAYER, *p. 65)*

EUCHARISTIC PRAYER FOR MASS WITH CHILDREN II

Preface

God, our loving Father, we are glad to give you thanks and praise because you love us. With Jesus we sing your praise:

> **Glory to God in the highest.**
> *or:* **Hosanna in the highest.**

Because you love us, you gave us this great and beautiful world. With Jesus we sing your praise:

> **Glory to God in the highest.**
> *or:* **Hosanna in the highest.**

Because you love us, you sent Jesus your Son to bring us to you and to gather us around him as the children of one family. With Jesus we sing your praise:

> **Glory to God in the highest.**
> *or:* **Hosanna in the highest.**

For such great love we thank you with the angels and saints as they praise you and sing:

Holy, holy, holy Lord, God of power and might, heaven and earth are full of your glory. Hosanna in the highest. Blessed is he who comes in the name of the Lord. Hosanna in the highest.

Blessed be Jesus, whom you sent to be the friend of children and of the poor.

He came to show us how we can love you, Father, by loving one another. He came to take away sin, which keeps us from being friends, and hate, which makes us all unhappy.

He promised to send the Holy Spirit, to be with us always so that we can live as your children.

Blessed is he who comes in the name of the Lord. Hosanna in the highest.

God our Father, we now ask you to send your Holy Spirit to change these gifts of bread and wine into the body and blood of Jesus Christ, our Lord.

The night before he died, Jesus your Son showed us how much you love us. When he was at supper with his disciples, he took bread, and gave you thanks and praise. Then he broke the bread, gave it to his friends, and said:

> Take this, all of you, and eat it:
> this is my body which will be given up for you.

Jesus has given his life for us.

When supper was ended, Jesus took the cup that was filled with wine. He thanked you, gave it to his friends, and said:

Take this, all of you, and drink from it:
this is the cup of my blood,
the blood of the new and everlasting covenant.
It will be shed for you and for all
so that sins may be forgiven.

Jesus has given his life for us.

Then he said to them:

Do this in memory of me.

And so, loving Father, we remember that Jesus died and rose again to save the world. He put himself into our hands to be the sacrifice we offer you.

We praise you. We bless you. We thank you.

Lord our God, listen to our prayer. Send the Holy Spirit to all of us who share in this meal. May this Spirit bring us closer together in the family of the Church, with N., our pope, N., our bishop, all other bishops, and all who serve your people.

We praise you. We bless you. We thank you.

Remember, Father, our families and friends and all those we do not love as we should. Remember those who have died. Bring them home to you, to be with you for ever.

We praise you. We bless you. We thank you.

Gather us all together into your kingdom. There we shall be happy for ever with the Virgin Mary, Mother of God and our mother. There all the friends of Jesus the Lord will sing a song of joy.

We praise you. We bless you. We thank you.

Through him, with him, in him, in the unity of the Holy Spirit, all glory and honour is yours, almighty Father, for ever and ever. **Amen**.

(Turn to the LORD'S PRAYER, *p. 65)*

EUCHARISTIC PRAYER FOR MASS FOR VARIOUS NEEDS AND OCCASIONS IV
Jesus, the Compassion of God

Preface

It is truly right to give you thanks, it is fitting that we offer you praise, Father of mercy, faithful God.

You sent Jesus Christ your Son among us as redeemer and Lord. He was moved with compassion for the poor and the powerless, for the sick and the sinner; he made himself neighbour to the oppressed. By his words and actions he proclaimed to the world that you care for us as a father cares for his children.

And so, with all the angels and saints we sing the joyful hymn of your praise: **Holy, Holy** *(p. 33)*

Praise

You are truly blessed, O God of holiness: you accompany us with love as we journey through life. Blessed too is your Son, Jesus Christ, who is present among us and whose love gathers us together. As once he did for his disciples, Christ now opens the scriptures for us and breaks the bread.

Invocation of the Holy Spirit

Great and merciful Father, we ask you to send down your Holy Spirit to hallow these gifts of bread and wine, that they may become for us the body and blood of our Lord, Jesus Christ.

The Lord's Supper

On the eve of his passion and death, while at table with those he loved, he took bread and gave you thanks; he broke the bread, gave it to his disciples, and said:

> Take this, all of you, and eat it:
> this is my body which will be given up for you.

When supper was ended, he took the cup; again he gave you thanks and, handing the cup to his disciples, he said:

> Take this, all of you, and drink from it:
> this is the cup of my blood,
> the blood of the new and everlasting covenant.
> It will be shed for you and for all
> so that sins may be forgiven.
> Do this in memory of me.

Memorial Acclamation

Let us proclaim the mystery of faith:

1 **Christ has died, Christ is risen, Christ will come again.**

2 **Dying you destroyed our death, rising you restored our life. Lord Jesus, come in glory.**

3 **When we eat this bread and drink this cup, we proclaim your death, Lord Jesus, until you come in glory.**

4 **Lord, by your cross and resurrection you have set us free. You are the Saviour of the world.**

Memorial Prayer

And so, Father most holy, we celebrate the memory of Christ, your Son, whom you led through suffering and death on the cross to the glory of the resurrection and place at your right hand. Until Jesus, our Saviour, comes again, we proclaim the work of your love, and we offer you the bread of life and the cup of eternal blessing.

Look with favour on the offering of your Church in which we show forth the paschal sacrifice of Christ entrusted to us. Through the power of your Spirit of love include us now and for ever among the members of your Son, whose body and blood we share.

For the Church

Lord, perfect your Church in faith and love together with N. our pope, N. our bishop, with all bishops, priests, and deacons, and all those your son has gained for you.

Open our eyes to the needs of all; inspire us with words and deeds to comfort those who labour and are burdened; keep our service of others faithful to the example and command of Christ.

Let your Church be a living witness to truth and freedom, to justice and peace, that all people may be lifted up by the hope of a world made new.

For the dead

Be mindful of our brothers and sisters [N. and N.], who have fallen asleep in the peace of Christ, and all the dead whose faith only you can know. Lead them to the fullness of the resurrection and gladden them with the light of your face.

In communion with the saints

When our pilgrimage on earth is complete, welcome us into your heavenly home, where we shall dwell with you for ever. There, with Mary, the Virgin Mother of God, with the apostles, the martyrs, [Saint N.,] and all the saints, we shall praise you and give you glory through Jesus Christ, your Son.

In praise of God

Through him, with him, in him, in the unity of the Holy Spirit, all glory and honour is yours, almighty Father, for ever and ever. **Amen.**

LORD'S PRAYER

Let us pray with confidence to the Father in the words our Saviour gave us:

Our Father, who art in heaven, hallowed be thy name; thy kingdom come; thy will be done on earth as it is in heaven. Give us this day our daily bread; and forgive us our trespasses as we forgive those who trespass against us; and lead us not into temptation, but deliver us from evil.

Deliver us, Lord, from every evil, and grant us peace in our day. In your mercy keep us free from sin and protect us from all anxiety as we wait in joyful hope for the coming of our Saviour, Jesus Christ.

For the kingdom, the power and the glory are yours, now and forever.

SIGN OF PEACE

Lord Jesus Christ, you said to your apostles: I leave you peace, my peace I give you. Look not on our sins, but on the faith of your Church, and grant us the peace and unity of your kingdom where you live for ever and ever. **Amen**.

The peace of the Lord be with you always. **And also with you.**

Let us offer each other a sign of peace.

BREAKING OF THE BREAD

Lamb of God, you take away the sins of the world: have mercy on us.

Lamb of God, you take away the sins of the world: have mercy on us.

Lamb of God, you take away the sins of the world: grant us peace.

May this mingling of the body and blood of our Lord Jesus Christ bring eternal life to us who receive it.

COMMUNION

1 Lord Jesus Christ, Son of the living God, by the will of the Father and the work of the Holy Spirit your death brought life to the world. By your holy body and blood free me from all my sins and from every evil. Keep me faithful to your teaching and never let me be parted from you.

2 Lord Jesus Christ, with faith in your love and mercy, I eat your body and drink your blood. Let it not bring me condemnation, but health in mind and body.

This is the Lamb of God who takes away the sins of the world. Happy are those who are called to his supper.

Lord, I am not worthy to receive you, but only say the word and I shall be healed.

May the body (blood) of Christ bring me to everlasting life.

The body of Christ. **Amen.**

The blood of Christ. **Amen.**

COMMUNION ANTIPHON

(Turn to the appropriate day)

PRAYER AFTER COMMUNION

(Turn to the appropriate day)

CONCLUDING RITE

BLESSING

The Lord be with you. **And also with you.**

May almighty God bless you, the Father, and the Son, and the Holy Spirit. **Amen.**

DISMISSAL

During Easter octave, add the double alleluia.

1 Go in the peace of Christ. **Thanks be to God.**

2 The Mass is ended, go in peace.
   Thanks be to God.

3 Go in peace to love and serve the Lord.
   Thanks be to God.

The first reading of this new liturgical year opens with "The word that Isaiah son of Amoz saw." This reminds me of a bumper sticker I've seen that reads "Visualize Peace." Isaiah *saw* a message from God: a vision of peace, a time when people would turn swords into ploughshares and no one would "learn war" any more.

Of course, it takes more than visualizing. That's part of Paul's message in the second reading: to "wake from sleep" — not just to dream about doing good, but to put our dreams into practice. "The day is near," Paul says. There are things that should not be put off, opportunities for good that shouldn't be missed. In the gospel, too, is this sense of urgency: "Keep awake... for you do not know on what day your Lord is coming." As both Paul and Jesus insist, we don't know how much time we have, so we must be prepared to act. We can't just dream.

We must go beyond visualizing peace to actually working for peace. What are the steps we can take, the attitudes we can adopt, the organizations we can support, the lessons we can learn in the cause of peace?

For the Church, Advent is the beginning of a new year. This year, let us make a new year's resolution to become more fully people of peace.

Dinah Simmons, Halifax, NS

ENTRANCE ANTIPHON *(Psalm 25.1-3)*

To you, my God, I lift my soul, I trust in you; let me never come to shame. Do not let my enemies laugh at me. No one who waits for you is ever put to shame.

INTRODUCTORY RITES *(p. 7)*

OPENING PRAYER

All-powerful God, increase our strength of will for doing good that Christ may find an eager welcome at his coming and call us to his side in the kingdom of heaven.

FIRST READING *(Isaiah 2.1-5)*

The word that Isaiah son of Amoz saw concerning Judah and Jerusalem. In days to come the mountain of the Lord's house shall be established as the highest of the mountains, and shall be raised above the hills; all the nations shall stream to it.

Many peoples shall come and say, "Come, let us go up to the mountain of the Lord, to the house of the God of Jacob; that he may teach us his ways and that we may walk in his paths."

For out of Zion shall go forth instruction, and the word of the Lord from Jerusalem. He shall judge between the nations, and shall arbitrate for many peoples; they shall beat their swords into ploughshares, and their spears into pruning hooks; nation shall not lift up sword against nation, neither shall they learn war any more.

O house of Jacob, come, let us walk in the light of the Lord!

The word of the Lord. **Thanks be to God.**

RESPONSORIAL PSALM *(Psalm 122)*

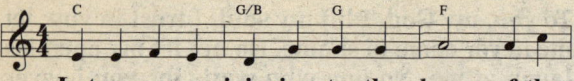

Let us go re‑joic‑ing to the house of the

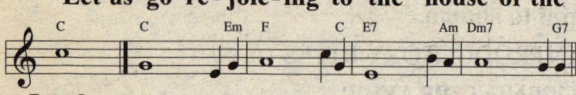

Lord.

℟. **Let us go rejoicing to the house of the Lord.**

I was glad when they said · **to** me,
"Let us go to the house of · **the** Lord!"
Our feet · **are** standing
within your gates, O · **Je**‑rusalem. ℟.

To it the tribes go up, the tribes · **of_the** Lord,
as it was decreed for Israel,
   to give thanks to the name of · **the** Lord.
For there the thrones
   for judgment · **were_set** up,
the thrones of the · **house_of** David. ℟.

Pray for the peace of · **Je**‑rusalem:
"May they prosper · **who** love_you.
Peace be within · **your** walls,
and security within · **your** towers." ℟.

For the sake of my relatives · **and** friends
I will say, "Peace be · **with**‑in_you."
For the sake of the house of the Lord · **our** God,
I will seek · **your** good. ℟.

SECOND READING *(Romans 13.11-14)*

Brothers and sisters, you know what time it is, how it is now the moment for you to wake from sleep. For salvation is nearer to us now than when we became believers; the night is far gone, the day is near. Let us then lay aside the works of darkness and put on the armour of light; let us live honourably as in the day, not in revelling and drunkenness, not in debauchery and licentiousness, not in quarrelling and jealousy.

Instead, put on the Lord Jesus Christ, and make no provision for the flesh, to gratify its desires.

The word of the Lord. **Thanks be to God.**

GOSPEL ACCLAMATION *(Psalm 85.7)*

Alleluia. Alleluia. Show us your steadfast love, O Lord, and grant us your salvation. **Alleluia.**

GOSPEL *(Matthew 24.37-44)*

A reading from the holy Gospel according to Matthew. **Glory to you, Lord.**

Jesus spoke to his disciples: "As the days of Noah were, so will be the coming of the Son of Man. For as in those days before the flood they were eating and drinking, marrying and giving in marriage, until the day Noah entered the ark, and they knew nothing until the flood came and swept them all away, so too will be the coming of the Son of Man. Then two will be in the field; one will be taken and one will be left. Two women will be grinding meal together; one will be taken and one will be left.

71

"Keep awake, therefore, for you do not know on what day your Lord is coming. But understand this: if the owner of the house had known in what part of the night the thief was coming, he would have stayed awake and would not have let his house be broken into. Therefore you also must be ready, or the Son of Man is coming at an unexpected hour."

The Gospel of the Lord. **Praise to you, Lord Jesus Christ.**

PROFESSION OF FAITH *(p. 13-14)*

PRAYER OF THE FAITHFUL

The following intentions are suggestions only.

R. **Lord, hear our prayer.**

For the Church, witness to God's word in the world, we pray to the Lord: R.

For government leaders guided by principles of justice and mercy, we pray to the Lord: R.

For those who search for hope amidst despair, we pray to the Lord: R.

For ourselves, God's people, called to welcome those who have lost hope, we pray to the Lord: R.

PREPARATION OF THE GIFTS *(p. 15)*

PRAYER OVER THE GIFTS

Father, from all you give us we present this bread and wine. As we serve you now, accept our offering and sustain us with your promise of eternal life.

PREFACE *(Advent I, p. 16)*

COMMUNION ANTIPHON *(Psalm 85.12)*

The Lord will shower his gifts, and our land will yield its fruit.

PRAYER AFTER COMMUNION

Father, may our communion teach us to love heaven. May its promise and hope guide our way on earth.

SOLEMN BLESSING — Advent *(Optional)*

Bow your heads and pray for God's blessing.

You believe that the Son of God once came to us; you look for him to come again. May his coming bring you the light of his holiness and free you with his blessing. **Amen.**

May God make you steadfast in faith, joyful in hope, and untiring in love all the days of your life. **Amen.**

You rejoice that our Redeemer came in the flesh. When he comes again in glory, may he reward you with endless life. **Amen.**

May almighty God bless you, the Father, and the Son, and the Holy Spirit. **Amen.**

DISMISSAL *(p. 67)*

December 5   2nd Sunday of Advent

The Alaska Highway runs 2,237 km between Dawson Creek, BC to Delta Junction, Alaska. War and the fear of an imminent invasion launched this road in 1942. In under eight months a pioneer road twisted and turned its way over mountains, through deep muskeg and dark forests.

Today wartime enemies are friends. Death gave way to life. Now snow-covered spruce trees line this lifeline to remote northern communities. Peace reigns along its route.

Today more than a trillion dollars are spent world-wide every year on weapons and military forces. Fear once again grips us. Will we ever see the world Isaiah speaks of in the first reading? Can we build peace on earth?

Paul tells us in his epistle that by steadfastness and the encouragement of the scriptures we will find hope and harmony. In the gospel, John the Baptist urges us on, "Prepare the way of the Lord, make his paths straight."

John calls us to repent. We must reject our global culture of death. He tells us of someone coming after him baptizing with the Holy Spirit and fire. Can we hear John's voice in today's gospel and turn from the path we are on?

Hunger, disease and poverty — both the source and result of conflicts today — have to be vanquished. We must forsake age old hatreds and intolerance. Through Jesus we can truly hope that the wolf will live with the lamb.

Michael Dougherty, Whitehorse, YT

ENTRANCE ANTIPHON *(See Isaiah 30.19, 30)*

People of Zion, the Lord will come to save all nations, and your hearts will exult to hear his majestic voice.

INTRODUCTORY RITES *(p. 7)*

OPENING PRAYER

God of power and mercy, open our hearts in welcome. Remove the things that hinder us from receiving Christ with joy, so that we may share his wisdom and become one with him when he comes in glory.

FIRST READING *(Isaiah 11.1-10)*

On that day:
A shoot shall come out from the stump of Jesse,
and a branch shall grow out of his roots.
The spirit of the Lord shall rest on him,
the spirit of wisdom and understanding,
the spirit of counsel and might,
the spirit of knowledge and the fear of the Lord.
His delight shall be in the fear of the Lord.

He shall not judge by what his eyes see,
or decide by what his ears hear;
but with righteousness he shall judge the poor,
and decide with equity for the meek of the earth;
he shall strike the earth with the rod of his mouth,
and with the breath of his lips
    he shall kill the wicked.
Righteousness shall be the belt around his waist,
and faithfulness the belt around his loins.

Second Sunday of Advent

The wolf shall live with the lamb,
the leopard shall lie down with the kid,
the calf and the lion and the fatling together,
and a little child shall lead them.
The cow and the bear shall graze,
their young shall lie down together;
and the lion shall eat straw like the ox.
The nursing child shall play over the hole
    of the asp,
and the weaned child shall put its hand
    on the adder's den.
They will not hurt or destroy
on all my holy mountain;
for the earth will be full of the knowledge
    of the Lord
as the waters cover the sea.

On that day the root of Jesse shall stand
as a signal to the peoples;
the nations shall inquire of him,
and his dwelling shall be glorious.

The word of the Lord. **Thanks be to God.**

RESPONSORIAL PSALM *(Psalm 72)*

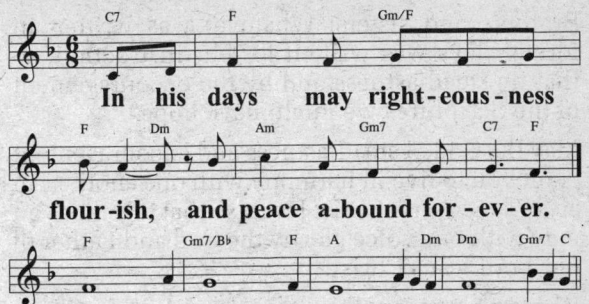

In his days   may right-eous-ness flour-ish, and peace a-bound for-ev-er.

℟. **In his days may righteousness flourish,
and peace abound forever.**

Give the king your justice, O · **God,**
and your righteousness to a king's · **son.**
May he judge your · **people**
    with righteousness,
and your · **poor** with justice. ℟.

In his days may righteousness · **flourish**
and peace abound, until the moon is no · **more.**
May he have dominion from · **sea** to sea,
and from the River to the · **ends_of** the earth. ℟.

For he delivers the needy one who · **calls,**
the poor and the one who has no · **helper.**
He has pity on the · **weak_and** the needy,
and saves the · **lives_of** the needy. ℟.

May his name endure for-·**ever,**
his fame continue as long as the · **sun.**
May all nations be · **blessed** in him;
may they pro-·**nounce** him happy. ℟.

©2010 Gordon Johnston/Novalis

SECOND READING *(Romans 15.4-9)*

Brothers and sisters: Whatever was written in former days was written for our instruction, so that by steadfastness and by the encouragement of the Scriptures we might have hope.

May the God of steadfastness and encouragement grant you to live in harmony with one another, in accordance with Christ Jesus, so that together you may with one voice glorify the God and Father of our Lord Jesus Christ.

Welcome one another, therefore, just as Christ has welcomed you, for the glory of God. For I tell you that Christ has become a servant of the circumcised on behalf of the truth of God in order that he might confirm the promises given to the patriarchs, and in order that the Gentiles might glorify God for his mercy. As it is written, "Therefore I will confess you among the Gentiles, and sing praises to your name."

The word of the Lord. **Thanks be to God.**

GOSPEL ACCLAMATION *(Luke 3.4, 6)*

Alleluia. Alleluia. Prepare the way of the Lord, make straight his paths: all flesh shall see the salvation of God. **Alleluia.**

GOSPEL *(Matthew 3.1-12)*

A reading from the holy Gospel according to Matthew. **Glory to you, Lord.**

In those days John the Baptist appeared in the wilderness of Judea, proclaiming, "Repent, for the kingdom of heaven has come near." This is the one of whom the Prophet Isaiah spoke when he said, "The voice of one crying out in the wilderness: 'Prepare the way of the Lord, make his paths straight.'"

Now John wore clothing of camel's hair with a leather belt around his waist, and his food was locusts and wild honey. Then the people of Jerusalem and all Judea were going out to him, and all the region along the Jordan, and they were baptized by him in the river Jordan, confessing their sins.

But when he saw many Pharisees and Sadducees coming for baptism, John said to them, "You brood of vipers! Who warned you to flee from the wrath to come? Bear fruit worthy of repentance. Do not presume to say to yourselves, 'We have Abraham as our father'; for I tell you, God is able from these stones to raise up children to Abraham. Even now the axe is lying at the root of the trees; every tree therefore that does not bear good fruit is cut down and thrown into the fire.

"I baptize you with water for repentance, but one who is more powerful than I is coming after me; I am not worthy to carry his sandals. He will baptize you with the Holy Spirit and fire. His winnowing fork is in his hand, and he will clear his threshing floor and will gather his wheat into the granary; but the chaff he will burn with unquenchable fire."

The Gospel of the Lord. **Praise to you, Lord Jesus Christ.**

PROFESSION OF FAITH *(p. 13-14)*

PRAYER OF THE FAITHFUL

The following intentions are suggestions only.

R̰ **Lord, hear our prayer.**

For all Christians, called to work together to prepare the Lord's way, we pray to the Lord: R̰

For an end to persecution and wars, we pray to the Lord: R̰

For those caught up in turmoil and uncertainty, and for all who assist them, we pray to the Lord: R̰

For us, God's people gathered here, called to walk the path of new life in the face of despair and darkness, we pray to the Lord: R̰

PREPARATION OF THE GIFTS *(p. 15)*

PRAYER OVER THE GIFTS

Lord, we are nothing without you. As you sustain us with your mercy, receive our prayers and offerings.

PREFACE *(Advent I, p. 16)*

COMMUNION ANTIPHON *(Baruch 5.5; 4.36)*

Rise up, Jerusalem, stand on the heights, and see the joy that is coming to you from God.

PRAYER AFTER COMMUNION

Father, you give us food from heaven. By our sharing in this mystery, teach us to judge wisely the things of earth and to love the things of heaven.

SOLEMN BLESSING AND DISMISSAL *(p. 73)*

What a difference between last Sunday's gospel and this Sunday's! Last week, it was a confident, assertive John the Baptist who exploded onto the scene preaching repentance, judgment and the coming Messiah. Today, we see a much different John. Imprisoned and disheartened, John questions whether Jesus is actually the One whose coming he had foretold.

But who can blame him? After all, the Messiah whose coming John had promised was to chop down the unworthy and burn the "chaff." Instead, Jesus was healing the lame and cleansing the lepers. He certainly wasn't the kind of Messiah John had expected.

And what about our own expectations? If we are honest with ourselves, there may be times when Jesus doesn't fit into the nice, neat mould we have for him. Times, perhaps, when a prayer isn't answered the way we would like, or our idea about what is right and fair doesn't fit with gospel teachings. Then what do we do?

As the beginning of the new Church year, Advent invites us to start over, to leave behind the familiar and venture into the unknown. Part of that can be letting go of preconceived notions about who Jesus is and how he should work in our lives, and opening ourselves up to new possibilities. With John the Baptist as our guide, let us begin today to discover anew the Jesus born into the world at Christmas.

Teresa Whalen Lux, Regina, SK

ENTRANCE ANTIPHON *(Philippians 4.4, 5)*

Rejoice in the Lord always; again I say, rejoice! The Lord is near.

INTRODUCTORY RITES *(p. 7)*

OPENING PRAYER

Lord God, may we your people, who look forward to the birthday of Christ, experience the joy of salvation and celebrate that feast with love and thanksgiving.

FIRST READING *(Isaiah 35.1-6, 10)*

The wilderness and the dry land shall be glad,
the desert shall rejoice and blossom;
like the crocus it shall blossom abundantly,
and rejoice with joy and singing.
The glory of Lebanon shall be given to it,
the majesty of Carmel and Sharon.
They shall see the glory of the Lord,
the majesty of our God.

Strengthen the weak hands,
and make firm the feeble knees.
Say to those who are of a fearful heart,
"Be strong, do not fear!
Here is your God.
He will come with vengeance,
with terrible recompense.
He will come and save you."

Then the eyes of the blind shall be opened,
and the ears of the deaf unstopped;
then the lame shall leap like a deer,
and the tongue of the mute sing for joy.

And the ransomed of the Lord shall return,
and come to Zion with singing;
everlasting joy shall be upon their heads;
they shall obtain joy and gladness,
and sorrow and sighing shall flee away.

The word of the Lord. **Thanks be to God.**

RESPONSORIAL PSALM *(Psalm 146)*

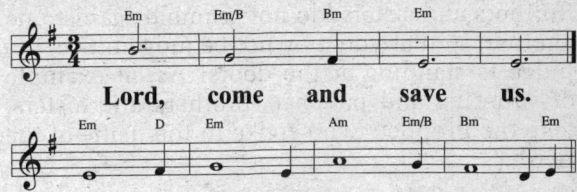

℟. **Lord, come and save us.**

or **Alleluia!**

It is the Lord who keeps faith for-·**ever**,
who executes justice for the op-·**pressed**;
who gives food to the · **hungry**.
The Lord sets the · **prisoners** free. ℟.

The Lord opens the eyes of the · **blind**
and lifts up those who are bowed · **down**;
the Lord loves the · **righteous**
and watches over · **the** strangers. ℟.

The Lord upholds the orphan and the · **widow**,
but the way of the wicked he brings to · **ruin**.
The Lord will reign for-·**ever**,
your God, O Zion, for all · **gener**-ations. ℟.

©2010 Gordon Johnston/Novalis

SECOND READING *(James 5.7-10)*

Be patient, brothers and sisters, until the coming of the Lord. The farmer waits for the precious crop from the earth, being patient with it until it receives the early and the late rains. You also must be patient. Strengthen your hearts, for the coming of the Lord is near.

Brothers and sisters, do not grumble against one another, so that you may not be judged. See, the Judge is standing at the doors! As an example of suffering and patience, brothers and sisters, take the Prophets who spoke in the name of the Lord.

The word of the Lord. **Thanks be to God.**

GOSPEL ACCLAMATION *(Luke 4.18 [see Is 61.1])*

Alleluia. Alleluia. The Spirit of the Lord is upon me; he has sent me to bring good news to the poor. **Alleluia.**

GOSPEL *(Matthew 11.2-11)*

A reading from the holy Gospel according to Matthew. **Glory to you, Lord.**

When John the Baptist heard in prison about the deeds of the Christ, he sent word by his disciples who said to Jesus, "Are you the one who is to come, or are we to wait for another?"

Jesus answered them, "Go and tell John what you hear and see: the blind receive their sight, the lame walk, the lepers are cleansed, the deaf hear, the dead are raised, and the poor have good news brought to them. And blessed is anyone who takes no offence at me."

As they went away, Jesus began to speak to the crowds about John: "What did you go out into the wilderness to look at? A reed shaken by the wind? What then did you go out to see? Someone dressed in soft robes? Look, those who wear soft robes are in royal palaces. What then did you go out to see? A Prophet? Yes, I tell you, and more than a Prophet. This is the one about whom it is written, 'See, I am sending my messenger ahead of you, who will prepare your way before you.'

"Truly I tell you, among those born of women no one has arisen greater than John the Baptist; yet the least in the kingdom of heaven is greater than he."

The Gospel of the Lord. **Praise to you, Lord Jesus Christ.**

PROFESSION OF FAITH *(p. 13-14)*

PRAYER OF THE FAITHFUL

The following intentions are suggestions only.

℟ **Lord, hear our prayer.**

For Christians everywhere, called to witness to God's love by joyful and practical service in the world, we pray to the Lord: ℟

For the swift coming of God's rule of peace and justice among all nations, we pray to the Lord: ℟

For people among us who are lonely or separated from family and friends, we pray to the Lord: ℟

For all who work to help families experience true peace and joy, we pray to the Lord: ℟

PREPARATION OF THE GIFTS *(p. 15)*

PRAYER OVER THE GIFTS

Lord, may the gift we offer in faith and love be a continual sacrifice in your honour and truly become our eucharist and our salvation.

PREFACE *(Advent I, p. 16)*

COMMUNION ANTIPHON *(See Isaiah 35.4)*

Say to the anxious: be strong and fear not, our God will come to save us.

PRAYER AFTER COMMUNION

God of mercy, may this eucharist bring us your divine help, free us from our sins, and prepare us for the birthday of our Saviour, who is Lord for ever and ever.

SOLEMN BLESSING AND DISMISSAL *(p. 73)*

Even very young children know that being a king or queen is something remarkable. All that power! All those jewels and crowns and thrones and servants! Kings and queens are born of kings and queens, generation after generation. Except in today's gospel, that is.

Instead of being born of a royal couple, Jesus, the Christ, is to be born to a teenage girl and a labourer who isn't his father. This surprising story of Jesus' family tree turns our ideas about kingship upside down. The intriguing details about Jesus' conception and birth are the first of many signs of big changes in how we understand God. This long-awaited king is born in modest circumstances, with no earthly power, no jewels or crowns or thrones, no servants. In fact, as we know, this king *becomes* a servant to all.

Instead of being remote from the people, living in luxury, this king — Jesus, Emmanuel — lives as one of us. God is with us in the chaos and sadness and joy and messiness of our lives, not looking down from on high, but here on the ground, among us. As the story unfolds, we come to see Jesus as the model king: humble, compassionate, prayerful, loving, willing to sacrifice life itself for the good of the people. With the psalmist, we call for the Lord to enter, for truly he is king of glory.

A. L. Mahoney, Ottawa, ON

ENTRANCE ANTIPHON *(Isaiah 45.8)*

Let the clouds rain down the Just One, and the earth bring forth a Saviour.

INTRODUCTORY RITES *(p. 7)*

OPENING PRAYER

Lord, fill our hearts with your love, and as you revealed to us by an angel the coming of your Son as man, so lead us through his suffering and death to the glory of his resurrection.

FIRST READING *(Isaiah 7.10-14)*

The Lord spoke to Ahaz, saying, "Ask a sign of the Lord your God; let it be deep as Sheol or high as heaven." But Ahaz said, "I will not ask, and I will not put the Lord to the test."

Then Isaiah said: "Hear then, O house of David! Is it too little for you to weary the people, that you weary my God also? Therefore the Lord himself will give you a sign. Look, the young woman is with child and shall bear a son, and shall name him Emmanuel."

The word of the Lord. **Thanks be to God.**

RESPONSORIAL PSALM *(Psalm 24)*

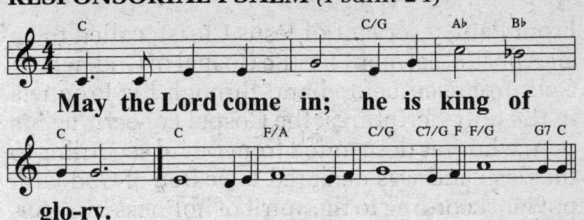

May the Lord come in; he is king of

glo-ry.

R. **May the Lord come in; he is king of glory.**

The earth is the Lord's and all that · **is** in_it,
the world, and those · **who** live_in_it;
for he has founded it · **on_the** seas,
and established it · **on_the** rivers. R.

Who shall ascend the hill · **of_the** Lord?
And who shall stand in his · **holy** place?
Someone who has clean hands
　and a · **pure** heart,
who does not lift up their soul
　to · **what_is** false. R.

That person will receive blessing
　· **from_the** Lord,
and vindication from the God
　of their · **sal**-vation.
Such is the company of those · **who** seek_him,
who seek the face of the God · **of** Jacob. R.

Fourth Sunday of Advent

SECOND READING *(Romans 1.1-7)*

From Paul, a servant of Jesus Christ, called to be an Apostle, set apart for the Gospel of God, which God promised beforehand through his Prophets in the holy Scriptures: the Gospel concerning his Son, who was descended from David according to the flesh and was declared to be Son of God with power according to the spirit of holiness by resurrection from the dead, Jesus Christ our Lord.

Through Christ we have received grace and apostleship to bring about the obedience of faith among all the Gentiles for the sake of his name, including yourselves who are called to belong to Jesus Christ.

To all God's beloved in Rome, who are called to be saints: Grace to you and peace from God our Father and the Lord Jesus Christ.

The word of the Lord. **Thanks be to God.**

GOSPEL ACCLAMATION *(Matthew 1.23)*

Alleluia. Alleluia. The virgin shall be with child and bear a son; and they shall name him Emmanuel: God is with us. **Alleluia.**

GOSPEL *(Matthew 1.18-24)*

A reading from the holy gospel according to Matthew. **Glory to you, Lord.**

The birth of Jesus the Christ took place in this way. When his mother Mary had been engaged to Joseph, but before they lived together, she was found to be with child from the Holy Spirit. Her husband Joseph, being a righteous man and unwilling to expose her to public disgrace, planned to dismiss her quietly.

But just when he had resolved to do this, an Angel of the Lord appeared to him in a dream and said, "Joseph, son of David, do not be afraid to take Mary as your wife, for the child conceived in her is from the Holy Spirit. She will bear a son, and you are to name him Jesus, for he will save his people from their sins."

All this took place to fulfill what had been spoken by the Lord through the Prophet: "Look, the virgin shall conceive and bear a son, and they shall name him Emmanuel," which means, "God is with us." When Joseph awoke from sleep, he did as the Angel of the Lord commanded him; he took her as his wife.

The Gospel of the Lord. **Praise to you, Lord Jesus Christ.**

PROFESSION OF FAITH *(p. 13-14)*

PRAYER OF THE FAITHFUL

The following intentions are suggestions only.

R. **Lord, hear our prayer.**

For the Church, called as Mary was, to give Christ to the world, we pray to the Lord: R.

For all the world's children, born and unborn, signs of God's gift of life, we pray to the Lord: R.

For people in our midst who reach out for our love and our hope, we pray to the Lord: R.

For us, God's people gathered here, called to bring the presence of Christ to each other, we pray to the Lord: R.

PREPARATION OF THE GIFTS *(p. 15)*

PRAYER OVER THE GIFTS

Lord, may the power of the Spirit, which sancti-fied Mary the mother of your Son, make holy the gifts we place upon this altar.

PREFACE *(Advent II, p. 17)*

COMMUNION ANTIPHON *(Isaiah 7.14)*

The Virgin is with child and shall bear a son, and she will call him Emmanuel.

PRAYER AFTER COMMUNION

Lord, in this sacrament we receive the promise of salvation; as Christmas draws near make us grow in faith and love to celebrate the coming of Christ our Saviour, who is Lord for ever and ever.

SOLEMN BLESSING AND DISMISSAL *(p. 73)*

Take a moment to remember a Christmas celebration that was deeply meaningful...

The Christmases of deepest meaning for me took place where there was no snow, Christmas tree decorations, family, fruit cake or eggnog. When I lived in Latin America, I spent three Christmases picking coffee in the mountains, sleeping on the schoolhouse floor and eating only rice, tortillas and beans. We worked to assist peasant cooperatives bring in their harvest, the best of which was exported to North America.

One year, as we celebrated Christmas by preparing a *piñata* game for the children of the community, we received word that a baby had died. Visiting the simple hut of the grieving family, we discovered that due to unsanitary living conditions — no running water, no electricity, no medical care — worms had infected and eventually killed the infant.

Thousands of years before, a young virgin mother gave birth in similar conditions, wrapped her firstborn son in swaddling rags and laid him in a manger because there was no place for them in the inn. Mary's heart must have been breaking to have had to receive the Son of God in this manner, and yet the new mother was no doubt also bursting with joy. Christmas is a time to open our hearts to God. This Christmas let us also resolve to make room in our hearts for all the children of the world.

Joseph Gunn, Ottawa, ON

Mass during the Night

ENTRANCE ANTIPHON *(Psalm 2.7)*

The Lord said to me: You are my Son; this day have I begotten you.

or

Let us all rejoice in the Lord, for our Saviour is born to the world. True peace has descended from heaven.

INTRODUCTORY RITES *(p. 7)*

OPENING PRAYER

Father, you make this holy night radiant with the splendour of Jesus Christ our light. We welcome him as Lord, the true light of the world. Bring us to eternal joy in the kingdom of heaven.

FIRST READING *(Isaiah 9.2-4, 6-7)*

The people who walked in darkness
   have seen a great light;
those who lived in a land of deep darkness —
on them light has shone.
You have multiplied the nation,
you have increased its joy;
they rejoice before you
as with joy at the harvest,
as people exult when dividing plunder.

For the yoke of their burden,
and the bar across their shoulders,
the rod of their oppressor,
you have broken as on the day of Midian.

For a child has been born for us,
a son given to us;
authority rests upon his shoulders;
and he is named
Wonderful Counsellor, Mighty God,
Everlasting Father, Prince of Peace.

His authority shall grow continually,
and there shall be endless peace
for the throne of David and his kingdom.
He will establish and uphold it
with justice and with righteousness
from this time onward and forevermore.
The zeal of the Lord of hosts will do this.

The word of the Lord. **Thanks be to God.**

RESPONSORIAL PSALM *(Psalm 96)*

R. **Today is born our Saviour, Christ the Lord.**

O sing to the Lord a · **new** song;
sing to the Lord, · **all_the** earth.
Sing to the Lord, · **bless_his** name;
tell of his salvation from day · **to** day. R. →

Declare his glory among · **the** nations,
his marvellous works among
   all · **the** peoples.
For great is the Lord,
   and greatly · **to_be** praised;
he is to be revered above · **all** gods. R.

R. **Today is born our Saviour, Christ the Lord.**

Let the heavens be glad,
   and let the earth · **re**-joice;
let the sea roar, and all · **that** fills_it;
let the field exult, and every-**thing** in_it.
Then shall all the trees of the forest
   sing · **for** joy. R.

Rejoice before the Lord; for · **he_is** coming,
for he is coming to judge · **the** earth.
He will judge the world · **with** righteousness,
and the peoples · **with_his** truth. R.

©2009 Gordon Johnston/Novalis

SECOND READING *(Titus 2.11-14)*

Beloved: The grace of God has appeared, bringing
salvation to all, training us to renounce impiety
and worldly passions, and in the present age to
live lives that are self-controlled, upright, and
godly, while we wait for the blessed hope and the
manifestation of the glory of our great God and
Saviour, Jesus Christ.

He it is who gave himself for us that he might
redeem us from all iniquity and purify for himself a people of his own who are zealous for good
deeds.

The word of the Lord. **Thanks be to God.**

GOSPEL ACCLAMATION *(Luke 2.10-11)*

Alleluia. Alleluia. Good news and great joy to all the world: today is born our Saviour, Christ the Lord. **Alleluia.**

GOSPEL *(Luke 2.1-16)*

A reading from the holy Gospel according to Luke. **Glory to you, Lord.**

In those days a decree went out from Caesar Augustus that all the world should be registered. This was the first registration and was taken while Quirinius was governor of Syria. All went to their own towns to be registered. Joseph also went from the town of Nazareth in Galilee to Judea, to the city of David called Bethlehem, because he was descended from the house and family of David. He went to be registered with Mary, to whom he was engaged and who was expecting a child.

While they were there, the time came for her to deliver her child. And she gave birth to her firstborn son and wrapped him in swaddling clothes, and laid him in a manger, because there was no place for them in the inn.

In that region there were shepherds living in the fields, keeping watch over their flock by night. Then an Angel of the Lord stood before them, and the glory of the Lord shone around them, and they were terrified. But the Angel said to them, "Do not be afraid; for see — I am bringing you good news of great joy for all the people: to you is born this day in the city of David a Saviour, who is the

Christ, the Lord. This will be a sign for you: you will find a child wrapped in swaddling clothes and lying in a manger."

And suddenly there was with the Angel a multitude of the heavenly host, praising God and saying, "Glory to God in the highest heaven, and on earth peace among those whom he favours!"

When the Angels had left them and gone into heaven, the shepherds said to one another, "Let us go now to Bethlehem and see this thing that has taken place, which the Lord has made known to us." So they went with haste and found Mary and Joseph, and the child lying in the manger.

The Gospel of the Lord. **Praise to you, Lord Jesus Christ.**

PROFESSION OF FAITH *(Nicene Creed, p. 14)*

PRAYER OF THE FAITHFUL

The following intentions are suggestions only.

R. **Lord, hear our prayer.**

For the Church, called to see with the eyes of faith God's living presence in our midst, we pray to the Lord: R.

For all the world's children, gracious sacraments of God's gift of life, we pray to the Lord: R.

For people in our midst who, in this season of joyful light, walk in darkness, loneliness and despair, we pray to the Lord: R.

For us, God's people gathered here, called to proclaim God's love to the world, we pray to the Lord: R.

PREPARATION OF THE GIFTS *(p. 15)*

PRAYER OVER THE GIFTS

Lord, accept our gifts on this joyful feast of our salvation. By our communion with God made man, may we become more like him who joins our lives to yours.

PREFACE *(Christmas I-III, p. 17)*

COMMUNION ANTIPHON *(John 1.14)*

The Word of God became man; we have seen his glory.

PRAYER AFTER COMMUNION

God our Father, we rejoice in the birth of our Saviour. May we share his life completely by living as he has taught.

SOLEMN BLESSING — Christmas *(Optional)*

Bow your heads and pray for God's blessing.

When he came to us as our brother, the Son of God scattered the darkness of this world, and filled this holy night (day) with his glory. May the God of infinite goodness scatter the darkness of sin and brighten your hearts with holiness. **Amen.**

God sent his angels to shepherds to herald the great joy of our Saviour's birth. May he fill you with joy and make you heralds of his gospel. **Amen.**

When the Word became flesh, earth was joined to heaven. May he give you his peace and good will, and fellowship with all the heavenly host. **Amen.**

May almighty God bless you, the Father, and the Son, and the Holy Spirit. **Amen.**

DISMISSAL *(p. 67)*

Mass at Dawn

ENTRANCE ANTIPHON *(See Isaiah 9; Luke 1)*

A light will shine on us this day, the Lord is born for us: he shall be called Wonderful God, Prince of Peace, Father of the world to come; and his kingship will never end.

INTRODUCTORY RITES *(p. 7)*

OPENING PRAYER

Father, we are filled with the new light by the coming of your Word among us. May the light of faith shine in our words and actions.

FIRST READING *(Isaiah 62.11-12)*

The Lord has proclaimed to the end of the earth:
"Say to daughter Zion,
See, your salvation comes;
his reward is with him,
and his recompense before him.

"They shall be called 'The Holy People,'
'The Redeemed of the Lord';
and you shall be called 'Sought Out,'
'A City Not Forsaken.'"

The word of the Lord. **Thanks be to God.**

RESPONSORIAL PSALM *(Psalm 97)*

A light will shine on us this day:

The Lord is born for us.

℟ **A light will shine on us this day:**
The Lord is born for us.

The Lord is king! Let the earth re·-**joice;**
let the many coastlands be · **glad!**
Clouds and thick darkness
   are all a·-**round_him;**
righteousness and justice are the foundation
   of his · **throne.** ℟

The mountains melt like wax
   before the · **Lord,**
before the Lord of all the · **earth.**
The heavens proclaim his · **righteousness;**
and all the peoples behold his · **glory.** ℟

Light dawns for the · **righteous,**
and joy for the upright in · **heart.**
Rejoice in the Lord, O you · **righteous,**
and give thanks to his holy · **name!** ℟

SECOND READING (*Titus 3.4-7*)

When the goodness and loving kindness of God our Saviour appeared, he saved us, not because of any works of righteousness that we had done, but according to his mercy, through the water of rebirth and renewal by the Holy Spirit. This Spirit he poured out on us richly through Jesus Christ our Saviour, so that, having been justified by his grace, we might become heirs according to the hope of eternal life.

The word of the Lord. **Thanks be to God.**

GOSPEL ACCLAMATION (*Luke 2.14*)

Alleluia. Alleluia. Glory to God in the highest heaven; peace on earth to people of good will. **Alleluia.**

GOSPEL (*Luke 2.15-20*)

A reading from the holy Gospel according to Luke. **Glory to you, Lord.**

When the Angels had left them and gone into heaven, the shepherds said to one another, "Let us go now to Bethlehem and see this thing that has taken place, which the Lord has made known to us."

So they went with haste and found Mary and Joseph, and the child lying in the manger. When they saw this, they made known what had been told them about this child; and all who heard it were amazed at what the shepherds told them.

But Mary treasured all these words and pondered them in her heart. The shepherds returned, glorifying and praising God for all they had heard and seen, as it had been told them.

The Gospel of the Lord. **Praise to you, Lord Jesus Christ.**

PROFESSION OF FAITH *(Nicene Creed, p. 14)*

PRAYER OF THE FAITHFUL *(p. 98)*

PREPARATION OF THE GIFTS *(p. 15)*

PRAYER OVER THE GIFTS

Father, may we follow the example of your Son who became man and lived among us. May we receive the gift of divine life through these offerings here on earth.

PREFACE *(Christmas I-III, p. 17)*

COMMUNION ANTIPHON *(See Zechariah 9.9)*

Daughter of Zion, exult; shout aloud, daughter of Jerusalem! Our King is coming, the Holy One, the Saviour of the world.

PRAYER AFTER COMMUNION

Lord, with faith and joy we celebrate the birthday of your Son. Increase our understanding and our love of the riches you have revealed in him.

SOLEMN BLESSING AND DISMISSAL *(p. 99)*

Mass during the Day

ENTRANCE ANTIPHON *(Isaiah 9.6)*

A child is born for us, a son given to us; dominion is laid on his shoulder, and he shall be called Wonderful Counsellor.

INTRODUCTORY RITES *(p. 7)*

OPENING PRAYER

Lord God, we praise you for creating us, and still more for restoring us in Christ. Your Son shared our weakness: may we share his glory.

FIRST READING *(Isaiah 52.7-10)*

How beautiful upon the mountains are the feet of the messenger who announces peace, who brings good news, who announces salvation, who says to Zion, "Your God reigns."

Listen! Your watchmen lift up their voices, together they sing for joy; for in plain sight they see the return of the Lord to Zion.

Break forth together into singing, you ruins of Jerusalem; for the Lord has comforted his people, he has redeemed Jerusalem. The Lord has bared his holy arm before the eyes of all the nations; and all the ends of the earth shall see the salvation of our God.

The word of the Lord. **Thanks be to God.**

RESPONSORIAL PSALM *(Psalm 98)*

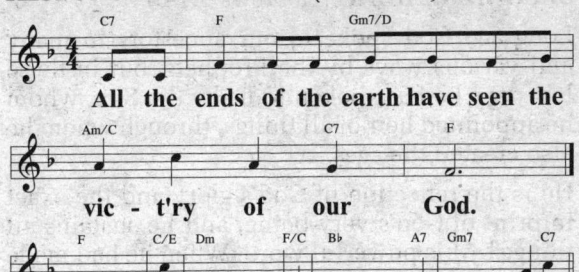

All the ends of the earth have seen the vic - t'ry of our God.

℟. **All the ends of the earth have seen
the victory of our God.**

O sing to the Lord a · **new** song,
for he has done · **marvellous** things.
His right hand and his holy · **arm**
have brought · **him** victory. ℟.

The Lord has made known · **his** victory;
he has revealed his vindication
  in the sight of · **the** nations.
He has remembered his steadfast love
  and · **faithfulness**
to the house · **of** Israel. ℟.

All the ends of the earth · **have** seen
the victory of · **our** God.
Make a joyful noise to the Lord, all the · **earth;**
break forth into joyous song
  and · **sing** praises. ℟.

Sing praises to the Lord with · **the** lyre,
with the lyre and the sound · **of** melody.
With trumpets and the sound of the · **horn**
make a joyful noise before the King,
  · **the** Lord. ℟.

©2009 Gordon Johnston/Novalis

SECOND READING *(Hebrews 1.1-6)*

Long ago God spoke to our ancestors in many and various ways by the Prophets, but in these last days he has spoken to us by the Son, whom he appointed heir of all things, through whom he also created the ages.

He is the reflection of God's glory and the exact imprint of God's very being, and he sustains all things by his powerful word. When he had made purification for sins, he sat down at the right hand of the Majesty on high, having become as much superior to Angels as the name he has inherited is more excellent than theirs.

For to which of the Angels did God ever say, "You are my Son; today I have begotten you"? Or again, "I will be his Father, and he will be my Son"? And again, when he brings the firstborn into the world, he says, "Let all God's Angels worship him."

The word of the Lord. **Thanks be to God.**

GOSPEL GOSPEL ACCLAMATION

Alleluia. Alleluia. A holy day has dawned upon us. Come you nations and adore the Lord. Today a great light has come down upon the earth. **Alleluia.**

GOSPEL *(John 1.1-18)*

For the shorter version, omit the indented parts.

A reading from the holy gospel according to John. **Glory to you, Lord.**

In the beginning was the Word, and the Word was with God, and the Word was God. He was in the beginning with God. All things came into being through him, and without him not one thing came into being. What has come into being in him was life, and the life was the light of the human race.

The light shines in the darkness, and the darkness did not overcome it.

> There was a man sent from God, whose name was John. He came as a witness to testify to the light, so that all might believe through him. He himself was not the light, but he came to testify to the light.

The true light, which enlightens everyone, was coming into the world. He was in the world, and the world came into being through him; yet the world did not know him. He came to what was his own, and his own people did not accept him. But to all who received him, who believed in his name, he gave power to become children of God, who were born, not of blood or of the will of the flesh or of the will of man, but of God.

And the Word became flesh and lived among us, and we have seen his glory, the glory as of a father's only-begotten son, full of grace and truth.

> John testified to him and cried out, "This was he of whom I said, 'He who comes after me ranks ahead of me because he was before me.'"

From his fullness we have all received, grace upon grace. The law indeed was given through Moses; grace and truth came through Jesus Christ. No one has ever seen God. It is

God the only-begotten Son, who is close to the Father's heart, who has made him known.

The Gospel of the Lord. **Praise to you, Lord Jesus Christ.**

PROFESSION OF FAITH *(Nicene Creed, p. 14)*

PRAYER OF THE FAITHFUL *(p. 98)*

PREPARATION OF THE GIFTS *(p. 15)*

PRAYER OVER THE GIFTS

Almighty God, the saving work of Christ made our peace with you. May our offering today renew that peace within us and give you perfect praise.

PREFACE *(Christmas I-III, p. 17)*

COMMUNION ANTIPHON *(Psalm 98.3)*

All the ends of the earth have seen the saving power of God.

PRAYER AFTER COMMUNION

Father, the child born today is the Saviour of the world. He made us your children. May he welcome us into your kingdom.

SOLEMN BLESSING AND DISMISSAL *(p. 99)*

The gospel today is theology in story form. Matthew's purpose is to root the life and teaching of Jesus in the story of Israel. He is building a bridge between the Old and New Testaments.

The evangelist knew the legend of how the Pharaoh of Exodus was forewarned by his own 'magi' about the birth of a Hebrew child who would threaten his authority, and how his murderous plans were frustrated by the dreams of Moses' father who acted on them to protect his son. The quote from Hosea, "Out of Egypt I have called my son," refers to this biblical story. Moses grew up to lead Israel from slavery at the hands of Pharaoh to freedom in the hands of God.

It is Matthew's purpose to show that Jesus' life and teaching bring a new dimension to traditional biblical contrasts between human and divine ways, between slavery and freedom, and between life and death.

We cannot help, however, letting our imaginations be drawn beyond biblical symbolism into the 'real life' relationship that must have existed between Jesus and Joseph. That Jesus' favourite way of naming God was 'Abba,' literally 'Daddy,' is itself a remarkable tribute to Joseph. It was in Joseph's protective and challenging embrace that Jesus developed the profoundly intimate relationship with the Almighty that would sustain him throughout his life.

Corbin Eddy, Hancock, MI

ENTRANCE ANTIPHON *(Luke 2.16)*

The shepherds hastened to Bethlehem, where they found Mary and Joseph, and the baby lying in a manger.

INTRODUCTORY RITES *(p. 7)*

OPENING PRAYER

Father, help us to live as the holy family, united in respect and love. Bring us to the joy and peace of your eternal home.

FIRST READING *(Sirach 3.2-6, 12-14)*

The Lord honours a father above his children,
and he confirms a mother's rights over her sons.
Whoever honours their father atones for sins
and gains preservation from them;
when they pray, they will be heard.
Whoever respects their mother
is like one who lays up treasure.
The person who honours their father
will have joy in their own children,
and when they pray they will be heard.
Whoever respects their father will have a long life,
and whoever honours their mother
      obeys the Lord.

My child, help your father in his old age,
and do not grieve him as long as he lives.
Even if his mind fails, be patient with him;
because you have all your faculties,
do not despise him all the days of his life.
For kindness to your father will not be forgotten,
and will be credited to you against your sins —
a house raised in justice for you.

The word of the Lord. **Thanks be to God.**

RESPONSORIAL PSALM *(Psalm 128)*

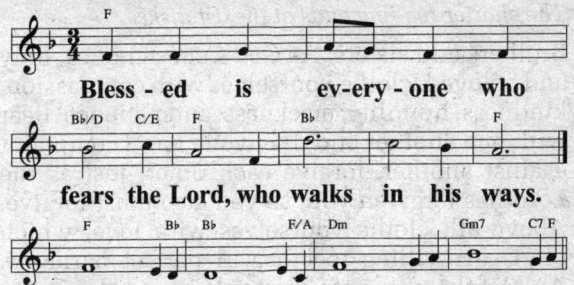

Bless - ed   is   ev-ery - one   who

fears the Lord, who walks   in   his ways.

R̥ **Blessed is everyone who fears the Lord.**

or **Blessed is everyone who fears the Lord,
who walks in his ways.**

Blessed is everyone who fears · **the** Lord,
who walks in · **his** ways.
You shall eat the fruit of the labour
    of · **your** hands;
you shall be happy,
    and it shall go well · **with** you. R̥

Your wife will be like a fruit·-**ful** vine
within · **your** house;
your children will be · **like** olive_shoots
around · **your** table. R̥

Thus shall the man be blessed
    who fears · **the** Lord.
The Lord bless you · **from** Zion.
May you see the prosperity of · **Je**-rusalem
all the days of · **your** life. R̥

SECOND READING *(Colossians 3.12-21)*

The shorter reading ends at the asterisks.

Brothers and sisters: As God's chosen ones, holy and beloved, clothe yourselves with compassion, kindness, humility, meekness, and patience. Bear with one another and, if anyone has a complaint against another, forgive each other; just as the Lord has forgiven you, so you also must forgive. Above all, clothe yourselves with love, which binds everything together in perfect harmony. And let the peace of Christ rule in your hearts, to which indeed you were called in the one body. And be thankful.

Let the word of Christ dwell in you richly; teach and admonish one another in all wisdom; and with gratitude in your hearts sing Psalms, hymns, and spiritual songs to God. And whatever you do, in word or deed, do everything in the name of the Lord Jesus, giving thanks to God the Father through him.

***

Wives, be subject to your husbands, as is fitting in the Lord. Husbands, love your wives and never treat them harshly. Children, obey your parents in everything, for this is your acceptable duty in the Lord. Fathers, do not provoke your children, or they may lose heart.

The word of the Lord. **Thanks be to God.**

GOSPEL ACCLAMATION *(Colossians 3.15, 16)*

Alleluia. Alleluia. Let the peace of Christ rule in your hearts, and the word of Christ dwell in you richly. **Alleluia.**

GOSPEL *(Matthew 2.13-15, 19-23)*

A reading from the holy Gospel according to Matthew. **Glory to you, Lord.**

After the wise men had left, an Angel of the Lord appeared to Joseph in a dream and said, "Get up, take the child and his mother, and flee to Egypt, and remain there until I tell you; for Herod is about to search for the child, to destroy him." Then Joseph got up, took the child and his mother by night, and went to Egypt, and remained there until the death of Herod. This was to fulfill what had been spoken by the Lord through the Prophet, "Out of Egypt I have called my son."

When Herod died, an Angel of the Lord suddenly appeared in a dream to Joseph in Egypt and said, "Get up, take the child and his mother, and go to the land of Israel, for those who were seeking the child's life are dead." Then Joseph got up, took the child and his mother, and went to the land of Israel.

But when he heard that Archelaus was ruling over Judea in place of his father Herod, he was afraid to go there. And after being warned in a dream, he went away to the district of Galilee. There he made his home in a town called Nazareth, so that what had been spoken through the Prophets might be fulfilled, "He will be called a Nazorean."

The Gospel of the Lord. **Praise to you, Lord Jesus Christ.**

PROFESSION OF FAITH *(p. 13-14)*

PRAYER OF THE FAITHFUL

The following intentions are suggestions only.

R. **Lord, hear our prayer.**

For the Church, building the community of love and faith that God desires for the world, we pray to the Lord: R.

For peace on earth, we pray to the Lord: R.

For refugees and those who welcome them, we pray to the Lord: R.

For ourselves, gathered together, seeking to be a community of brothers and sisters, we pray to the Lord: R.

PREPARATION OF THE GIFTS *(p. 15)*

PRAYER OVER THE GIFTS

Lord, accept this sacrifice and through the prayers of Mary, the virgin Mother of God, and of her husband, Joseph, unite our families in peace and love.

PREFACE *(Christmas I-III, p. 17)*

COMMUNION ANTIPHON *(Baruch 3.38)*

Our God has appeared on earth, and lived among us.

PRAYER AFTER COMMUNION

Eternal Father, we want to live as Jesus, Mary and Joseph, in peace with you and one another. May this communion strengthen us to face the troubles of life.

SOLEMN BLESSING AND DISMISSAL *(p. 99)*

January 1   Mary, Mother of God
World Day of Prayer for Peace

Shakespeare's Juliet asks Romeo, her boyfriend who has a hated last name, "What's in a name?" Today the Church answers, "Plenty!" Have you ever noticed how often in scripture a person is introduced by name along with the reason or meaning of that name? For example, Eve is named because she will be mother of all living; Moses is named because he was drawn from the water. Sometimes God changes a person's name to suit the new role they have been given. Abram becomes Abraham because he will be the ancestor of many nations; Simon becomes Peter, a rock upon whom the Church will be built.

Today the Church celebrates a handful of names. The woman who gave birth is Mary; the child born is Jesus, so named because he would save his people from their sins. Those he saved name him the Christ and God. Mary gave birth to a little baby boy. Those he saved call her Mother of God. But today's scriptures also speak of our name. Whatever family we were born into, whatever name they have given us, we are children of God and heirs with Christ: we bear the name 'Christian.'

Isaiah names the promised child the Prince of Peace. Our sign of peace before communion pledges us, as members of God's royal family, to seek peace within ourselves and to work and pray for peace in the world.

Margaret Bick, Toronto, ON

ENTRANCE ANTIPHON *(See Luke 1.33)*

Hail, holy Mother! The child to whom you gave birth is the King of heaven and earth for ever.

or (See Isaiah 9.2, 6)

A light will shine on us this day, the Lord is born for us: he shall be called Wonderful God, Prince of Peace, Father of the world to come; and his kingship will never end.

INTRODUCTORY RITES *(p. 7)*

OPENING PRAYER

God our Father, may we always profit by the prayers of the Virgin Mother Mary, for you bring us life and salvation through Jesus Christ her Son.

FIRST READING *(Numbers 6.22-27)*

The Lord spoke to Moses: Speak to Aaron and his sons, saying, Thus you shall bless the children of Israel: You shall say to them,

The Lord bless you and keep you;
the Lord make his face to shine upon you,
and be gracious to you;
the Lord lift up his countenance upon you,
and give you peace.

So they shall put my name on the children of Israel, and I will bless them.

The word of the Lord. **Thanks be to God.**

RESPONSORIAL PSALM *(Psalm 67)*

R. **May God be gracious to us and bless us.**

May God be gracious to us · **and** bless_us
and make his face to shine · **up**-on_us,
that your way may be known up-**on** earth,
your saving power a-**mong** all nations. R.

Let the nations be glad and sing · **for** joy,
for you judge the peoples with equity
   and guide the nations up-**on** earth.
Let the peoples praise you, · **O** God;
let all the · **peo**-ples praise_you. R.

The earth has yielded · **its** increase;
God, our God, · **has** blessed_us.
May God continue · **to** bless_us;
let all the ends of the · **earth** re-vere_him. R.

SECOND READING *(Galatians 4.4-7)*

Brothers and sisters: When the fullness of time had come, God sent his Son, born of a woman, born under the law, in order to redeem those who were under the law, so that we might receive adoption to sonship.

And because you are sons and daughters, God has sent the Spirit of his Son into our hearts, crying, "Abba! Father!" So you are no longer slave but son, and if son then also heir, through God.

The word of the Lord. **Thanks be to God.**

GOSPEL ACCLAMATION *(Hebrews 1.1-2)*

Alleluia. Alleluia. Long ago God spoke to our ancestors by the Prophets; in these last days he has spoken to us by the Son. **Alleluia.**

GOSPEL *(Luke 2.16-21)*

A reading from the holy Gospel according to Luke. **Glory to you, Lord.**

The shepherds went with haste to Bethlehem and found Mary and Joseph, and the child lying in the manger. When they saw this, they made known what had been told them about this child; and all who heard it were amazed at what the shepherds told them.

But Mary treasured all these words and pondered them in her heart.

The shepherds returned, glorifying and praising God for all they had heard and seen, as it had been told them.

After eight days had passed, it was time to circumcise the child; and he was called Jesus, the name given by the Angel before he was conceived in the womb.

The Gospel of the Lord. **Praise to you, Lord Jesus Christ.**

PROFESSION OF FAITH *(p. 13-14)*

PRAYER OF THE FAITHFUL

The following intentions are suggestions only.

℟. **Lord, hear our prayer.**

For all Christians, called to be a sign of unity as we work together for justice, we pray to the Lord: ℟.

For peace in our world broken by violence, abuse, hatred and the misuse of the world's resources, we pray to the Lord: ℟.

For all who hunger and thirst for freedom from poverty, unemployment and prejudice, we pray to the Lord: ℟.

For all those who, like Mary, display strength, courage and perseverance, we pray to the Lord: ℟.

PREPARATION OF THE GIFTS *(p. 15)*

PRAYER OVER THE GIFTS

God our Father, we celebrate at this season the beginning of our salvation. On this feast of Mary, the Mother of God, we ask that our salvation will be brought to its fulfillment.

PREFACE *(Blessed Virgin Mary I, p. 18)*

COMMUNION ANTIPHON *(Hebrews 13.8)*

Jesus Christ is the same yesterday, today, and for ever.

PRAYER AFTER COMMUNION

Father, as we proclaim the Virgin Mary to be the mother of Christ and the mother of the Church, may our communion with her Son bring us to salvation.

SOLEMN BLESSING — New Year *(Optional)*

Bow your heads and pray for God's blessing.

Born of the Blessed Virgin Mary, the Son of God redeemed mankind. May he enrich you with his blessings. **Amen.**

You received the author of life through Mary. May you always rejoice in her loving care. **Amen.**

You have come to rejoice at Mary's feast. May you be filled with the joys of the Spirit and the gifts of your eternal home. **Amen.**

May almighty God bless you, the Father, and the Son, and the Holy Spirit. **Amen.**

DISMISSAL *(p. 67)*

In the Jewish tradition, the scriptures were not taken literally; rather, they were searched for a deeper meaning which spoke to the current situation. Rabbis taught that the scriptures could be examined and interpreted for every generation. God was constantly being revealed. We can ask ourselves: what is God revealing to us in this feast?

To begin, we might focus on the foreign visitors to the stable. We can imagine they left the safety and security of their homeland, travelled with no modern mapping devices and gave up control of their lives to follow a voice deep within themselves that was leading them to an unknown destination. They may have felt totally vulnerable, as vulnerable as the poor, defenceless child they sought to worship.

By choosing to be vulnerable and to risk a leap of faith, they discovered an unexpected gift much greater than the ones they were ready to offer. They discovered the fulfillment of a 'holy longing.' Each day, we are called to leave the safety and security of what we know, the conventions which rule our lives, the control we think we have. We are called to leave it all behind and step out into the unknown, to let go and be vulnerable in order to discover the answer to our 'holy longing.'

Today, let us celebrate a feast for risk-takers by taking a leap of faith which will lead us to the kingdom.

Anthony Chezzi, Sudbury, ON

ENTRANCE ANTIPHON *(See Malachi 3.1)*

The Lord and ruler is coming; kingship is his, and government and power.

INTRODUCTORY RITES *(p. 7)*

OPENING PRAYER

Father, you revealed your Son to the nations by the guidance of a star. Lead us to your glory in heaven by the light of faith.

FIRST READING *(Isaiah 60.1-6)*

Arise, shine, for your light has come,
and the glory of the Lord has risen upon you!
For darkness shall cover the earth,
and thick darkness the peoples;
but the Lord will arise upon you,
and his glory will appear over you.
Nations shall come to your light,
and kings to the brightness of your dawn.
Lift up your eyes and look around;
they all gather together, they come to you;
your sons shall come from far away,
and your daughters shall be carried
on their nurses' arms.

Then you shall see and be radiant;
your heart shall thrill and rejoice,
because the abundance of the sea
shall be brought to you,
the wealth of the nations shall come to you.
A multitude of camels shall cover you,
the young camels of Midian and Ephah;
all those from Sheba shall come.
They shall bring gold and frankincense,
and shall proclaim the praise of the Lord.

The word of the Lord. **Thanks be to God.**

RESPONSORIAL PSALM *(Psalm 72)*

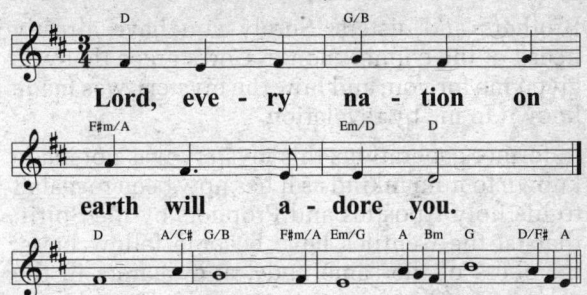

R. **Lord, every nation on earth will adore you.**

Give the king your justice, O · **God,**
and your righteousness to a king's · **son.**
May he judge your · **people** with righteousness,
and your · **poor** with justice. R.

In his days may righteousness · **flourish**
and peace abound, until the moon is no · **more.**
May he have dominion from · **sea** to sea,
and from the River to the · **ends_of** the earth. R.

May the kings of Tarshish
and of the isles render him · **tribute,**
may the kings of Sheba and Seba bring · **gifts.**
May all kings fall · **down** be-fore_him,
all nations · **give** him service. R.

For he delivers the needy one who · **calls,**
the poor and the one who has no · **helper.**
He has pity on the · **weak_and** the needy,
and saves the · **lives_of** the needy. R.

©2009 Gordon Johnston/Novalis

SECOND READING *(Ephesians 3.2-3, 5-6)*

Brothers and sisters: Surely you have already heard of the commission of God's grace that was given me for you, and how the mystery was made known to me by revelation.

In former generations this mystery was not made known to humankind as it has now been revealed to his holy Apostles and Prophets by the Spirit: that is, the Gentiles have become fellow heirs, members of the same body, and sharers in the promise in Christ Jesus through the Gospel.

The word of the Lord. **Thanks be to God.**

GOSPEL ACCLAMATION *(Matthew 2.2)*

Alleluia. Alleluia. We observed his star at its rising, and have come to pay homage to the Lord. **Alleluia.**

GOSPEL *(Matthew 2.1-12)*

A reading from the holy Gospel according to Matthew. **Glory to you, Lord.**

In the time of King Herod, after Jesus was born in Bethlehem of Judea, wise men from the East came to Jerusalem, asking, "Where is the child who has been born king of the Jews? For we observed his star at its rising, and have come to pay him homage."

When King Herod heard this, he was frightened, and all Jerusalem with him; and calling together all the chief priests and scribes of the people, he inquired of them where the Messiah was to be born. They told him, "In Bethlehem of Judea;

for so it has been written by the Prophet: 'And you, Bethlehem, in the land of Judah, are by no means least among the rulers of Judah; for from you shall come a ruler who is to shepherd my people Israel.'"

Then Herod secretly called for the wise men and learned from them the exact time when the star had appeared. Then he sent them to Bethlehem, saying, "Go and search diligently for the child; and when you have found him, bring me word so that I may also go and pay him homage."

When they had heard the king, they set out; and there, ahead of them, went the star that they had seen at its rising, until it stopped over the place where the child was. When they saw that the star had stopped, they were overwhelmed with joy.

On entering the house, they saw the child with Mary his mother; and they knelt down and paid him homage. Then, opening their treasure chests, they offered him gifts of gold, frankincense, and myrrh.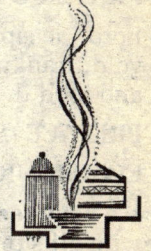

And having been warned in a dream not to return to Herod, they left for their own country by another road.

The Gospel of the Lord. **Praise to you, Lord Jesus Christ.**

PROFESSION OF FAITH *(Nicene Creed, p. 14)*

PRAYER OF THE FAITHFUL

The following intentions are suggestions only.

R. **Lord, hear our prayer.**

For the Church, light of the nations, witness to the message of Jesus, we pray to the Lord: R.

For a deep and mutual respect for all faith traditions among all leaders and teachers, we pray to the Lord: R.

For those who seek a welcome at our table and a place in our communities, we pray to the Lord: R.

For us, God's people, yearning for fresh hope as we seek the Light, we pray to the Lord: R.

PREPARATION OF THE GIFTS (*p. 15*)

PRAYER OVER THE GIFTS

Lord, accept the offerings of your Church, not gold, frankincense and myrrh, but the sacrifice and food they symbolize: Jesus Christ.

PREFACE (*Epiphany, p. 19*)

COMMUNION ANTIPHON (*See Matthew 2.2*)

We have seen his star in the east and have come with gifts to adore the Lord.

PRAYER AFTER COMMUNION

Father, guide us with your light. Help us to recognize Christ in this eucharist and welcome him with love.

SOLEMN BLESSING — Epiphany *(Optional)*

Bow your heads and pray for God's blessing.

God has called you out of darkness, into his wonderful light. May you experience his kindness and blessings, and be strong in faith, in hope, and in love. **Amen.**

Because you are followers of Christ, who appeared on this day as a light shining in darkness, may he make you a light to all your sisters and brothers. **Amen.**

The wise men followed the star, and found Christ, who is light from light. May you too find the Lord when your pilgrimage is ended. **Amen.**

May almighty God bless you, the Father, and the Son, and the Holy Spirit. **Amen.**

DISMISSAL *(p. 67)*

At the end of her email messages, one of my friends includes a quote, ancient wisdom reminding the reader to be kind because everybody has great struggles or burdens. Her note may well have been inspired by today's beautiful first reading from Isaiah.

As we celebrate Jesus' baptism, Isaiah reminds us that the message Jesus brings to our world is a message of justice and tenderness: God will not crush those who are "bruised," nor quench the light that is "dimly burning" in anyone. Today, if we are feeling "bruised" by the injustices of life, our hope dimmed, let us take time to listen and allow the comfort and strength of these words to sink deep into our being.

At the same time, let us be mindful of others struggling around us, whether we know their struggles or not — perhaps a confident young person, or a fellow worker, a neighbour, an elderly person, a family member. Let us resolve to crush no one, nor to put out anyone's light by our impatience or dismissal or gossip, or by participating in injustice. Let us reach out with care and stand always for justice. When we do, we join ourselves to Jesus' ministry. And just as the Father is well pleased with Jesus, and the Holy Spirit comes to strengthen him for the challenges ahead, so too we will receive God's blessing and strength for our journey.

Beth Porter, Richmond Hill, ON

ENTRANCE ANTIPHON *(See Matthew 3.16-17)*

When the Lord had been baptized, the heavens opened and the Spirit came down like a dove to rest on him. Then the voice of the Father thundered: This is my beloved Son, with him I am well pleased.

INTRODUCTORY RITES *(p. 7)*

OPENING PRAYER

Almighty, eternal God, when the Spirit descended upon Jesus at his baptism in the Jordan, you revealed him as your own beloved Son. Keep us, your children born of water and the Spirit, faithful to our calling.

FIRST READING *(Isaiah 42.1-4, 6-7)*

Thus says the Lord:
"Here is my servant, whom I uphold,
my chosen, in whom my soul delights;
I have put my spirit upon him;
he will bring forth justice to the nations.
He will not cry or lift up his voice,
or make it heard in the street;
a bruised reed he will not break,
and a dimly burning wick he will not quench;
he will faithfully bring forth justice.
He will not grow faint or be crushed
until he has established justice in the earth;
and the coastlands wait for his teaching.

"I am the Lord, I have called you
     in righteousness,
I have taken you by the hand and kept you;
I have given you as a covenant to the people,
a light to the nations,

to open the eyes that are blind,
to bring out the prisoners from the dungeon,
from the prison those who sit in darkness."

The word of the Lord. **Thanks be to God.**

RESPONSORIAL PSALM *(Psalm 29)*

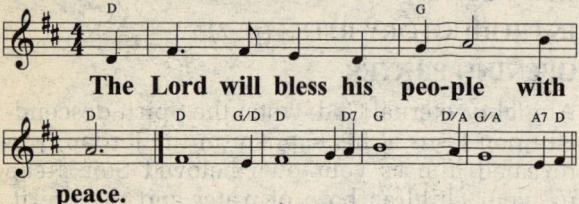

The Lord will bless his peo-ple with peace.

R̸. **The Lord will bless his people with peace.**

Ascribe to the Lord, O heavenly · **beings,**
ascribe to the Lord glory · **and** strength.
Ascribe to the Lord the glory of his · **name;**
worship the Lord in · **holy** splendour. R̸.

The voice of the Lord is over the · **waters;**
the Lord, over · **mighty** waters.
The voice of the Lord is · **powerful;**
the voice of the Lord is · **full_of** majesty. R̸.

The God of glory · **thunders,**
and in his temple all · **say,** "Glory!"
The Lord sits enthroned over the · **flood;**
the Lord sits enthroned as king · **for**-ever. R̸.

©2009 Gordon Johnston/Novalis

SECOND READING *(Acts 10.34-38)*

Peter began to speak:

"I truly understand that God shows no partiality, but in every nation anyone who fears him

and does what is right is acceptable to him. You know the message he sent to the people of Israel, preaching peace by Jesus Christ — he is Lord of all. That message spread throughout Judea, beginning in Galilee after the baptism that John announced: how God anointed Jesus of Nazareth with the Holy Spirit and with power; how he went about doing good and healing all who were oppressed by the devil, for God was with him."

The word of the Lord. **Thanks be to God.**

GOSPEL ACCLAMATION *(See Mark 9.7)*

Alleluia. Alleluia. The heavens were opened and the Father's voice was heard: this is my Son, the beloved; listen to him! **Alleluia.**

GOSPEL *(Matthew 3.13-17)*

A reading from the holy Gospel according to Matthew. **Glory to you, Lord.**

Jesus came from Galilee to John at the Jordan, to be baptized by him. John would have prevented him, saying, "I need to be baptized by you, and do you come to me?" But Jesus answered him, "Let it be so for now; for it is proper for us in this way to fulfill all righteousness." Then John consented.

And when Jesus had been baptized, just as he came up from the water, suddenly the heavens were opened to him and he saw the Spirit of God descending like a dove and alighting on him. And a voice from heaven said, "This is my Son, the Beloved, with whom I am well pleased."

The Gospel of the Lord. **Praise to you, Lord Jesus Christ.**

PROFESSION OF FAITH *(p. 13-14)*

PRAYER OF THE FAITHFUL

The following intentions are suggestions only.

R̥. **Lord, hear our prayer.**

For the Church, community of the baptized, entrusted to continue the mission and ministry of Jesus, we pray to the Lord: R̥.

For a deeper awareness of and respect for the dignity of all human beings, we pray to the Lord: R̥.

For those among us who suffer any kind of pain, we pray to the Lord: R̥.

For us, God's priestly people gathered here, called to bless the Lord for all his gifts, we pray to the Lord: R̥.

PREPARATION OF THE GIFTS *(p. 15)*

PRAYER OVER THE GIFTS

Lord, we celebrate the revelation of Christ your Son who takes away the sins of the world. Accept our gifts and let them become one with his sacrifice, for he is Lord for ever and ever.

PREFACE *(Baptism of the Lord, p. 19)*

COMMUNION ANTIPHON *(John 1.32, 34)*

This is he of whom John said: I have seen and have given witness that this is the Son of God.

PRAYER AFTER COMMUNION

Lord, you feed us with bread from heaven. May we hear your Son with faith and become your children in name and in fact.

BLESSING AND DISMISSAL *(p. 67)*

"You have given me an open ear." This marvellous line in today's psalm evokes the basis for any witness, the 'how' of all discipleship, the possibility of vocation, 'call.' Just as the instrumentalists in a band or orchestra need an open ear so that they can tune together, so the Christian body needs an open ear so it can be attuned to God's call and presence, and respond.

That openness is, of course, a challenge in our noisy, busy, distracting world. But if we are to create a 'culture of vocations' — an ambiance in which believers *can* hear God's call — those open ears are absolutely necessary. But the ears may just be an image of the whole person — eyes, heart and mind — whose openness is needed. God's voice speaks in the poor, and asks for justice and generosity in response to their needs. God's voice speaks in the lonely and marginalized, and invites our compassion. God's voice speaks in the cries of those oppressed by war, by violence and by injustice, and asks for our solidarity.

A culture of vocations cannot be limited to hearing a call to a state of life. For such a culture to thrive, our ears need lots of practice at hearing the divine voice wherever it calls. Whether our ears are seven years old or seventy, the better tuned they are, the more fully we can respond.

Bernadette Gasslein, Edmonton, AB

ENTRANCE ANTIPHON *(Psalm 66.4)*

May all the earth give you worship and praise, and break into song to your name, O God, Most High.

INTRODUCTORY RITES *(p. 7)*

OPENING PRAYER

Father of heaven and earth, hear our prayers, and show us the way to peace in the world.

FIRST READING *(Isaiah 49.3, 5-6)*

The Lord said to me,
"You are my servant, Israel, in whom
    I will be glorified."

And now the Lord says,
who formed me in the womb to be his servant,
to bring Jacob back to him,
and that Israel might be gathered to him,
for I am honoured in the sight of the Lord,
and my God has become my strength.

He says,
"It is too small a thing that you should be
    my servant
to raise up the tribes of Jacob
and to restore the survivors of Israel;
I will give you as a light to the nations,
that my salvation may reach
    to the end of the earth."

The word of the Lord. **Thanks be to God.**

RESPONSORIAL PSALM *(Psalm 40)*

Here I am, Lord; I come to do your will.

℟ **Here I am, Lord; I come to do your will.**

I waited patiently for the · **Lord;**
he inclined to me and · **heard** my cry.
He put a new song in · **my** mouth,
a song of praise · **to** our God. ℟

Sacrifice and offering you do not de--**sire,**
but you have given me an · **o**-pen ear.
Burnt offering · **and** sin_offering
you have · **not** re-quired. ℟

Then I said, "Here I · **am;**
in the scroll of the book it is · **written** of me.
I delight to do your will, O · **my** God;
your law is with--**in** my heart." ℟

I have told the glad news of de--**liverance**
in the great · **con**-gre-gation;
see, I have not restrained · **my** lips,
as you · **know,** O Lord. ℟

©2010 Gordon Johnston/Novalis

SECOND READING *(1 Corinthians 1.1-3)*

From Paul, called to be an Apostle of Christ Jesus by the will of God, and from our brother Sosthenes. To the Church of God that is in Corinth, to those who are sanctified in Christ Jesus, called to be saints, together with all those who in every place call on the name of our Lord Jesus Christ, both their Lord and ours:

Grace to you and peace from God our Father and the Lord Jesus Christ.

The word of the Lord. **Thanks be to God.**

GOSPEL ACCLAMATION *(John 1.14, 12)*

Alleluia. Alleluia. The Word became flesh and lived among us. To all who received him, he gave the power to become children of God. **Alleluia.**

GOSPEL *(John 1.29-34)*

A reading from the holy Gospel according to John. **Glory to you, Lord.**

John the Baptist saw Jesus coming toward him and declared, "Here is the Lamb of God who takes away the sin of the world! This is he of whom I said, 'After me comes a man who ranks ahead of me because he was before me.' I myself did not know him; but I came baptizing with water for this reason, that he might be revealed to Israel."

And John testified, "I saw the Spirit descending from heaven like a dove, and remain on him. I myself did not know him, but the one who sent me to baptize with water said to me, 'He on whom you see the Spirit descend and remain is the one who baptizes with the Holy Spirit.' And I myself have seen and have testified that this is the Son of God."

The Gospel of the Lord. **Praise to you, Lord Jesus Christ.**

PROFESSION OF FAITH *(p. 13-14)*

PRAYER OF THE FAITHFUL

The following intentions are suggestions only.

R̞ **Lord, hear our prayer.**

For the Church, called to share the gifts received from the Spirit for the good of all, we pray to the Lord: R̞

For leaders of nations and peoples, from whom is expected prudent, just and wise action, we pray to the Lord: R̞

For the elderly among us who are lonely, shut-in or ignored, we pray to the Lord: R̞

For us, your people gathered here, seeking healing and renewal in this celebration of the Lord's death and resurrection, we pray to the Lord: R̞

PREPARATION OF THE GIFTS *(p. 15)*

PRAYER OVER THE GIFTS

Father, may we celebrate the eucharist with reverence and love, for when we proclaim the death of the Lord you continue the work of his redemption, who is Lord for ever and ever.

PREFACE *(Sundays in Ordinary Time, p. 20)*

COMMUNION ANTIPHON *(1 John 4.16)*

We know and believe in God's love for us.

PRAYER AFTER COMMUNION

Lord, you have nourished us with bread from heaven. Fill us with your Spirit, and make us one in peace and love.

BLESSING AND DISMISSAL *(p. 67)*

January 23   **3rd Sunday**
Week of Prayer for Christian Unity **in Ordinary Time**
"One in the apostles' teaching"

This week we are praying that our desire to be united as Christians will become more tangible. We hear Jesus say, "Follow me." Four fishermen spontaneously drop their nets and follow Jesus. For a brief and precious moment there is unity in Jesus' community. This unity is the result of each person freely letting go of their past and embracing a new future.

Unity is gained, in part, when each person voluntarily *gives up* something that hinders them from being included in the community. Parents' long-held beliefs and traditions may be challenged. Spouses and good friends may be asked to change and move from *my* way to *our* way or risk ending up alone. Unity among Christians (and all religions) will be realized through authentic re-examination of perspectives and positions that cause the current disunity. In this way, we will demonstrate that we value communion over being right.

The challenge is to recognize which conviction we can let go of without compromising our integrity. Creating unity involves taking risks like the ones the disciples took by following Jesus. It is only in the act of letting go that we discover we were holding on too tightly.

Joe Vorstermans, Richmond Hill, ON

Mass for the Unity of Christians (#517) may be celebrated during the week. However, for pastoral reasons, it may be celebrated on Sunday.

ENTRANCE ANTIPHON *(Psalm 96.1, 6)*

Sing a new song to the Lord! Sing to the Lord, all the earth. Truth and beauty surround him, he lives in holiness and glory.

> *Christian Unity (Psalm 106.47):*
> **Save us, Lord our God, and gather us together from the nations, that we may proclaim your holy name, and glory in your praise.**

INTRODUCTORY RITES *(p. 7)*

OPENING PRAYER

All-powerful and ever-living God, direct your love that is within us, that our efforts in the name of your Son may bring the human family to unity and peace.

> *Christian Unity:*
> Lord, hear the prayers of your people and bring the hearts of believers together in your praise and in common sorrow for their sins. Heal all divisions among Christians that we may rejoice in the perfect unity of your Church and move together as one to eternal life in your kingdom.

FIRST READING *(Isaiah 9.1-4)*

There will be no gloom for those who were in anguish. In the former time the Lord brought into contempt the land of Zebulun and the land of Naphtali, but in the latter time he will make glorious the way of the sea, the land beyond the Jordan, Galilee of the nations.

The people who walked in darkness have seen a great light; those who lived in a land of deep darkness — on them light has shone. You have multiplied the nation, you have increased its joy; they rejoice before you as with joy at the harvest, as people exult when dividing plunder.

For the yoke of their burden, and the bar across their shoulders, the rod of their oppressor, you have broken as on the day of Midian.

The word of the Lord. **Thanks be to God.**

RESPONSORIAL PSALM *(Psalm 27)*

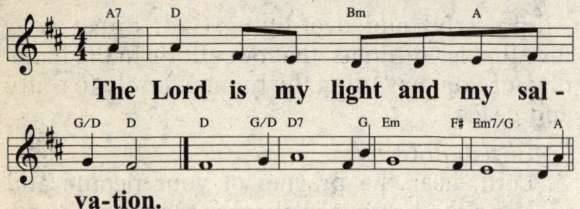

The Lord is my light and my sal-va-tion.

R. **The Lord is my light and my salvation.**

The Lord is my light and my sal-**vation;**
whom shall · **I** fear?
The Lord is the stronghold of my · **life;**
of whom shall I be · **a**-fraid? R.

One thing I asked of the Lord,
     that will I · **seek_after:**
to live in the house of the Lord all the days
     of · **my** life,
to behold the beauty of the · **Lord,**
and to inquire in · **his** temple. R.

I believe that I shall see the goodness
   of the · **Lord**
in the land of · **the** living.
Wait for the Lord; be · **strong,**
and let your heart take courage;
   wait · **for_the** Lord! R.

©2010 Gordon Johnston/Novalis

SECOND READING *(1 Cor 1.10-13, 17-18)*

I appeal to you, brothers and sisters, by the name of our Lord Jesus Christ, that all of you be in agreement and that there be no divisions among you, but that you be united in the same mind and the same purpose.

For it has been reported to me by Chloe's people that there are quarrels among you, my brothers and sisters. What I mean is that each of you says, "I belong to Paul," or "I belong to Apollos," or "I belong to Cephas," or "I belong to Christ."

Has Christ been divided? Was Paul crucified for you? Or were you baptized in the name of Paul?

For Christ did not send me to baptize but to proclaim the Gospel, and not with eloquent wisdom so that the Cross of Christ might not be emptied of its power.

For the message about the Cross is foolishness to those who are perishing, but to us who are being saved it is the power of God.

The word of the Lord. **Thanks be to God.**

GOSPEL ACCLAMATION *(See Matthew 4.23)*

Alleluia. Alleluia. Jesus proclaimed the good news of the kingdom curing every sickness among the people. **Alleluia.**

GOSPEL *(Matthew 4.12-23)*

The shorter version ends at the asterisks.

A reading from the holy Gospel according to Matthew. **Glory to you, Lord.**

When Jesus heard that John had been arrested, he withdrew to Galilee. He left Nazareth and made his home in Capernaum by the sea, in the territory of Zebulun and Naphtali, so that what had been spoken through the Prophet Isaiah might be fulfilled: "Land of Zebulun, land of Naphtali, on the road by the sea, across the Jordan, Galilee of the Gentiles — the people who sat in darkness have seen a great light, and for those who sat in the region and shadow of death light has dawned."

From that time Jesus began to proclaim, "Repent, for the kingdom of heaven has come near."

* * *

As he walked by the Sea of Galilee, he saw two brothers, Simon, who is called Peter, and Andrew his brother, casting a net into the sea, for they were fishermen. And he said to them, "Come, follow me, and I will make you fishers of people." Immediately they left their nets and followed him.

As he went from there, he saw two other brothers, James son of Zebedee and his brother John, in the boat with their father Zebedee, mending their nets, and he called them. Immediately they left the boat and their father, and followed him.

Jesus went throughout Galilee, teaching in their synagogues and proclaiming the good news of the kingdom and curing every disease and every sickness among the people.

The Gospel of the Lord. **Praise to you, Lord Jesus Christ.**

PROFESSION OF FAITH *(p. 13-14)*

PRAYER OF THE FAITHFUL

The following intentions are suggestions only.

R̲ **Lord, hear our prayer.**

For the Church, called to proclaim faithfully the mission of Jesus, we pray to the Lord: R̲

For leaders of nations, entrusted with the political and economic futures of their peoples, we pray to the Lord: R̲

For those in our global community who, poor, unemployed and oppressed, seek justice, we pray to the Lord: R̲

For our parish community, called in baptism to be responsible for one another, we pray to the Lord: R̲

PREPARATION OF THE GIFTS *(p. 15)*

PRAYER OVER THE GIFTS

Lord, receive our gifts. Let our offerings make us holy and bring us salvation.

> *Christian Unity:*
> Lord, hear our prayer for your mercy as we celebrate this memorial of our salvation. May

143

this sacrament of your love be our sign of unity
and our bond of charity.

PREFACE *(Sundays in Ordinary Time, p. 20 or
Christian Unity, p. 23)*

COMMUNION ANTIPHON *(Psalm 34.5)*

**Look up at the Lord with gladness and smile;
your face will never be ashamed.**

Christian Unity (Colossians 3.14-15):
**To crown all things there must be love, to
bind them together and bring them to completion; and may the peace of Christ rule in
your hearts, that peace to which all of you are
called as one body.**

PRAYER AFTER COMMUNION

God, all-powerful Father, may the new life you
give us increase our love and keep us in the joy
of your kingdom.

Christian Unity:
Lord, fill us with the Spirit of love; by the
power of this sacrifice bring together in love
and peace all who believe in you.

BLESSING AND DISMISSAL *(p. 67)*

Before my nieces and nephews could walk, I loved to stand them on my feet and 'walk' them. Perhaps this is one of our first experiences of walking in someone else's shoes, but it is certainly not the last. The individual Christian — and, indeed, the whole Church — always strives to follow faithfully in the footsteps of Christ.

When the Christian community hears the joyful proclamation of the Beatitudes in today's gospel reading, then, it neither takes pride in how meek or humble it is, nor becomes discouraged by what may appear to be a very daunting task. Rather, it has an 'aha!' moment, realizing that, when it follows in Christ's footsteps, it experiences what Christ experiences: the blessedness of the kingdom of heaven. The Christian community, knowing the final outcome of the passion and death of Christ, is able to rejoice: it has it on the very best authority that sin and death, injustice and persecution, are not all there is. Just as Jesus Christ was vindicated and is now risen from the dead, so Christians who live with the single-minded purpose of 'doing God's will' will also be vindicated.

Paul reminds us we have only God to thank for our participation in this plan of divine wisdom. Chosen, called and guided by God alone, we make our boast in the One Source of Life.

Christine Mader, Calgary, AB

ENTRANCE ANTIPHON *(Psalm 106.47)*

Save us, Lord our God, and gather us together from the nations, that we may proclaim your holy name and glory in your praise.

INTRODUCTORY RITES *(p. 7)*

OPENING PRAYER

Lord our God, help us to love you with all our hearts and to love all people as you love them.

FIRST READING *(Zephaniah 2.3; 3.12-13)*

Seek the Lord, all you humble of the land,
who do his commands;
seek righteousness, seek humility;
perhaps you may be hidden on the day
    of the Lord's wrath.

For I will leave in the midst of you
a people humble and lowly.
They shall seek refuge in the name
    of the Lord —
the remnant of Israel;
they shall do no wrong and utter no lies,
nor shall a deceitful tongue be found
    in their mouths.
Then they will pasture and lie down,
and no one shall make them afraid.

The word of the Lord. **Thanks be to God.**

RESPONSORIAL PSALM *(Psalm 146)*

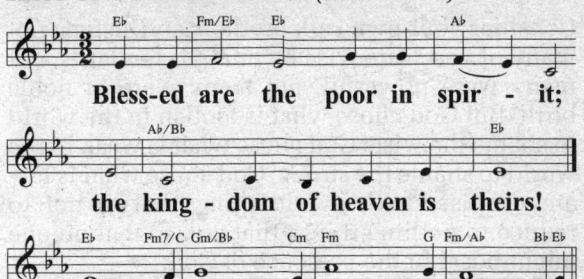

℞. **Blessed are the poor in spirit;
the kingdom of heaven is theirs!**

or **Alleluia!**

It is the Lord who keeps faith for··**ever,**
who executes justice for the op··**pressed;**
who gives food to the · **hungry.**
The Lord sets the · **prisoners** free. ℞.

The Lord opens the eyes of the · **blind**
and lifts up those who are bowed · **down;**
the Lord loves the · **righteous**
and watches over · **the** strangers. ℞.

The Lord upholds the orphan and the · **widow,**
but the way of the wicked he brings to · **ruin.**
The Lord will reign for··**ever,**
your God, O Zion, for all · **gener**-ations. ℞.

©2010 Gordon Johnston/Novalis

147

SECOND READING *(1 Corinthians 1.26-31)*

Consider your own call, brothers and sisters: not many of you were wise by human standards, not many were powerful, not many were of noble birth. But God chose what is foolish in the world to shame the wise; God chose what is weak in the world to shame the strong; God chose what is low and despised in the world, things that are not, to reduce to nothing things that are, so that no one might boast in the presence of God.

God is the source of your life in Christ Jesus, who became for us wisdom from God, and righteousness and sanctification and redemption, in order that, as it is written, "Let the one who boasts, boast in the Lord."

The word of the Lord. **Thanks be to God.**

GOSPEL ACCLAMATION *(Matthew 5.12)*

Alleluia. Alleluia. Rejoice and be glad, for your reward is great in heaven. **Alleluia.**

GOSPEL *(Matthew 5.1-12)*

A reading from the holy Gospel according to Matthew. **Glory to you, Lord.**

When Jesus saw the crowds, he went up the mountain; and after he sat down, his disciples came to him. Then he began to speak, and taught them, saying:

"Blessed are the poor in spirit,
for theirs is the kingdom of heaven.
Blessed are those who mourn,
for they will be comforted.

Blessed are the meek,
for they will inherit the earth.
Blessed are those who hunger and thirst
    for righteousness,
for they will be filled.

"Blessed are the merciful,
for they will receive mercy.
Blessed are the pure in heart,
for they will see God.
Blessed are the peacemakers,
for they will be called children of God.
Blessed are those who are persecuted
    for righteousness' sake,
for theirs is the kingdom of heaven.

"Blessed are you when people revile you and persecute you and utter all kinds of evil against you falsely on my account. Rejoice and be glad, for your reward is great in heaven, for in the same way they persecuted the Prophets who were before you."

The Gospel of the Lord. **Praise to you, Lord Jesus Christ.**

PROFESSION OF FAITH *(p. 13-14)*

PRAYER OF THE FAITHFUL

The following intentions are suggestions only.

R. **Lord, hear our prayer.**

For the Church, called to serve all nations, we pray to the Lord: R.

For open and ongoing dialogue between nations, we pray to the Lord: R.

For those who suffer persecution and loneliness, we pray to the Lord: R.

For us, called in baptism to be prophets of God's word, we pray to the Lord: R̞.

PREPARATION OF THE GIFTS *(p. 15)*

PRAYER OVER THE GIFTS

Lord, be pleased with the gifts we bring to your altar, and make them the sacrament of our salvation.

PREFACE *(Sundays in Ordinary Time, p. 20)*

COMMUNION ANTIPHON *(Matthew 5.3-4)*

Blessed are the poor in spirit; the kingdom of heaven is theirs! Blessed are the lowly; they shall inherit the land.

PRAYER AFTER COMMUNION

Lord, you invigorate us with this help to our salvation. By this eucharist give the true faith continued growth throughout the world.

BLESSING AND DISMISSAL *(p. 67)*

Today's gospel about salt and light presents one of Jesus' most vivid teachings. In the ancient biblical world, salt was a precious commodity, associated with longevity and permanence. It served as the principal way to preserve food. Loyalty and friendship were sealed with salt because its essence does not change. In both Islam and Judaism, salt seals a bargain because it is immutable. In Christianity, salt is associated not only with longevity and permanence but, by extension, with truth and wisdom. Our Church dispenses not only holy water but holy salt, *sal sapientia*, the Salt of Wisdom.

Salt gives flavour and zest to food; it also makes people thirst for something more. Jesus wanted his disciples to give flavour and zest to the world through his teaching — to preserve the truth as he proclaimed it and to make the world thirst for more. Salt is an appropriate metaphor for discipleship, which can and does lose its vigour over time if care is not taken to preserve it.

In addition to salt for the earth, Jesus calls his followers to be the light of the world. He transfers his light to those who follow him: "You are the light of the world." We are called to follow the Lord Jesus, to be salt and light for the world, to bring to the world the flavour of the gospel and the light of Christ.

Thomas Rosica, Toronto, ON

ENTRANCE ANTIPHON *(Psalm 95.6-7)*

Come, let us worship the Lord. Let us bow down in the presence of our maker, for he is the Lord our God.

INTRODUCTORY RITES *(p. 7)*

OPENING PRAYER

Father, watch over your family and keep us safe in your care, for all our hope is in you.

FIRST READING *(Isaiah 58.6-10)*

Thus says the Lord:
Is this not the fast that I choose:
to loose the bonds of injustice,
to undo the thongs of the yoke,
to let the oppressed go free,
and to break every yoke?
Is it not to share your bread with the hungry,
and bring the homeless poor into your house;
when you see the naked, to cover them,
and not to hide yourself from your own kin?

Then your light shall break forth like the dawn,
and your healing shall spring up quickly;
your vindicator shall go before you,
the glory of the Lord shall be your rear guard.
Then you shall call, and the Lord will answer;
you shall cry for help, and he will say, Here I am.

If you remove the yoke from among you,
the pointing of the finger, the speaking of evil,
if you offer your food to the hungry
and satisfy the needs of the afflicted,
then your light shall rise in the darkness
and your gloom be like the noonday.

The word of the Lord. **Thanks be to God.**

RESPONSORIAL PSALM *(Psalm 112)*

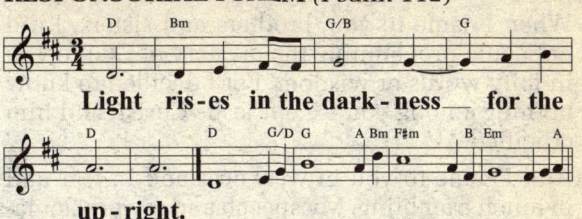

Light ris-es in the dark-ness___ for the

up - right.

℟ **Light rises in the darkness for the upright.**

or **Alleluia!**

Light rises in the darkness · **for_the** upright:
gracious, merciful · **and** righteous.
It is well with the person
    who deals generously · **and** lends,
who conducts their af-**fairs** with justice. ℟

For the righteous person·will never · **be** moved;
they will be remembered · **for**-ever.
Unafraid of · **evil** tidings;
their heart is firm, secure · **in** the Lord. ℟

That person's heart is steady
    and will not · **be_a**-fraid.
One who has distributed freely,
    who has given · **to_the** poor,
their righteousness endures · **for**-ever:
their name is ex-**alted** in honour. ℟

©2010 Gordon Johnston/Novalis

Fifth Sunday in Ordinary Time

SECOND READING *(1 Corinthians 2.1-5)*

When I came to you, brothers and sisters, I did not come proclaiming the mystery of God to you in lofty words or wisdom. For I decided to know nothing among you except Jesus Christ, and him crucified.

And I came to you in weakness and in fear and in much trembling. My speech and my proclamation were not with plausible words of wisdom, but with a demonstration of the Spirit and of power, so that your faith might rest not on human wisdom but on the power of God.

The word of the Lord. **Thanks be to God.**

GOSPEL ACCLAMATION *(John 8.12)*

Alleluia. Alleluia. I am the light of the world, says the Lord; whoever follows me will have the light of life. **Alleluia.**

GOSPEL *(Matthew 5.13-16)*

A reading from the holy Gospel according to Matthew. **Glory to you, Lord.**

Jesus said to his disciples: "You are the salt of the earth; but if salt has lost its taste, how can its saltiness be restored? It is no longer good for anything, but is thrown out and trampled under foot.

"You are the light of the world. A city built on a hill cannot be hidden. No one after lighting a lamp puts it under the bushel basket, but on the lampstand, and it gives light to all in the house. In the same way, let your light shine before human beings, so that they may see your good works and give glory to your Father in heaven."

The Gospel of the Lord. **Praise to you, Lord Jesus Christ.**

154

PROFESSION OF FAITH *(p. 13-14)*

PRAYER OF THE FAITHFUL

The following intentions are suggestions only.

R. **Lord, hear our prayer.**

For the Church, community of disciples, called to follow Jesus in all things, we pray to the Lord: R.

For nations and peoples as they struggle to build a world of peace and justice, we pray to the Lord: R.

For those among us who seek healing, sustenance and peace, we pray to the Lord: R.

For us, God's people, invited to discover God in the routine of our lives, we pray to the Lord: R.

PREPARATION OF THE GIFTS *(p. 15)*

PRAYER OVER THE GIFTS

Lord our God, may the bread and wine you give us for our nourishment on earth become the sacrament of our eternal life.

PREFACE *(Sundays in Ordinary Time, p. 20)*

COMMUNION ANTIPHON *(Psalm 107.8-9)*

Give praise to the Lord for his kindness, for his wonderful deeds toward men. He has filled the hungry with good things, he has satisfied the thirsty.

or (Matthew 5.5-6)

Blessed are the sorrowing; they shall be consoled. Blessed those who hunger and thirst for what is right; they shall be satisfied.

PRAYER AFTER COMMUNION

God our Father, you give us a share in the one bread and the one cup and make us one in Christ. Help us to bring your salvation and joy to all the world.

BLESSING AND DISMISSAL *(p. 67)*

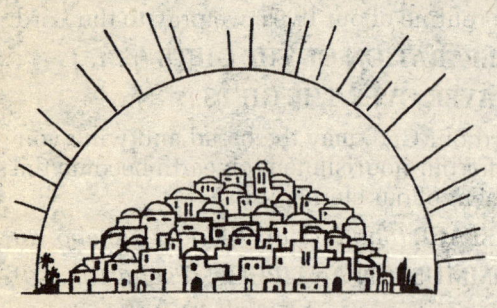

God summons us to a radical way of living. We are called to be more than just moral: God invites us to be virtuous. We become virtuous by habitually choosing to do good. Naturally, we are not perfect, but God calls us to reflect on how we live and to understand what has gone right and wrong for us. Such reflection can lead us to insight that will help us to live better — be virtuous — in the future. Therefore, by reflecting on our experiences in the light of our faith, we grow in wisdom.

Sirach affirms that God knows every human action; Paul reminds us that God has many riches for those who love him; and Jesus, in Matthew's Gospel, says that he has come not to abolish but to fulfill the Law and the Prophets. What we see clearly in the readings today is that there are repercussions, consequences — good or bad — for all our actions. Our challenge is to avoid the opportunities that do harm and to choose what directs us to God.

Sirach, the Psalmist, Paul and Jesus embraced this way of life; they are examples of how it is possible for us to become virtuous and wise. If we take to heart their messages from the readings this Sunday, we too, like them, will be true beacons of virtue — people of faith, hope and love.

Caroline Nolan, Edmonton, AB

ENTRANCE ANTIPHON *(Psalm 31.3)*

Lord, be my rock of safety, the stronghold that saves me. For the honour of your name, lead me and guide me.

INTRODUCTORY RITES *(p. 7)*

OPENING PRAYER

God our Father, you have promised to remain for ever with those who do what is just and right. Help us to live in your presence.

FIRST READING *(Sirach 15.15-20)*

If you choose, you can keep the commandments, and they will save you. If you trust in God, you too shall live, and to act faithfully is a matter of your own choice.

The Lord has placed before you fire and water; stretch out your hand for whichever you choose. Before each person are life and death, good and evil and whichever one chooses, that shall be given.

For great is the wisdom of the Lord; he is mighty in power and sees everything; his eyes are on those who fear him, and he knows every human action. He has not commanded anyone to be wicked, and he has not given anyone permission to sin.

The word of the Lord. **Thanks be to God.**

RESPONSORIAL PSALM *(Psalm 119)*

Bless-ed are those who walk in the law of the

Lord!

R̥ **Blessed are those who walk in the law
of the Lord!**

Blessed are those whose way · **is** blameless,
who walk in the law of · **the** Lord.
Blessed are those who · **keep_his** de-crees,
who seek him · **with** their whole heart. R̥

You have commanded · **your** precepts
to be · **kept** diligently.
O that my ways · **may** be steadfast
in · **keep**-ing your statutes! R̥

Deal bountifully with · **your** servant,
so that I may live and observe · **your** word.
Open my eyes, so that I · **may** be-hold
wondrous things · **out** of your law. R̥

Teach me, O Lord, the way of · **your** statutes,
and I will observe it · **to_the** end.
Give me understanding,
    that I may · **keep** your law
and observe it · **with** my whole heart. R̥

©2010 Gordon Johnston/Novalis

SECOND READING *(1 Corinthians 2.6-10)*

Brothers and sisters: Among the mature we do speak wisdom, though it is not a wisdom of this age or of the rulers of this age, who are doomed to perish. But we speak God's wisdom, secret and hidden, which God decreed before the ages for our glory. None of the rulers of this age understood this; for if they had, they would not have crucified the Lord of glory.

As it is written, "What no eye has seen, nor ear heard, nor the human heart conceived, what God has prepared for those who love him." These things God has revealed to us through the Spirit; for the Spirit searches everything, even the depths of God.

The word of the Lord. **Thanks be to God.**

GOSPEL ACCLAMATION *(See Matthew 11.25)*

Alleluia. Alleluia. Blessed are you, Father, Lord of heaven and earth; you have revealed to little ones the mysteries of the kingdom. **Alleluia.**

GOSPEL *(Matthew 5.17-37)*

For the shorter version, omit the indented parts.

A reading from the holy Gospel according to Matthew. **Glory to you, Lord.**

Jesus said to his disciples: "Do not think that I have come to abolish the Law or the Prophets; I have come not to abolish but to fulfill.

> For truly I tell you, until heaven and earth pass away, not one letter, not one stroke of a letter, will pass from the Law until all is accomplished. Therefore, whoever breaks

one of the least of these commandments, and teaches others to do the same, will be called least in the kingdom of heaven; but whoever does them and teaches them will be called great in the kingdom of heaven.

"For I tell you, unless your righteousness exceeds that of the scribes and Pharisees, you will never enter the kingdom of heaven.

"You have heard that it was said to those of ancient times, 'You shall not murder'; and 'whoever murders shall be liable to judgment.' But I say to you that the one who is angry with their brother or sister, will be liable to judgment; and whoever insults their brother or sister, will be liable to the council; and whoever says, 'You fool,' will be liable to the hell of fire.

"So when you are offering your gift at the altar, if you remember that your brother or sister has something against you, leave your gift there before the altar and go; first be reconciled to your brother or sister, and then come and offer your gift.

"Come to terms quickly with your accuser while the two of you are on the way to court, or your accuser may hand you over to the judge, and the judge to the guard, and you will be thrown into prison. Truly I tell you, you will never get out until you have paid the last penny.

"You have heard that it was said, 'You shall not commit adultery.' But I say to you that everyone who looks at a woman with lust has already committed adultery with her in his heart.

"If your right eye causes you to sin, tear it out and throw it away; it is better for you to lose one of your members than for your whole body to be thrown into hell. And if your right hand causes you to sin, cut it off and throw it away; it is better for you to lose one of your members than for your whole body to go into hell.

"It was also said, 'Whoever divorces his wife, let him give her a certificate of divorce.' But I say to you that anyone who divorces his wife, except on the ground of unchastity, causes her to commit adultery; and whoever marries a divorced woman commits adultery.

"Again, you have heard that it was said to those of ancient times, 'You shall not swear falsely, but carry out the vows you have made to the Lord.' But I say to you: Do not swear at all.

either by heaven, for it is the throne of God, or by the earth, for it is his footstool, or by Jerusalem, for it is the city of the great King. And do not swear by your head, for you cannot make one hair white or black.

"Let your word be 'Yes,' if 'Yes,' or 'No,' if 'No'; anything more than this comes from the evil one."

The Gospel of the Lord. **Praise to you, Lord Jesus Christ.**

PROFESSION OF FAITH *(p. 13-14)*

PRAYER OF THE FAITHFUL

The following intentions are suggestions only.

R. **Lord, hear our prayer.**

For the Church, called to trust in the Lord, who alone brings salvation, we pray to the Lord: R.

For those who shoulder the burden of public service and the challenge of promoting the good of all, we pray to the Lord: R.

For those whose riches, power and success have left them unsatisfied, we pray to the Lord: R.

For us, baptized into discipleship, called to stand with the poor, the hungry and the unemployed in their search for justice, we pray to the Lord: R.

PREPARATION OF THE GIFTS *(p. 15)*

PRAYER OVER THE GIFTS

Lord, we make this offering in obedience to your word. May it cleanse and renew us, and lead us to our eternal reward.

PREFACE *(Sundays in Ordinary Time, p. 20)*

COMMUNION ANTIPHON *(Psalm 78.29-30)*

They ate and were filled; the Lord gave them what they wanted: they were not deprived of their desire.

or (John 3.16) **God loved the world so much, he gave his only Son, that all who believe in him might not perish, but might have eternal life.**

PRAYER AFTER COMMUNION

Lord, you give us food from heaven. May we always hunger for the bread of life.

BLESSING AND DISMISSAL *(p. 67)*

The Sermon on the Mount expresses the very best of Jesus' message: the good news of God who is a loving, caring, comforting and forgiving Father. Such great news entails great revelation too about who we are — children of God — and called to become "salt of the earth" and "light of the world." Knowing who God is for us and who we are to him can only be an illuminating and wonder-filled experience.

What Jesus tells us now is that we ought to rise up to attitudes and deeds that will mirror in day-to-day life our understanding of the God he is revealing to us. Jesus' teaching is first and foremost good news about the heavenly Father. Yet Jesus keeps inviting us to nothing less than imitating God. God is merciful? Be merciful to others. God is kind to all? Be likewise kind to all. God is love only? Be love only, even toward your enemies and those who persecute you.

So when Jesus says "Be perfect as your heavenly Father is perfect," he sets the standard pretty high. But why be satisfied with lower standards and lesser achievements? Jesus himself has given us a shining example that living in the spirit of the Beatitudes not only gets us closer to God, but contributes also to making this world more humane. Isn't that a most thrilling and stimulating mission?

Jean-Pierre Prévost, Chénéville, QC

ENTRANCE ANTIPHON *(Psalm 13.5-6)*

Lord, your mercy is my hope, my heart rejoices in your saving power. I will sing to the Lord for his goodness to me.

INTRODUCTORY RITES *(p. 7)*

OPENING PRAYER

Father, keep before us the wisdom and love you have revealed in your Son. Help us to be like him in word and deed.

FIRST READING *(Leviticus 19.1-2, 17-18)*

The Lord spoke to Moses:
"Speak to all the congregation of the children of Israel and say to them:
'You shall be holy,
    for I the Lord your God am holy.
You shall not hate in your heart
    anyone of your kin;
you shall reprove your neighbour,
or you will incur guilt yourself.
You shall not take vengeance
or bear a grudge against any of your people,
but you shall love your neighbour as yourself:
I am the Lord.'"

The word of the Lord. **Thanks be to God.**

RESPONSORIAL PSALM *(Psalm 103)*

The Lord is mer-ci-ful and gra-cious.

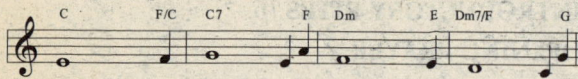

℟. **The Lord is merciful and gracious.**

Bless the Lord, O my · **soul,**
and all that is within me, bless his · **holy** name.
Bless the Lord, O my · **soul,**
and do not forget all · **his** benefits. ℟.

It is the Lord who forgives all your in-·**iquity,**
who heals all your · **dis**-eases,
who redeems your life from the · **Pit,**
who crowns you with steadfast love
· **and** mercy. ℟.

The Lord is merciful and · **gracious,**
slow to anger and abounding
in stead-·**fast** love.
He does not deal with us according
to our · **sins,**
nor repay us according to our · **in**-iquities. ℟.

As far as the east is from the · **west,**
so far he removes our transgressions · **from** us.
As a father has compassion for his · **children,**
so the Lord has compassion
for those · **who** fear_him. ℟.

SECOND READING *(1 Corinthians 3.16-23)*

Brothers and sisters: Do you not know that you are God's temple and that God's Spirit dwells in you? If anyone destroys God's temple, God will destroy that person. For God's temple is holy, and you are that temple.

Do not deceive yourselves. If you think that you are wise in this age, you should become fools so that you may become wise. For the wisdom of this world is foolishness with God. For it is written, "He catches the wise in their craftiness," and again, "The Lord knows the thoughts of the wise, that they are futile."

So let no one boast about human beings. For all things are yours — whether Paul or Apollos or Cephas, or the world or life or death, or the present or the future — all belong to you, and you belong to Christ, and Christ belongs to God.

The word of the Lord. **Thanks be to God.**

GOSPEL ACCLAMATION *(1 John 2.5)*

Alleluia. Alleluia. Whoever obeys the word of Christ, grows perfect in the love of God. **Alleluia.**

GOSPEL *(Matthew 5.38-48)*

A reading from the holy Gospel according to Matthew. **Glory to you, Lord.**

Jesus said to his disciples, "You have heard that it was said, 'An eye for an eye and a tooth for a tooth.' But I say to you, Do not resist an evildoer. But if anyone strikes you on the right cheek, turn the other also; and if anyone wants to sue you and take your coat, give your cloak as well; and if anyone forces you to go one mile, go with them also the second mile. Give to everyone who begs from you, and do not refuse anyone who wants to borrow from you.

"You have heard that it was said, 'You shall love your neighbour and hate your enemy.' But I say to you, Love your enemies and pray for those who persecute you, so that you may be children of your Father in heaven; for he makes his sun rise on the evil and on the good, and sends rain on the righteous and on the unrighteous.

"For if you love those who love you, what reward do you have? Do not even the tax collectors do the same? And if you greet only your brothers and sisters, what more are you doing than others? Do not even the Gentiles do the same? Be perfect, therefore, as your heavenly Father is perfect."

The Gospel of the Lord. **Praise to you, Lord Jesus Christ.**

PROFESSION OF FAITH *(p. 13-14)*

PRAYER OF THE FAITHFUL

The following intentions are suggestions only.

R. **Lord, hear our prayer.**

For the Church and its leaders, called to stand in solidarity with victims of oppression and abuse, we pray to the Lord: R.

For world peace built on non-violence, we pray to the Lord: R.

For the healing and empowerment of victims of violence and oppression, we pray to the Lord: R.

For us, God's holy people, challenged to love our enemies, we pray to the Lord: R.

PREPARATION OF THE GIFTS *(p. 15)*

PRAYER OVER THE GIFTS

Lord, as we make this offering, may our worship in Spirit and truth bring us salvation.

PREFACE *(Sundays in Ordinary Time, p. 20)*

COMMUNION ANTIPHON *(Psalm 9.1-2)*

I will tell all your marvellous works. I will rejoice and be glad in you, and sing to your name, Most High.

or (John 11.27)

Lord, I believe that you are the Christ, the Son of God, who was to come into this world.

PRAYER AFTER COMMUNION

Almighty God, help us to live the example of love we celebrate in this eucharist, that we may come to its fulfilment in your presence.

BLESSING AND DISMISSAL *(p. 67)*

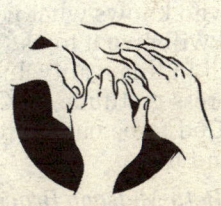

The pursuit of wealth drives the ups and downs of our economies. We are all affected by stock market speculation, the price of oil, the value of the dollar and interest rates. Some of us are dependent on excessive credit to feed our over-consumption. We can get caught up in a desire for more money and things to improve our life-styles. Many of us try to keep up with the cultural expectation that success, security and fulfillment can be found by pursuing wealth.

Today's gospel challenges this narrow focus on wealth. Jesus tells us not to worry, as nature's abundance clearly demonstrates how much God loves us. When, as Jesus suggests, I reflect on the splendour of flowers with their breathtaking detail and beauty, I am deeply moved by the wonder of God's generosity and care. I am also humbled by Jesus' insight that if God so clothes the grass of the field, God will surely take care of us even more so.

Jesus' teaching reminds me that all Christians are called to a distinct way of life. We are called to trust in God who knows what we need and to believe that God will give it to us. The challenge is to put our faith in this reality. In the eucharist today, let us express gratitude for God's amazing love and allow God to be our source of nourishment, security and hope.

Beth McIsaac Bruce, Halifax, NS

ENTRANCE ANTIPHON *(Psalm 17.19-20)*

The Lord has been my strength; he has led me into freedom. He saved me because he loves me.

INTRODUCTORY RITES *(p. 7)*

OPENING PRAYER

Lord, guide the course of world events and give your Church the joy and peace of serving you in freedom.

FIRST READING *(Isaiah 49.14-15)*

Zion said, "The Lord has forsaken me,
my Lord has forgotten me."
Can a woman forget her nursing child,
or show no compassion for the child
    of her womb?
Even these may forget,
yet I will not forget you.

The word of the Lord. **Thanks be to God.**

RESPONSORIAL PSALM *(Psalm 62)*

℟. **For God alone my soul waits in silence.**

For God alone my soul waits in · **silence;**
from him comes my sal--**vation.**
He alone is my rock and my salvation,
    my · **fortress;**
I shall never · **be** shaken. ℟.

→

For God alone my soul waits in · **silence,**
for my hope is from · **him.**
He alone is my rock and my salvation,
    my · **fortress;**
I shall not · **be** shaken. ℟

℟ **For God alone my soul waits in silence.**

On God rests my deliverance and my · **honour;**
my mighty rock, my refuge is in · **God.**
Trust in him at all times, O · **people;**
pour out your heart · **be**-fore_him. ℟

SECOND READING *(1 Corinthians 4.1-5)*

Brothers and sisters: Think of us in this way, as servants of Christ and stewards of God's mysteries. Moreover, it is required of stewards that they be found trustworthy.

But with me it is a very small thing that I should be judged by you or by any human court. I do not even judge myself. I am not aware of anything against myself, but I am not thereby acquitted. It is the Lord who judges me.

Therefore do not pronounce judgment before the time, before the Lord comes, who will bring to light the things now hidden in darkness and will disclose the purposes of the heart. Then each one will receive commendation from God.

The word of the Lord. **Thanks be to God.**

GOSPEL ACCLAMATION *(See Hebrews 4.12)*

Alleluia. Alleluia. The word of God is living and active; it judges the thoughts and intentions of the heart. **Alleluia.**

GOSPEL *(Matthew 6.24-34)*

A reading from the holy Gospel according to Matthew. **Glory to you, Lord.**

Jesus taught his disciples, saying. "No one can serve two masters; for a slave will either hate the one and love the other, or be devoted to the one and despise the other. You cannot serve God and wealth.

"Therefore I tell you, do not worry about your life, what you will eat or what you will drink, or about your body, what you will wear. Is not life more than food, and the body more than clothing?

"Look at the birds of the air; they neither sow nor reap nor gather into barns, and yet your heavenly Father feeds them. Are you not of more value than they? And can any one of you by worrying add a single hour to their span of life?

"And why do you worry about clothing? Consider the lilies of the field, how they grow; they neither toil nor spin, yet I tell you, even Solomon in all his glory was not clothed like one of these. But if God so clothes the grass of the field, which is alive today and tomorrow is thrown into the oven, will he not much more clothe you — you of little faith?

"Therefore do not worry, saying, 'What will we eat?' or 'What will we drink?' or 'What will we wear?' For it is the Gentiles who strive for all these things; and indeed your heavenly Father knows that you need all these things. But strive first for the kingdom of God and his righteousness, and all these things will be given to you as well.

"So do not worry about tomorrow, for tomorrow will bring worries of its own. Today's trouble is enough for today."

The Gospel of the Lord. **Praise to you, Lord Jesus Christ.**

PROFESSION OF FAITH *(p. 13-14)*

PRAYER OF THE FAITHFUL

The following intentions are suggestions only.

R. **Lord, hear our prayer.**

For the Church, a community called to integrity of speech and action, we pray to the Lord: R.

For peace and justice among nations, built on mutual assistance, we pray to the Lord: R.

For the healing of those who suffer harsh and unfair criticism, we pray to the Lord: R.

For us, God's people gathered here, called to speak words of goodness and love, we pray to the Lord: R.

PREPARATION OF THE GIFTS *(p. 15)*

174

PRAYER OVER THE GIFTS

God our creator, may this bread and wine we offer as a sign of our love and worship lead us to salvation.

PREFACE *(Sundays in Ordinary Time, p. 20)*

COMMUNION ANTIPHON *(Psalm 12.6)*

I will sing to the Lord for his goodness to me, I will sing the name of the Lord, Most High.

or (Matthew 28.20)

I, the Lord, am with you always, until the end of the world.

PRAYER AFTER COMMUNION

God of salvation, may this sacrament which strengthens us here on earth bring us to eternal life.

BLESSING AND DISMISSAL *(p. 67)*

What does it mean to follow God? How can we be sure we are on the right path? What does it take to enter into heaven? These are questions that believers have asked for centuries. They are at the root of the readings today.

Moses told the Israelites what the Lord required of them: to love and serve God with their entire being. There could be no half-measures. Their obedience to the commandments had to come from their heart, and not be just a matter of external observances. If they do this, they will be blessed. If they do not, they will be cursed.

Jesus told his followers much the same thing. Proclaiming their faith in Jesus is not enough. Not even performing miracles in Jesus' name is enough. They have to do his Father's will if they expect Jesus to recognize them at the time of judgment. Once again, doing this will enable them to withstand great storms, but failure to follow his words will result in destruction.

We gather to worship God, proclaiming in song, prayer and the eucharist that Jesus is our Lord and Saviour. But that is not enough. Nourished by our common worship, we also must go forth and live out Jesus' teachings in our daily lives. Otherwise, Jesus may not recognize us when the time comes.

John L. McLaughlin, Toronto, ON

ENTRANCE ANTIPHON *(Psalm 25.16, 18)*

O look at me and be merciful, for I am wretched and alone. See my hardship and my poverty, and pardon all my sins.

INTRODUCTORY RITES *(p. 7)*

OPENING PRAYER

Father, your love never fails. Hear our call. Keep us from danger and provide for all our needs.

FIRST READING *(Deuteronomy 11.18, 26-28, 32)*

Moses said to the people: "You shall put these words of mine in your heart and soul, and you shall bind them as a sign on your hand, and fix them as an emblem on your forehead.

"See, I am setting before you today a blessing and a curse: the blessing, if you obey the commandments of the Lord your God that I am commanding you today; and the curse, if you do not obey the commandments of the Lord your God, but turn from the way that I am commanding you today, to follow other gods that you have not known.

"You must diligently observe all the statutes and ordinances that I am setting before you today."

The word of the Lord. **Thanks be to God.**

RESPONSORIAL PSALM *(Psalm 31)*

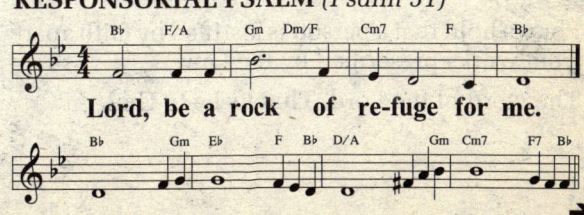

Lord, be a rock of re-fuge for me.

R. **Lord, be a rock of refuge for me.**

In you, O Lord, I · **seek** refuge;
do not let me ever be · **put** to shame;
in your · **righteousness** de-liver_me.
Incline your ear to me; · **rescue** me speedily. R.

Be a rock of refuge · **for** me,
a strong · **fortress** to save_me.
You are indeed my rock · **and** my fortress;
for your name's sake · **lead_me**
   and guide_me. R.

Let your face shine upon · **your** servant;
save me in your · **stead**-fast love.
Be strong, and let your · **heart** take courage,
all you who · **wait** for_the Lord. R.

©2010 Gordon Johnston/Novalis

SECOND READING *(Romans 3.21-25, 28)*

Brothers and sisters: Now, apart from Law, the righteousness of God has been disclosed, and is attested by the Law and the Prophets, the righteousness of God through faith in Jesus Christ for all who believe.

For there is no distinction, since all have sinned and fall short of the glory of God; they are now justified by his grace as a gift, through the redemption that is in Christ Jesus, whom God put forward as a sacrifice of atonement by his blood.

For we hold that a person is justified by faith apart from works prescribed by the Law.

The word of the Lord. **Thanks be to God.**

GOSPEL ACCLAMATION *(See John 15.5)*

Alleluia. Alleluia. I am the vine, you are the branches. Whoever abides in me and I in them bears much fruit. **Alleluia.**

GOSPEL *(Matthew 7.21-27)*

A reading from the holy Gospel according to Matthew. **Glory to you, Lord.**

Jesus went up the mountain with his disciples. He sat down and began to teach them: "Not everyone who says to me, 'Lord, Lord,' will enter the kingdom of heaven, but only the one who does the will of my Father in heaven. On that day many will say to me, 'Lord, Lord, did we not prophesy in your name, and cast out demons in your name, and do many deeds of power in your name?' Then I will declare to them, 'I never knew you; go away from me, you evildoers.'

"Everyone then who hears these words of mine and acts on them will be like a wise man who built his house on rock. The rain fell, the floods came, and the winds blew and beat on that house, but it did not fall, because it had been founded on rock. And everyone who hears these words of mine and does not act on them will be like a foolish man who built his house on sand. The rain fell, and the floods came, and the winds blew and beat against that house, and it fell — and great was its fall!"

The Gospel of the Lord. **Praise to you, Lord Jesus Christ.**

PROFESSION OF FAITH *(p. 13-14)*

PRAYER OF THE FAITHFUL

The following intentions are suggestions only.

R. **Lord, hear our prayer.**

For the leaders of the Church, shepherds of God's people, we pray to the Lord: R.

For the gifts of respect and caring in our leaders, we pray to the Lord: R.

For the sick and the dying and for those who care for them, we pray to the Lord: R.

For all of us here today, called to break down walls of injustice and intolerance in the world, we pray to the Lord: R.

PREPARATION OF THE GIFTS *(p. 15)*

PRAYER OVER THE GIFTS

Lord, as we gather to offer our gifts, confident in your love, make us holy by sharing your life with us and by this eucharist forgive our sins.

PREFACE *(Sundays in Ordinary Time, p. 20)*

COMMUNION ANTIPHON *(Psalm 17.6)*

I call upon you, God, for you will answer me; bend your ear and hear my prayer.

or (Mark 11.23-24) **I tell you solemnly, whatever you ask for in prayer, believe that you have received it, and it will be yours, says the Lord.**

PRAYER AFTER COMMUNION

Lord, as you give us the body and blood of your Son, guide us with your Spirit that we may honour you not only with our lips, but also with the lives we lead, and so enter your kingdom.

BLESSING AND DISMISSAL *(p. 67)*

There are three simple — and sensible — things to do as Lent begins:

Pray. Find that quiet, private space where you can be alone with your thoughts and alone with God. It could be when you go for a walk, while you are folding the laundry, when you are working on a hobby, on your bus commute to or from work, or in that precious time after the kids are in bed and before you start making tomorrow's lunches. Taking time for yourself isn't selfish; it is about making room in your life to nurture your relationship with God.

Fast. Think about what you eat and drink, and why. Try to make healthy choices and support local producers. If you are able, take a short pause from consuming your favourite foods. Take an objective look at your words and actions. Consider fasting from criticism, impatience, inflexibility. Thoughtful self-denial cleanses both the body and the spirit.

Give alms. With a generous spirit, share what you have with those who have less. And share often. Know that acts of justice and compassion bless both the giver and the recipient.

Three simple things: prayer, fasting and almsgiving. They stand the test of time because they are pleasing to God and they are good for us as well.

Susan Eaton, Antigonish, NS

Or Ash Wednesday Service, p. 188.

ENTRANCE ANTIPHON *(Wisdom 11.24-25, 27)*

Lord, you are merciful to all, and hate nothing you have created. You overlook the sins of men to bring them to repentance. You are the Lord our God.

GREETING *(p. 7)*

The Penitential Rite *and the* Glory to God *are omitted today.*

OPENING PRAYER

Lord, protect us in our struggle against evil. As we begin the discipline of Lent, make this day holy by our self-denial.

or

Let us pray in quiet remembrance of our need for redemption. *(Pause)* Father in heaven, the light of your truth bestows sight to the darkness of sinful eyes. May this season of repentance bring us the blessing of your forgiveness and the gift of your light.

*Ash Wed. Service: Liturgy of the Word begins here.

FIRST READING *(Joel 2.12-18)*

Even now, says the Lord, return to me with all your heart, with fasting, with weeping, and with mourning; rend your hearts and not your clothing.

Return to the Lord, your God, for he is gracious and merciful, slow to anger, and abounding in steadfast love, and relents from punishing.

Who knows whether the Lord will not turn and relent, and leave a blessing behind him: a grain offering and a drink offering to be presented to the Lord, your God?

Blow the trumpet in Zion; sanctify a fast; call a solemn assembly; gather the people. Sanctify the congregation; assemble the aged; gather the children, even infants at the breast. Let the bridegroom leave his room, and the bride her canopy.

Between the vestibule and the altar let the priests, the ministers of the Lord, weep. Let them say, "Spare your people, O Lord, and do not make your heritage a mockery, a byword among the nations. Why should it be said among the peoples, 'Where is their God?'"

Then the Lord became jealous for his land, and had pity on his people.

The word of the Lord. **Thanks be to God.**

RESPONSORIAL PSALM *(Psalm 51)*

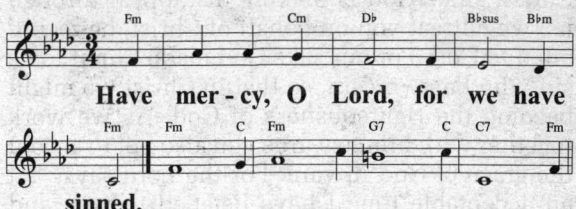

Have mer-cy, O Lord, for we have sinned.

R. **Have mercy, O Lord, for we have sinned.**

Have mercy on me, O God,
    according to your steadfast · **love;**
according to your abundant mercy
    blot out my trans·-**gressions.**
Wash me thoroughly from my in·-**iquity,**
and cleanse me from my · **sin.** R.

→

183

For I know my trans--**gressions,**
and my sin is ever be--**fore_me.**
Against you, you alone, have I · **sinned,**
and done what is evil in your · **sight.** R̶

R̶ **Have mercy, O Lord, for we have sinned.**

Create in me a clean heart, O · **God,**
and put a new and right spirit with--**in_me.**
Do not cast me away from your · **presence,**
and do not take your holy spirit from · **me.** R̶

Restore to me the joy of your sal--**vation,**
and sustain in me a willing · **spirit.**
O Lord, open my · **lips,**
and my mouth will declare your · **praise.** R̶

©2009 Gordon Johnston/Novalis

SECOND READING (*2 Corinthians 5.20 – 6.2*)

Brothers and sisters: We are ambassadors for
Christ, since God is making his appeal through
us; we entreat you on behalf of Christ, be reconciled to God. For our sake God made Christ to be
sin who knew no sin, so that in Christ we might
become the righteousness of God. As we work
together with him, we urge you also not to accept
the grace of God in vain. For the Lord says, "At
an acceptable time I have listened to you, and
on a day of salvation I have helped you." See,
now is the acceptable time; see, now is the day
of salvation!

The word of the Lord. **Thanks be to God.**

GOSPEL ACCLAMATION *(Psalm 95.7-8)*

Praise to you, Lord, king of eternal glory! Today, do not harden your hearts, but listen to the voice of the Lord. **Praise to you, Lord, king of eternal glory!**

GOSPEL *(Matthew 6.1-6, 16-18)*

A reading from the holy Gospel according to Matthew. **Glory to you, Lord.**

Jesus said to the disciples: "Beware of practising your piety before people in order to be seen by them; for then you have no reward from your Father in heaven.

"So whenever you give alms, do not sound a trumpet before you, as the hypocrites do in the synagogues and in the streets, so that they may be praised by others. Truly I tell you, they have received their reward. But when you give alms, do not let your left hand know what your right hand is doing, so that your alms may be done in secret; and your Father who sees in secret will reward you.

"And whenever you pray, do not be like the hypocrites; for they love to stand and pray in the synagogues and at the street corners, so that they may be seen by others. Truly I tell you, they have received their reward. But whenever  you pray, go into your room and shut the door and pray to your Father who is in secret; and your Father who sees in secret will reward you.

185

"And whenever you fast, do not look dismal, like the hypocrites, for they disfigure their faces so as to show others that they are fasting. Truly I tell you, they have received their reward. But when you fast, put oil on your head and wash your face, so that your fasting may be seen not by others but by your Father who is in secret; and your Father who sees in secret will reward you."

The Gospel of the Lord. **Praise to you, Lord Jesus Christ.**

The Profession of Faith *is omitted today.*

BLESSING AND GIVING OF ASHES

Dear friends in Christ, let us ask our Father to bless these ashes which we will use as the mark of our repentance. *(Pause)* Lord, bless the sinner who asks for your forgiveness and bless all those who receive these ashes. May they keep this Lenten season in preparation for the joy of Easter.

While the faithful come forward to receive ashes, an appropriate song may be sung.

1 Turn away from sin and be faithful to the gospel.

2 Remember that you are dust and to dust you will return.

PRAYER OF THE FAITHFUL

The following intentions are suggestions only.

℟. **Lord, hear our prayer.**

For the Church, called in this season of Lent to open our hearts to God's kingdom among us, we pray to the Lord: ℟.

For renewed generosity among nations for the sake of our brothers and sisters who are poor and dispossessed, we pray to the Lord: R.

For all who suffer loneliness and loss, we pray to the Lord: R.

For us, God's people gathered here, called to care for each other as God cares for us, we pray to the Lord: R.

Ash Wed. Service: Liturgy of the Word ends here.

PREPARATION OF THE GIFTS *(p. 15)*

PRAYER OVER THE GIFTS

Lord, help us to resist temptation by our Lenten works of charity and penance. By this sacrifice may we be prepared to celebrate the death and resurrection of Christ our Saviour and be cleansed from sin and renewed in spirit.

PREFACE *(Lent IV, p. 24)*

COMMUNION ANTIPHON *(Psalm 1.2-3)*

The man who meditates day and night on the law of the Lord will yield fruit in due season.

PRAYER AFTER COMMUNION

Lord, through this communion may our Lenten penance give you glory and bring us your protection.

BLESSING AND DISMISSAL *(p. 67)*

ASH WEDNESDAY SERVICE

When ashes are blessed outside Mass, the ceremony consists of a brief scripture service as outlined here.

GATHERING SONG

SIGN OF THE CROSS — GREETING

OPENING PRAYER

Father in heaven, the light of your truth bestows sight to the darkness of sinful eyes. May this season of repentance bring us the blessing of your forgiveness and the gift of your light.

LITURGY OF THE WORD *(p. 182)*

LORD'S PRAYER *(p. 65)*

CLOSING HYMN *or* RECESSIONAL POSTLUDE

March 13   1st Sunday of Lent

Years ago I was travelling across India on a train that ran along a high embankment. The region was flooded, and water stretched as far as the eye could see. People lined the railway track, begging to get on. A man got in our carriage carrying a sack of potatoes and holding his small daughter by the hand. It was all he had managed to save.

With climate change, floods, droughts and famines will become more and more common. The environmental crisis tempts us to despair, but Jesus shows the way in the wilderness.

The devil faced Jesus with three familiar temptations: to use his power to be materially secure (never hungry), physically safe (comfortable) and politically successful (in control). The desires for wealth, comfort or political power are normal human impulses, and Jesus is human — but he rejects them. He centres himself in another kind of power, far greater and more mysterious than what the devil offers. It is the power of love. This is the power that will save us, ultimately, from destroying ourselves.

This Lent, Jesus asks us to 'give up' acquiring more stuff, and 'give up' seeking comfort and control so we can experience his kind of power. We're all on this train together.

Louisa Blair, Québec, QC

Parishes engaged in the Rite of Christian Initiation of Adults (RCIA) *may celebrate the* Rite of Election *today.*

First Sunday of Lent

ENTRANCE ANTIPHON *(Psalm 91.15-16)*

When he calls to me, I will answer; I will rescue him and give him honour. Long life and contentment will be his.

INTRODUCTORY RITES *(p. 7)*

OPENING PRAYER

Father, through our observance of Lent, help us to understand the meaning of your Son's death and resurrection, and teach us to reflect it in our lives.

FIRST READING *(Genesis 2.7-9, 16-18, 25; 3.1-7)*

The Lord God formed man from the dust of the ground, and breathed into his nostrils the breath of life; and the man became a living being. And the Lord God planted a garden in Eden, in the east; and there he put the man whom he had formed. Out of the ground the Lord God made to grow every tree that is pleasant to the sight and good for food, the tree of life also in the midst of the garden, and the tree of the knowledge of good and evil.

And the Lord God commanded the man, "You may freely eat of every tree of the garden; but of the tree of the knowledge of good and evil you shall not eat, for in the day that you eat of it you shall die."

Then the Lord God said, "It is not good that the man should be alone; I will make him a helper as his partner." And the man and his wife were both naked, and were not ashamed.

Now the serpent was more crafty than any other wild animal that the Lord God had made. He said to the woman, "Did God say, 'You shall not eat from any tree in the garden'?" The woman said to the serpent, "We may eat of the fruit of the trees in the garden; but God said, 'You shall not eat of the fruit of the tree that is in the middle of the garden, nor shall you touch it, or you shall die.'" But the serpent said to the woman, "You will not die; for God knows that when you eat of it your eyes will be opened, and you will be like God, knowing good and evil." So when the woman saw that the tree was good for food, and that it was a delight to the eyes, and that the tree was to be desired to make one wise, she took of its fruit and ate; and she also gave some to her husband, who was with her, and he ate.

Then the eyes of both were opened, and they knew that they were naked; and they sewed fig leaves together and made loincloths for themselves.

The word of the Lord. **Thanks be to God.**

RESPONSORIAL PSALM *(Psalm 51)*

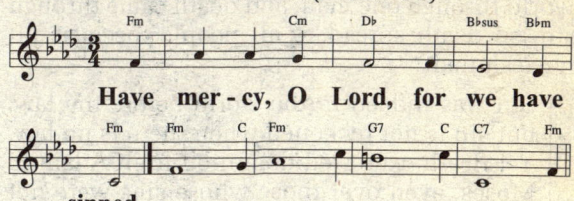

Have mer - cy, O Lord, for we have sinned.

R. **Have mercy, O Lord, for we have sinned.**

Have mercy on me, O God,
    according to your steadfast · **love;**
according to your abundant mercy
    blot out my trans-·**gressions.**
Wash me thoroughly from my in-·**iquity,**
and cleanse me from my · **sin.** R.

➜

For I know my trans-·**gressions,**
and my sin is ever be-·**fore_me.**
Against you, you alone, have I · **sinned,**
and done what is evil in your · **sight.** R.

R. **Have mercy, O Lord, for we have sinned.**

Create in me a clean heart, O · **God,**
and put a new and right spirit with-·**in_me.**
Do not cast me away from your · **presence,**
and do not take your holy spirit from · **me.** R.

Restore to me the joy of your sal-·**vation,**
and sustain in me a willing · **spirit.**
O Lord, open my · **lips,**
and my mouth will declare your · **praise.** R.

©2009 Gordon Johnston/Novalis

SECOND READING *(Romans 5.12-19)*

For the shorter version, omit the indented parts.

Brothers and sisters: Just as sin came into the
world through one man, and death came through
sin, so death spread to all people, because all
have sinned.

Sin was indeed in the world before the law,
but sin is not reckoned when there is no law.
Yet death exercised dominion from Adam to
Moses, even over those whose sins were not
like the transgression of Adam, who is a type
of the one who was to come.

But the free gift is not like the trespass. For
if the many died through the one man's trespass, much more surely have the grace of God
and the free gift in the grace of the one man,
Jesus Christ, abounded for the many. And the

free gift is not like the effect of the one man's sin. For the judgment following one trespass brought condemnation, but the free gift following many trespasses brings justification.

If, because of the one man's trespass, death exercised dominion through that one, much more surely will those who receive the abundance of grace and the free gift of righteousness exercise dominion in life through the one man, Jesus Christ.

Therefore just as one man's trespass led to condemnation for all people, so one man's act of righteousness leads to justification and life for all people. For just as by the one man's disobedience the many were made sinners, so by the one man's obedience the many will be made righteous.

The word of the Lord. **Thanks be to God.**

GOSPEL ACCLAMATION (*Matthew 4.4*)

Praise to you, Lord, king of eternal glory! Man does not live by bread alone, but by every word that comes from the mouth of God. **Praise to you, Lord, king of eternal glory!**

GOSPEL (*Matthew 4.1-11*)

A reading from the holy Gospel according to Matthew. **Glory to you, Lord.**

Jesus was led up by the Spirit into the wilderness to be tempted by the devil. He fasted forty days and forty nights, and afterwards he was famished. The tempter came and said to him, "If you are the Son of God, command these stones to become loaves of bread." But he answered, "It is written,

'Man does not live by bread alone, but by every word that comes from the mouth of God.'"

Then the devil took him to the holy city and placed him on the pinnacle of the temple, saying to him, "If you are the Son of God, throw yourself down; for it is written, 'He will command his Angels concerning you,' and 'On their hands they will bear you up, so that you will not dash your foot against a stone.'" Jesus said to him, "Again it is written, 'Do not put the Lord your God to the test.'"

Again, the devil took him to a very high mountain and showed him all the kingdoms of the world and their splendour; and he said to him, "All these I will give you, if you will fall down and worship me." Jesus said to him, "Away with you, Satan! for it is written, 'Worship the Lord your God, and serve only him.'"

Then the devil left him, and suddenly Angels came and waited on him.

The Gospel of the Lord. **Praise to you, Lord Jesus Christ.**

PROFESSION OF FAITH *(Nicene Creed, p. 14)*

PRAYER OF THE FAITHFUL

The following intentions are suggestions only.

R̰ **Lord, hear our prayer.**

For the Church, cherished community to whom the Lord speaks, we pray to the Lord: R̰

For leaders of nations, entrusted with the political and economic futures of their peoples, we pray to the Lord: R̰

For those who are discouraged by temptation, we pray to the Lord: R̰

For us, God's people gathered here, called to conversion at the start of our Lenten journey, we pray to the Lord: R̰

PREPARATION OF THE GIFTS *(p. 15)*

PRAYER OVER THE GIFTS

Lord, make us worthy to bring you these gifts. May this sacrifice help to change our lives.

PREFACE *(1st Sunday of Lent or Lent I-II, p. 23)*

COMMUNION ANTIPHON *(Matthew 4.4)*

Man does not live on bread alone, but on every word that comes from the mouth of God.

or (Psalm 91.4) **The Lord will overshadow you, and you will find refuge under his wings.**

PRAYER AFTER COMMUNION

Father, you increase our faith and hope, you deepen our love in this communion. Help us to live by your words and to seek Christ, our bread of life.

BLESSING AND DISMISSAL *(p. 67)*

Change is hard; we fear it, we resist it, we deny it. Whether we are sent, summoned or called to accompany someone, we are often reluctant to strike out on a new and unfamiliar path. We take comfort in the familiar, even if it is sometimes difficult. "Better the devil you know," runs the refrain we tell ourselves.

But as much as we resist, change is a part of life. We grow from infant to child to adult. We move away from our parents; we find new partners. We get sick, we grow old, we die — the same happens to all of us.

"Go from your country and your kindred and your father's house to the land that I will show you" is a frightening command — but Abram obeys. He becomes a nomad travelling far and enduring much, but in the end he is rewarded with the destiny promised him, becoming the father of the Chosen People.

And so it is with us; we face change, much of it hard, whether we like it or not. But it is in the hard times especially that we grow, that we become transformed. Sometimes change is a gradual process: in setting aside time for quiet reflection on the meaning of our lives in faith, we become aware of the crucible in which our faith is refined and purified. Lent offers us such an opportunity.

Patrick Doyle, Carleton Place, ON

ENTRANCE ANTIPHON *(Psalm 25.6, 3, 22)*

Remember your mercies, Lord, your tenderness from ages past. Do not let our enemies triumph over us; O God, deliver Israel from all her distress.

or (Psalm 27.8-9) **My heart has prompted me to seek your face; I seek it, Lord; do not hide from me.**

INTRODUCTORY RITES *(p. 7)*

OPENING PRAYER

God our Father, help us to hear your Son. Enlighten us with your word, that we may find the way to your glory.

FIRST READING *(Genesis 12.1-4)*

The Lord said to Abram, "Go from your country and your kindred and your father's house to the land that I will show you. I will make of you a great nation, and I will bless you, and make your name great, so that you will be a blessing. I will bless those who bless you, and the one who curses you I will curse; and in you all the families of the earth shall be blessed."

So Abram went, as the Lord had told him.

The word of the Lord. **Thanks be to God.**

RESPONSORIAL PSALM *(Psalm 33)*

Let your love be up-on us, Lord,
e-ven as we hope in you.

R. **Let your love be upon us, Lord,
even as we hope in you.**

The word of the Lord is · **upright,**
and all his work is done in · **faithfulness.**
He loves righteousness and · **justice;**
the earth is full of the steadfast love
    of the · **Lord.** R.

Truly the eye of the Lord is on those
    who · **fear_him,**
on those who hope in his steadfast · **love,**
to deliver their soul from · **death,**
and to keep them alive in · **famine.** R.

Our soul waits for the · **Lord;**
he is our help and · **shield.**
Let your steadfast love, O Lord, be up-·**on_us,**
even as we hope in · **you.** R.

SECOND READING *(2 Timothy 1.8-10)*

Brothers and sisters: Join with me in suffering for the Gospel, relying on the power of God, who saved us and called us with a holy calling, not according to our works but according to his own purpose and grace.

This grace was given to us in Christ Jesus before the ages began, but it has now been revealed through the appearing of our Saviour Christ Jesus, who abolished death and brought life and immortality to light through the Gospel.

The word of the Lord. **Thanks be to God.**

GOSPEL ACCLAMATION *(See Luke 9.35)*

Praise to you, Lord, king of eternal glory! From the bright cloud the Father's voice is heard: This is my Son, the Beloved; listen to him. **Praise to you, Lord, king of eternal glory!**

GOSPEL *(Matthew 17.1-9)*

A reading from the holy Gospel according to Matthew. **Glory to you, Lord.**

Jesus took with him Peter and James and his brother John and led them up a high mountain, by themselves. And he was transfigured before them, and his face shone like the sun, and his clothes became dazzling white. Suddenly there appeared to them Moses and Elijah, talking with him.

Then Peter said to Jesus, "Lord, it is good for us to be here; if you wish, I will make three dwellings here, one for you, one for Moses, and one for Elijah."

199

While he was still speaking, suddenly a bright cloud overshadowed them, and from the cloud a voice said, "This is my Son, the Beloved; with him I am well pleased; listen to him!"

When the disciples heard this, they fell to the ground and were overcome by fear. But Jesus came and touched them, saying, "Get up and do not be afraid." And when they looked up, they saw no one except Jesus himself alone.

As they were coming down the mountain, Jesus ordered them, "Tell no one about the vision until after the Son of Man has been raised from the dead."

The Gospel of the Lord. **Praise to you, Lord Jesus Christ.**

PROFESSION OF FAITH *(p. 13-14)*

PRAYER OF THE FAITHFUL

The following intentions are suggestions only.

R. **Lord, hear our prayer.**

For the Church, journeying toward Easter rebirth in fasting and prayer, we pray to the Lord: R.

For the liberation of those who suffer poverty and cruel political and economic oppression, we pray to the Lord: R.

For those among us who are sick, lonely, unemployed, we pray to the Lord: R.

For us, God's people gathered here, called to be a transforming presence to our neighbours, we pray to the Lord: R.

PREPARATION OF THE GIFTS *(p. 15)*

PRAYER OVER THE GIFTS

Lord, make us holy. May this eucharist take away our sins that we may be prepared to celebrate the resurrection.

PREFACE *(2nd Sunday of Lent or Lent I-II, p. 23)*

COMMUNION ANTIPHON *(Matthew 17.5)*

This is my Son, my beloved, in whom is all my delight: listen to him.

PRAYER AFTER COMMUNION

Lord, we give thanks for these holy mysteries which bring to us here on earth a share in the life to come, through Christ our Lord.

BLESSING AND DISMISSAL *(p. 67)*

In John's gospel we encounter a Samaritan woman preparing to draw water from a well during the hottest time of the day. This daily, ordinary ritual becomes an extraordinary, transformative life experience for her. At the well she encounters one not bound by the legalism of religious authorities, but instead by the law of love written on his heart by God who led him to her. As a woman, a Samaritan and one married five times, she was an outcast. Not blinded by categories, imperfections or sins, Jesus models for us all how to satisfy the deepest human thirsts. This is Jesus the pastoral minister whose words water the human soul.

The Samaritan woman, like all of us, thirsts for understanding and acceptance, which are hard to find in a patriarchal society marked by rigid religious laws. Jesus offers her cleansing water of the truth of her life experience. There is no harsh, judgmental rebuke. This truthful encounter is tempered by loving acceptance.

We all thirst for meaning in life. Our faith needs watering. Jesus encounters each of us at the well of our lives and offers unconditional love. With all catechumens preparing for baptism, let us join the entire community in answering Jesus' renewed invitation to selfless service.

Judy Morris, Louisville, KY

Parishes engaged in the Rite of Christian Initiation of Adults (RCIA) *may celebrate the* 1st Scrutiny *today.*

ENTRANCE ANTIPHON *(Psalm 25.15-16)*

My eyes are ever fixed on the Lord, for he releases my feet from the snare. O look at me and be merciful, for I am wretched and alone.

> *Scrutiny (Ezekiel 36.23-26):*
> **I will prove my holiness through you. I will gather you from the ends of the earth; I will pour clean water on you and wash away all your sins. I will give you a new spirit within you, says the Lord.**

INTRODUCTORY RITES *(p. 7)*

OPENING PRAYER

Father, you have taught us to overcome our sins by prayer, fasting and works of mercy. When we are discouraged by our weakness, give us confidence in your love.

> *Scrutiny:*
> Lord, you call these chosen ones to the glory of a new birth in Christ, the second Adam. Help them grow in wisdom and love as they prepare to profess their faith in you.

FIRST READING *(Exodus 17.3-7)*

In the wilderness the people thirsted for water; and the people complained against Moses and said, "Why did you bring us out of Egypt, to kill us and our children and livestock with thirst?" So Moses cried out to the Lord, "What shall I do with this people? They are almost ready to stone me."

The Lord said to Moses, "Go on ahead of the people, and take some of the elders of Israel with you; take in your hand the staff with which you struck the Nile, and go. I will be standing there in front of you on the rock at Horeb. Strike the rock, and water will come out of it, so that the people may drink." Moses did so, in the sight of the elders of Israel.

He called the place Massah and Meribah, because the children of Israel quarrelled and tested the Lord, saying, "Is the Lord among us or not?"

The word of the Lord. **Thanks be to God.**

RESPONSORIAL PSALM *(Psalm 95)*

O that to-day you would lis-ten to the voice of the Lord. Do not hard-en your hearts!

R. **O that today you would listen to the voice of the Lord. Do not harden your hearts!**

O come, let us sing to · **the** Lord;
let us make a joyful noise to the rock
   of our · **sal**-vation!
Let us come into his presence
   with · **thanks**-giving;
let us make a joyful noise to him
   with songs · **of** praise! R.

O come, let us worship and · **bow** down,
let us kneel before the Lord, · **our** Maker!
For he is our God, and we are the people
   of · **his** pasture,
and the sheep of · **his** hand. R.

O that today you would listen to · **his** voice!
Do not harden your hearts, as at Meribah,
   as on the day at Massah in · **the** wilderness,
when your ancestors tested me,
   and put me to · **the** proof,
though they had seen · **my** work. R.

©2009 Gordon Johnston/Novalis

SECOND READING *(Romans 5.1-2, 5-8)*

Brothers and sisters: Since we are justified by
faith, we have peace with God through our Lord
Jesus Christ, through whom we have obtained
access to this grace in which we stand; and we
boast in our hope of sharing the glory of God.

And hope does not disappoint us, because God's
love has been poured into our hearts through the
Holy Spirit that has been given to us. For while
we were still weak, at the right time Christ died
for the ungodly. Indeed, rarely will anyone die for
a righteous person — though perhaps for a good
person someone might actually dare to die. But
God proves his love for us in that while we still
were sinners Christ died for us.

The word of the Lord. **Thanks be to God.**

GOSPEL ACCLAMATION *(John 4.42, 15)*

Praise to you, Lord, king of eternal glory! Lord, you are truly the Saviour of the world; give me living water, that I may never be thirsty. **Praise to you, Lord, king of eternal glory!**

GOSPEL *(John 4.5-42)*

For the shorter reading, omit the indented parts.

A reading from the holy Gospel according to John. **Glory to you, Lord.**

Jesus came to a Samaritan city called Sychar, near the plot of ground that Jacob had given to his son Joseph. Jacob's well was there, and Jesus, tired out by his journey, was sitting by the well. It was about noon.

A Samaritan woman came to draw water, and Jesus said to her, "Give me a drink." (His disciples had gone to the city to buy food.)

The Samaritan woman said to him, "How is it that you, a Jew, ask a drink of me, a woman of Samaria?" (Jews do not share things in common with Samaritans.) Jesus answered her, "If you knew the gift of God, and who it is that is saying to you, 'Give me a drink,' you would have asked him, and he would have given you living water."

The woman said to him, "Sir, you have no bucket, and the well is deep. Where do you get that living water? Are you greater than our father Jacob, who gave us the well, and with his children and his flocks drank from it?" Jesus said to her, "Everyone who drinks of this water will be thirsty again, but the one who drinks of the water that I will give will never be thirsty. The water that I will give him will become in him a spring of water gushing up to eternal life." The woman said to him, "Sir, give me this water, so that I may never be thirsty or have to keep coming here to draw water."

> Jesus said to her, "Go, call your husband, and come back." The woman answered him, "I have no husband." Jesus said to her, "You are right in saying, 'I have no husband'; for you have had five husbands, and the one you have now is not your husband. What you have said is true!" The woman said to him, "Sir,

"I see that you are a Prophet. Our ancestors worshipped on this mountain, but you say that the place where people must worship is in Jerusalem."

Jesus said to her, "Woman, believe me, the hour is coming when you will worship the Father neither on this mountain nor in Jerusalem. You worship what you do not know; we worship what we know, for salvation is from the Jews. But the hour is coming, and is now here, when the true worshippers will worship the Father in spirit and truth, for the Father seeks such as these to worship him. God is spirit, and those who worship him must worship in spirit and truth."

The woman said to him, "I know that the Messiah is coming" (who is called the Christ). "When he comes, he will proclaim all things to us." Jesus said to her, "I am he, the one who is speaking to you."

Just then his disciples came. They were astonished that he was speaking with a woman, but no one said, "What do you want?" or, "Why are you speaking with her?" Then the woman left her water jar and went back to the city. She said to the people, "Come and see a man who told me everything I have ever done! He cannot be the Messiah, can he?" They left the city and were on their way to him. Meanwhile the disciples were urging him, "Rabbi, eat something." But he said to them, "I have food to eat that you do not know about." So the disciples said to one another, "Surely no one has brought him something to eat?"

Jesus said to them, "My food is to do the will of him who sent me and to complete his work. Do you not say, 'Four months more, then comes the harvest'? But I tell you, look around you, and see how the fields are ripe for harvesting. The reaper is already receiving wages and is gathering fruit for eternal life, so that sower and reaper may rejoice together. For here the saying holds true, 'One sows and another reaps.' I sent you to reap that for which you did not labour. Others have laboured, and you have entered into their labour."

Many Samaritans from that city believed in Jesus because of the woman's testimony, "He told me everything I have ever done." So when the Samaritans came to him, they asked him to stay with them; and he stayed there two days. And many more believed because of his word. They said to the woman, "It is no longer because of what you said that we believe, for we have heard for ourselves, and we know that this is truly the Saviour of the world."

The Gospel of the Lord. **Praise to you, Lord Jesus Christ.**

PROFESSION OF FAITH *(p. 13-14)*

PRAYER OF THE FAITHFUL

The following intentions are suggestions only.

R̶ **Lord, hear our prayer.**

For the Church, herald of the good news of God's love for all creation, we pray to the Lord: R̶

For the world's peoples who seek safe haven, and for our own country, strong in its tradition of welcoming strangers, we pray to the Lord: R̶

For God's beloved sons and daughters who are in pain and distress, or enslaved by fear or depression, we pray to the Lord: R̶

For us, God's people gathered here, invited to grow in caring and fidelity to our families and our Christian communities, we pray to the Lord: R̶

PREPARATION OF THE GIFTS *(p. 15)*

PRAYER OVER THE GIFTS

Lord, by the grace of this sacrifice may we who ask forgiveness be ready to forgive one another.

> *Scrutiny:*
> Lord God, give faith and love to your children and lead them safely to the banquet you have prepared for them.

PREFACE *(3rd Sunday of Lent, p. 25)*

COMMUNION ANTIPHON *(John 4.13-14)*

Whoever drinks the water that I shall give him, says the Lord, will have a spring inside him, welling up for eternal life.

PRAYER AFTER COMMUNION

Lord, in sharing this sacrament may we receive your forgiveness and be brought together in unity and peace.

> *Scrutiny:*
> Lord, be present in our lives with your gifts of salvation. Prepare these men and women for your sacraments and protect them in your love.

BLESSING AND DISMISSAL *(p. 67)*

Seeing with the eyes, with the heart... seeing afresh... seeing for the first time, not seeing... these are images — evocative metaphors — of spiritual vision. Images of vision and blindness, of light and darkness inform our Lenten readings today by asking us to look within.

Today's reading from John's gospel of the man born blind invites us to reflect on how we receive Jesus. Do we, with the Pharisees, attempt to limit God with rules and judgments? Or are we open to possibility, to transformation, as we journey with Jesus into the Easter mysteries? Together with the man born blind, we see anew through our encounter with Jesus; we learn to view everything through the lens of committed discipleship.

Later in his gospel, John uses the familiar and rich image of Jesus as light of the world. Yet earlier this year, in Matthew's gospel, we heard Jesus tell us that we *too* are light of the world. In the second reading today, Paul assures us that "in the Lord" we are light. Not a light that is nebulous, diffused, soft-focused. But light embodied, light incarnated — light with a purpose. We become a people who reflect Christ in our words and attitudes, through our actions, here... now.

With the man born blind, let us affirm with confidence, "Lord, I believe."

Ella Allen, Saint John, NB

Parishes engaged in the Rite of Christian Initiation of Adults (RCIA) *may celebrate the* 2nd Scrutiny *today.*

ENTRANCE ANTIPHON *(See Isaiah 66.10-11)*

Rejoice, Jerusalem! Be glad for her, you who love her; rejoice with her, you who mourned for her, and you will find contentment at her consoling breasts.

Scrutiny (Ezekiel 36.23-26):
I will prove my holiness through you. I will gather you from the ends of the earth; I will pour clean water on you and wash away all your sins. I will give you a new spirit within you, says the Lord.

INTRODUCTORY RITES *(p. 7)*

OPENING PRAYER

Father of peace, we are joyful in your Word, your Son Jesus Christ, who reconciles us to you. Let us hasten toward Easter with the eagerness of faith and love.

Scrutiny:
Almighty and eternal God, may your Church increase in true joy. May these candidates for baptism, and all the family of man, be reborn into the life of your kingdom.

FIRST READING *(1 Samuel 16.1, 6-7, 10-13)*

The Lord said to Samuel, "Fill your horn with oil and set out; I will send you to Jesse of Bethlehem, for I have provided for myself a king among his sons."

When the sons of Jesse came, Samuel looked on Eliab and thought, "Surely the Lord's anointed is now before the Lord." But the Lord said to Samuel, "Do not look on his appearance or on the height of his stature, because I have rejected him; for the Lord does not see as the human sees; the human looks on the outward appearance, but the Lord looks on the heart."

Jesse made seven of his sons pass before Samuel, and Samuel said to Jesse, "The Lord has not chosen any of these." Samuel said to Jesse, "Are all your sons here?" And he said, "There remains yet the youngest, but he is keeping the sheep." And Samuel said to Jesse, "Send and bring him; for we will not sit down until he comes here." Jesse sent and brought David in. Now he was ruddy, and had beautiful eyes, and was handsome. The Lord said, "Rise and anoint him; for this is the one."

Then Samuel took the horn of oil, and anointed him in the presence of his brothers; and the spirit of the Lord came mightily upon David from that day forward.

The word of the Lord. **Thanks be to God.**

RESPONSORIAL PSALM *(Psalm 23)*

℟ **The Lord is my shepherd; I shall not want.**

The Lord is my shepherd, I shall · **not** want.
He makes me lie down in · **green** pastures;
he leads me be-·**side** still waters;
he re-·**stores** my soul. ℟

→

He leads me in right paths for his · **name's** sake.
Even though I walk through the darkest valley,
    I fear · **no** evil;
for · **you** are with_me;
your rod and your · **staff** — they comfort_me. R.

R. **The Lord is my shepherd; I shall not want.**

You prepare a table · **be**-fore_me
in the presence · **of_my** enemies;
you anoint my · **head** with oil;
my · **cup** over-flows. R.

Surely goodness and mercy · **shall** follow_me
all the days of · **my** life,
and I shall dwell in the · **house_of** the Lord
my · **whole** life long. R.

©2009 Gordon Johnston/Novalis

SECOND READING *(Ephesians 5.8-14)*

Brothers and sisters: Once you were darkness, but now in the Lord you are light. Live as children of light — for the fruit of the light is found in all that is good and right and true.

Try to find out what is pleasing to the Lord. Take no part in the unfruitful works of darkness, but instead expose them. For it is shameful even to mention what such people do secretly; but everything exposed by the light becomes visible, for everything that becomes visible is light. Therefore it is said, "Sleeper, awake! Rise from the dead, and Christ will shine on you."

The word of the Lord. **Thanks be to God.**

GOSPEL ACCLAMATION *(John 8.12)*

Praise to you, Lord, king of eternal glory! I am the light of the world, says the Lord; whoever follows me will have the light of life. **Praise to you, Lord, king of eternal glory!**

GOSPEL *(John 9.1-41)*

For the shorter version, omit the indented parts.

A reading from the holy Gospel according to John. **Glory to you, Lord.**

As Jesus walked along, he saw a man blind from birth.

> His disciples asked him, "Rabbi, who sinned, this man or his parents, that he was born blind?"
>
> Jesus answered, "Neither this man nor his parents sinned; he was born blind so that God's works might be revealed in him. We must work the works of him who sent me while it is day; night is coming when no one can work. As long as I am in the world, I am the light of the world." When he had said this,

He spat on the ground and made mud with the saliva and spread the mud on the man's eyes, saying to him, "Go, wash in the pool of Siloam" (which means Sent).

Then the man who was blind went and washed, and came back able to see. The neighbours and those who had seen him before as a beggar began to ask, "Is this not the man who used to sit and beg?" Some were saying, "It is he." Others were saying, "No, but it is someone like him." He kept saying, "I am the man."

But they kept asking him, "Then how were your eyes opened?" He answered, "The man called Jesus made mud, spread it on my eyes, and said to me, 'Go to Siloam and wash.' Then I went and washed and received my sight." They said to him, "Where is he?" He said, "I do not know."

They brought to the Pharisees the man who had formerly been blind. Now it was a Sabbath day when Jesus made the mud and opened his eyes. Then the Pharisees also began to ask him how he had received his sight. He said to them, "He put mud on my eyes. Then I washed, and now I see." Some of the Pharisees said, "This man is not from God, for he does not observe the Sabbath." But others said, "How can a man who is a sinner perform such signs?" And they were divided. So they said again to the blind man, "What do you say about him? It was your eyes he opened." He said, "He is a Prophet."

They did not believe that he had been blind and had received his sight until they called the parents of the man who had received his sight and asked them, "Is this your son, who you say was born blind? How then does he now see?" His parents answered, "We know that this is our son, and that he was born blind; but we do not know how it is that now he sees, nor do we know who opened his eyes. Ask him; he is of age. He will speak for himself." His parents said this because they were afraid of the Jewish authorities, who had already agreed that anyone who confessed Jesus to be the Messiah would be put out of the synagogue. Therefore his parents said, "He is of age; ask him."

So for the second time they called the man who had been blind, and they said to him, "Give glory to God! We know that this man is a sinner." He answered, "I do not know whether he is a sinner. One thing I do know, that though I was blind, now I see." They said to him, "What did he do to you? How did he open your eyes?" He answered them, "I have told you already, and you would not listen. Why do you want to hear it again? Do you also want to become his disciples?" Then they reviled him, saying, "You are his disciple, but we are disciples of Moses. We know that God has spoken to Moses, but as for this man, we do not know where he comes from."

The man answered, "Here is an astonishing thing! You do not know where he comes from, and yet he opened my eyes. We know that God does not listen to sinners, but he does listen to one who worships him and obeys his will. Never since the world began has it been heard that anyone opened the eyes of a person born blind. If this man were not from God, he could do nothing."

They answered him, "You were born entirely in sins, and are you trying to teach us?" And they drove him out.

Jesus heard that they had driven him out, and when he found him, he said, "Do you believe in the Son of Man?" He answered, "And who is he, sir? Tell me, so that I may believe in him." Jesus said to him, "You have seen him, and the one speaking with you is he." He said, "Lord, I believe." And he worshipped him.

> Jesus said, "I came into this world for judgment so that those who do not see may see, and those who do see may become blind." Some of the Pharisees near him heard this and said to him, "Surely we are not blind, are we?" Jesus said to them, "If you were blind, you would have no sin. But now that you say, 'We see,' your sin remains."

The Gospel of the Lord. **Praise to you, Lord Jesus Christ.**

PROFESSION OF FAITH *(p. 13-14)*

PRAYER OF THE FAITHFUL

The following intentions are suggestions only.

R. **Lord, hear our prayer.**

For the Church, broken yet strong, healing yet seeking wholeness, we pray to the Lord: R.

For leaders of nations, struggling to witness to love and compassion in a world of suffering and loneliness, we pray to the Lord: R.

For those who are searching for a word of hope, we pray to the Lord: R.

For those seeking initiation into the Christian community and the outstretched arms of God's love and forgiveness, we pray to the Lord: R.

PREPARATION OF THE GIFTS *(p. 15)*

PRAYER OVER THE GIFTS

Lord, we offer you these gifts which bring us peace and joy. Increase our reverence by this eucharist, and bring salvation to the world.

> *Scrutiny:*
> Lord, we offer these gifts in joy and thanksgiving for our salvation. May the example of our faith and love help your chosen ones on their way to salvation.

PREFACE *(4th Sunday of Lent, p. 26)*

COMMUNION ANTIPHON *(See John 9.11)*

The Lord rubbed my eyes: I went away and washed; then I could see, and I believed in God.

PRAYER AFTER COMMUNION

Father, you enlighten all who come into the world. Fill our hearts with the light of your gospel, that our thoughts may please you, and our love be sincere.

> *Scrutiny:*
> Lord, be close to your family. Rule and guide us on our way to your kingdom and bring us to the joy of salvation.

BLESSING AND DISMISSAL *(p. 67)*

Dear God, so far today, I haven't complained, been selfish, or argued with anyone. But I'm going to get up now, and I'm probably going to need a lot of help. We smile, perhaps recognizing that without God's life-giving Spirit we can become bound in negativity, binding others as well.

The psalmist calls us to hope in God's steadfast love that will breathe life into us. What makes us want to get up in the morning? Or would we rather hide back under the covers?

Like Martha, we are sometimes overwhelmed by the "stench" of both our own and the world's needs, fearing hope and meaning are impossible. But impossible is not in Jesus' vocabulary. He first expresses gratitude and unwavering trust in God's love. "Father, I thank you for having heard me. I knew that you always hear me." Then Jesus expresses trust in *us*: "Unbind him." We are to give to others freedom from whatever imprisons them.

Acknowledging our need and trusting in God's help is a good place to start. With a grateful heart, we respond to others in a more compassionate and meaningful way. On this Solidarity Sunday, our support of Development and Peace is a concrete means of helping to 'unbind' others in desperate need of new life.

Sherie Rusler Croft, Gatineau, QC

Parishes engaged in the Rite of Christian Initiation of Adults (RCIA) *may celebrate the* 3rd Scrutiny *today.*
National Collection for Development and Peace

ENTRANCE ANTIPHON *(Psalm 43.1-2)*

Give me justice, O God, and defend my cause against the wicked; rescue me from deceitful and unjust men. You, O God, are my refuge.

> *Scrutiny (Ezekiel 36.23-26):*
> **I will prove my holiness through you. I will gather you from the ends of the earth; I will pour clean water on you and wash away all your sins. I will give you a new spirit within you, says the Lord.**

INTRODUCTORY RITES *(p. 7)*

OPENING PRAYER

Father, help us to be like Christ your Son, who loved the world and died for our salvation. Inspire us by his love, guide us by his example.

> *Scrutiny:*
> Lord, enlighten your chosen ones with the word of life. Give them a new birth in the waters of baptism and make them living members of the Church.

FIRST READING *(Ezekiel 37.12-14)*

Thus says the Lord God: "I am going to open your graves, and bring you up from your graves, O my people; and I will bring you back to the land of Israel. And you shall know that I am the Lord, when I open your graves, and bring you up from your graves, O my people.

"I will put my spirit within you, and you shall live, and I will place you on your own soil; then you shall know that I, the Lord, have spoken and will act," says the Lord.

The word of the Lord. **Thanks be to God.**

RESPONSORIAL PSALM *(Psalm 130)*

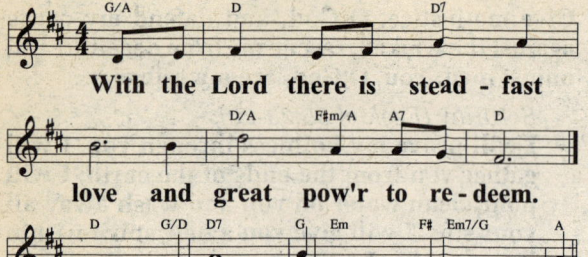

With the Lord there is stead - fast
love and great pow'r to re - deem.

R. **With the Lord there is steadfast love
and great power to redeem.**

Out of the depths I cry to you, O · **Lord.**
Lord, hear · **my** voice!
Let your ears be at·-**tentive**
to the voice of my sup·-**pli**-cations! R.

If you, O Lord, should mark in·-**iquities,**
Lord, who · **could** stand?
But there is forgiveness with · **you,**
so that you may be · **re**-vered. R.

I wait for the · **Lord,**
my soul waits, and in his word · **I** hope;
my soul waits for the · **Lord**
more than watchmen for · **the** morning. R.

For with the Lord there is steadfast · **love,**
and with him is great power to · **re**-deem.
It is he who will redeem · **Israel**
from all its · **in**-iquities. R.

SECOND READING *(Romans 8.8-11)*

Brothers and sisters: Those who are in the flesh cannot please God. But you are not in the flesh; you are in the Spirit, since the Spirit of God dwells in you. Anyone who does not have the Spirit of Christ does not belong to him.

But if Christ is in you, though the body is dead because of sin, the Spirit is life because of righteousness.

If the Spirit of God who raised Jesus from the dead dwells in you, he who raised Christ from the dead will give life to your mortal bodies also through his Spirit that dwells in you.

The word of the Lord. **Thanks be to God.**

GOSPEL ACCLAMATION *(John 11.25, 26)*

Praise to you, Lord, king of eternal glory! I am the resurrection and the life, says the Lord; whoever believes in me will never die. **Praise to you, Lord, king of eternal glory!**

GOSPEL *(John 11.1-45)*

For the shorter version, omit the indented parts.

A reading from the holy Gospel according to John. **Glory to you, Lord.**

> Now a certain man, Lazarus, was ill. He was from Bethany, the village of Mary and her sister Martha. Mary was the one who anointed the Lord with perfume and wiped his feet with her hair; her brother Lazarus was ill. So

The sisters [of Lazarus] sent a message to Jesus, "Lord, he whom you love is ill." But when Jesus heard this, he said, "This illness does not lead to death; rather it is for God's glory, so that the Son of God may be glorified through it." Accordingly, though Jesus loved Martha and her sister and Lazarus, after having heard that Lazarus was ill, he stayed two days longer in the place where he was. Then after this he said to the disciples, "Let us go to Judea again."

> The disciples said to him, "Rabbi, the people there were just now trying to stone you, and are you going there again?" Jesus answered, "Are there not twelve hours of daylight? Those who walk during the day do not stumble, because they see the light of this world. But those who walk at night stumble, because the light is not in them."

> After saying this, he told them, "Our friend Lazarus has fallen asleep, but I am going there to awaken him." The disciples said to him, "Lord, if he has fallen asleep, he will be all right." Jesus, however, had been speaking about his death, but they thought that he was referring merely to sleep. Then Jesus told them plainly, "Lazarus is dead. For your sake I am glad I was not there, so that you may believe. But let us go to him." Thomas, who was called the Twin, said to his fellow disciples, "Let us also go, that we may die with him."

When Jesus arrived, he found that Lazarus had already been in the tomb four days.

> Now Bethany was near Jerusalem, some two miles away, and many Jews had come to Martha and Mary to console them about their brother.

When Martha heard that Jesus was coming, she went and met him, while Mary stayed at home. Martha said to Jesus, "Lord, if you had been here, my brother would not have died. But even now I know that God will give you whatever you ask of him." Jesus said to her, "Your brother will rise again." Martha said to him, "I know that he will rise again in the resurrection on the last day." Jesus said to her, "I am the resurrection and the life. Whoever believes in me, even though they die, will live, and everyone who lives and believes in me will never die. Do you believe this?" She said to him, "Yes, Lord, I believe that you are the Christ, the Son of God, the one coming into the world."

When she had said this, she went back and called her sister Mary, and told her privately, "The Teacher is here and is calling for you." And when Mary heard it, she got up quickly and went to him. Now Jesus had not yet come to the village, but was still at the place where Martha had met him. The Jews who were with her in the house, consoling her, saw Mary get up quickly and go out. They followed her because they thought that she was going to the tomb to weep there.

When Mary came where Jesus was and saw him, she knelt at his feet and said to him, "Lord, if you had been here, my brother would not have died." When Jesus saw her weeping, and the Jews who came with her also weeping, he

[Jesus] was greatly disturbed in spirit and deeply moved. He said, "Where have you laid him?" They said to him, "Lord, come and see." Jesus began to weep. So the Jews said, "See how he loved him!" But some of them said, "Could not he who opened the eyes of the blind man have kept this man from dying?"

Then Jesus, again greatly disturbed, came to the tomb. It was a cave, and a stone was lying against it. Jesus said, "Take away the stone." Martha, the sister of the dead man, said to him, "Lord, already there is a stench because he has been dead four days." Jesus said to her, "Did I not tell you that if you believed, you would see the glory of God?" So they took away the stone. And Jesus looked upward and said, "Father, I thank you for having heard me. I knew that you always hear me, but I have said this for the sake of the crowd standing here, so that they may believe that you sent me."

When he had said this, he cried with a loud voice, "Lazarus, come out!" The dead man came out, his hands and feet bound with strips of cloth, and his face wrapped in a cloth. Jesus said to them, "Unbind him, and let him go."

Many of the Jews therefore, who had come with Mary and had seen what Jesus did, believed in him.

The Gospel of the Lord. **Praise to you, Lord Jesus Christ.**

PROFESSION OF FAITH *(p. 13-14)*

PRAYER OF THE FAITHFUL

The following intentions are suggestions only.

℟ **Lord, hear our prayer.**

For the Church, called to be a community of solidarity with those who are oppressed, we pray to the Lord: ℟

For leaders of nations, entrusted with the task of building a just world, we pray to the Lord: ℟

For our brothers and sisters in Asia, Africa and Latin America, as they teach us how we can support their efforts to improve their lives, we pray to the Lord: ℟

For us, God's holy people, witnesses to the dignity and respect owed each human person, we pray to the Lord: ℟

PREPARATION OF THE GIFTS *(p. 15)*

PRAYER OVER THE GIFTS

Almighty God, may the sacrifice we offer take away the sins of those whom you enlighten with the Christian faith.

> *Scrutiny:*
> Almighty God, hear our prayers for these men and women who have begun to learn the Christian faith, and by this sacrifice prepare them for baptism.

PREFACE *(5th Sunday of Lent, p. 26)*

COMMUNION ANTIPHON *(John 11.26)*

He who lives and believes in me will not die for ever, said the Lord.

PRAYER AFTER COMMUNION

Almighty Father, by this sacrifice may we always remain one with your Son, Jesus Christ, whose body and blood we share.

> *Scrutiny:*
> Lord, may your people be one in spirit and serve you with all their heart. Free them from all fear. Give them joy in your gifts and love for those who are reborn as your children.

BLESSING AND DISMISSAL *(p. 67)*

On that day, says the Lord God, I will make the sun set at midday and cover the earth with darkness in broad daylight. (Amos 8.9)

From noon on, darkness came over the whole land until three in the afternoon. (Matthew 27.45)

In Matthew's gospel, events in the life of Jesus are often interpreted with direct reference to the Old Testament. The prophet Amos had described noonday darkness falling on God's great day of judgment. Temple observances would cease and those who "trample the needy" would be called to account. However paradoxical, it is the evangelist's faith conviction that judgment day had come with the passion and death of Jesus.

In a sense this is Jesus' darkest hour; in another sense it is his brightest. Jesus stands before the chief priests and Pilate who think that they are passing judgment on him. Instead his luminous presence overshadows them, and it is he who passes judgment on them and on the values and institutions they represent.

Shining in the midst of darkness, the crucified Jesus continues to challenge those who "look but do not see" as he affirms and "blesses those with eyes to see what prophets longed to see." (Mt 13)

The liturgy of Passion Sunday invites us to confidently reaffirm with the whole Church: "Jesus Christ is the light of the world, a light no darkness can extinguish."

Corbin Eddy, Hancock, MI

COMMEMORATION OF THE LORD'S ENTRANCE INTO JERUSALEM

FIRST FORM: THE PROCESSION

INTRODUCTION

The people, carrying palm branches, gather in a suitable place distinct from the church to which the procession will move. As they gather, they may sing:

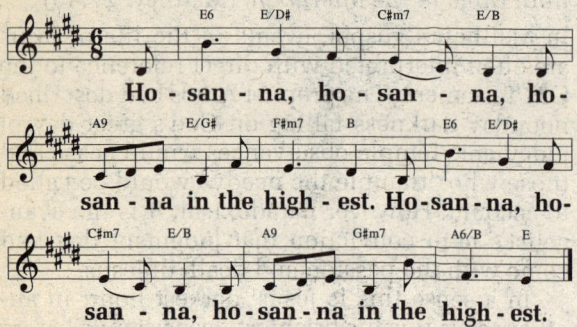

Ho - san - na, ho - san - na, ho - san - na in the high - est. Ho - san - na, ho - san - na, ho - san - na in the high - est.

© *Michel Guimont*

Dear friends in Christ, for five weeks of Lent we have been preparing, by works of charity and self-sacrifice, for the celebration of our Lord's paschal mystery. Today we come together to begin this solemn celebration in union with the whole Church throughout the world. Christ entered in triumph into his own city, to complete his work as our Messiah: to suffer, to die, and to rise again. Let us remember with devotion this entry which began his saving work and follow him with a lively faith. United with him in his suffering on the cross, may we share his resurrection and new life.

Let us pray.

1   Almighty God, we pray you, bless these branches and make them holy. Today we joyfully acclaim Jesus, our Messiah and King. May we reach one day the happiness of the new and everlasting Jerusalem by faithfully following him who lives and reigns for ever and ever. **Amen.**

2   Lord, increase the faith of your people and listen to our prayers. Today we honour Christ our triumphant King by carrying these branches. May we honour you every day by living always in him, for he is Lord for ever and ever. **Amen.**

GOSPEL *(Matthew 21.1-11)*

A reading from the holy Gospel according to Matthew. **Glory to you, Lord.**

When they had come near Jerusalem and had reached Bethphage, at the Mount of Olives, Jesus sent two disciples, saying to them, "Go into the village ahead of you, and immediately you will find a donkey tied, and a colt with her; untie them and bring them to me. If anyone says anything to you, just say this, 'The Lord needs them.' And he will send them immediately."

This took place to fulfill what had been spoken through the Prophet, saying, "Tell the daughter of Zion, Look, your king is coming to you, humble, and mounted on a donkey, and on a colt, the foal of a donkey."

The disciples went and did as Jesus had directed them; they brought the donkey and the colt, and put their cloaks on them, and he sat on them. A very large crowd spread their cloaks on the road, and others cut branches from the trees and spread them on the road. The crowds that went ahead of him and that followed were shouting, "Hosanna to the Son of David! Blessed is the one who comes in the name of the Lord! Hosanna in the highest heaven!"

When Jesus entered Jerusalem, the whole city was in turmoil, asking, "Who is this?" The crowds were saying, "This is the Prophet Jesus from Nazareth in Galilee."

The Gospel of the Lord. **Praise to you, Lord Jesus Christ.**

PROCESSION

Let us go forth in peace, praising Jesus our Messiah, as did the crowds who welcomed him to Jerusalem.

All process to the church, singing a hymn in honour of Christ the King. Mass continues with the Opening Prayer *(p. 233).*

SECOND FORM: THE SOLEMN ENTRANCE

The blessing of branches and proclamation of the gospel take place, as above, but in the church. After the gospel, the priest moves solemnly through the church to the sanctuary, while all sing. Mass continues with the Opening Prayer *(p. 233).*

THIRD FORM: THE SIMPLE ENTRANCE

The people gather in the church as usual. While the priest goes to the altar, the following Entrance Antiphon *or a suitable hymn is sung.*

ENTRANCE ANTIPHON *(See Psalm 24)*

Six days before the solemn Passover, the Lord came to Jerusalem, and children waving palm branches ran out to welcome him. They loudly praised the Lord:

> **Blessed are you who have come to us**
> **So rich in love and mercy.**

Open wide the doors and gates.
Lift high the ancient portals.
The King of glory enters.

Who is this King of glory?
He is God the mighty Lord.
Hosanna in the highest.
Blessed are you who have come to us
So rich in love and mercy.

INTRODUCTORY RITES *(p. 7)*

OPENING PRAYER

Almighty, ever-living God, you have given the human race Jesus Christ our Saviour as a model of humility. He fulfilled your will by becoming man and giving his life on the cross. Help us to bear witness to you by following his example of suffering and make us worthy to share in his resurrection.

FIRST READING *(Isaiah 50.4-7)*

The servant of the Lord said: "The Lord God has given me the tongue of a teacher, that I may know how to sustain the weary with a word. Morning by morning he wakens — wakens my ear to listen as those who are taught.

"The Lord God has opened my ear, and I was not rebellious, I did not turn backward.

"I gave my back to those who struck me, and my cheeks to those who pulled out the beard; I did not hide my face from insult and spitting.

"The Lord God helps me; therefore I have not been disgraced; therefore I have set my face like flint, and I know that I shall not be put to shame."

The word of the Lord. **Thanks be to God.**

RESPONSORIAL PSALM *(Psalm 22)*

My God, my God, why have you for - sak - en me?

R. **My God, my God,
why have you forsaken me?**

All who see me · **mock_at_me**;
they make mouths at me,
   they shake · **their** heads;
"Commit your cause to the Lord;
   let him de--**liver**;
let him rescue the one in whom
   he · **de**-lights!" R.

For dogs are all a--**round_me**;
a company of evildoers · **en**-circles_me.
My hands and feet have · **shrivelled**;
I can count all · **my** bones. R.

They divide my clothes a--**mong_themselves**,
and for my clothing they · **cast** lots.
But you, O Lord, do not be far a--**way**!
O my help, come quickly · **to_my** aid! R.

I will tell of your name to my brothers and
   sisters; in the midst of the congregation
   I will · **praise_you**:
You who fear the · **Lord**, praise_him!
All you offspring of Jacob, · **glorify_him**;
stand in awe of him, all you offspring
   · **of** Israel! R.

SECOND READING *(Philippians 2.6-11)*

Christ Jesus, though he was in the form of God, did not regard equality with God as something to be exploited, but emptied himself, taking the form of a slave, being born in human likeness. And being found in human form, he humbled himself and became obedient to the point of death — even death on a cross.

Therefore God highly exalted him and gave him the name that is above every name, so that at the name of Jesus every knee should bend, in heaven and on earth and under the earth, and every tongue should confess that Jesus Christ is Lord, to the glory of God the Father.

The word of the Lord. **Thanks be to God.**

GOSPEL ACCLAMATION *(Philippians 2.8-9)*

Praise to you, Lord, king of eternal glory! Christ became obedient for us to death, even death on a Cross. Therefore God exalted him and gave him the name above every name. **Praise to you, Lord, king of eternal glory!**

GOSPEL *(Matthew 26.14 – 27.66)*

Several readers may proclaim the passion narrative today. N indicates the narrator, J the words of Jesus, and S the words of other speakers. The shorter version begins (p. 244) and ends (p. 249) at the asterisks.

N The Passion of our Lord Jesus Christ according to Matthew.

One of the twelve, who was called Judas Iscariot, went to the chief priests and said,

S *What will you give me if I betray him to you?*

N They paid him thirty pieces of silver. And from that moment he began to look for an opportunity to betray him.

On the first day of Unleavened Bread the disciples came to Jesus, saying,

S *Where do you want us to make the preparations for you to eat the Passover?*

J **Go into the city to a certain man, and say to him, "The Teacher says, My time is near; I will keep the Passover at your house with my disciples."**

N So the disciples did as Jesus had directed them, and they prepared the Passover meal.

When it was evening, he took his place with the twelve; and while they were eating, he said,

J **Truly I tell you, one of you will betray me.**

N And they became greatly distressed and began to say to him one after another,

S *Surely not I, Lord?*

J **The one who has dipped his hand into the bowl with me will betray me. The Son of Man goes as it is written of him, but woe to that one by whom the Son of Man is betrayed! It would have been better for that one not to have been born.**

N Judas, who betrayed him, said,

S *Surely not I, Rabbi?*

J **You have said so.**

N While they were eating, Jesus took a loaf of bread, and after blessing it he broke it, gave it to the disciples, and said,

J **Take, eat; this is my Body**.

N Then he took a cup, and after giving thanks he gave it to them, saying,

J **Drink from it, all of you; for this is my Blood of the covenant, which is poured out for many for the forgiveness of sins. I tell you, I will never again drink of this fruit of the vine until that day when I drink it new with you in my Father's kingdom.**

N When they had sung the hymn, they went out to the Mount of Olives. Then Jesus said to them,

J **You will all become deserters because of me this night; for it is written, "I will strike the shepherd, and the sheep of the flock will be scattered."**

   But after I am raised up, I will go ahead of you to Galilee.

N Peter said to him,

S *Though all become deserters because of you, I will never desert you.*

J **Truly I tell you, this very night, before the cock crows, you will deny me three times.**

N Peter said to him,

S *Even though I must die with you, I will not deny you.*

N And so said all the disciples.

*At this point all may join in singing
an appropriate acclamation.*

Ky - ri - e, Chris - te, Ky - ri - e e - le - i - son!

Text: Didier Rimaud, © *CNPL*. Music: Jacques Berthier
Source: © *Éditions Musicales Studio SM*, 060794-2

N   Then Jesus went with them to a place called Gethsemane; and he said to his disciples,

J   **Sit here while I go over there and pray.**

N   He took with him Peter and the two sons of Zebedee, and began to be grieved and agitated. Then he said to them,

J   **I am deeply grieved, even to death; remain here, and stay awake with me.**

N   And going a little farther, he threw himself on the ground and prayed,

J   **My Father, if it is possible, let this cup pass from me; yet not what I want, but what you want.**

N   Then he came to the disciples and found them sleeping; and he said to Peter,

J   **So, could you not stay awake with me one hour? Stay awake and pray that you may not come into temptation; for the spirit indeed is willing, but the flesh is weak.**

N   Again he went away for the second time and prayed,

J   **My Father, if this cannot pass unless I drink it, your will be done.**

N Again he came and found them sleeping, for their eyes were heavy. So leaving them again, he went away and prayed for the third time, saying the same words. Then he came to the disciples and said to them,

J **Are you still sleeping and taking your rest? See, the hour is at hand, and the Son of Man is betrayed into the hands of sinners. Get up, let us be going. See, my betrayer is at hand.**

N While he was still speaking, Judas, one of the twelve, arrived; with him was a large crowd with swords and clubs, from the chief priests and the elders of the people. Now the betrayer had given them a sign, saying,

S *The one I will kiss is the man; arrest him.*

N At once he came up to Jesus and said,

S *Greetings, Rabbi!*

N and kissed him. Jesus said to him,

J **Friend, do what you are here to do.**

N Then they came and laid hands on Jesus and arrested him.

Suddenly, one of those with Jesus put his hand on his sword, drew it, and struck the slave of the high priest, cutting off his ear. Then Jesus said to him,

J **Put your sword back into its place; for all who take the sword will perish by the sword.**

Do you think that I cannot appeal to my Father, and he will at once send me more than twelve legions of Angels? But how then would the Scriptures be fulfilled, which say it must happen in this way?

N   At that hour Jesus said to the crowds,

J   **Have you come out with swords and clubs to arrest me as though I were a bandit? Day after day I sat in the temple teaching, and you did not arrest me. But all this has taken place so that the Scriptures of the Prophets may be fulfilled.**

N   Then all the disciples deserted him and fled.

Those who had arrested Jesus took him to Caiaphas the high priest, in whose house the scribes and the elders had gathered.

But Peter was following him at a distance, as far as the courtyard of the high priest; and going inside, he sat with the guards in order to see how this would end.

Now the chief priests and the whole council were looking for false testimony against Jesus so that they might put him to death, but they found none, though many false witnesses came forward. At last two came forward and said,

S   *This fellow said, "I am able to destroy the temple of God and to build it in three days."*

N   The high priest stood up and said,

S   *Have you no answer? What is it that they testify against you?*

N But Jesus was silent.

Then the high priest said to him,

S *I put you under oath before the living God, tell us if you are the Christ, the Son of God.*

N Jesus said to him,

J **You have said so. But I tell you, from now on you will see the Son of Man seated at the right hand of Power and coming on the clouds of heaven.**

N Then the high priest tore his clothes and said,

S *He has blasphemed! Why do we still need witnesses? You have now heard his blasphemy. What is your verdict?*

N They answered,

S *He deserves death.*

N Then they spat in his face and struck him; and some slapped him, saying,

S *Prophesy to us, Christ! Who is it that struck you?*

N Now Peter was sitting outside in the courtyard. A servant girl came to him and said,

S *You also were with Jesus the Galilean.*

N But he denied it before all of them, saying,

S *I do not know what you are talking about.*

N When Peter went out to the porch, another servant girl saw him, and she said to the bystanders,

S **This man was with Jesus of Nazareth.**

N Again he denied it with an oath,

S **I do not know the man.**

N After a little while the bystanders came up and said to Peter,

S **Certainly you are also one of them, for your accent betrays you.**

N Then he began to curse, and he swore an oath,

S **I do not know the man!**

N At that moment the cock crowed. Then Peter remembered what Jesus had said: "Before the cock crows, you will deny me three times." And he went out and wept bitterly.

At this point all may join in singing
an appropriate acclamation.

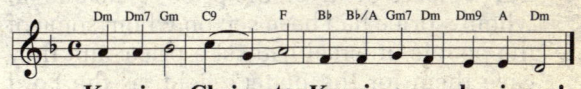

Ky-ri-e, Chris-te, Ky-ri-e e-le-i-son!

Text: Didier Rimaud, © *CNPL*. Music: Jacques Berthier
Source: © *Éditions Musicales Studio SM*, 060794-2

N When morning came, all the chief priests and the elders of the people conferred together against Jesus in order to bring about his death. They bound him, led him away, and handed him over to Pilate the governor.

When Judas, his betrayer, saw that Jesus was condemned, he repented and brought back the thirty pieces of silver to the chief priests and the elders.

S **I have sinned by betraying innocent blood.**

N But they said,

S **What is that to us? See to it yourself.**

N Throwing down the pieces of silver in the temple, he departed; and he went and hanged himself.

But the chief priests, taking the pieces of silver, said,

S **It is not lawful to put them into the treasury, since they are blood money.**

N After conferring together, they used them to buy the potter's field as a place to bury foreigners. For this reason that field has been called the Field of Blood to this day. Then was fulfilled what had been spoken through the Prophet Jeremiah, "And they took the thirty pieces of silver, the price of the one on whom a price had been set, on whom some of the people of Israel had set a price, and they gave them for the potter's field, as the Lord commanded me."

* * *

N Now Jesus stood before the governor; and the governor asked him,

S **Are you the King of the Jews?**

J **You say so.**

N But when he was accused by the chief priests and elders, he did not answer. Then Pilate said to him,

S **Do you not hear how many accusations they make against you?**

N But Jesus gave him no answer, not even to a single charge, so that the governor was greatly amazed.

Now at the festival the governor was accustomed to release a prisoner for the crowd, anyone they wanted. At that time they had a notorious prisoner, called Barabbas. So after they had gathered, Pilate said to them,

S **Whom do you want me to release for you, Barabbas or Jesus who is called the Christ?**

N For he realized that it was out of jealousy that they had handed him over.

While he was sitting on the judgment seat, his wife sent word to him,

S **Have nothing to do with that innocent man, for today I have suffered a great deal because of a dream about him.**

N Now the chief priests and the elders persuaded the crowds to ask for Barabbas and to have Jesus killed. The governor again said to them,

S **Which of the two do you want me to release for you?**

N And they said,

S **Barabbas.**

N Pilate said to them,

S ***Then what should I do with Jesus who is called the Christ?***

N All of them said,

S ***Let him be crucified!***

N Then he asked,

S ***Why, what evil has he done?***

N But they shouted all the more,

S ***Let him be crucified!***

N So when Pilate saw that he could do nothing, but rather that a riot was beginning, he took some water and washed his hands before the crowd, saying,

S ***I am innocent of this man's blood; see to it yourselves.***

N Then the people as a whole answered,

S ***His blood be on us and on our children!***

N So he released Barabbas for them; and after flogging Jesus, he handed him over to be crucified.

Then the soldiers of the governor took Jesus into the governor's headquarters, and they gathered the whole cohort around him. They stripped him and put a scarlet robe on him, and after twisting some thorns into a crown, they put it on his head. They put a reed in his right hand and knelt before him and mocked him, saying,

S ***Hail, King of the Jews!***

N They spat on him, and took the reed and struck him on the head. After mocking him, they stripped him of the robe and put his own clothes on him. Then they led him away to crucify him.

As they went out, they came upon a man from Cyrene named Simon; they compelled this man to carry his Cross.

*At this point all may join in singing
an appropriate acclamation.*

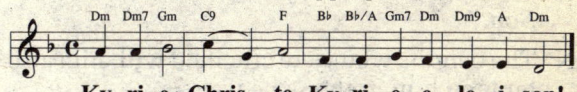

Ky-ri-e, Chris - te, Ky-ri - e e - le - i - son!

Text: Didier Rimaud, © *CNPL*. Music: Jacques Berthier
Source: © *Éditions Musicales Studio SM*, 060794-2

N And when they came to a place called Golgotha which means Place of a Skull, they offered him wine to drink, mixed with gall; but when he tasted it, he would not drink it.

And when they had crucified him, they divided his clothes among themselves by casting lots; then they sat down there and kept watch over him.

Over his head they put the charge against him, which read, "This is Jesus, the King of the Jews."

Then two bandits were crucified with him, one on his right and one on his left. Those who passed by derided him, shaking their heads and saying,

S ***You who would destroy the temple and build***

it in three days, save yourself! If you are the Son of God, come down from the Cross.

N   In the same way the chief priests also, along with the scribes and elders, were mocking him, saying,

S   *He saved others; he cannot save himself. He is the King of Israel; let him come down from the Cross now, and we will believe in him. He trusts in God; let God deliver him now, if he wants to; for he said, "I am God's Son."*

N   The bandits who were crucified with him also taunted him in the same way.

From noon on, darkness came over the whole land until three in the afternoon. And about three o'clock Jesus cried with a loud voice,

J   **Eli, Eli, lema sabachthani?**

N   that is, "My God, my God, why have you forsaken me?" When some of the bystanders heard it, they said,

S   *This man is calling for Elijah.*

N   At once one of them ran and got a sponge, filled it with sour wine, put it on a stick, and gave it to him to drink. But the others said,

S   *Wait, let us see whether Elijah will come to save him.*

N   Then Jesus cried again with a loud voice and breathed his last.

> *Here all kneel and pause for a short time.*

N   At that moment the curtain of the temple was torn in two, from top to bottom. The earth shook, and the rocks were split. The tombs also were opened, and many bodies of the saints who had fallen asleep were raised. After his resurrection they came out of the tombs and entered the holy city and appeared to many.

Now when the centurion and those with him, who were keeping watch over Jesus, saw the earthquake and what took place, they were terrified and said,

S **Truly this man was God's Son!**

* * *

N Many women were also there, looking on from a distance; they had followed Jesus from Galilee and had provided for him. Among them were Mary Magdalene, and Mary the mother of James and Joseph, and the mother of the sons of Zebedee.

When it was evening, there came a rich man from Arimathea, named Joseph, who was also a disciple of Jesus. He went to Pilate and asked for the body of Jesus; then Pilate ordered it to be given to him. So Joseph took the body and wrapped it in a clean linen cloth and laid it in his own new tomb, which he had hewn in the rock. He then rolled a great stone to the door of the tomb and went away.

Mary Magdalene and the other Mary were there, sitting opposite the tomb. The next day, that is, after the day of Preparation, the chief priests and the Pharisees gathered before Pilate and said,

S *Sir, we remember what that impostor said while he was still alive, "After three days I will rise again." Therefore command the tomb to be made secure until the third day; otherwise his disciples may go and steal him away, and tell the people, "He has been raised from the dead," and the last deception would be worse than the first.*

N Pilate said to them,

S *You have a guard of soldiers; go, make it as secure as you can.*

N So they went with the guard and made the tomb secure by sealing the stone.

> *The readers return to their places in silence.*

PROFESSION OF FAITH *(p. 13-14)*

PRAYER OF THE FAITHFUL

The following intentions are suggestions only.

℟ **Lord, hear our prayer.**

For the Church, community of the crucified Christ, manifesting his solidarity with the poor and oppressed, we pray to the Lord: ℟

For leaders of nations and peoples, struggling to implement policies that promote development, justice and peace, we pray to the Lord: ℟

For those whom we, as a Church or a society, have rejected, we pray to the Lord: ℟

For us, God's people, struggling to see the world through the eyes of the crucified Christ, we pray to the Lord: ℟

PREPARATION OF THE GIFTS *(p. 15)*

PRAYER OVER THE GIFTS

Lord, may the suffering and death of Jesus, your only Son, make us pleasing to you. Alone we can do nothing, but may this perfect sacrifice win us your mercy and love.

PREFACE *(Passion Sunday, p. 26)*

COMMUNION ANTIPHON *(Matthew 26.42)*

Father, if this cup may not pass, but I must drink it, then your will be done.

PRAYER AFTER COMMUNION

Lord, you have satisfied our hunger with this eucharistic food. The death of your Son gives us hope and strengthens our faith. May his resurrection give us perseverance and lead us to salvation.

SOLEMN BLESSING — Passion *(Optional)*

Bow your heads and pray for God's blessing.

The Father of mercies has given us an example of unselfish love in the sufferings of his only Son. Through your service of God and neighbour may you receive his countless blessings. **Amen.**

You believe that by his dying Christ destroyed death for ever. May he give you everlasting life. **Amen.**

He humbled himself for our sakes. May you follow his example and share in his resurrection. **Amen.**

May almighty God bless you, the Father, and the Son, and the Holy Spirit. **Amen.**

DISMISSAL *(p. 67)*

On that first Holy Thursday, a profound sacredness accompanied every gesture of Jesus. After sharing his last supper with his friends, Jesus humbly removed his outer garment and taking up a basin of water and a towel, he began to wash the feet of his disciples. They were all caught by surprise. No master was expected to wash his disciples' feet. When Peter objected, Jesus challenged him, "Unless I wash you, you have no share with me."

In surrendering to Jesus, Peter was showing us how we too must live out our discipleship with Christ. Only by being totally united with him are we able to faithfully serve his mission. With him we will always have hope, whatever trials or suffering we may have to face.

Even as he was about to be handed over to his passion and death, Jesus never stopped loving his disciples, even when out of fear they would temporarily abandon him. We too receive that same love today as we struggle to live our faith. With one humble gesture, washing the feet of his disciples, Jesus has shown us how to *be* eucharist, making his presence alive and real in a world that hungers for God's compassion, justice and peace. Our vocation as his present-day disciples is truly a revolutionary commitment to the life of the world.

Michael Traher, Scarborough, ON

ENTRANCE ANTIPHON *(Galatians 6.14)*

It is our duty to glory in the cross of our Lord Jesus Christ. He saves us and sets us free; through him we find salvation, life, and resurrection.

INTRODUCTORY RITES *(p. 7)*

OPENING PRAYER

God our Father, we are gathered here to share in the supper which your only Son left to his Church to reveal his love. He gave it to us when he was about to die and commanded us to celebrate it as the new and eternal sacrifice. We pray that in this eucharist we may find the fullness of love and life.

FIRST READING *(Exodus 12.1-8, 11-14)*

The Lord said to Moses and Aaron in the land of Egypt: This month shall mark for you the beginning of months; it shall be the first month of the year for you. Tell the whole congregation of Israel that on the tenth of this month they are to take a lamb for each family, a lamb for each household. If a household is too small for a whole lamb, it shall join its closest neighbour in obtaining one; the lamb shall be divided in proportion to the number of people who eat of it.

Your lamb shall be without blemish, a year-old male; you may take it from the sheep or from the goats. You shall keep it until the fourteenth day of this month; then the whole assembled congregation of Israel shall slaughter it at twilight. They shall take some of the blood and put it on the two doorposts and the lintel of the houses in which they eat it. They shall eat the lamb that same night; they shall eat it roasted over the fire with unleavened bread and bitter herbs.

This is how you shall eat it: your loins girded, your sandals on your feet, and your staff in your hand; and you shall eat it hurriedly. It is the Passover of the Lord. For I will pass through the land of Egypt that night, and I will strike down every firstborn in the land of Egypt, both human beings and animals; on all the gods of Egypt I will execute judgments: I am the Lord.

The blood shall be a sign for you on the houses where you live: when I see the blood, I will pass over you, and no plague shall destroy you when I strike the land of Egypt.

This day shall be a day of remembrance for you. You shall celebrate it as a festival to the Lord; throughout your generations you shall observe it as a perpetual ordinance.

The word of the Lord. **Thanks be to God.**

RESPONSORIAL PSALM *(Psalm 116)*

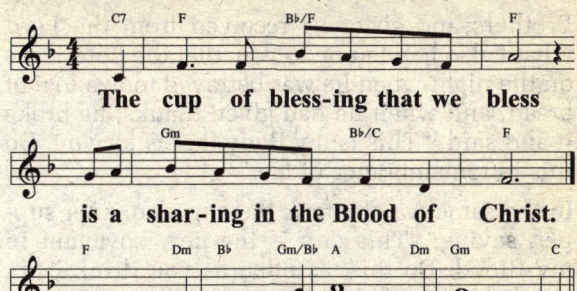

The cup of bless-ing that we bless
is a shar-ing in the Blood of Christ.

R̝. **The cup of blessing that we bless
is a sharing in the Blood of Christ.**

What shall I return to the · **Lord**
for all his bounty to · **me?**
I will lift up the cup of sal-**vation**
and call on the name · **of_the** Lord. R̝.

Precious in the sight of the · **Lord**
is the death of his · **faithful_ones.**
I am your servant,
    the son of your · **serving_girl.**
You have loosed · **my** bonds. R̝.

I will offer to you a thanksgiving · **sacrifice**
and call on the name of the · **Lord.**
I will pay my vows to the · **Lord**
in the presence of all · **his** people. R̝.

SECOND READING *(1 Corinthians 11.23-26)*

Brothers and sisters: I received from the Lord what I also handed on to you, that the Lord Jesus on the night when he was betrayed took a loaf of bread, and when he had given thanks, he broke it and said, "This is my Body that is for you. Do this in remembrance of me."

In the same way he took the cup also, after supper, saying, "This cup is the new covenant in my Blood. Do this, as often as you drink it, in remembrance of me." For as often as you eat this bread and drink the cup, you proclaim the Lord's death until he comes.

The word of the Lord. **Thanks be to God.**

GOSPEL ACCLAMATION *(John 13.34)*

Praise to you, Lord, king of eternal glory! I give you a new commandment: love one another as I have loved you. **Praise to you, Lord, king of eternal glory!**

GOSPEL *(John 13.1-15)*

A reading from the holy Gospel according to John. **Glory to you, Lord.**

Before the festival of the Passover, Jesus knew that his hour had come to depart from this world and go to the Father. Having loved his own who were in the world, he loved them to the end.

The devil had already put it into the heart of Judas, son of Simon Iscariot, to betray him. And during supper Jesus, knowing that the Father had given all things into his hands, and that he had come from God and was going to God, got up from the table, took off his outer robe, and tied a towel around himself. Then he poured water into a basin and began to wash the disciples' feet and to wipe them with the towel that was tied around him.

He came to Simon Peter, who said to him, "Lord, are you going to wash my feet?" Jesus answered, "You do not know now what I am doing, but later you will understand." Peter said to him, "You will never wash my feet." 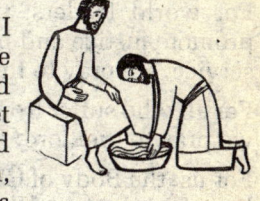 Jesus answered, "Unless I wash you, you have no share with me." Simon Peter said to him, "Lord, not my feet only but also my hands and my head!" Jesus said to him, "One who has bathed does not need to wash, except for the feet, but is entirely clean. And you are clean, though not all of you." For he knew who was to betray him; for this reason he said, "Not all of you are clean."

After he had washed their feet, put on his robe, and returned to the table, Jesus said to them, "Do you know what I have done to you? You call me Teacher and Lord — and you are right, for that is what I am. So if I, your Lord and Teacher, have washed your feet, you also ought to wash one another's feet. For I have set you an example, that you also should do as I have done to you."

The Gospel of the Lord. **Praise to you, Lord Jesus Christ.**

The Profession of Faith *is omitted.*

THE WASHING OF THE FEET

During the washing of the feet, the assembly may sing an appropriate song.

PRAYER OF THE FAITHFUL

The following intentions are suggestions only.

R̲ **Lord, hear our prayer.**

For the Church, witness to true love and service in Christ, we pray to the Lord: R̲

For world leaders, trusted by their people to promote justice and human dignity through true service, we pray to the Lord: R̲

For all who suffer from our greed and selfishness, we pray to the Lord: R̲

For us, the Body of Christ, called to pour out our lives for others as Jesus did for us, we pray to the Lord: R̲

PREPARATION OF THE GIFTS *(p. 15)*

PRAYER OVER THE GIFTS

Lord, make us worthy to celebrate these mysteries. Each time we offer this memorial sacrifice, the work of our redemption is accomplished.

PREFACE *(Holy Eucharist I, p. 31)*

COMMUNION ANTIPHON *(1 Cor.11.24-25)*

This body will be given for you. This is the cup of the new covenant in my blood; whenever you receive them, do so in remembrance of me.

PRAYER AFTER COMMUNION

Almighty God, we receive new life from the supper your Son gave us in this world. May we find full contentment in the meal we hope to share in your eternal kingdom.

The Blessing and Dismissal *are omitted tonight.*

TRANSFER OF THE HOLY EUCHARIST

The Blessed Sacrament is carried through the church to the place of reposition. During the procession, the hymn Pange lingua *(p. 638, stanzas 1-4) or another eucharistic song is sung. At the place of reposition, the presider incenses the Blessed Sacrament, while* Tantum ergo (Pange lingua, *stanzas 5-6) is sung. The tabernacle of repose is then closed.*

After a few moments of silent adoration, the priests and ministers of the altar retire. The faithful are encouraged to continue adoration before the Blessed Sacrament for a suitable period of time. There should be no solemn adoration after midnight.

The portrait of the Suffering Servant as depicted in today's first reading is not an easy one to contemplate. Beaten, bruised and broken, the Redeemer has become an object of scorn and disgust. Once crowds followed him in search of his words of wisdom or his healing touch. Now, whether recoiling in horror or overwhelmed by helplessness, they turn away. Do we, too, turn away?

I am reminded of a powerful homily I heard during a retreat several years ago. The speaker was reflecting on recognizing the face of Jesus in others. She used the examples of some public figures in the news, political leaders promoting questionable policies, and asked if we could see Jesus in them. She then left us with the haunting question: In whom do *you* find it most difficult to see the face of Jesus?

We are called daily to see Jesus in others, but not only in those who are immediately attractive or to whom we are easily drawn. Jesus is equally present in those people whom we find annoying or hurtful, who seem close-minded, who reject our efforts to reach them, who are broken in body or in spirit.

Let us begin each new day with a prayer for the wisdom and humility to see the face of Jesus in everyone whom we encounter, especially when it is most difficult for us.

Krystyna Higgins, Fredericton, NB

National Collection for the Church in the Holy Land

PRAYER

Lord, by shedding his blood for us, your Son, Jesus Christ, established the paschal mystery. In your goodness, make us holy and watch over us always.

LITURGY OF THE WORD

FIRST READING *(Isaiah 52.13 – 53.12)*

See, my servant shall prosper; he shall be exalted and lifted up, and shall be very high.

Just as there were many who were astonished at him — so marred was his appearance, beyond human semblance, and his form beyond that of the sons of man — so he shall startle many nations; kings shall shut their mouths because of him; for that which had not been told them they shall see, and that which they had not heard they shall contemplate. Who has believed what we have heard? And to whom has the arm of the Lord been revealed?

For he grew up before the Lord like a young plant, and like a root out of dry ground; he had no form or majesty that we should look at him, nothing in his appearance that we should desire him. He was despised and rejected by men; a man of suffering and acquainted with infirmity; and as one from whom others hide their faces he was despised, and we held him of no account.

Surely he has borne our infirmities and carried our diseases; yet we accounted him stricken, struck down by God, and afflicted. But he was wounded for our transgressions, crushed for our iniquities; upon him was the punishment that made us whole, and by his bruises we are healed.

All we like sheep have gone astray; each has turned to their own way and the Lord has laid on him the iniquity of us all.

He was oppressed, and he was afflicted, yet he did not open his mouth; like a lamb that is led to the slaughter, and like a sheep that before its shearers is silent, so he did not open his mouth.

By a perversion of justice he was taken away. Who could have imagined his future? For he was cut off from the land of the living, stricken for the transgression of my people. They made his grave with the wicked and his tomb with the rich, although he had done no violence, and there was no deceit in his mouth.

Yet it was the will of the Lord to crush him with pain. When you make his life an offering for sin, he shall see his offspring, and shall prolong his days; through him the will of the Lord shall prosper. Out of his anguish he shall see light; he shall find satisfaction through his knowledge. The righteous one, my servant, shall make many righteous, and he shall bear their iniquities.

Therefore I will allot him a portion with the great, and he shall divide the spoil with the strong; because he poured out himself to death, and was numbered with the transgressors; yet he bore the sin of many, and made intercession for the transgressors.

The word of the Lord. **Thanks be to God.**

RESPONSORIAL PSALM *(Psalm 31)*

Fa - ther, in - to your hands
I com - mend my spir - it.

℟. **Father, into your hands**
I commend my spirit.

In you, O Lord, I seek refuge;
do not let me ever be put · **to** shame;
in your righteousness · **de**-liver_me.
Into your hand I commit · **my** spirit;
you have redeemed me,
O Lord, · **faith**-ful God. ℟.

I am the scorn of all my adversaries,
a horror to my neighbours,
an object of dread to my · **ac**-quaintances.
Those who see me in the · **street** flee_from_me.
I have passed out of mind like one
who · **is** dead;
I have become like a · **bro**-ken vessel. ℟.

But I trust in you, · **O** Lord;
I say, "You are · **my** God."
My times are in · **your** hand;
deliver me from the hand
of my · **enemies** and persecutors. ℟. **→**

Let your face shine upon · **your** servant;
save me in your stead·-**fast** love.
Be strong, and let your heart · **take** courage,
all you who wait · **for** the Lord. R.

R. **Father, into your hands
I commend my spirit.**

©2009 Gordon Johnston/Novalis

SECOND READING *(Hebrews 4.14-16; 5.7-9)*

Brothers and sisters: Since we have a great high priest who has passed through the heavens, Jesus, the Son of God, let us hold fast to our confession. For we do not have a high priest who is unable to sympathize with our weaknesses, but we have one who in every respect has been tested as we are, yet without sin. Let us therefore approach the throne of grace with boldness, so that we may receive mercy and find grace to help in time of need.

In the days of his flesh, Jesus offered up prayers and supplications, with loud cries and tears, to the one who was able to save him from death, and he was heard because of his reverent submission. Although he was a Son, he learned obedience through what he suffered; and having been made perfect, he became the source of eternal salvation for all who obey him.

The word of the Lord. **Thanks be to God.**

GOSPEL ACCLAMATION *(Philippians 2.8-9)*

Praise to you, Lord, king of eternal glory! Christ became obedient for us to death, even death on a Cross. Therefore God exalted him and gave him the name above every name. **Praise to you, Lord, king of eternal glory!**

GOSPEL *(John 18.1 – 19.42)*

Several readers may proclaim the passion narrative today. N indicates the narrator, J the words of Jesus, and S the words of other speakers.

N   The Passion of our Lord Jesus Christ according to John.

After they had eaten the supper, Jesus went out with his disciples across the Kidron valley to a place where there was a garden, which he and his disciples entered. Now Judas, who betrayed him, also knew the place, because Jesus often met there with his disciples. So Judas brought a detachment of soldiers together with police from the chief priests and the Pharisees, and they came there with lanterns and torches and weapons.

Then Jesus, knowing all that was to happen to him, came forward and asked them,

J   **Whom are you looking for?**

N   They answered,

S   *Jesus of Nazareth.*

J   **I am he.**

N   Judas, who betrayed him, was standing with them. When Jesus said to them, "I am he," they stepped back and fell to the ground. Again he asked them,

J   **Whom are you looking for?**

S   *Jesus of Nazareth.*

J   **I told you that I am he. So if you are looking for me, let these men go.**

N This was to fulfill the word that he had spoken, "I did not lose a single one of those whom you gave me."

Then Simon Peter, who had a sword, drew it, struck the high priest's slave, and cut off his right ear. The slave's name was Malchus. Jesus said to Peter,

J **Put your sword back into its sheath. Am I not to drink the cup that the Father has given me?**

N So the soldiers, their officer, and the Jewish police arrested Jesus and bound him. First they took him to Annas, who was the father-in-law of Caiaphas, the high priest that year. Caiaphas was the one who had advised the Jews that it was better to have one person die for the people.

Simon Peter and another disciple followed Jesus. Since that disciple was known to the high priest, he went with Jesus into the courtyard of the high priest, but Peter was standing outside at the gate. So the other disciple, who was known to the high priest, went out, spoke to the woman who guarded the gate, and brought Peter in. The woman said to Peter,

S *You are not also one of this man's disciples, are you?*

N Peter said,

S *I am not.*

N Now the slaves and the police had made a charcoal fire because it was cold, and they were standing around it and warming themselves. Peter also was standing with them and warming himself.

Then the high priest questioned Jesus about his disciples and about his teaching. Jesus answered,

J **I have spoken openly to the world; I have always taught in synagogues and in the temple, where all the Jews come together. I have said nothing in secret. Why do you ask me? Ask those who heard what I said to them; they know what I said.**

N When he had said this, one of the police standing nearby struck Jesus on the face, saying,

S *Is that how you answer the high priest?*

J **If I have spoken wrongly, testify to the wrong. But if I have spoken rightly, why do you strike me?**

N Then Annas sent him bound to Caiaphas the high priest.

Now Simon Peter was standing and warming himself. They asked him,

S *You are not also one of his disciples, are you?*

N He denied it and said,

S *I am not.*

N One of the slaves of the high priest, a relative of the man whose ear Peter had cut off, asked,

S *Did I not see you in the garden with him?*

N Again Peter denied it, and at that moment the cock crowed.

*At this point all may join in singing
an appropriate acclamation.*

Ky - ri - e, Chris - te, Ky - ri - e e - le - i - son!

Text: Didier Rimaud, © *CNPL*. Music: Jacques Berthier
Source: © *Éditions Musicales Studio SM, 060794-2*

N Then they took Jesus from Caiaphas to Pilate's headquarters. It was early in the morning. They themselves did not enter the headquarters, so as to avoid ritual defilement and to be able to eat the Passover. So Pilate went out to them and said,

S *What accusation do you bring against this man?*

N They answered,

S *If this man were not a criminal, we would not have handed him over to you.*

N Pilate said to them,

S *Take him yourselves and judge him according to your law.*

N They replied,

S *We are not permitted to put anyone to death.*

N This was to fulfill what Jesus had said when he indicated the kind of death he was to die.

Then Pilate entered the headquarters again, summoned Jesus, and asked him,

S *Are you the King of the Jews?*

J   Do you ask this on your own, or did others tell you about me?

S   *I am not a Jew, am I? Your own nation and the chief priests have handed you over to me. What have you done?*

J   My kingdom is not from this world. If my kingdom were from this world, my followers would be fighting to keep me from being handed over to the Jews. But as it is, my kingdom is not from here.

S   *So you are a king?*

J   You say that I am a king. For this I was born, and for this I came into the world, to testify to the truth. Everyone who belongs to the truth listens to my voice.

S   *What is truth?*

N   After he had said this, Pilate went out to the Jews again and told them,

S   *I find no case against him. But you have a custom that I release someone for you at the Passover. Do you want me to release for you the King of the Jews?*

N   They shouted in reply,

S   *Not this man, but Barabbas!*

N   Now Barabbas was a bandit. Then Pilate took Jesus and had him flogged. And the soldiers wove a crown of thorns and put it on his head, and they dressed him in a purple robe. They kept coming up to him, saying,

S   *"Hail, King of the Jews!"*

N and they struck him on the face. Pilate went out again and said to them,

S *Look, I am bringing him out to you to let you know that I find no case against him.*

N So Jesus came out, wearing the crown of thorns and the purple robe. Pilate said to them,

S *Here is the man!*

N When the chief priests and the police saw him, they shouted,

S *Crucify him! Crucify him!*

N Pilate said to them,

S *Take him yourselves and crucify him; I find no case against him.*

N They answered him,

S *We have a law, and according to that law he ought to die because he has claimed to be the Son of God.*

N Now when Pilate heard this, he was more afraid than ever. He entered his headquarters again and asked Jesus,

S *Where are you from?*

N But Jesus gave him no answer. Pilate therefore said to him,

S *Do you refuse to speak to me? Do you not know that I have power to release you, and power to crucify you?*

J **You would have no power over me unless it had been given you from above; therefore the**

one who handed me over to you is guilty of a greater sin.

N From then on Pilate tried to release him, but the Jews cried out,

S *If you release this man, you are no friend of the emperor. Everyone who claims to be a king sets himself against the emperor.*

N When Pilate heard these words, he brought Jesus outside and sat on the judge's bench at a place called "The Stone Pavement," or in Hebrew "Gabbatha."

Now it was the day of Preparation for the Passover; and it was about noon. Pilate said to the Jews,

S *Here is your King!*

N They cried out,

S *Away with him! Away with him! Crucify him!*

N Pilate asked them,

S *Shall I crucify your King?*

N The chief priests answered,

S *We have no king but the emperor.*

> *At this point all may join in singing an appropriate acclamation.*

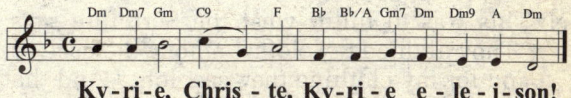

Ky-ri-e, Chris-te, Ky-ri-e e-le-i-son!

Text: Didier Rimaud, © *CNPL*. Music: Jacques Berthier
Source: © *Éditions Musicales Studio SM, 060794-2*

N Then Pilate handed Jesus over to them to be crucified. So they took Jesus; and carrying the Cross by himself, he went out to what is called The Place of the Skull, which in Hebrew is called Golgotha. There they crucified him, and with him two others, one on either side, with Jesus between them.

Pilate also had an inscription written and put on the Cross. It read, "Jesus of Nazareth, the King of the Jews." Many of the people read this inscription, because the place where Jesus was crucified was near the city; and it was written in Hebrew, in Latin, and in Greek. Then the chief priests of the Jews said to Pilate,

S *Do not write, "The King of the Jews," but, "This man said, I am King of the Jews."*

N Pilate answered,

S *What I have written I have written.*

N When the soldiers had crucified Jesus, they took his clothes and divided them into four parts, one for each soldier. They also took his tunic; now the tunic was seamless, woven in one piece from the top. So they said to one another,

S *Let us not tear it, but cast lots for it to see who will get it.*

N This was to fulfill what the Scripture says, "They divided my clothes among themselves, and for my clothing they cast lots." And that is what the soldiers did.

Meanwhile, standing near the Cross of Jesus

were his mother, and his mother's sister, Mary the wife of Clopas, and Mary Magdalene. When Jesus saw his mother and the disciple whom he loved standing beside her, he said to his mother,

J **Woman, here is your son.**

N Then he said to the disciple,

J **Here is your mother.**

N And from that hour the disciple took her into his own home.

After this, when Jesus knew that all was now finished, in order to fulfill the Scripture, he said,

J **I am thirsty.**

N A jar full of sour wine was standing there. So they put a sponge full of the wine on a branch of hyssop and held it to his mouth.

When Jesus had received the wine, he said,

J **It is finished.**

N Then he bowed his head and gave up his spirit.

Here all kneel and pause for a short time.

N Since it was the day of Preparation, the Jews did not want the bodies left on the cross during the Sabbath, especially because that Sabbath was a day of great Solemnity. So they asked Pilate to have the legs of the crucified men broken and the bodies removed.

Then the soldiers came and broke the legs of the first and of the other who had been crucified with him. But when they came to Jesus and saw that he was already dead, they did not break his legs. Instead, one of the soldiers pierced his side with a spear, and at once blood and water came out.

(He who saw this has testified so that you also may believe. His testimony is true, and he knows that he tells the truth.) These things occurred so that the Scripture might be fulfilled, "None of his bones shall be broken." And again another passage of Scripture says, "They will look on the one whom they have pierced."

After these things, Joseph of Arimathea, who was a disciple of Jesus, though a secret one because of his fear of the Jews, asked Pilate to let him take away the body of Jesus. Pilate gave him permission; so he came and removed his body.

Nicodemus, who had at first come to Jesus by night, also came, bringing a mixture of myrrh and aloes, weighing about a hundredweight. They took the body of Jesus and wrapped it with the spices in linen cloths, according to the burial custom of the Jews. Now there was a garden in the place where he was crucified, and in the garden there was a new tomb in which no one had ever been laid. And so, because it was the Jewish day of Preparation, and the tomb was nearby, they laid Jesus there.

The readers return to their places in silence.

PRAYER OF THE FAITHFUL

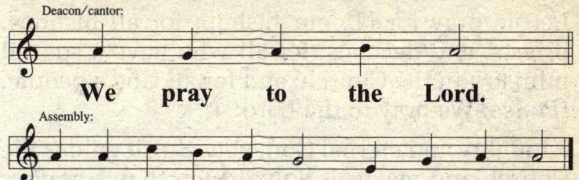

R. **For the sake of your Son, have mercy, Lord.**

For the Church

Let us pray, dear friends, for the holy Church of God throughout the world, that God the almighty Father guide it and gather it together so that it may worship him in peace and tranquillity. *(Pause)* We pray to the Lord: **R.**

Almighty and eternal God, you have shown your glory to all nations in Christ, your Son. Guide the work of your Church. Help it to persevere in faith, proclaim your name and bring your salvation to people everywhere. We ask this through Christ our Lord. **Amen.**

For the Pope

Let us pray for our Holy Father, Pope N., that God who chose him to be bishop may give him health and strength to guide and govern God's holy people. *(Pause)* We pray to the Lord: **R.**

Almighty and eternal God, you guide all things by your word, you govern all Christian people. In your love protect the Pope you have chosen for us. Under his leadership deepen our faith and make us better Christians. We ask this through Christ our Lord. **Amen.**

For the clergy and laity of the Church

Let us pray for N., our bishop; for all bishops, priests, and deacons; for all who have a special ministry in the Church; and for all God's people. *(Pause)* We pray to the Lord: R.

Almighty and eternal God, your Spirit guides the Church and makes it holy. Listen to our prayers and help each of us in his own vocation to do your work more faithfully. We ask this through Christ our Lord. **Amen.**

For those preparing for baptism

Let us pray for those (among us) preparing for baptism, that God in his mercy make them responsive to his love, forgive their sins through the waters of new birth, and give them life in Jesus Christ our Lord. *(Pause)* We pray to the Lord: R.

Almighty and eternal God, you continually bless your Church with new members. Increase the faith and understanding of those (among us) preparing for baptism. Give them a new birth in these living waters and make them members of your chosen family. We ask this through Christ our Lord. **Amen.**

For the unity of Christians

Let us pray for all our brothers and sisters who share our faith in Jesus Christ, that God may gather and keep together in one Church all those who seek the truth with sincerity. *(Pause)* We pray to the Lord: R.

Almighty and eternal God, you keep together those you have united. Look kindly on all who follow Jesus your Son. We are all consecrated to you by our common baptism. Make us one in the fullness of faith, and keep us in the fellowship of love. We ask this through Christ our Lord. **Amen.**

For the Jewish people

Let us pray for the Jewish people, the first to hear the word of God, that they may continue to grow in the love of his name and in faithfulness to his covenant. *(Pause)* We pray to the Lord: ℞

Almighty and eternal God, long ago you gave your promise to Abraham and his posterity. Listen to your Church as we pray that the people you first made your own may arrive at the fullness of redemption. We ask this through Christ our Lord. **Amen.**

For those who do not believe in Christ

Let us pray for those who do not believe in Christ, that the light of the Holy Spirit may show them the way to salvation. *(Pause)* We pray to the Lord: ℞

Almighty and eternal God, enable those who do not acknowledge Christ to find the truth as they walk before you in sincerity of heart. Help us to grow in love for one another, to grasp more fully the mystery of your godhead, and to become more perfect witnesses of your love in the sight of men. We ask this through Christ our Lord. **Amen.**

For those who do not believe in God

Let us pray for those who do not believe in God, that they may find him by sincerely following all that is right. *(Pause)* We pray to the Lord: ℞

Almighty and eternal God, you created mankind so that all might long to find you and have peace when you are found. Grant that, in spite of the hurtful things that stand in their way, they may all recognize in the lives of Christians the tokens of your love and mercy, and gladly acknowledge you as the one true God and Father of us all. We ask this through Christ our Lord. **Amen.**

For all in public office

Let us pray for those who serve us in public office, that God may guide their minds and hearts, so that all men may live in true peace and freedom. *(Pause)* We pray to the Lord: R.

Almighty and eternal God, you know the longings of men's hearts and you protect their rights. In your goodness, watch over those in authority, so that your people everywhere may enjoy religious freedom, security, and peace. We ask this through Christ our Lord. **Amen.**

For those in special need

Let us pray, dear friends, that God the almighty Father may heal the sick, comfort the dying, give safety to travellers, free those unjustly deprived of liberty, and rid the world of falsehood, hunger, and disease. *(Pause)* We pray to the Lord: R.

Almighty, ever-living God, you give strength to the weary and new courage to those who have lost heart. Hear the prayers of all who call on you in any trouble that they may have the joy of receiving your help in their need. We ask this through Christ our Lord. **Amen.**

VENERATION OF THE CROSS

Three times, the priest or deacon invites the assembly to proclaim its faith:

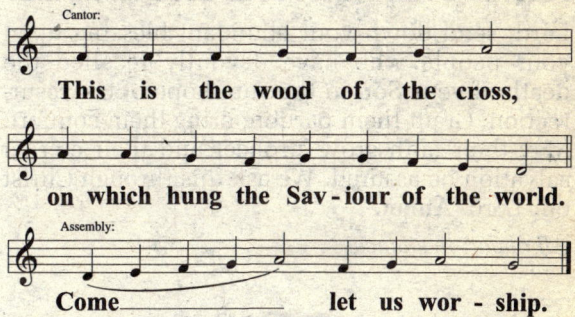

This is the wood of the cross,

on which hung the Sav-iour of the world.

Come___ let us wor - ship.

After each response all venerate the cross briefly in silence. After the third response, the cross and the candles are placed at the entrance to the sanctuary and the people approach to venerate the cross. They may make a simple genuflection or perform some other appropriate sign of reverence according to local custom.

During the veneration, suitable songs are sung (see pages 640, 641). All who have venerated the cross return to their places. Where large numbers of people make individual veneration difficult, the presider may raise the cross briefly for all to venerate in silence.

COMMUNION RITE

LORD'S PRAYER *(p. 65)*

PRAYER AFTER COMMUNION

Almighty and eternal God, you have restored us to life by the triumphant death and resurrection of Christ. Continue this healing work within us.

May we who participate in this mystery never cease to serve you. We ask this through Christ our Lord. **Amen.**

PRAYER OVER THE PEOPLE and DISMISSAL

Lord, send down your abundant blessing upon your people who have devoutly recalled the death of your Son in the sure hope of the resurrection. Grant them pardon; bring them comfort. May their faith grow stronger and their eternal salvation be assured. We ask this through Christ our Lord. **Amen.**

All depart in silence.

April 23   **Holy Saturday**

There is no liturgical action on Holy Saturday. The very absence of celebration is the Church's way of expressing that it waits at the Lord's tomb, meditating on his suffering and death.

Holy Saturday is also a day of hope. We know that Jesus did not remain in the tomb. We anticipate his resurrection during this holy night when the joy of Easter will burst forth and overflow into the 50 days of celebration of the Easter Season.

In the Easter gospel for the "Mother of all Liturgies," Matthew announces the resurrection using the imagery of a severe earthquake. We have heard that story once before. At Jesus' death, the curtain of the Temple was torn in two, the earth shook and the tombs of the dead burst open. The image of an earthquake is an attempt to express the inexpressible. Jesus' breaking the bonds of death has cosmic and human resonances, which can be only picked up in faith.

What happens when we experience earthquakes in our own lives? Just when we thought that everything in our world was dying or ended, the Lord enters forcefully and reminds us that despair and destruction do not have the final word. Sinfulness, darkness and death are overcome by the living and present Jesus whose words startle, console and renew us: "Do not be afraid!"

In this marvellous earth-shattering liturgy of Easter night, let us hear once again those consoling words. Tonight, having encountered the Risen One in Word and Sacrament, let us bow down and worship him.

Who is the Risen Jesus for me? From what do I need to be liberated? What earthquakes have I experienced in my life that have allowed me to encounter the powerful presence of God and his Son Jesus breaking through my history? How do I carry the good news of his resurrection to others?

Thomas Rosica, Toronto, ON

THE SERVICE OF LIGHT

BLESSING OF THE FIRE

Dear friends in Christ, on this most holy night, when our Lord Jesus Christ passed from death to life, the Church invites her children throughout the world to come together in vigil and prayer. This is the passover of the Lord: if we honour the memory of his death and resurrection by hearing his word and celebrating his mysteries, then we may be confident that we shall share his victory over death and live with him for ever in God.

Let us pray. Father, we share in the light of your glory through your Son, the light of the world. Make this new fire holy, and inflame us with new hope. Purify our minds by this Easter celebration, and bring us one day to the feast of eternal light. We ask this through Christ our Lord. **Amen.**

PREPARATION OF THE CANDLE *(Optional)*

The priest cuts a cross in the Easter candle and traces the Greek letters alpha (A) and omega (Ω) and the numerals 2011, saying:

Christ yesterday and today, the beginning and the end, Alpha and Omega; all time belongs to him, and all the ages; to him be glory and power through every age and for ever. **Amen.**

When the marks have been made, the priest may insert five grains of incense in the candle.

By his holy and glorious wounds may Christ our Lord guard us and keep us. **Amen.**

LIGHTING OF THE CANDLE

The priest lights the Easter candle from the new fire, saying:

May the light of Christ, rising in glory, dispel the darkness of our hearts and minds.

PROCESSION WITH THE EASTER CANDLE

The priest or deacon takes the Easter candle and, three times during the procession to the altar, lifts it high and sings alone. The people respond.

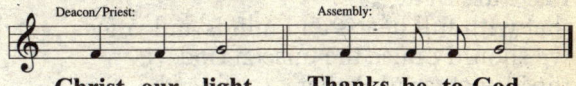

Christ our light.   Thanks be to God.

Christ our Light. **Thanks be to God.**

After the second such response all the people light their candles with a flame taken from the Easter candle.

EASTER PROCLAMATION (EXSULTET)

For the shorter version, omit the indented parts.

Rejoice, heavenly powers! Sing, choirs of angels!
Exult, all creation around God's throne!
Jesus Christ, our King, is risen!
Sound the trumpet of salvation!

Rejoice, O earth, in shining splendour,
radiant in the brightness of your King!
Christ has conquered! Glory fills you!
Darkness vanishes for ever!

Rejoice, O Mother Church! Exult in glory!
The risen Saviour shines upon you!
Let this place resound with joy,
echoing the mighty song of all God's people!

> My dearest friends, standing with me in this
> holy light, join me in asking God for mercy,
> that he may give his unworthy minister grace
> to sing his Easter praises.

The Lord be with you. **And also with you.**

Lift up your hearts. **We lift them up to the Lord.**

Let us give thanks to the Lord our God.
It is right to give him thanks and praise.

It is truly right
that with full hearts and minds and voices
we should praise the unseen God,
the all-powerful Father,
and his only Son, our Lord Jesus Christ.
For Christ has ransomed us with his blood,
and paid for us the price of Adam's sin
to our eternal Father!

This is our passover feast,
when Christ, the true Lamb, is slain,
whose blood consecrates the homes
of all believers.

This is the night when first you saved our fathers:
you freed the people of Israel from their slavery
and led them dry-shod through the sea.

> This is the night when the pillar of fire
> destroyed the darkness of sin!

This is the night when Christians everywhere,
washed clean of sin
and freed from all defilement,
are restored to grace
and grow together in holiness.

This is the night when Jesus Christ
broke the chains of death
and rose triumphant from the grave.

> What good would life have been to us,
> had Christ not come as our Redeemer?

Father, how wonderful your care for us!
How boundless your merciful love!
To ransom a slave you gave away your Son.

O happy fault, O necessary sin of Adam,
which gained for us so great a Redeemer!

> Most blessed of all nights, chosen by God
> to see Christ rising from the dead!

> Of this night scripture says:
> "The night will be as clear as day:
> it will become my light, my joy."

The power of this holy night
dispels all evil, washes guilt away,
restores lost innocence, brings mourners joy;

> it casts out hatred, brings us peace,
> and humbles earthly pride.

Night truly blessed
when heaven is wedded to earth
and man is reconciled with God!

Therefore, heavenly Father,
in the joy of this night,
receive our evening sacrifice of praise,
your Church's solemn offering.

longer version:

Accept this Easter candle,
a flame divided but un-
dimmed, a pillar of fire that
glows to the honour of God.

Let it mingle with the lights
of heaven and continue
bravely burning to dispel
the darkness of this night!

shorter version:

Accept this
Easter candle.
May it always
dispel the dark-
ness of this
night!

May the Morning Star which never sets
find this flame still burning:
Christ, that Morning Star,
who came back from the dead,
and shed his peaceful light on all mankind,
your Son who lives and reigns for ever and ever.
Amen.

LITURGY OF THE WORD

Dear friends in Christ, we have begun our solemn
vigil. Let us now listen attentively to the word of
God, recalling how he saved his people throughout history and, in the fullness of time, sent his
own Son to be our Redeemer. Through this Easter
celebration, may God bring to perfection the saving work he has begun in us.

FIRST READING *(Genesis 1.1 – 2.2)*

For the shorter version, omit the indented parts.

In the beginning when God created the heavens and the earth,

> the earth was a formless void and darkness covered the face of the deep, while the spirit of God swept over the face of the waters. Then God said, "Let there be light"; and there was light. And God saw that the light was good; and God separated the light from the darkness. God called the light "Day," and the darkness he called "Night." And there was evening and there was morning, the first day.
>
> And God said, "Let there be a dome in the midst of the waters, and let it separate the waters from the waters." So God made the dome and separated the waters that were under the dome from the waters that were above the dome. And it was so. God called the dome "Sky." And there was evening and there was morning, the second day.
>
> And God said, "Let the waters under the sky be gathered together into one place, and let the dry land appear." And it was so. God called the dry land "Earth," and the waters that were gathered together he called "Seas." And God saw that it was good.
>
> Then God said, "Let the earth put forth vegetation: plants yielding seed, and fruit trees of every kind on earth that bear fruit with the seed in it." And it was so. The earth brought forth vegetation: plants yielding seed of every

kind, and trees of every kind bearing fruit with the seed in it. And God saw that it was good. And there was evening and there was morning, the third day.

And God said, "Let there be lights in the dome of the sky to separate the day from the night; and let them be for signs and for seasons and for days and years, and let them be lights in the dome of the sky to give light upon the earth." And it was so.

God made the two great lights — the greater light to rule the day and the lesser light to rule the night — and the stars. God set them in the dome of the sky to give light upon the earth, to rule over the day and over the night, and to separate the light from the darkness. And God saw that it was good. And there was evening and there was morning, the fourth day.

And God said, "Let the waters bring forth swarms of living creatures, and let birds fly above the earth across the dome of the sky." So God created the great sea monsters and every living creature that moves, of every kind, with which the waters swarm, and every winged bird of every kind. And God saw that it was good. God blessed them, saying, "Be fruitful and multiply and fill the waters in the seas, and let birds multiply on the earth." And there was evening and there was morning, the fifth day.

And God said, "Let the earth bring forth living creatures of every kind: cattle and creeping things and wild animals of the earth of every kind." And it was so. God made the wild animals of the earth of every kind, and the cattle of every kind, and everything that creeps upon the ground of every kind. And God saw that it was good. Then

God said, "Let us make man in our image, according to our likeness; and let them have dominion over the fish of the sea, and over the birds of the air, and over the cattle, and over all the wild animals of the earth, and over every creeping thing that creeps upon the earth." So God created man in his image, in the image of God he created him; male and female he created them.

God blessed them, and God said to them, "Be fruitful and multiply, and fill the earth and subdue it; and have dominion over the fish of the sea and over the birds of the air and over every living thing that moves upon the earth."

God said, "See, I have given you every plant yielding seed that is upon the face of all the earth, and every tree with seed in its fruit; you shall have them for food. And to every beast of the earth, and to every bird of the air, and to everything that creeps on the earth, everything that has the breath of life, I have given every green plant for food." And it was so.

God saw everything that he had made, and indeed, it was very good. And there was evening and there was morning, the sixth day.

Thus the heavens and the earth were finished, and all their multitude. And on the seventh day God finished the work that he had done,

and he rested on the seventh day from all the
work that he had done.

The word of the Lord. **Thanks be to God.**

An alternate psalm follows.

RESPONSORIAL PSALM *(Psalm 104)*

Lord, send forth your Spir - it,
and re - new the face of the earth.

R̥. **Lord, send forth your Spirit,**
   and renew the face of the earth.

Bless the Lord, O · **my** soul.
O Lord my God, you are very · **great.**
You are clothed with · **honour** and majesty,
wrapped in light as with · **a** garment. R̥.

You set the earth on its · **foun**-dations,
so that it shall never be · **shaken.**
You cover it with the deep as · **with** a garment;
the waters stood above · **the** mountains. R̥.

You make springs gush forth in · **the** valleys;
they flow between the · **hills.**
By the streams the birds of the air
   have their · **ha**-bi-tation;
they sing among · **the** branches. R̥.

From your lofty abode
    you water · **the** mountains;
the earth is satisfied with the fruit
    of your · **work.**
You cause the grass to · **grow_for** the cattle,
and plants for people to use,
    to bring forth food from · **the** earth. ℟.

O Lord, how manifold are · **your** works!
In wisdom you have made them · **all;**
the earth is · **full_of** your creatures.
Bless the Lord, O · **my** soul. ℟.

©2009 Gordon Johnston/Novalis

or

RESPONSORIAL PSALM *(Psalm 33)*

℟. **The earth is full of the steadfast love
of the Lord.**

The word of the Lord · **is** upright,
and all his work is done · **in** faithfulness.
He loves righteousness · **and** justice;
the earth is full of the steadfast love
    of · **the** Lord. ℟.

→

By the word of the Lord
  the heavens · **were** made,
and all their host by the breath of · **his** mouth.
He gathered the waters of the sea
  as in · **a** bottle;
he put the deeps · **in** storehouses. R.

R. **The earth is full of the steadfast love
of the Lord.**

Blessed is the nation whose God is · **the** Lord,
the people whom he has chosen
  as · **his** heritage.
The Lord looks down · **from** heaven;
he sees all · **human** beings. R.

Our soul waits for · **the** Lord;
he is our help · **and** shield.
Let your steadfast love, O Lord, be · **up**-on_us,
even as we hope · **in** you. R.

©2009 Gordon Johnston/Novalis

PRAYER

Let us pray. Almighty and eternal God, you created all things in wonderful beauty and order. Help us now to perceive how still more wonderful is the new creation by which in the fullness of time you redeemed your people through the sacrifice of our passover, Jesus Christ, who lives and reigns for ever and ever. **Amen.**

SECOND READING *(Genesis 22.1-18)*

For the shorter version, omit the indented parts.

God tested Abraham. He said to him, "Abraham!" And Abraham said, "Here I am." God said, "Take your son, your only son Isaac, whom you love, and go to the land of Moriah, and offer him there as a burnt offering on one of the mountains that I shall show you."

So Abraham rose early in the morning, saddled his donkey, and took two of his young men with him, and his son Isaac; he cut the wood for the burnt offering, and set out and went to the place in the distance that God had shown him.

On the third day Abraham looked up and saw the place far away. Then Abraham said to his young men, "Stay here with the donkey; the boy and I will go over there; we will worship, and then we will come back to  you." Abraham took the wood of the burnt offering and laid it on his son Isaac, and he himself carried the fire and the knife. So the two of them walked on together.

Isaac said to his father Abraham, "Father!" And Abraham said, "Here I am, my son." Isaac said, "The fire and the wood are here, but where is the lamb for a burnt offering?" Abraham said, "God himself will provide the lamb for a burnt offering, my son." So the two of them walked on together.

When Abraham and Isaac came to the place that God had shown him, Abraham built an altar there and laid the wood in order. He bound his son Isaac, and laid him on the altar, on top of the wood. Then Abraham reached out his hand and took the knife to kill his son.

But the Angel of the Lord called to him from heaven, and said, "Abraham, Abraham!" And he said, "Here I am." The Angel said, "Do not lay your hand on the boy or do anything to him; for now I know that you fear God, since you have not withheld your son, your only son, from me." And Abraham looked up and saw a ram, caught in a thicket by its horns. Abraham went and took the ram and offered it up as a burnt offering instead of his son.

> So Abraham called that place "The Lord will provide"; as it is said to this day, "On the mount of the Lord it shall be provided."

The Angel of the Lord called to Abraham a second time from heaven, and said, "By myself I have sworn, says the Lord: Because you have done this, and have not withheld your son, your only son, I will indeed bless you, and I will make your offspring as numerous as the stars of heaven and as the sand that is on the seashore. And your offspring shall possess the gate of their enemies, and by your offspring shall all the nations of the earth gain blessing for themselves, because you have obeyed my voice."

The word of the Lord. **Thanks be to God.**

RESPONSORIAL PSALM *(Psalm 16)*

℟. **Protect me, O God, for in you I take refuge.**

The Lord is my chosen portion · **and_my** cup;
you hold · **my** lot.
I keep the Lord always · **be**-fore_me;
because he is at my right hand,
    I shall · **not** be moved. ℟.

Therefore my heart is glad,
    and my soul · **re**-joices;
my body also rests · **se**-cure.
For you do not give me up · **to** Sheol,
or let your faithful one · **see** the Pit. ℟.

You show me the path · **of** life.
In your presence there is fullness · **of** joy;
in your right hand · **are** pleasures
for--**ev**-er-more. ℟.

©2009 Gordon Johnston/Novalis

PRAYER

Let us pray. God and Father of all who believe
in you, you promised Abraham that he would
become the father of all nations, and through the
death and resurrection of Christ you fulfill that

promise: everywhere throughout the world you increase your chosen people. May we respond to your call by joyfully accepting your invitation to the new life of grace. We ask this in the name of Jesus the Lord. **Amen.**

THIRD READING *(Exodus 14.15-31; 15.20, 1)*

The Lord said to Moses, "Why do you cry out to me? Tell the children of Israel to go forward. But you, lift up your staff, and stretch out your hand over the sea and divide it, that the children of Israel may go into the sea on dry ground. Then I will harden the hearts of the Egyptians so that they will go in after them; and so I will gain glory for myself over Pharaoh and all his army, his chariots, and his chariot drivers. And the Egyptians shall know that I am the Lord, when I have gained glory for myself over Pharaoh, his chariots, and his chariot drivers."

The Angel of God who was going before the Israelite army moved and went behind them; and the pillar of cloud moved from in front of them and took its place behind them. It came between the army of Egypt and the army of Israel. And so the cloud was there with the darkness, and it lit up the night; one did not come near the other all night. Then Moses stretched out his hand over the sea. The Lord  drove the sea back by a strong east wind all night, and turned the sea into dry land; and the waters were divided. The children of Israel went into the sea on dry ground, the waters forming a wall for them on their right and on their left.

The Egyptians pursued, and went into the sea after them, all of Pharaoh's horses, chariots, and chariot drivers. At the morning watch, the Lord in the pillar of fire and cloud looked down upon the Egyptian army, and threw the Egyptian army into panic. He clogged their chariot wheels so that they turned with difficulty. The Egyptians said, "Let us flee from the children of Israel, for the Lord is fighting for them against Egypt."

Then the Lord said to Moses, "Stretch out your hand over the sea, so that the water may come back upon the Egyptians, upon their chariots and chariot drivers." So Moses stretched out his hand over the sea, and at dawn the sea returned to its normal depth. As the Egyptians fled before it, the Lord tossed the Egyptians into the sea. The waters returned and covered the chariots and the chariot drivers, the entire army of Pharaoh that had followed them into the sea; not one of them remained.

But the children of Israel walked on dry ground through the sea, the waters forming a wall for them on their right and on their left. Thus the Lord saved Israel that day from the Egyptians; and Israel saw the Egyptians dead on the seashore. Israel saw the great work that the Lord did against the Egyptians. So the people feared the Lord and believed in the Lord and in his servant Moses.

The Prophet Miriam, Aaron's sister, took a tambourine in her hand; and all the women went out after her with tambourines and with dancing. Moses and the children of Israel sang this song to the Lord:

RESPONSORIAL PSALM *(Exodus 15)*

Let us sing to the Lord; he has covered himself in glory.

℟ **Let us sing to the Lord;
he has covered himself in glory.**

I will sing to the Lord,
     for he has triumphed · **gloriously;**
horse and rider he has thrown into · **the** sea.
The Lord is my strength and my · **might,**
and he has become my · **sal**-vation;
this is my God, and I will · **praise_him,**
my father's God, and I will · **ex**-alt_him. ℟

The Lord is a · **warrior;**
the Lord is · **his** name.
Pharaoh's chariots and his army
     he cast into the · **sea;**
his picked officers were sunk in the · **Red** Sea.
The floods · **covered_them;**
they went down into the depths
     · **like_a** stone. ℟

Your right hand, O Lord, glorious in · **power;**
your right hand, O Lord, shattered · **the** enemy.
In the greatness of your · **majesty**
you overthrew · **your** adversaries;
you sent out your · **fury,**
it consumed them · **like** stubble. ℟

You brought your people · **in**
and plant·-**ed** them
on the mountain of your own pos·-**session,**
the place, O Lord, that you made your · **a**-bode,
the sanctuary, O Lord, that your hands
    have es·-**tablished.**
The Lord will reign forever · **and** ever. R̞.

PRAYER

Let us pray.

1 Father, even today we see the wonders of the miracles you worked long ago. You once saved a single nation from slavery, and now you offer that salvation to all through baptism. May the peoples of the world become true sons of Abraham and prove worthy of the heritage of Israel. Grant this through Christ our Lord. **Amen.**

2 Lord God, in the new covenant you shed light on the miracles you worked in ancient times: the Red Sea is a symbol of our baptism, and the nation you freed from slavery is a sign of your Christian people. May every nation share the faith and privilege of Israel and come to new birth in the Holy Spirit. Grant this through Christ our Lord. **Amen.**

FOURTH READING *(Isaiah 54.5-14)*

Thus says the Lord, the God of hosts. Your Maker is your husband, the Lord of hosts is his name; the Holy One of Israel is your Redeemer, the God of the whole earth he is called. For the Lord has called you like a wife forsaken and grieved in spirit, like the wife of a man's youth when she is cast off, says your God.

For a brief moment I abandoned you, but with great compassion I will gather you. In overflowing wrath for a moment I hid my face from you, but with everlasting love I will have compassion on you, says the Lord, your Redeemer.

This is like the days of Noah to me: Just as I swore that the waters of Noah would never again go over the earth, so I have sworn that I will not be angry with you and will not rebuke you. For the mountains may depart and the hills be removed, but my steadfast love shall not depart from you, and my covenant of peace shall not be removed, says the Lord, who has compassion on you.

O afflicted one, storm-tossed, and not comforted, I am about to set your stones in antimony, and lay your foundations with sapphires. I will make your pinnacles of rubies, your gates of jewels, and all your walls of precious stones.

All your children shall be taught by the Lord, and great shall be the prosperity of your children. In righteousness you shall be established; you shall be far from oppression, for you shall not fear; and from terror, for it shall not come near you.

The word of the Lord. **Thanks be to God.**

RESPONSORIAL PSALM *(Psalm 30)*

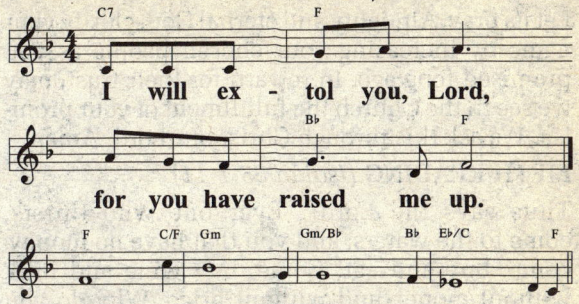

I will ex - tol you, Lord,

for you have raised me up.

℟ **I will extol you, Lord,
for you have raised me up.**

I will extol you, O Lord, for you have
    drawn me · **up,**
and did not let my foes rejoice · **over_me.**
O Lord, you brought up my soul from · **Sheol,**
restored me to life from among those gone
    down · **to_the** Pit. ℟

Sing praises to the Lord,
    O you his · **faithful_ones,**
and give thanks to his holy · **name.**
For his anger is but for a moment;
    his favour is for a · **lifetime.**
Weeping may linger for the night,
    but joy comes · **with_the** morning. ℟

Hear, O Lord, and be gracious to · **me!**
O Lord, be my · **helper!**
You have turned my mourning into · **dancing.**
O Lord my God, I will give thanks
    to you · **for**-ever. ℟

©2009 Gordon Johnston/Novalis

PRAYER

Let us pray. Almighty and eternal God, glorify your name by increasing your chosen people as you promised long ago. In reward for their trust, may we see in the Church the fulfillment of your promise. We ask this through Christ our Lord. **Amen.**

FIFTH READING *(Isaiah 55.1-11)*

Thus says the Lord: "Everyone who thirsts, come to the waters; and you that have no money, come, buy and eat! Come, buy wine and milk without money and without price. Why do you spend your money for that which is not bread, and your labour for that which does not satisfy? Listen carefully to me, and eat what is good, and delight yourselves in rich food. Incline your ear, and come to me; listen, so that you may live. I will make with you an everlasting covenant, my steadfast, sure love for David.

"See, I made him a witness to the peoples, a leader and commander for the peoples. See, you shall call nations that you do not know, and nations that do not know you shall run to you, because of the Lord your God, the Holy One of Israel, for he has glorified you.

"Seek the Lord while he may be found, call upon him while he is near; let the wicked person forsake their way, and the unrighteous person their thoughts; let that person return to the Lord that he may have mercy on them, and to our God, for he will abundantly pardon.

"For my thoughts are not your thoughts, nor are your ways my ways, says the Lord. For as the heavens are higher than the earth, so are my ways higher than your ways and my thoughts than your thoughts. For as the rain and the snow come down from heaven, and do not return there until they have watered the earth, making it bring forth and sprout, giving seed to the sower and bread to the one who eats, so shall my word be that goes out from my mouth; it shall not return to me empty, but it shall accomplish that which I purpose, and succeed in the thing for which I sent it."

The word of the Lord. **Thanks be to God.**

RESPONSORIAL PSALM *(Isaiah 12)*

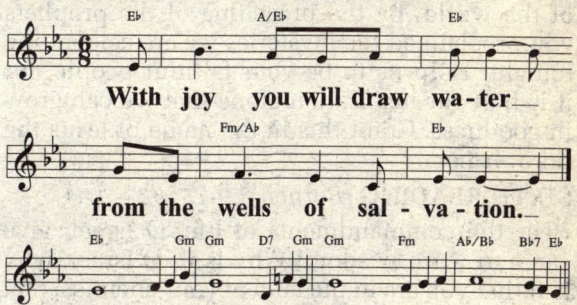

R̟ **With joy you will draw water**
   from the wells of salvation.

Surely God is my salvation;
   I will trust, and will not · **be** a-fraid,
for the Lord God is my strength and my might;
   he has be·-**come_my** sal-vation.
With joy · **you_will** draw water
from the wells · **of** sal-vation. R̟

Give thanks · **to** the Lord,
call · **on** his name;
make known his deeds a·-**mong** the nations;
proclaim that his · **name_is** ex-alted. R̟ ➔

Sing praises to the Lord,
for he · **has** done gloriously;
let this be known in · **all** the earth.
Shout aloud and sing for joy, O · **roy**-al Zion,
for great in your midst
is the Holy · **One** of Israel. ℟

℟ **With joy you will draw water
from the wells of salvation.**

©2009 Gordon Johnston/Novalis

PRAYER

Let us pray. Almighty, ever-living God, only hope
of the world, by the preaching of the prophets
you proclaimed the mysteries we are celebrating
tonight. Help us to be your faithful people, for
it is by your inspiration alone that we can grow
in goodness. Grant this in the name of Jesus the
Lord. **Amen.**

SIXTH READING *(Baruch 3.9-15, 32 – 4.4)*

Hear the commandments of life, O Israel; give
ear, and learn wisdom! Why is it, O Israel, why
is it that you are in the land of your enemies, that
you are growing old in a foreign country, that
you are defiled with the dead, that you are counted
among those in Hades? You have forsaken the
fountain of wisdom. If you had walked in the way
of God, you would be living in peace forever.

Learn where there is wisdom, where there is
strength, where there is understanding, so that
you may at the same time discern where there is
length of days, and life, where there is light for
the eyes, and peace. Who has found her place?
And who has entered her storehouses?

But the one who knows all things knows her, he
found her by his understanding. The one who pre-

pared the earth for all time filled it with four-footed creatures; the one who sends forth the light, and it goes; he called it, and it obeyed him, trembling; the stars shone in their watches, and were glad; he called them, and they said, "Here we are!" They shone with gladness for him who made them.

This is our God; no other can be compared to him. He found the whole way to knowledge, and gave her to his servant Jacob and to Israel, whom he loved. Afterward she appeared on earth and lived with humanity. She is the book of the commandments of God, the law that endures forever. All who hold her fast will live, and those who forsake her will die. Turn, O Jacob, and take her; walk toward the shining of her light. Do not give your glory to another, or your advantages to an alien people.

Happy are we, O Israel, for we know what is pleasing to God.

The word of the Lord. **Thanks be to God.**

RESPONSORIAL PSALM *(Psalm 19)*

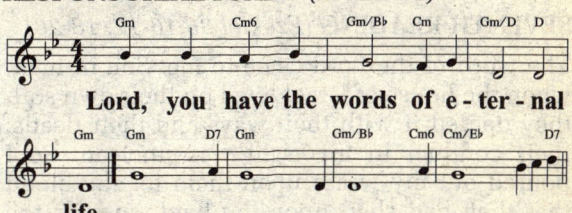

℟. **Lord, you have the words of eternal life.**

The law of the Lord is · **perfect,**
reviving the · **soul;**
the decrees of the Lord are · **sure,**
making · **wise** the simple. ℟.

→

The precepts of the Lord are · **right,**
rejoicing the · **heart;**
the commandment of the Lord is · **clear,**
en-·**lightening** the eyes. ℟

℟ **Lord, you have the words of eternal life.**

The fear of the Lord is · **pure,**
enduring for-·**ever;**
the ordinances of the Lord are · **true**
and righteous · **al**-to-gether. ℟

More to be desired are they than · **gold,**
even much fine · **gold;**
sweeter also than · **honey,**
and drippings · **of** the honeycomb. ℟

©2009 Gordon Johnston/Novalis

PRAYER

Let us pray. Father, you increase your Church by continuing to call all people to salvation. Listen to our prayers and always watch over those you cleanse in baptism. We ask this through Christ our Lord. **Amen.**

SEVENTH READING *(Ezekiel 36.16-17, 18-28)*

The word of the Lord came to me: Son of man, when the house of Israel lived on their own soil, they defiled it with their ways and their deeds; their conduct in my sight was unclean. So I poured out my wrath upon them for the blood that they had shed upon the land, and for the idols with which they had defiled it. I scattered them among the nations, and they were dispersed through the countries; in accordance with their conduct and their deeds I judged them.

But when they came to the nations, wherever they came, they profaned my holy name, in that it was said of them, "These are the people of the Lord, and yet they had to go out of his land."

But I had concern for my holy name, which the house of Israel had profaned among the nations to which they came. Therefore say to the house of Israel, Thus says the Lord God: It is not for your sake, O house of Israel, that I am about to act, but for the sake of my holy name, which you have profaned among the nations to which you came.

I will sanctify my great name, which has been profaned among the nations, and which you have profaned among them; and the nations shall know that I am the Lord, says the Lord God, when through you I display my holiness before their eyes.

I will take you from the nations, and gather you from all the countries, and bring you into your own land.

I will sprinkle clean water upon you, and you shall be clean from all your uncleanness, and from all your idols I will cleanse you.

A new heart I will give you, and a new spirit I will put within you; and I will remove from your body the heart of stone and give you a heart of flesh. I will put my spirit within you, and make you follow my statutes and be careful to observe my ordinances. Then you shall live in the land that I gave to your ancestors; and you shall be my people, and I will be your God.

The word of the Lord. **Thanks be to God.**

An alternate psalm follows.
When baptism is celebrated, sing Isaiah 12, p. 303.

RESPONSORIAL PSALM *(Psalm 42; 43)*

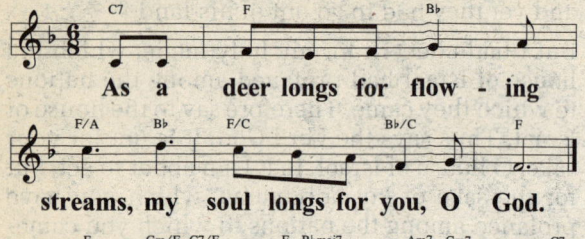

As a deer longs for flow - ing streams, my soul longs for you, O God.

R. **As a deer longs for flowing streams,**
my soul longs for you, O God.

My soul thirsts for · **God,**
for the living · **God.**
When shall I · **come**
and behold the face · **of** God? R.

I went with the · **throng,**
and led them in procession
        to the house of · **God,**
with glad shouts and songs of · **thanksgiving,**
a multitude · **keeping** festival. R.

O send out your light and your · **truth;**
let them · **lead_me;**
let them bring me to your holy · **mountain**
and to · **your** dwelling. R.

Then I will go to the altar of · **God,**
to God my exceeding · **joy;**
and I will praise you with the · **harp,**
O God, · **my** God. R.

or

RESPONSORIAL PSALM *(Psalm 51)*

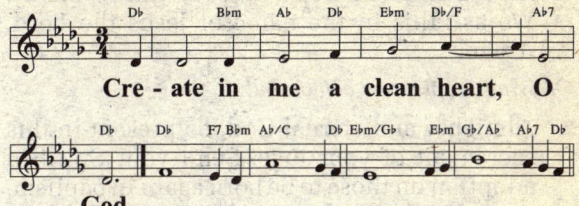

Cre - ate in me a clean heart, O God.

℟. **Create in me a clean heart, O God.**

Create in me a clean heart, · **O** God,
and put a new and right spirit · **with**-in_me.
Do not cast me away from · **your** presence,
and do not take your holy · **spirit** from me. ℟.

Restore to me the joy of your · **sal**-vation,
and sustain in me a will--**ing** spirit.
Then I will teach transgressors · **your** ways,
and sinners will re--**turn** to you. ℟.

For you have no delight · **in** sacrifice;
if I were to give a burnt offering,
    you would not · **be** pleased.
The sacrifice acceptable to God
    is a bro--**ken** spirit;
a broken and contrite heart, O God,
    you will · **not** de-spise. ℟.

©2009 Gordon Johnston/Novalis

PRAYER

Let us pray.

1 Father, you teach us in both the Old and the
New Testament to celebrate this passover

mystery. Help us to understand your great love for us. May the goodness you now show us confirm our hope in your future mercy. We ask this in the name of Jesus the Lord. **Amen.**

Or, when baptism is celebrated:

2 Almighty and eternal God, be present in this sacrament of your love. Send your Spirit of adoption on those to be born again in baptism. And may the work of our humble ministry be brought to perfection by your mighty power. We ask this in the name of Jesus the Lord. **Amen.**

GLORY TO GOD *(p. 12)*

OPENING PRAYER

Lord God, you have brightened this night with the radiance of the risen Christ. Quicken the spirit of sonship in your Church; renew us in mind and body to give you whole-hearted service.

EPISTLE *(Romans 6.3-11)*

Brothers and sisters: Do you not know that all of us who have been baptized into Christ Jesus were baptized into his death? Therefore we have been buried with him by baptism into death, so that, just as Christ was raised from the dead by the glory of the Father, so we too might walk in newness of life. For if we have been united with him in a death like his, we will certainly be united with him in a resurrection like his.

We know that our old self was crucified with him so that the body of sin might be destroyed, and we might no longer be enslaved to sin. For whoever has died is freed from sin. But if we have died with Christ, we believe that we will also live with him.

We know that Christ, being raised from the dead, will never die again; death no longer has dominion over him. The death he died, he died to sin, once for all; but the life he lives, he lives to God. So you also must consider yourselves dead to sin and alive to God in Christ Jesus.

The word of the Lord. **Thanks be to God.**

SOLEMN ALLELUIA *(Psalm 118)*

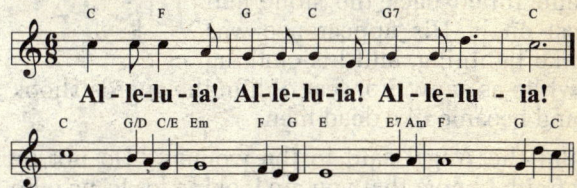

R. **Alleluia! Alleluia! Alleluia!**

O give thanks to the Lord, for · **he** is good;
his steadfast love en-**dures** for-ever.
Let Is-**rael** say,
"His steadfast love en-**dures** for-ever." R.

"The right hand of the Lord · **is** ex-alted;
the right hand of the · **Lord** does valiantly."
I shall not die, but · **I shall** live,
and recount the · **deeds of** the Lord. R.

The stone that the · **builders** re-jected
has become · **the** chief cornerstone.
This is the · **Lord's** doing;
it is marvellous · **in** our eyes. R.

GOSPEL *(Matthew 28.1-10)*

A reading from the holy Gospel according to Matthew. **Glory to you, Lord.**

After the Sabbath, as the first day of the week was dawning, Mary Magdalene and the other Mary went to see the tomb. And suddenly there was a great earthquake; for an Angel of the Lord, descending from heaven, came and rolled back the stone and sat on it. His appearance was like lightning, and his clothing  white as snow. For fear of him the guards shook and became like dead men.

But the Angel said to the women, "Do not be afraid; I know that you are looking for Jesus who was crucified. He is not here; for he has been raised, as he said. Come, see the place where he lay. Then go quickly and tell his disciples, 'He has been raised from the dead, and indeed he is going ahead of you to Galilee; there you will see him.' This is my message for you."

So they left the tomb quickly with fear and great joy, and ran to tell his disciples. Suddenly Jesus met them and said, "Greetings!" And they came to him, took hold of his feet, and worshipped him. Then Jesus said to them, "Do not be afraid; go and tell my brothers to go to Galilee; there they will see me."

The Gospel of the Lord. **Praise to you, Lord Jesus Christ.**

CELEBRATION OF THE SACRAMENTS OF INITIATION AND THE RITE OF RECEPTION

This celebration follows the Rite of Christian Initiation of Adults *(CCCB, 1987). If there is no baptism, proceed to the* BLESSING OF THE WATER, *p. 319.*

CELEBRATION OF BAPTISM

INVITATION

Dear friends, let us pray to almighty God for our brothers and sisters, N. and N., who are asking for baptism. He has called them and brought them to this moment; may he grant them light and strength to follow Christ with resolute hearts and to profess the faith of the Church. May he give them the new life of the Holy Spirit, whom we are about to call down on this water.

LITANY OF THE SAINTS

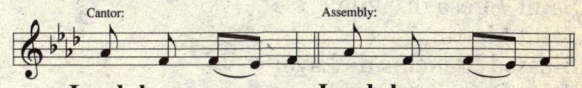

Lord, have mer - cy. Lord, have mer - cy.

Lord, have mercy. **Lord, have mercy.**
Christ, have mercy. **Christ, have mercy.**
Lord, have mercy. **Lord, have mercy.**

Holy Mary, Mother of God: pray for us.

Holy Mary, Mother of <u>God</u>, **pray for us.**
Saint <u>Mi</u>chael
Holy angels of <u>God</u>

Abraham, Moses and Elijah
Saint Joachim and Saint Anne
Saint Joseph
Saint John the Baptist
Saint Peter and Saint Paul
Saint Andrew
Saint John
Saint Mary Magdalene
Saint Stephen
Saint Ignatius
Saint Lawrence
Saint John de Brébeuf and
    the holy Canadian Martyrs
Saint Perpetua and Saint Felicity
Saint Agnes
Saint Gregory
Saint Augustine
Saint Athanasius
Saint Basil
Saint Catherine of Siena
Saint Teresa of Avila
Saint Martin
Blessed François de Laval
Saint Benedict
Saint Francis and Saint Dominic
Saint Francis Xavier
Saint John Vianney
Saint Marguerite Bourgeoys
Saint Marguerite d'Youville
Saint Monica
Saint Louis
Blessed Kateri Tekakwitha
(other saints)
All holy men and women

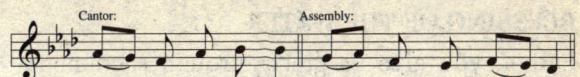

Lord, be mer-ci-ful. Lord, save your peo-ple.

Lord, be merciful. **Lord, save your people.**
From all harm
From ev'ry sin
From all temptations
From everlasting death
By your coming among us
By your death and rising to new life
By your gift of the Holy Spirit

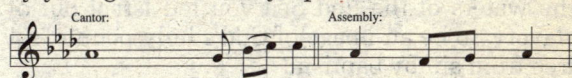

Be merciful to us sin-ners. Lord, hear our prayer.

Be merciful to us sinners. **Lord, hear our prayer.**
Give new life to these chosen ones
　　by the grace of baptism
Jesus, Son of the living God

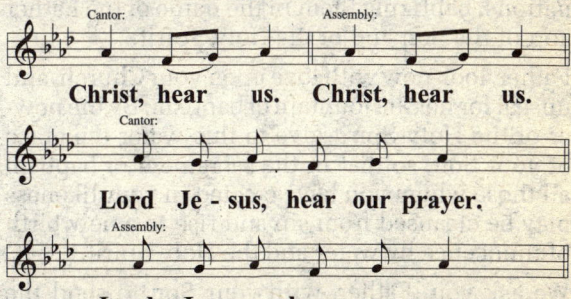

Christ, hear us. Christ, hear us.

Lord Je-sus, hear our prayer.

Lord Je-sus, hear our prayer.

Christ, hear us. **Christ, hear us.**
Lord Jesus, hear our prayer.
Lord Jesus, hear our prayer.

BLESSING OF THE WATER

Father, you give us grace through sacramental signs, which tell us of the wonders of your unseen power. In baptism we use your gift of water, which you have made a rich symbol of the grace you give us in this sacrament.

At the very dawn of creation your Spirit breathed on the waters, making them the wellspring of all holiness. The waters of the great flood you made a sign of the waters of baptism, that make an end of sin and a new beginning of goodness. Through the waters of the Red Sea you led Israel out of slavery, to be an image of God's holy people, set free from sin by baptism.

In the waters of the Jordan your Son was baptized by John and anointed with the Spirit. Your Son willed that water and blood should flow from his side as he hung upon the cross. After his resurrection he told his disciples: "Go out and teach all nations, baptizing them in the name of the Father and of the Son and of the Holy Spirit."

Father, look now with love upon your Church, and unseal for her the fountain of baptism. By the power of the Holy Spirit give to this water the grace of your Son, so that in the sacrament of baptism all those whom you have created in your likeness may be cleansed from sin and rise to a new birth of innocence by water and the Holy Spirit.

We ask you, Father, with your Son to send the Holy Spirit upon the waters of this font. May all who are buried with Christ in the death of baptism rise also with him to newness of life. We ask this through Christ our Lord. **Amen.**

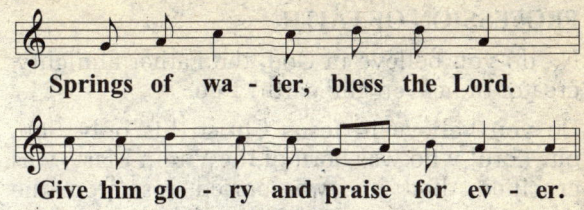

Springs of wa-ter, bless the Lord.

Give him glo-ry and praise for ev-er.

Springs of water, bless the Lord.
Give him glory and praise for ever.

RENUNCIATION OF SIN

Using one of the following formularies, the priest questions all the candidates together or individually.

1   Do you reject sin so as to live in the freedom of God's children? **I do.**

Do you reject the glamour of evil, and refuse to be mastered by sin? **I do.**

Do you reject Satan, father of sin and prince of darkness? **I do.**

2   Do you reject Satan, and all his works, and all his empty promises? **I do.**

3   Do you reject Satan? **I do.**
And all his works? **I do.**
And all his empty promises? **I do.**

ANOINTING
WITH THE OIL OF CATECHUMENS

We anoint you with the oil of salvation in the name of Christ our Saviour. May he strengthen you with his power, who lives and reigns for ever and ever. **Amen.**

PROFESSION OF FAITH

N., do you believe in God, the Father almighty, creator of heaven and earth? **I do.**

Do you believe in Jesus Christ, his only Son, our Lord, who was born of the Virgin Mary, was crucified, died, and was buried, rose from the dead, and is now seated at the right hand of the Father? **I do.**

Do you believe in the Holy Spirit, the holy catholic Church, the communion of saints, the forgiveness of sins, the resurrection of the body, and the life everlasting? **I do.**

BAPTISM

The priest baptizes each candidate either by immersion or by the pouring of water.

N., I baptize you in the name of the Father, and of the Son, and of the Holy Spirit.

ANOINTING AFTER BAPTISM

The newly baptized who will be confirmed at another time are anointed now with chrism.

The God of power and Father of our Lord Jesus Christ has freed you from sin and brought you to new life through water and the Holy Spirit.

He now anoints you with the chrism of salvation, so that, united with his people, you may remain for ever a member of Christ who is Priest, Prophet, and King. **Amen.**

CLOTHING WITH A BAPTISMAL GARMENT

N. and N., you have become a new creation and have clothed yourselves in Christ. Receive this baptismal garment and bring it unstained to the judgement seat of our Lord Jesus Christ, so that you may have everlasting life. **Amen.**

PRESENTATION OF A LIGHTED CANDLE

Godparents, please come forward to give to the newly baptized the light of Christ.

A godparent of each of the newly baptized lights a candle from the Easter candle and presents it to the newly baptized.

You have been enlightened by Christ. Walk always as children of the light and keep the flame of faith alive in your hearts. When the Lord comes, may you go out to meet him with all the saints in the heavenly kingdom. **Amen.**

(Turn to RENEWAL, p. 320)

BLESSING OF THE WATER *(without baptism)*

My brothers and sisters, let us ask the Lord our God to bless this water he has created, which we shall use to recall our baptism. May he renew us and keep us faithful to the Spirit we have all received.

Lord our God, this night your people keep prayerful vigil. Be with us as we recall the wonder of our creation and the greater wonder of our redemption. Bless this water: it makes the seed grow, it refreshes us and makes us clean. You have made of it a servant of your loving kindness: through water you set your people free, and quenched their thirst in the desert. With water the prophets announced a new covenant that you would make with humankind. By water, made holy by Christ in the Jordan, you made our sinful nature new in the bath that gives rebirth. Let this water remind us of our baptism; let us share the joys of our brothers and sisters who are baptized this Easter. We ask this through Christ our Lord. **Amen.**

RENEWAL OF BAPTISMAL PROMISES

INVITATION

The community renews its baptismal promises. Candidates for reception into full communion join in this renunciation of sin and profession of faith.

Dear friends, through the paschal mystery we have been buried with Christ in baptism, so that we may rise with him to newness of life. Now that we have completed our Lenten observance, let us renew the promises we made in baptism, when we rejected Satan and his works and promised to serve God faithfully in his holy catholic Church.

RENUNCIATION OF SIN

1   Do you reject sin so as to live in the freedom of God's children? **I do.**

    Do you reject the glamour of evil, and refuse to be mastered by sin? **I do.**

    Do you reject Satan, father of sin and prince of darkness? **I do.**

2   Do you reject Satan? **I do.**
    And all his works? **I do.**
    And all his empty promises? **I do.**

PROFESSION OF FAITH

Do you believe in God, the Father almighty, creator of heaven and earth? **I do.**

Do you believe in Jesus Christ, his only Son, our Lord, who was born of the Virgin Mary, was crucified, died, and was buried, rose from the dead, and is now seated at the right hand of the Father? **I do.**

Do you believe in the Holy Spirit, the holy catholic Church, the communion of saints, the forgiveness of sins, the resurrection of the body, and the life everlasting? **I do.**

SPRINKLING WITH BAPTISMAL WATER

During this sprinkling rite, an appropriate song may be sung (see page 594).

God, the all-powerful Father of our Lord Jesus Christ, has given us a new birth by water and the Holy Spirit and forgiven all our sins. May he also keep us faithful to our Lord Jesus Christ for ever and ever. **Amen.**

If there are no candidates for reception or confirmation, proceed to the PRAYER OF THE FAITHFUL, *p. 324.*

CELEBRATION OF RECEPTION

INVITATION

The priest invites the candidates for reception, along with their sponsors, to come into the sanctuary and join the newly baptized and their godparents.

N. and N., of your own free will you have asked to be received into the full communion of the Catholic Church. You have made your decision after careful thought under the guidance of the Holy Spirit. I now invite you to come forward with your sponsors and in the presence of this community to profess the Catholic faith. In this faith you will be one with us for the first time at the eucharistic table of the Lord Jesus, the sign of the Church's unity.

PROFESSION BY THE CANDIDATES

The priest asks the candidates to make the following profession of faith. The candidates say:

I believe and profess all that the holy Catholic Church believes, teaches and proclaims to be revealed by God.

ACT OF RECEPTION

Then the candidates with their sponsors go individually to the priest, who says to each candidate:

N., the Lord receives you into the Catholic Church. His loving kindness has led you here, so that in the unity of the Holy Spirit you may have full communion with us in the faith that you have professed in the presence of his family.

CELEBRATION OF CONFIRMATION

INVITATION

The newly baptized with their godparents and, if they have not received the sacrament of confirmation, the newly received with their sponsors stand before the priest.

My dear candidates for confirmation, by your baptism you have been born again in Christ and you have become members of Christ and of his priestly people. Now you are to share in the outpouring of the Holy Spirit among us, the Spirit sent by the Lord upon his apostles at Pentecost and given by them and their successors to the baptized.

The promised strength of the Holy Spirit, which you are to receive, will make you more like Christ and help you to be witnesses to his suffering, death, and resurrection. It will strengthen you to be active members of the Church and to build up the Body of Christ in faith and love.

My dear friends, let us pray to God our Father, that he will pour out the Holy Spirit on these candidates for confirmation to strengthen them with his gifts and anoint them to be more like Christ, the Son of God.

LAYING ON OF HANDS

All-powerful God, Father of our Lord Jesus Christ, by water and the Holy Spirit you freed your sons and daughters from sin and gave them new life. Send your Holy Spirit upon them to be their helper and guide.

Give them the spirit of wisdom and understanding, the spirit of right judgment and courage, the spirit of knowledge and reverence. Fill them with the spirit of wonder and awe in your presence.

We ask this through Christ our Lord. **Amen.**

ANOINTING WITH CHRISM

During the conferral of the sacrament an appropriate song may be sung.

N., be sealed with the Gift of the Holy Spirit. **Amen.**

Peace be with you. **And also with you.**

PRAYER OF THE FAITHFUL

The following intentions are suggestions only.

℟ **Lord, hear our prayer.**

For the Church, joyful witness to the resurrection of the Lord, we pray to the Lord: ℟

For the world's nations and peoples, to whom Christ's resurrection offers the fullness of God's peace, we pray to the Lord: ℟

For those baptized this night into Christ's death and resurrection, called as Christ's body to witness to the Good News, we pray to the Lord: ℟

For Christian communities everywhere, embodying the triumph of life over death in their neighbourhoods and cities, we pray to the Lord: ℟

LITURGY OF THE EUCHARIST

PREPARATION OF THE GIFTS *(p. 15)*

PRAYER OVER THE GIFTS

Lord, accept the prayers and offerings of your people. With your help may this Easter mystery of our redemption bring to perfection the saving work you have begun in us.

PREFACE *(Easter I, p. 27)*

COMMUNION ANTIPHON *(1 Corinthians 5.7-8)*

Christ has become our paschal sacrifice; let us feast with the unleavened bread of sincerity and truth, alleluia.

PRAYER AFTER COMMUNION

Lord, you have nourished us with your Easter sacraments. Fill us with your Spirit, and make us one in peace and love.

SOLEMN BLESSING — Easter *(Optional)*

Bow your heads and pray for God's blessing.

May almighty God bless you on this solemn feast of Easter, and may he protect you against all sin. **Amen.**

Through the resurrection of his Son, God has granted us healing. May he fulfill his promises, and bless you with eternal life. **Amen.**

You have mourned for Christ's sufferings; now you celebrate the joy of his resurrection. May you come with joy to the feast which lasts for ever. **Amen.**

May almighty God bless you, the Father, and the Son, and the Holy Spirit. **Amen.**

DISMISSAL

1 Go in the peace of Christ, alleluia, alleluia!

2 The Mass is ended, go in peace, alleluia, alleluia!

3 Go in peace to love and serve the Lord, alleluia, alleluia!

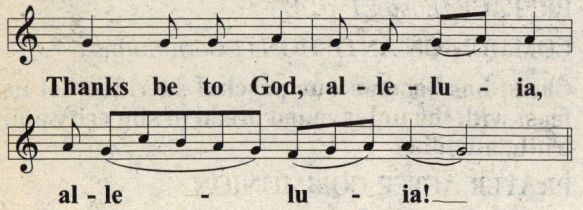

Thanks be to God, al - le - lu - ia,

al - le - lu - ia!

R̷. **Thanks be to God, alleluia, alleluia!**

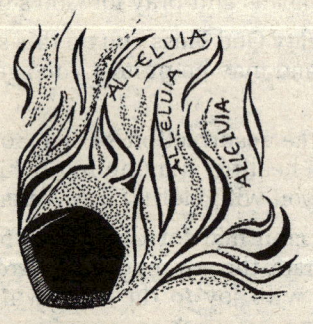

It is Easter! After forty days of fasting and Lenten observance, we are bathed in the light of the resurrection. Easter is about life: life where we least expect to find it, life that overcomes the power of evil and death. Today's gospel hints at this in showing us the disciples looking for Jesus in the tomb. Mary Magdalene had seen Jesus die on the cross and wanted to honour him one last time. She looked for Jesus who had died and found only emptiness. Peter and the other disciple saw only the linen that had wrapped Jesus' body. There was no sign of life.

The disciples were invited to change their way of thinking: to see life in a new way, with new eyes. Mary recognized Jesus when he addressed her by name, but she still had to learn that although Jesus was alive and present to her, his risen life was different. She had to let go of what had been familiar and accept Jesus' new way of being with her. Death had changed everything, but it did not extinguish the life that is God's gift.

As Christians we are Easter people, people who support, uphold and proclaim life. Like Mary and Peter and the other witnesses to the resurrection, we are invited to recognize life in new ways, even where all seems to be darkness, for our God is the God of resurrection, the God of life.

Barbara Bozak, Windsor, CT

ENTRANCE ANTIPHON *(Psalm 139.18, 5-6)*

I have risen: I am with you once more; you placed your hand on me to keep me safe. How great is the depth of your wisdom, alleluia.

INTRODUCTORY RITES *(p. 7)*

OPENING PRAYER

God our Father, by raising Christ your Son you conquered the power of death and opened for us the way to eternal life. Let our celebration today raise us up and renew our lives by the Spirit that is within us.

FIRST READING *(Acts 10.34, 37-43)*

Peter began to speak: "You know the message that spread throughout Judea, beginning in Galilee after the baptism that John announced: how God anointed Jesus of Nazareth with the Holy Spirit and with power; how he went about doing good and healing all who were oppressed by the devil, for God was with him.

"We are witnesses to all that he did both in Judea and in Jerusalem. They put him to death by hanging him on a tree; but God raised him on the third day and allowed him to appear, not to all the people but to us who were chosen by God as witnesses, and who ate and drank with him after he rose from the dead.

"He commanded us to preach to the people and to testify that he is the one ordained by God as judge of the living and the dead. All the Prophets testify about him that everyone who believes in him receives forgiveness of sins through his name."

The word of the Lord. **Thanks be to God.**

RESPONSORIAL PSALM *(Psalm 118)*

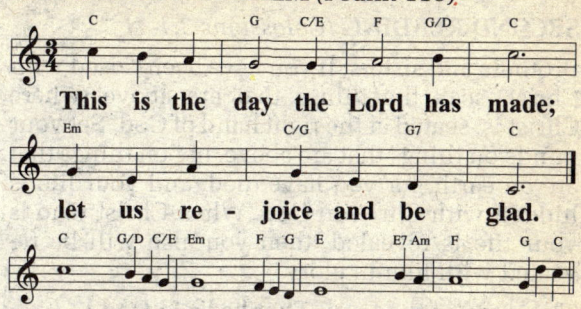

This is the day the Lord has made;
let us re - joice and be glad.

R. **This is the day the Lord has made;**
   let us rejoice and be glad.

or **Alleluia! Alleluia! Alleluia!**

O give thanks to the Lord, for · **he** is good;
his steadfast love en--**dures** for-ever.
Let Is--**rael** say,
"His steadfast love en--**dures** for-ever." R.

"The right hand of the Lord · **is** ex-alted;
the right hand of the · **Lord** does valiantly."
I shall not die, but · **I_shall** live,
and recount the · **deeds_of** the Lord. R.

The stone that the · **builders** re-jected
has become · **the** chief cornerstone.
This is the · **Lord's** doing;
it is marvellous · **in** our eyes. R.

An alternate reading follows.

SECOND READING *(Colossians 3.1-4)*

Brothers and sisters: If you have been raised with Christ, seek the things that are above, where Christ is, seated at the right hand of God. Set your minds on things that are above, not on things that are on earth, for you have died, and your life is hidden with Christ in God. When Christ who is your life is revealed, then you also will be revealed with him in glory.

The word of the Lord. **Thanks be to God.**

or

SECOND READING *(1 Corinthians 5.6-8)*

Do you not know that a little yeast leavens the whole batch of dough? Clean out the old yeast so that you may be a new batch, as you really are unleavened. For our paschal lamb, Christ, has been sacrificed. Therefore, let us celebrate the festival, not with the old yeast, the yeast of malice and evil, but with the unleavened bread of sincerity and truth.

The word of the Lord. **Thanks be to God.**

SEQUENCE

On this day the following sequence is sung. It may also be used during the Easter Octave.

1. Christians, praise the paschal victim!
   Offer thankful sacrifice!

2. Christ the Lamb has saved the sheep,
   Christ the just one paid the price,
   Reconciling sinners to the Father.

3. Death and life fought bitterly
   For this wondrous victory;
   The Lord of life who died reigns glorified!

4. "O Mary, come and say
   what you saw at break of day."

5. "The empty tomb of my living Lord!
   I saw Christ Jesus risen and adored!

6. "Bright Angels testified,
   Shroud and grave clothes side by side!

7. "Yes, Christ my hope rose gloriously.
   He goes before you into Galilee."

8. Share the Good News, sing joyfully:
   His death is victory!
   Lord Jesus, Victor King, show us mercy.

Text: *Victimae Paschali Laudes;* tr. © 1983 *Peter J. Scagnelli.*
Tune: VICTIMAE PASCHALI LAUDES. Music: *CBW III* 690

GOSPEL ACCLAMATION *(1 Corinthians 5.7-8)*

Alleluia. Alleluia. Christ, our Paschal Lamb, has been sacrificed; let us feast with joy in the Lord. **Alleluia.**

The Gospel from the Easter Vigil (p. 312) may be read instead. For an afternoon or evening mass, see p. 333.

GOSPEL *(John 20.1-18)*

The shorter version ends at the asterisks.

A reading from the holy Gospel according to John.
Glory to you, Lord.

Early on the first day of the week, while it was still dark, Mary Magdalene came to the tomb and saw that the stone had been removed from the tomb. So she ran and went to Simon Peter and the other disciple, the one whom Jesus loved, and said to them, "They have taken the Lord out of the tomb, and we do not know where they have laid him."

Then Peter and the other disciple set out and went toward the tomb. The two were running together, but the other disciple outran Peter and reached the tomb first. He bent down to look in and saw the linen wrappings lying there, but he did not go in.

Then Simon Peter came, following him, and went into the tomb. He saw the linen wrappings lying there, and the cloth that had been on Jesus' head, not lying with the linen wrappings but rolled up in a place by itself. Then the other disciple, who reached the tomb first, also went in, and he saw and believed; for as yet they did not understand the Scripture, that he must rise from the dead.

***

Then the disciples returned to their homes. But Mary Magdalene stood weeping outside the tomb. As she wept, she bent over to look into the tomb; and she saw two Angels in white, sitting where the body of Jesus had been lying, one at the head and the other at the feet. They said to her, "Woman, why are you weeping?" She said to them, "They have taken away my Lord, and I do not know where they have laid him."

When she had said this, she turned around and saw Jesus standing there, but she did not know that it was Jesus. Jesus said to her, "Woman, why are you weeping? Whom are you looking for?" Supposing him to be the gardener, she said to him, "Sir, if you have carried him away, tell me where you have laid him, and I will take him away."

Jesus said to her, "Mary!" She turned and said to him in Hebrew, "Rabbouni!" which means Teacher. Jesus said to her, "Do not hold on to me, because I have not yet ascended to the Father. But go to my brothers and say to them, 'I am ascending to my Father and your Father, to my God and your God.'"

Mary Magdalene went and announced to the disciples, "I have seen the Lord," and she told them that he had said these things to her.

The Gospel of the Lord. **Praise to you, Lord Jesus Christ.**

Alternate Gospel for an afternoon or evening mass:

GOSPEL *(Luke 24.13-35)*

A reading from the holy Gospel according to Luke. **Glory to you, Lord.**

On the first day of the week, two of the disciples were going to a village called Emmaus, about eleven kilometres from Jerusalem, and talking with each other about all these things that had happened. While they were talking and discussing, Jesus himself came near and went with them, but their eyes were kept from recognizing him.

And he said to them, "What are you discussing with each other while you walk along?" They stood still, looking sad. Then one of them, whose name was Cleopas, answered him, "Are you the only stranger in Jerusalem who does not know the things that have taken place there in these days?"

He asked them, "What things?" They replied, "The things about Jesus of Nazareth, who was a Prophet mighty in deed and word before God and all the people, and how our chief priests and leaders handed him over to be condemned to death and crucified him. But we had hoped that he was the one to redeem Israel. Yes, and besides all this, it is now the third day since these things took place. Moreover, some women of our group astounded us. They were at the tomb early this morning, and when they did not find his body there, they came back and told us that they had indeed seen a vision of Angels who said that he was alive. Some of those who were with us went to the tomb and found it just as the women had said; but they did not see him."

Then he said to them, "Oh, how foolish you are, and how slow of heart to believe all that the Prophets have declared! Was it not necessary that the Christ should suffer these things and then enter into his glory?"

Then beginning with Moses and all the Prophets, he interpreted to them the things about himself in all the Scriptures. As they came near the village to which they were going, he walked ahead as if he were going on. But they urged him strongly, saying, "Stay with us, because it is almost evening and the day is now nearly over." So he went in to stay with them.

When he was at the table with them, he took bread, blessed and broke it, and gave it to them. Then their eyes were opened, and they recognized him; and he vanished from their sight.

They said to each other, "Were not our hearts burning within us while he was talking to us on the road, while he was opening the Scriptures to us?"

That same hour they got up and returned to Jerusalem; and they found the eleven and their companions gathered together. These were saying, "The Lord has risen indeed, and he has appeared to Simon!"

Then they told what had happened on the road, and how he had been made known to them in the breaking of the bread.

The Gospel of the Lord. **Praise to you, Lord Jesus Christ.**

RENEWAL OF BAPTISMAL PROMISES *(p. 320)*

As at the Vigil, this rite replaces the Profession of Faith.

PRAYER OF THE FAITHFUL

The following intentions are suggestions only.

R̥ **Lord, hear our prayer.**

For the Church, witness to Jesus risen and present among us in our everyday lives, we pray to the Lord: R̥

For peace among nations and between peoples, we pray to the Lord: R̥

For those among us, in our homes, our cities, our parishes, who are in need of caring and compassion, and for those who reach out to them, we pray to the Lord: R̥

For us, your people gathered here, called to be a community that recognizes and celebrates the presence of the risen Jesus, we pray to the Lord: R̥

PREPARATION OF THE GIFTS *(p. 15)*

PRAYER OVER THE GIFTS

Lord, with Easter joy we offer you the sacrifice by which your Church is reborn and nourished through Christ our Lord.

PREFACE *(Easter I, p. 27)*

COMMUNION ANTIPHON *(1 Corinthians 5.7-8)*

Christ has become our paschal sacrifice; let us celebrate the feast with the unleavened bread of sincerity and truth, alleluia.

PRAYER AFTER COMMUNION

Father of love, watch over your Church and bring us to the glory of the resurrection promised by this Easter sacrament.

SOLEMN BLESSING AND DISMISSAL *(p. 325)*

The apostles and disciples of Christ, through their preaching, table-fellowship and prayers, passed on to others their faith and trust in God's plan of salvation. The readings this Sunday indicate that if we, like the apostles and disciples, live charitably and selflessly, we too can enter the kingdom of heaven. Central to this are the elements of faith and trust.

Just as it was difficult for the apostle Thomas to believe in a resurrected Christ without seeing him and touching him, so too it may be difficult for us at times to believe in heaven or in the plan of salvation. It was the same for the early Christians, as it is for us today: faith is an act of will. Faith is the result of our resolve that we are going to continue to believe in God in a spirit of trust. If we lose this trust, we will be left hopeless and sad. Today's readings urge us to be generous people who exude loving and joyful dispositions that are indicative of our faith and trust in God.

Let us be mindful this week that we too are called to be disciples of Christ with the important mandate to spread the good news of God's plan of salvation. The starting point for us is our conviction that through our belief we will have life — life to the full.

Caroline Nolan, Edmonton, AB

ENTRANCE ANTIPHON *(1 Peter 2.2)*

Like newborn children you should thirst for milk, on which your spirit can grow to strength, alleluia.

or

Rejoice to the full in the glory that is yours, and give thanks to God who called you to his kingdom, alleluia.

INTRODUCTORY RITES *(p. 7)*

OPENING PRAYER

God of mercy, you wash away our sins in water, you give us new birth in the Spirit, and redeem us in the blood of Christ. As we celebrate Christ's resurrection increase our awareness of these blessings, and renew your gift of life within us.

FIRST READING *(Acts 2.42-47)*

They devoted themselves to the Apostles' teaching and fellowship, to the breaking of bread and the prayers. Awe came upon everyone, because many wonders and signs were being done by the Apostles.

All who believed were together and had all things in common; they would sell their possessions and goods and distribute the proceeds to all, as any had need. Day by day, as they spent much time together in the temple, they broke bread in various houses and ate their food with glad and generous hearts, praising God and having the goodwill of all the people. And day by day the Lord added to their number those who were being saved.

The word of the Lord. **Thanks be to God.**

RESPONSORIAL PSALM *(Psalm 118)*

Give thanks to the Lord for he is good;

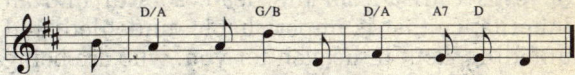

his stead-fast love en-dures for-ev-er.

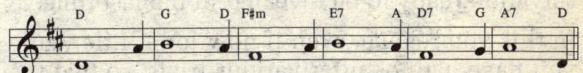

℞. **Give thanks to the Lord, for he is good;**
his steadfast love endures forever.

or **Alleluia!**

Let Israel · **say,**
"His steadfast love endures for··**ever.**"
Let the house of Aaron · **say,**
"His steadfast love endures for··**ever.**"
Let those who fear the Lord · **say,**
"His steadfast love endures for··**ever.**" ℞.

I was pushed hard, so that I was · **falling,**
but the Lord · **helped_me.**
The Lord is my strength and my · **might;**
he has become my sal-·**vation.**
There are glad songs of · **victory**
in the tents of the · **righteous.** ℞.

The stone that the builders re-·**jected**
has become the chief · **cornerstone.**
This is the Lord's · **doing;**
it is marvellous in our · **eyes.**
This is the day that the Lord has · **made;**
let us rejoice and be glad in · **it.** ℞.

©2010 Gordon Johnston/Novalis

SECOND READING *(1 Peter 1.3-9)*

Blessed be the God and Father of our Lord Jesus Christ! By his great mercy he has given us a new birth into a living hope through the resurrection of Jesus Christ from the dead: a birth into an inheritance that is imperishable, undefiled, and unfading, kept in heaven for you, who are being protected by the power of God through faith for a salvation ready to be revealed in the last time.

In this you rejoice, even if now for a little while you have had to suffer various trials, so that the genuineness of your faith — being more precious than gold that, though perishable, is tested by fire — may be found to result in praise and glory and honour when Jesus Christ is revealed.

Although you have not seen him, you love him; and even though you do not see him now, you believe in him and rejoice with an indescribable and glorious joy, for you are receiving the outcome of your faith, the salvation of your souls.

The word of the Lord. **Thanks be to God.**

GOSPEL ACCLAMATION *(See John 20.29)*

Alleluia. Alleluia. You believed, Thomas, because you have seen me; blessed are those who have not seen, and yet believe. **Alleluia.**

GOSPEL *(John 20.19-31)*

A reading from the holy Gospel according to John. **Glory to you, Lord.**

It was evening on the day Jesus rose from the dead, the first day of the week, and the doors of the house where the disciples had met were locked for fear of the Jews. Jesus came and stood among them and said, "Peace be with you." After he said this, he showed them his hands and his side. Then the disciples rejoiced when they saw the Lord.

Jesus said to them again, "Peace be with you. As the Father has sent me, so I send you."

When he had said this, he breathed on them and said to them, "Receive the Holy Spirit. If you forgive the sins of any, they are forgiven them; if you retain the sins of any, they are retained."

But Thomas, who was called the Twin, one of the twelve, was not with them when Jesus came. So the other disciples told him, "We have seen the Lord." But he said to them, "Unless I see the mark of the nails in his hands, and put my finger in the mark of the nails and my hand in his side, I will not believe."

After eight days his disciples were again in the house, and Thomas was with them. Although the doors were shut, Jesus came and stood among them and said, "Peace be with you." Then he said to Thomas, "Put your finger here and see my hands. Reach out your hand and put it in my side. Do not doubt but believe." Thomas answered him, "My Lord and my God!"

Jesus said to him, "Have you believed because you have seen me? Blessed are those who have not seen and yet have come to believe."

Now Jesus did many other signs in the presence of his disciples, which are not written in this book. But these are written so that you may come to believe that Jesus is the Christ, the Son of God, and that through believing you may have life in his name.

The Gospel of the Lord. **Praise to you, Lord Jesus Christ.**

PROFESSION OF FAITH *(p. 13-14)*

PRAYER OF THE FAITHFUL

The following intentions are suggestions only.

R̲. **Lord, hear our prayer.**

For the Church throughout the world, witness to God's kingdom in daily life, we pray to the Lord: R̲.

For elected officials and leaders of nations, to whom their peoples look for justice, we pray to the Lord: R̲.

For those who are hungry, lonely, abused, sick and dying, especially those who are abandoned or destitute, we pray to the Lord: R̲.

For us, God's people gathered here, fed from your table and called to feed all God's children, we pray to the Lord: R̲.

PREPARATION OF THE GIFTS *(p. 15)*

PRAYER OVER THE GIFTS

Lord, through faith and baptism we have become a new creation. Accept the offerings of your people (and of those born again in baptism) and bring us to eternal happiness.

PREFACE (*Easter I, p. 27*)

COMMUNION ANTIPHON (*See John 20.27*)

Jesus spoke to Thomas: Put your hand here, and see the place of the nails. Doubt no longer, but believe, alleluia.

PRAYER AFTER COMMUNION

Almighty God, may the Easter sacraments we have received live for ever in our minds and hearts.

SOLEMN BLESSING — Easter Season (*Opt.*)

Bow your heads and pray for God's blessing.

Through the resurrection of his Son God has redeemed you and made you his children. May he bless you with joy. **Amen.**

The Redeemer has given you lasting freedom. May you inherit his everlasting life. **Amen.**

By faith you rose with him in baptism. May your lives be holy, so that you will be united with him for ever. **Amen.**

May almighty God bless you, the Father, and the Son, and the Holy Spirit. **Amen.**

DISMISSAL (*p. 326*)

Like the friends walking to Emmaus, we like to use our minds to think, discuss, analyze and figure things out. Define the problem, put everything in some kind of order, and come up with the answer.

Sometimes, though, it doesn't work very well. The minds of these two travellers were engaged. They gave the unknown stranger a clear presentation of the 'facts' they were trying to understand. And even when he carefully explained what it meant, they still didn't get it. They didn't even recognize that the stranger was Jesus himself!

How could this be? How could intelligent and thoughtful people miss what seems so obvious?

The problem is that they were using their minds to try to grasp something beyond the mind. The path to understanding goes through the heart and its way of knowing truth, not the mind and its identification of truth with facts. Truth is encountered when the heart is open to a larger reality than the mind can grasp.

These travellers opened their hearts when they invited a stranger to stay with them because the day was nearly done. When the stranger broke and shared bread with them, their newly opened hearts were instantly able to see what their hard-working minds could not.

And, like them, we shall shortly share in the breaking of bread. What will we see?

Patrick Gallagher, Toronto, ON

ENTRANCE ANTIPHON *(Psalm 66.1-2)*

Let all the earth cry out to God with joy; praise the glory of his name; proclaim his glorious praise, alleluia.

INTRODUCTORY RITES *(p. 7)*

OPENING PRAYER

God our Father, may we look forward with hope to our resurrection, for you have made us your sons and daughters, and restored the joy of our youth.

FIRST READING *(Acts 2.14, 22-28)*

When the day of Pentecost had come, Peter, standing with the eleven, raised his voice and addressed the crowd, "Men of Judea and all who live in Jerusalem, let this be known to you, and listen to what I say. Jesus of Nazareth, a man attested to you by God with deeds of power, wonders, and signs that God did through him among you, as you yourselves know — this man, handed over to you according to the definite plan and foreknowledge of God, you crucified and killed by the hands of those outside the law.

"But God raised him up, having freed him from death, because it was impossible for him to be held in its power. For David says concerning him, 'I saw the Lord always before me, for he is at my right hand so that I will not be shaken; therefore my heart was glad, and my tongue rejoiced; moreover my flesh will live in hope. For you will not abandon my soul to Hades, or let your Holy One experience corruption. You have made known to me the ways of life; you will make me full of gladness with your presence.'"

The word of the Lord. **Thanks be to God.**

RESPONSORIAL PSALM *(Psalm 16)*

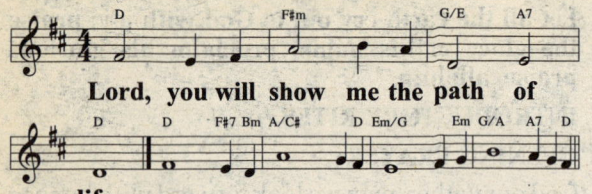

Lord, you will show me the path of life.

℟. **Lord, you will show me the path of life.**

or **Alleluia!**

Protect me, O God, for in you I · **take** refuge.
I say to the Lord, "You are · **my** Lord;
I have no good apart · **from** you."
The Lord is my chosen portion and my cup;
    you · **hold** my lot. ℟.

I bless the Lord who gives · **me** counsel;
in the night also my heart · **in**-structs_me.
I keep the Lord always · **be**-fore_me;
because he is at my right hand,
  I shall · **not** be moved. ℟.

Therefore my heart is glad,
    and my soul · **re**-joices;
my body also rests · **se**-cure.
For you do not give me up · **to** Sheol,
or let your faithful one · **see** the Pit. ℟.

1- You show me the path · **of** life.
2- In your presence there is fullness · **of** joy;
4- in your right hand are pleasures
    for--**ev**-er-more. ℟.

SECOND READING *(1 Peter 1.17-21)*

Beloved: If you invoke as Father the one who judges each person impartially according to each one's deeds, live in reverent fear during the time of your exile.

You know that you were ransomed from the futile ways inherited from your ancestors, not with perishable things like silver or gold, but with the precious blood of Christ, like that of a lamb without defect or blemish.

Christ was destined before the foundation of the world, but was revealed at the end of the ages for your sake. Through him you have come to trust in God, who raised him from the dead and gave him glory, so that your faith and hope are set on God.

The word of the Lord. **Thanks be to God.**

GOSPEL ACCLAMATION *(Luke 24.32)*

Alleluia. Alleluia. Lord Jesus, open the Scriptures to us; make our hearts burn with love when you speak. **Alleluia.**

GOSPEL *(Luke 24.13-35)*

A reading from the holy Gospel according to Luke. **Glory to you, Lord.**

On the first day of the week, two of the disciples were going to a village called Emmaus, about eleven kilometres from Jerusalem, and talking with each other about all these things that had happened. While they were talking and discussing, Jesus himself came near and went with them, but their eyes were kept from recognizing him.

And he said to them, "What are you discussing with each other while you walk along?" They stood still, looking sad. Then one of them, whose name was Cleopas, answered him, "Are you the only stranger in Jerusalem who does not know the things that have taken place there in these days?"

He asked them, "What things?" They replied, "The things about Jesus of Nazareth, who was a Prophet mighty in deed and word before God and all the people, and how our chief priests and leaders handed him over to be condemned to death and crucified him. But we had hoped that he was the one to redeem Israel. Yes, and besides all this, it is now the third day since these things took place. Moreover, some women of our group astounded us. They were at the tomb early this morning, and when they did not find his body there, they came back and told us that they had indeed seen a vision of Angels who said that he was alive. Some of those who were with us went to the tomb and found it just as the women had said; but they did not see him."

Then he said to them, "Oh, how foolish you are, and how slow of heart to believe all that the Prophets have declared! Was it not necessary that the Christ should suffer these things and then enter into his glory?"

Then beginning with Moses and all the Prophets, he interpreted to them the things about himself in all the Scriptures. As they came near the village to which they were going, he walked ahead as if he were going on. But they urged him strongly, saying, "Stay with us, because it is almost evening and the day is now nearly over." So he went in to stay with them.

When he was at the table with them, he took bread, blessed and broke it, and gave it to them. Then their eyes were opened, and they recognized him; and he vanished from their sight.

They said to each other, "Were not our hearts burning within us while he was talking to us on the road, while he was opening the Scriptures to us?"

That same hour they got up and returned to Jerusalem; and they found the eleven and their companions gathered together. These were saying, "The Lord has risen indeed, and he has appeared to Simon!"

Then they told what had happened on the road, and how he had been made known to them in the breaking of the bread.

The Gospel of the Lord. **Praise to you, Lord Jesus Christ.**

PROFESSION OF FAITH *(p. 13-14)*

PRAYER OF THE FAITHFUL

The following intentions are suggestions only.

R. **Lord, hear our prayer.**

For the Church, sacrament of Christ in the midst of the world's struggles, we pray to the Lord: R.

For an end to ethnic and religious hatreds, and the birth of understanding and peace among nations and peoples, we pray to the Lord: ℟

For those among us who are poor, lonely, sick and dying, we pray to the Lord: ℟

For all mothers today, in gratitude for their loving witness, we pray to the Lord: ℟

For us, God's holy people, embracing those who are nearing the end of life's journey, and supporting young people as they discover their life's direction, we pray to the Lord: ℟

PREPARATION OF THE GIFTS *(p. 15)*

PRAYER OVER THE GIFTS

Lord, receive these gifts from your Church. May the great joy you give us come to perfection in heaven.

PREFACE *(Easter II-V, p. 27)*

COMMUNION ANTIPHON *(Luke 24.35)*

The disciples recognized the Lord Jesus in the breaking of bread, alleluia.

PRAYER AFTER COMMUNION

Lord, look on your people with kindness and by these Easter mysteries bring us to the glory of the resurrection.

SOLEMN BLESSING *(p. 343)*

DISMISSAL *(p. 67)*

May 15   4th Sunday of Easter

World Day of Prayer for Vocations

In these times of rapid technological change and social stresses, it can sometimes be very challenging to establish our personal identity or to discover a sense of meaning in our lives. Amid this instability and confusion, Jesus offers us a clear alternative in today's gospel: he has come that we may have life, and have it abundantly.

This dynamic life that Jesus promises is one reason for which we choose to become his followers. What's more, the abundance of life made possible by Jesus' coming is not only remembered, it is also realized through our Christian communities. That is because, as the body of Christ, the Church witnesses to life in all its plenitude. And this begins with how each of us lives day-to-day — at home, at work, at school. We are now free from our sins, so that we may live for righteousness, as Peter writes today.

Jesus makes clear in today's gospel that the basis for this offer of abundant life is Jesus himself. He is the gate through whom we find nourishment and by whom we are saved. There may be other means by which we find comfort, pleasure and value, but we find fulfillment only through a personal relationship with Jesus. And we are faithful to this relationship in celebrating the eucharist, at which time we receive once again the abundant life promised us.

Armand Mercier, Edmonton, AB

ENTRANCE ANTIPHON *(Psalm 33.5-6)*

The earth is full of the goodness of the Lord; by the word of the Lord the heavens were made, alleluia.

INTRODUCTORY RITES *(p. 7)*

OPENING PRAYER

Almighty and ever-living God, give us new strength from the courage of Christ our shepherd, and lead us to join the saints in heaven.

FIRST READING *(Acts 2.14, 36-41)*

When the day of Pentecost had come, Peter, standing with the eleven, raised his voice and addressed the crowd. "Let the entire house of Israel know with certainty that God has made him both Lord and Christ, this Jesus whom you crucified."

Now when the people heard this, they were cut to the heart and said to Peter and to the other Apostles, "Brothers, what should we do?" Peter said to them, "Repent, and be baptized every one of you in the name of Jesus Christ so that your sins may be forgiven; and you will receive the gift of the Holy Spirit. For the promise is for you, for your children, and for all who are far away, everyone whom the Lord our God calls to him."

And he testified with many other arguments and exhorted them, saying, "Save yourselves from this corrupt generation." So those who welcomed his message were baptized, and that day were added about three thousand souls.

The word of the Lord. **Thanks be to God.**

RESPONSORIAL PSALM *(Psalm 23)*

R. **The Lord is my shepherd; I shall not want.**

or **Alleluia!**

The Lord is my shepherd, I shall · **not** want.
He makes me lie down in · **green** pastures;
he leads me be-·**side** still waters;
he re-·**stores** my soul. R.

He leads me in right paths for his · **name's** sake.
Even though I walk through the darkest valley,
   I fear · **no** evil;
for · **you** are with_me;
your rod and your · **staff** — they comfort_me. R.

You prepare a table · **be**-fore_me
in the presence · **of_my** enemies;
you anoint my · **head** with oil;
my · **cup** over-flows. R.

Surely goodness and mercy · **shall** follow_me
all the days of · **my** life,
and I shall dwell in the · **house_of** the Lord
my · **whole** life long. R.

©2009 Gordon Johnston/Novalis

SECOND READING *(1 Peter 2.20-25)*

Beloved: If you endure when you do right and suffer for it, you have God's approval. For to this you have been called, because Christ also suffered for you, leaving you an example, so that you should follow in his steps. "He committed no sin, and no deceit was found in his mouth." When he was abused, he did not return abuse; when he suffered, he did not threaten; but he entrusted himself to the one who judges justly.

Christ himself bore our sins in his body on the Cross, so that, free from sins, we might live for righteousness; by his wounds you have been healed. For you were going astray like sheep, but now you have returned to the shepherd and guardian of your souls.

The word of the Lord. **Thanks be to God.**

GOSPEL ACCLAMATION *(John 10.14)*

Alleluia. Alleluia. I am the good shepherd, says the Lord; I know my sheep, and my own know me. **Alleluia.**

GOSPEL *(John 10.1-10)*

A reading from the holy Gospel according to John. **Glory to you, Lord.**

Jesus said: "Very truly, I tell you, anyone who does not enter the sheepfold by the gate but climbs in by another way is a thief and a bandit. The one who enters by the gate is the shepherd of the sheep. The gatekeeper opens the gate for him, and the sheep hear his voice. He calls his own sheep by name and leads them out. When he has brought out all his own, he goes ahead of them, and the sheep follow him because they know his voice. They will not follow a stranger, but they will run from him because they do not know the voice of strangers."

Jesus used this figure of speech with them, but they did not understand what he was saying to them. So again Jesus said to them, "Very truly, I tell you, I am the gate for the sheep. All who came before me are thieves and bandits; but the sheep did not listen to them. I am the gate. Whoever enters by me will be saved, and will come in and go out and find pasture. The thief comes only to steal and kill and destroy. I came that they may have life, and have it abundantly."

The Gospel of the Lord. **Praise to you, Lord Jesus Christ.**

PROFESSION OF FAITH *(p. 13-14)*

PRAYER OF THE FAITHFUL

The following intentions are suggestions only.

R. **Lord, hear our prayer.**

For all who hold positions of authority in the Church, called to model their leadership on that of the Good Shepherd, we pray to the Lord: R.

For political leaders whose influence bears fruit in justice for all, we pray to the Lord: R.

For those among us struggling to resist peer pressure and stand up for our convictions, we pray to the Lord: R.

For us, God's holy people, striving to live out the challenges of our vocations with courage and joy, we pray to the Lord: R.

PREPARATION OF THE GIFTS *(p. 15)*

PRAYER OVER THE GIFTS

Lord, restore us by these Easter mysteries. May the continuing work of our redeemer bring us eternal joy.

PREFACE *(Easter II-V, p. 27)*

COMMUNION ANTIPHON

The Good Shepherd is risen! He who laid down his life for his sheep, who died for his flock, he is risen, alleluia.

PRAYER AFTER COMMUNION

Father, eternal shepherd, watch over the flock redeemed by the blood of Christ and lead us to the promised land.

SOLEMN BLESSING *(p. 343)*

DISMISSAL *(p. 67)*

In these Easter days we savour the message of Jesus' life, suffering, death and resurrection; we may be filled with the light, joy and hope of resurrection. Today's readings also point us toward the challenge of living as Easter people.

We hear that the apostles were receiving complaints — some widows were being neglected in their basic needs. In a society that regularly cast off widows as non-persons, the Church stood accused of doing the same. The cry of the widows is heard in our day — in those denied land rights, where access to clean water access is limited or not existent, when women and children live in fear of slavery or abuse, where war and violence are used to address difference and greed, in the earth and air as they groan under our exploitation.

The Church responds by teaching that the whole community must take responsibility for one another's needs. It takes the whole community, with each member playing their own part, to build and maintain the new order of care that Jesus calls for. The old ways of thinking have passed away. As our Way, Truth and Life, Jesus not only points out the way, he puts it into practice in a way that embraces us all. A church community long ago heard the cry and responded. We carry on, and we will respond, with the risen Jesus showing us the way.

Carmen Diston, Rome, Italy

ENTRANCE ANTIPHON *(Psalm 98.1-2)*

Sing to the Lord a new song, for he has done marvellous deeds; he has revealed to the nations his saving power, alleluia.

INTRODUCTORY RITES *(p. 7)*

OPENING PRAYER

God our Father, look upon us with love. You redeem us and make us your children in Christ. Give us true freedom and bring us to the inheritance you promised.

FIRST READING *(Acts 6.1-7)*

Now during those days, when the disciples were increasing in number, the Hellenists complained against the Hebrews because their widows were being neglected in the daily distribution of food. And the twelve called together the whole community of the disciples and said, "It is not right that we should neglect the word of God in order to wait on tables. Therefore, brothers, select from among yourselves seven men of good standing, full of the Spirit and of wisdom, whom we may appoint to this task, while we, for our part, will devote ourselves to prayer and to serving the word."

What they said pleased the whole community, and they chose Stephen, a man full of faith and the Holy Spirit, together with Philip, Prochorus, Nicanor, Timon, Parmenas, and Nicolaus, a convert of Antioch. They had these men stand before the Apostles, who prayed and laid their hands on them.

The word of God continued to spread; the number of the disciples increased greatly in Jerusalem, and a great many of the priests became obedient to the faith.

The word of the Lord. **Thanks be to God.**

RESPONSORIAL PSALM *(Psalm 33)*

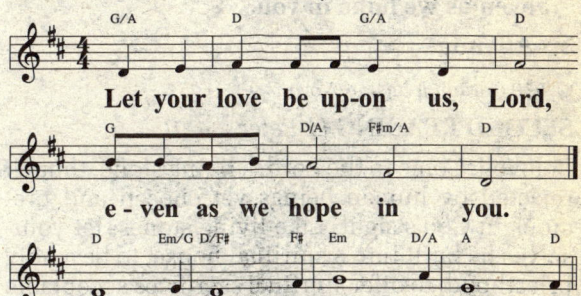

R. **Let your love be upon us, Lord,
even as we hope in you.**

or **Alleluia!**

Rejoice in the Lord, O you · **righteous,**
Praise befits the · **upright.**
Praise the Lord with the · **lyre;**
make melody to him with the harp
of ten · **strings.** R.

For the word of the Lord is · **upright,**
and all his work is done in · **faithfulness.**
He loves righteousness and · **justice;**
the earth is full of the steadfast love
of the · **Lord.** R.

→

Truly the eye of the Lord is on those
who · **fear_him,**
on those who hope in his steadfast · **love,**
to deliver their soul from · **death,**
and to keep them alive in · **famine.** R.

R. **Let your love be upon us, Lord,
even as we hope in you.**

or **Alleluia!**

©2010 Gordon Johnston/Novalis

SECOND READING *(1 Peter 2.4-9)*

Beloved: Come to the Lord, a living stone, though rejected by human beings yet chosen and precious in God's sight. Like living stones, let yourselves be built into a spiritual house, to be a holy priesthood, to offer spiritual sacrifices acceptable to God through Jesus Christ.

For it stands in Scripture: "See, I am laying in Zion a stone, a cornerstone chosen and precious; and whoever believes in him will not be put to shame." To you then who believe, he is precious; but for those who do not believe, "The stone that the builders rejected has become the very head of the corner," and "A stone that makes them stumble, and a rock that makes them fall." They stumble because they disobey the word, as they were destined to do.

But you are a chosen race, a royal priesthood, a holy nation, God's own people, in order that you may proclaim the mighty acts of him who called you out of darkness into his marvellous light.

The word of the Lord. **Thanks be to God.**

GOSPEL ACCLAMATION *(John 14.6)*

Alleluia. Alleluia. I am the way, the truth, and the life, says the Lord; no one comes to the Father, except through me. **Alleluia.**

GOSPEL *(John 14.1-12)*

A reading from the holy Gospel according to John. **Glory to you, Lord.**

Jesus said to his disciples: "Do not let your hearts be troubled. Believe in God, believe also in me. In my Father's house there are many dwelling places. If it were not so, would I have told you that I go to prepare a place for you? And if I go and prepare a place for you, I will come again and will take you to myself, so that where I am, there you may be also. And you know the way to the place where I am going."

Thomas said to him, "Lord, we do not know where you are going. How can we know the way?"

Jesus said to him, "I am the way, and the truth, and the life. No one comes to the Father except through me. If you know me, you will know my Father also. From now on you do know him and have seen him."

Philip said to him, "Lord, show us the Father, and we will be satisfied." Jesus said to him, "Have I been with you all this time, Philip, and you still do not know me? Whoever has seen me has seen the Father. How can you say, 'Show us the Father'? Do you not believe that I am in the Father and the Father is in me? The words that I say to you I do not speak on my own; but the Father who dwells in me does his works. Believe me

that I am in the Father and the Father is in me;
but if you do not, then believe me because of the
works themselves. Very truly, I tell you, the one
who believes in me will also do the works that I
do and, in fact, will do greater works than these,
because I am going to the Father."

The Gospel of the Lord. **Praise to you, Lord Jesus
Christ.**

PROFESSION OF FAITH *(p. 13-14)*

PRAYER OF THE FAITHFUL

The following intentions are suggestions only.

R. **Lord, hear our prayer.**

For the Church, community of the young and the
old, called to firm faith and enduring love, we
pray to the Lord: R.

For the end of persecution among nations and
between peoples, we pray to the Lord: R.

For those among us who are poor, lonely and
seeking God's consolation, we pray to the Lord:
R.

For us, God's people, called to manifest our discipleship by the love we have for one another, we
pray to the Lord: R.

PREPARATION OF THE GIFTS *(p. 15)*

PRAYER OVER THE GIFTS

Lord God, by this exchange of gifts you share with
us your divine life. Grant that everything we do
may be directed by the knowledge of your truth.

PREFACE *(Easter II-V, p. 27)*

COMMUNION ANTIPHON *(John 15.1, 5)*

I am the vine and you are the branches, says the Lord; he who lives in me, and I in him, will bear much fruit, alleluia.

PRAYER AFTER COMMUNION

Merciful Father, may these mysteries give us new purpose and bring us to a new life in you.

SOLEMN BLESSING *(p. 343)*

DISMISSAL *(p. 67)*

The Easter season invites testimonies of faith. Such testimonies are born from the experience of real places. I write these reflections as one living on the Mexico-U.S. border of Juarez/El Paso, a community divided by an ugly fence barrier.

If there is a place that needs prayers and action, it is Juarez. The place is lawless and ruled by the show of weapons. Violence abounds. The city is taken over by drug cartels due to a failed government attempt to take control. In 2008 there were 1,607 killings, an increase from 186 in 2003. Kidnappings have increased, extortion is out of hand, and theft is at its highest. Women and children have been murdered. Some 5,200 businesses have closed and over 90,000 people are unemployed. The army has been sent to the city to gain control, only to add to the abuses of illegal detention, torture and indiscriminate entry into private homes. Drug violence and the militarization of Juarez have created insecurity, fear and uncertainty, causing depression and trauma.

Easter is more than a commercial gimmick of bunnies and chocolate: it is about chaos in the lives of real people and real places. It is about *hope*. The letter of Peter presents the challenge to all: What is the reason "for the hope that is in you?" In Juarez, and places like it all over the world, it is the risen Christ.

Robert Dueweke, El Paso, TX

National Collection for Pope's Pastoral Works

ENTRANCE ANTIPHON *(See Isaiah 48.20)*

Speak out with a voice of joy; let it be heard to the ends of the earth: The Lord has set his people free, alleluia.

INTRODUCTORY RITES *(p. 7)*

OPENING PRAYER

Ever-living God, help us to celebrate our joy in the resurrection of the Lord and to express in our lives the love we celebrate.

FIRST READING *(Acts 8.5-8, 14-17)*

In those days: Philip went down to the city of Samaria and proclaimed the Christ to them. The crowds with one accord listened eagerly to what was said by Philip, hearing and seeing the signs that he did, for unclean spirits, crying with loud shrieks, came out of many who were possessed; and many others who were paralysed or lame were cured. So there was great joy in that city.

Now when the Apostles at Jerusalem heard that Samaria had accepted the word of God, they sent Peter and John to them. The two went down and prayed for them that they might receive the Holy Spirit; (for as yet the Spirit had not come upon any of them; they had only been baptized in the name of the Lord Jesus). Then Peter and John laid their hands on them, and they received the Holy Spirit.

The word of the Lord. **Thanks be to God.**

RESPONSORIAL PSALM *(Psalm 66)*

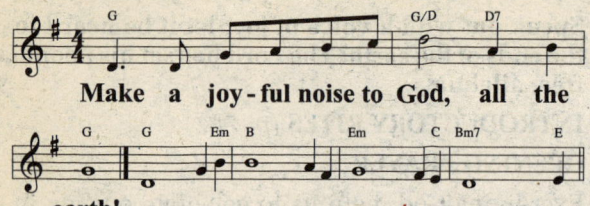

Make a joy-ful noise to God, all the earth!

R. **Make a joyful noise to God, all the earth!**

or **Alleluia!**

Make a joyful noise to God, all · **the** earth;
sing the glory · **of_his** name;
give to him · **glorious** praise.
Say to God, "How awesome
    are your · **deeds!"** R.

"All the earth · **worships** you;
they sing praises to you,
    sing praises · **to_your** name."
Come and see what God · **has** done:
he is awesome in his deeds
    among the children of · **Adam.** R.

He turned the sea into · **dry** land;
they passed through the river · **on** foot.
There we rejoiced · **in** him,
who rules by his might for-**ever.** R.

Come and hear, all you who · **fear** God,
and I will tell what he · **has** done_for_me.
Blessed be God, because he has not rejected ·
    my prayer
or removed his steadfast love from · **me.** R.

SECOND READING *(1 Peter 3.15-18)*

Beloved: In your hearts sanctify Christ as Lord. Always be ready to make your defence to anyone who demands from you an accounting for the hope that is in you; yet do it with gentleness and reverence. Keep your conscience clear, so that, when you are maligned, those who abuse you for your good conduct in Christ may be put to shame. For it is better to suffer for doing good, if suffering should be God's will, than to suffer for doing evil.

For Christ also suffered for sins once for all, the righteous for the unrighteous, in order to bring you to God. He was put to death in the flesh, but made alive in the spirit.

The word of the Lord. **Thanks be to God.**

GOSPEL ACCLAMATION *(John 14.23)*

Alleluia. Alleluia. All who love me will keep my word, and my Father will love them, and we will come to them. **Alleluia.**

GOSPEL *(John 14.15-21)*

A reading from the holy Gospel according to John. **Glory to you, Lord.**

Jesus said to his disciples: "If you love me, you will keep my commandments. And I will ask the Father, and he will give you another Advocate, to be with you forever. This is the Spirit of truth, whom the world cannot receive, because it neither sees him nor knows him. You know him, because he abides with you, and he will be in you.

"I will not leave you orphaned; I am coming to you. In a little while the world will no longer see me, but you will see me; because I live, you also will live. On that day you will know that I am in my Father, and you in me, and I in you.

"The one who has my commandments and keeps them is the one who loves me; and the one who loves me will be loved by my Father, and I will love them and reveal myself to them."

The Gospel of the Lord. **Praise to you, Lord Jesus Christ.**

PROFESSION OF FAITH *(p. 13-14)*

PRAYER OF THE FAITHFUL

The following intentions are suggestions only.

R. **Lord, hear our prayer.**

For the Church, temple of God's living word, we pray to the Lord: R.

For those who strive to make peace and justice part of everyday life in all nations, we pray to the Lord: R.

For those among us who do not recognize their worth as precious creatures fashioned in God's image, we pray to the Lord: R.

For us, the Body of Christ, as we minister to the sick, the lonely and those in any kind of need, we pray to the Lord: R.

PREPARATION OF THE GIFTS *(p. 15)*

PRAYER OVER THE GIFTS

Lord, accept our prayers and offerings. Make us worthy of your sacraments of love by granting us your forgiveness.

PREFACE *(Easter II-IV, p. 27)*

COMMUNION ANTIPHON *(John 14.15-16)*

If you love me, keep my commandments, says the Lord. The Father will send you the Holy Spirit, to be with you for ever, alleluia.

PRAYER AFTER COMMUNION

Almighty and ever-living Lord, you restored us to life by raising Christ from death. Strengthen us by this Easter sacrament; may we feel its saving power in our daily life.

SOLEMN BLESSING *(p. 343)*

DISMISSAL *(p. 67)*

World Communications Day

The last five verses of Matthew's gospel are tinged with great solemnity. The gathering of the eleven disciples takes place on a mountain — a great place to encounter God and be sent out for a mission. The encounter with the Risen Jesus reported by Matthew is not only the encounter of a lifetime for the disciples, but also the end of Jesus of Nazareth's earthly presence among us. Now in this momentous and historic farewell, while claiming total authority from God, Jesus gives us as well the assurance that he will be forever God-with-us, Emmanuel.

But what about the disciples and their commissioning? Their initial reaction to encountering the Risen Jesus is, to say the least, mixed. It is to these disciples — split between faith and doubt — that Jesus says: "Go therefore and make disciples of all nations!" At this stage, we would have liked to hear about the disciples' reaction to such great commissioning. Matthew has decided otherwise. By remaining silent on the immediate reaction of the eleven and thus leaving his gospel open-ended, Matthew is inviting all his readers up to this day to make Jesus' commissioning of the disciples their own and to tell the unwritten part of the story. Matthew wanted us to be part of that story: it is now up to each one of us to testify before the world to the unfailing and loving presence of God-with-us, Emmanuel.

Jean-Pierre Prévost, Chénéville, QC

ENTRANCE ANTIPHON *(Acts 1.11)*

Men of Galilee, why do you stand looking into the sky? The Lord will return, just as you have seen him ascend, alleluia.

INTRODUCTORY RITES *(p. 7)*

OPENING PRAYER

God our Father, make us joyful in the ascension of your Son Jesus Christ. May we follow him into the new creation, for his ascension is our glory and our hope.

FIRST READING *(Acts 1.1-11)*

In the first book, Theophilus, I wrote about all that Jesus did and taught from the beginning until the day when he was taken up to heaven, after giving instructions through the Holy Spirit to the Apostles whom he had chosen. After his suffering he presented himself alive to them by many convincing proofs, appearing to them during forty days and speaking about the kingdom of God.

While staying with them, he ordered them not to leave Jerusalem, but to wait there for the promise of the Father. "This," he said, "is what you have heard from me; for John baptized with water, but you will be baptized with the Holy Spirit not many days from now."

So when they had come together, they asked him, "Lord, is this the time when you will restore the kingdom to Israel?" He replied, "It is not for you to know the times or periods that the Father has set by his own authority. But you will receive power when the Holy Spirit has come upon you; and you will be my witnesses in Jerusalem, in all Judea and Samaria, and to the ends of the earth."

When he had said this, as they were watching, he was lifted up, and a cloud took him out of their sight. While he was going and they were gazing up toward heaven, suddenly two men in white robes stood by them. They said, "Men of Galilee, why do you stand looking up toward heaven? This Jesus, who has been taken up from you into heaven, will come in the same way as you saw him go into heaven."

The word of the Lord. **Thanks be to God.**

RESPONSORIAL PSALM *(Psalm 47)*

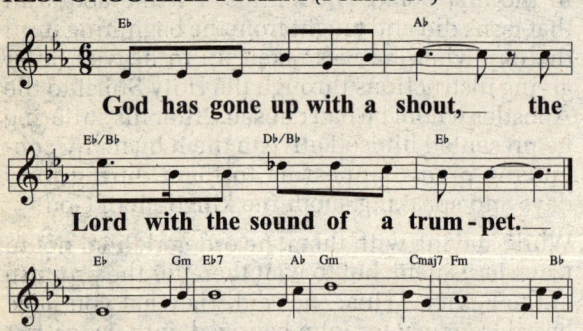

God has gone up with a shout, the Lord with the sound of a trum-pet.

R. **God has gone up with a shout,
the Lord with the sound of a trumpet.**

or **Alleluia!**

Clap your hands, all · **you** peoples;
shout to God with loud songs · **of** joy.
For the Lord, the Most High, · **is** awesome,
a great king over · **all** the earth. R.

God has gone up · **with_a** shout,
the Lord with the sound of · **a** trumpet.
Sing praises to God, · **sing** praises;
sing praises to our · **King,** sing praises. ℟

For God is the king of all · **the** earth;
sing praises · **with_a** Psalm.
God is king over · **the** nations;
God sits on his · **ho**-ly throne. ℟

©2009 Gordon Johnston/Novalis

SECOND READING (*Ephesians 1.17-23*)

Brothers and sisters: I pray that the God of our Lord Jesus Christ, the Father of glory, may give you a spirit of wisdom and revelation as you come to know him, so that, with the eyes of your heart enlightened, you may know what is the hope to which he has called you, what are the riches of his glorious inheritance among the saints, and what is the immeasurable greatness of his power for us who believe, according to the working of his great power.

God put this power to work in Christ when he raised him from the dead and seated him at his right hand in the heavenly places, far above all rule and authority and power and dominion, and above every name that is named, not only in this age but also in the age to come.

And he has put all things under his feet and has made him the head over all things for the Church, which is his body, the fullness of him who fills all in all.

The word of the Lord. **Thanks be to God.**

GOSPEL ACCLAMATION *(Matthew 28.19, 20)*

Alleluia. Alleluia. Go make disciples of all nations; I am with you always, to the end of the age. **Alleluia.**

GOSPEL *(Matthew 28.16-20)*

A reading from the holy Gospel according to Matthew. **Glory to you, Lord.**

The eleven disciples went to Galilee, to the mountain to which Jesus had directed them. When they saw him, they worshipped him; but some doubted.

And Jesus came and said to them, "All authority in heaven and on earth has been given to me. Go therefore and make disciples of all nations, baptizing them in the name of the Father and of the Son and of the Holy Spirit, and teaching them to obey everything that I have commanded you. And remember, I am with you always, to the end of the age."

The Gospel of the Lord. **Praise to you, Lord Jesus Christ.**

PROFESSION OF FAITH *(p. 13-14)*

PRAYER OF THE FAITHFUL

The following intentions are suggestions only.

℟. **Lord, hear our prayer.**

For the Church, community of disciples entrusted with authority and power to witness to the name of Jesus, we pray to the Lord: ℟.

For all leaders and teachers in the Church, we pray to the Lord: ℟.

For the poor and unemployed, at home and abroad, who seek the sustenance of our words and actions, we pray to the Lord: R.

For our parish community, called to act and speak courageously as we spread the Good News, we pray to the Lord: R.

PREPARATION OF THE GIFTS *(p. 15)*

PRAYER OVER THE GIFTS

Lord, receive our offering as we celebrate the ascension of Christ your Son. May his gifts help us rise with him to the joys of heaven.

PREFACE *(Ascension I-II, p. 29)*

COMMUNION ANTIPHON *(Matthew 28.20)*

I, the Lord, am with you always, until the end of the world, alleluia.

PRAYER AFTER COMMUNION

Father, in this eucharist we touch the divine life you give to the world. Help us to follow Christ with love to eternal life.

SOLEMN BLESSING — Ascension *(Optional)*

Bow your heads and pray for God's blessing.

May almighty God bless you on this day when his only Son ascended into heaven to prepare a place for you. **Amen.**

After his resurrection, Christ was seen by his disciples. When he appears as judge may you be pleasing for ever in his sight. **Amen.**

You believe that Jesus has taken his seat in majesty at the right hand of the Father. May you have the joy of experiencing that he is also with you to the end of time, according to his promise. **Amen.**

May almighty God bless you, the Father, and the Son, and the Holy Spirit. **Amen.**

DISMISSAL *(p. 67)*

As individuals and communities, we are sometimes like the Corinthians. We use the gifts we have received from God to divide, rather than unite. We prize some gifts over others, imagining that the more 'impressive' gifts (like speaking in tongues) provide better evidence of the Spirit's presence than more 'ordinary' gifts (like teaching or healing). By our personal and corporate behaviour, we often obscure the gospel message and make its reception difficult or impossible.

Today's readings, then, come as both a sober reminder and a great relief! We have been created *and* re-created by the breath of God. Filled with this Spirit of new life, the whole Church continues the work Jesus began, engaging in a new kind of speaking that powerfully proclaims the deeds of God so all can understand and believe. We can work for unity by putting an end to competition, strife and divisions in our communities, and valuing each one's God-given gifts. We can exercise the same power over sin that Jesus did, especially by the authentic and inviting witness of lives lived according to the truth about God, revealed in the life, death and resurrection of Jesus Christ.

All this may be accomplished when we are thankful for our dependence on God, rejoice that Jesus is Lord, and offer ourselves willingly to help renew the face of the earth.

Christine Mader, Calgary, AB

ENTRANCE ANTIPHON *(Wisdom 1.7)*

The Spirit of the Lord fills the whole world. It holds all things together and knows every word spoken by man, alleluia.

or (Romans 5.5; 8.11)

The love of God has been poured into our hearts by his Spirit living in us, alleluia.

INTRODUCTORY RITES *(p. 7)*

OPENING PRAYER

God our Father, let the Spirit you sent on your Church to begin the teaching of the gospel continue to work in the world through the hearts of all who believe.

FIRST READING *(Acts 2.1-11)*

When the day of Pentecost had come, they were all together in one place. And suddenly from heaven there came a sound like the rush of a violent wind, and it filled the entire house where they were sitting. Divided tongues, as of fire, appeared among them, and a tongue rested on each of them. All of them were filled with the Holy Spirit and began to speak in other languages, as the Spirit gave them ability.

Now there were devout Jews from every nation under heaven living in Jerusalem. And at this sound the crowd gathered and was bewildered, because each one heard them speaking in their own language. Amazed and astonished, they asked, "Are not all these who are speaking Galileans? And how is it that we hear, each of us, in our own language? Parthians, Medes, Elamites, and residents of Mesopotamia, Judea and Cappadocia, Pontus and Asia, Phrygia and Pamphylia, Egypt and the parts of Libya belonging to Cyrene, and visitors from Rome, both Jews and converts, Cretans and Arabs — in our own languages we hear them speaking about God's deeds of power."

The word of the Lord. **Thanks be to God.**

RESPONSORIAL PSALM *(Psalm 104)*

R̶. **Lord, send forth your Spirit,
and renew the face of the earth.**

or **Alleluia!**

Bless the Lord, O · **my** soul.
O Lord my God, you are very · **great.**
O Lord, how manifold · **are** your works!
The earth is full of · **your** creatures. R̶. →

When you take away · **their** breath,
they die and return to their · **dust.**
When you send forth your spirit,
    they · **are** cre-ated;
and you renew the face of · **the** earth. R̰

R̰ **Lord, send forth your Spirit,
and renew the face of the earth.**

or **Alleluia!**

May the glory of the Lord endure · **for-**ever;
may the Lord rejoice in his · **works.**
May my meditation be · **pleasing** to him,
for I rejoice in · **the** Lord. R̰

©2009 Gordon Johnston/Novalis

SECOND READING *(1 Corinthians 12.3-7, 12-13)*

Brothers and sisters: No one can say "Jesus is Lord" except by the Holy Spirit.

Now there are varieties of gifts, but the same Spirit; and there are varieties of services, but the same Lord; and there are varieties of activities, but it is the same God who activates all of them in everyone. To each is given the manifestation of the Spirit for the common good.

For just as the body is one and has many members, and all the members of the body, though many, are one body, so it is with Christ. For in the one Spirit we were all baptized into one body — Jews or Greeks, slaves or free — and we were all made to drink of one Spirit.

The word of the Lord. **Thanks be to God.**

SEQUENCE

1. Ho - ly Spir - it, Lord di - vine,
2. Come, O Fa - ther of the poor,

Come from heights of heav'n and shine,
Come, whose treas - ured gifts en - sure,

Come with bless - ed ra - diance bright.
Come, our heart's un - fail - ing light.

3. Of consolers, wisest, best,
   And our soul's most welcome guest,
   Sweet refreshment, sweet repose.

4. In our labour, rest most sweet,
   Pleasant coolness in the heat,
   Consolation in our woes.

5. Light most blessed, shine with grace
   In our heart's most secret place,
   Fill your faithful through and through.

6. Left without your presence here,
   Life itself would disappear,
   Nothing thrives apart from you!

7. Cleanse our soiled hearts of sin,
   Arid souls refresh within,
   Wounded lives to health restore.

→

8. On the faithful who are true
    And profess their faith in you,
    In your sev'nfold gift descend!

9. Bend the stubborn heart and will,
    Melt the frozen, warm the chill,
    Guide the wayward home once more!

10. Give us virtue's sure reward,
    Give us your salvation, Lord,
    Give us joys that never end!

Text: *Veni, Sancte Spiritus;* tr. © *Peter J. Scagnelli*
Tune: ©*1995 Albert Dunn*

GOSPEL ACCLAMATION

Alleluia. Alleluia. Come, Holy Spirit, fill the hearts of your faithful and kindle in them the fire of your love. **Alleluia.**

GOSPEL *(John 20.19-23)*

A reading from the holy Gospel according to John. **Glory to you, Lord.**

It was evening on the day Jesus rose from the dead, the first day of the week, and the doors of the house where the disciples had met were locked for fear of the Jews. Jesus came and stood among them and said, "Peace be with you." After he said this, he showed them his hands and his side. Then the disciples rejoiced when they saw the Lord.

Jesus said to them again, "Peace be with you. As the Father has sent me, so I send you."

When he had said this, he breathed on them and said to them, "Receive the Holy Spirit. If you forgive the sins of any, they are forgiven them; if you retain the sins of any, they are retained."

The Gospel of the Lord. **Praise to you, Lord Jesus Christ.**

PROFESSION OF FAITH *(Nicene Creed, p. 14)*

PRAYER OF THE FAITHFUL

The following intentions are suggestions only.

R. **Lord, hear our prayer.**

For the Church, carrying on the ministry of Jesus by mediating the mercy and compassion of God, we pray to the Lord: R.

For our world, longing for the peace and justice of God that ends violence against the human person, we pray to the Lord: R.

For those among us who are sick, homeless, hungry, unemployed or suffering in any way, we pray to the Lord: R.

For the outpouring of God's Spirit on our parish community as we love and serve God and each other, we pray to the Lord: R.

PREPARATION OF THE GIFTS *(p. 15)*

PRAYER OVER THE GIFTS

Lord, may the Spirit you promised lead us into all truth and reveal to us the full meaning of this sacrifice.

PREFACE *(Pentecost, p. 30)*

COMMUNION ANTIPHON *(Acts 2.4, 11)*

They were all filled with the Holy Spirit, and they spoke of the great things God had done, alleluia.

PRAYER AFTER COMMUNION

Father, may the food we receive in the eucharist help our eternal redemption. Keep within us the vigour of your Spirit and protect the gifts you have given to your Church.

SOLEMN BLESSING — Pentecost *(Optional)*

Bow your heads and pray for God's blessing

(This day) the Father of light has enlightened the minds of the disciples by the outpouring of the Holy Spirit. May he bless you and give you the gifts of the Spirit for ever. **Amen.**

May that fire which hovered over the disciples as tongues of flame burn out all evil from your hearts and make them glow with pure light. **Amen.**

God inspired speech in different tongues to proclaim one faith. May he strengthen your faith and fulfill your hope of seeing him face to face. **Amen.**

May almighty God bless you, the Father, and the Son, and the Holy Spirit. **Amen.**

DISMISSAL *(p. 326).*

"God so loved the world..." Love is the first step in the dance, and God always takes the lead. It's the dance into which we have been introduced at our baptism: life in the Trinity.

If you want to begin to approach the mystery of the Trinity as anything other than a mathematical equation, begin with love. It's love poured out, love given, love received and shared that is the essence of this mystery. Then, think love in motion — not a static equation, but love moving between persons whom we name as Father, Son and Spirit. Think of a dance between three equal lovers who have nothing else to do but love. That's the essence of Trinitarian life.

We tend to think of the Trinity as 'up there,' distant from us — a distance that absolves us from any obligation to participate! But Trinity, in fact, is our home address. We live *in* the Trinity. From the time of our baptism, we have been caught up in the dance that is love poured out, handed over, returned, shared. This love is our highest calling, our source of morality and our greatest delight.

That humanity is invited into the communion of love that is the God of Jesus Christ boggles our minds. But don't get caught in the boggle. Ignore your two left feet. Let God lead you in the best dance of your life.

Bernadette Gasslein, Edmonton, AB

ENTRANCE ANTIPHON

Blessed be God the Father and his only-begotten Son and the Holy Spirit: for he has shown that he loves us.

INTRODUCTORY RITES *(p. 7)*

OPENING PRAYER

Father, you sent your Word to bring us truth and your Spirit to make us holy. Through them we come to know the mystery of your life. Help us to worship you, one God in three Persons, by proclaiming and living our faith in you.

FIRST READING *(Exodus 34.4-6, 8-9)*

Moses rose early in the morning and went up on Mount Sinai, as the Lord had commanded him, and took in his hand the two tablets of stone. The Lord descended in the cloud and stood with him there, and proclaimed the name, "The Lord."

The Lord passed before Moses, and proclaimed, "The Lord, the Lord, a God merciful and gracious, slow to anger, and abounding in steadfast love and faithfulness."

And Moses quickly bowed his head toward the earth, and worshipped. He said, "If now I have found favour in your sight, O Lord, I pray, let the Lord go with us. Although this is a stiff-necked people, pardon our iniquity and our sin, and take us for your inheritance."

The word of the Lord. **Thanks be to God.**

RESPONSORIAL CANTICLE (*Daniel 3*)

Glo-ry and praise____ for ev - er!

℟. **Glory and praise for ever!**

Blessed are you, O Lord, God of our · **fathers**
and blessed is your glorious
    and · **holy** name. ℟.

Blessed are you in the temple
    of your holy · **glory,**
and to be extolled and highly glorified
    · **for**-ever. ℟.

Blessed are you on the throne
    of your · **kingdom,**
and to be extolled and highly exalted
    · **for**-ever. ℟.

Blessed are you who look into the · **depths**
from your throne on · **the** cherubim. ℟.

Blessed are you in the firmament
    of · **heaven,**
to be sung and glorified · **for**-ever. ℟.

SECOND READING *(2 Corinthians 13.11-13)*

Brothers and sisters, put things in order, listen to my appeal, agree with one another, live in peace; and the God of love and peace will be with you. Greet one another with a holy kiss. All the saints greet you.

The grace of the Lord Jesus Christ, the love of God, and the communion of the Holy Spirit be with all of you.

The word of the Lord. **Thanks be to God.**

GOSPEL ACCLAMATION *(See Revelation 1.8)*

Alleluia. Alleluia. Glory to the Father, the Son, and the Holy Spirit: to God who is, who was, and who is to come. **Alleluia.**

GOSPEL *(John 3.16-18)*

A reading from the holy Gospel according to John. **Glory to you. Lord.**

Jesus said to Nicodemus: "God so loved the world that he gave his only-begotten Son, so that everyone who believes in him may not perish but may have eternal life.

"Indeed, God did not send the Son into the world to condemn the world, but in order that the world might be saved through him. The one who believes in him is not condemned; but the one who does not believe is condemned already, for not having believed in the name of the only-begotten Son of God."

The Gospel of the Lord. **Praise to you, Lord Jesus Christ.**

PROFESSION OF FAITH *(Nicene Creed, p. 14)*

PRAYER OF THE FAITHFUL

The following intentions are suggestions only.

R̸ **Lord, hear our prayer.**

For the Church, called to deepen its understanding of the mystery of God, we pray to the Lord: R̸

For our nation's leaders, seeking to learn the ways of peace and gentleness, we pray to the Lord: R̸

For all who are oppressed because of race, gender or religion, and for those whose prejudice wounds them, we pray to the Lord: R̸

For all fathers today: in gratitude for their loving witness, we pray to the Lord: R̸

PREPARATION OF THE GIFTS *(p. 15)*

PRAYER OVER THE GIFTS

Lord our God, make these gifts holy, and through them make us a perfect offering to you.

PREFACE *(Trinity, p. 30)*

COMMUNION ANTIPHON *(Galatians 4.6)*

You are the sons of God, so God has given you the Spirit of his Son to form your hearts and make you cry out: Abba, Father.

PRAYER AFTER COMMUNION

Lord God, we worship you, a Trinity of Persons, one eternal God. May our faith and the sacrament we receive bring us health of mind and body.

BLESSING AND DISMISSAL *(p. 67)*

Today's gospel passage has one of Jesus' most extreme sayings. Jesus tells his listeners that unless they eat his flesh and drink his blood, they will not enter into eternal life. This sounds shocking enough, but it is even more graphic in the Greek, where the words have the nuance of "you must chew on the meat that makes up my body." It is no wonder that some of his followers left him after this episode. This was just too much to accept. But Jesus did not call them back and explain that he was only speaking symbolically. He let them go.

Early Christians took this passage very seriously too. They were often accused of practising cannibalism. Those who had not been at a eucharistic celebration took the words literally to mean that Christians were eating the body of a dead person. But just like Jesus, those early Christians never backed down from their beliefs. They never explained their actions as purely symbolic.

Our consumption of the Body and Blood of Christ today continues to affirm a powerful message. God came among us in the person of Jesus, and Jesus then gave his very self to us in order to give us eternal life. This is the act of a God whose love is truly outrageous, knowing no bounds.

John L. McLaughlin, Toronto, ON

ENTRANCE ANTIPHON *(Psalm 81.16)*

The Lord fed his people with the finest wheat and honey; their hunger was satisfied.

INTRODUCTORY RITES *(p. 7)*

OPENING PRAYER

Lord Jesus Christ, you gave us the eucharist as the memorial of your suffering and death. May our worship of this sacrament of your body and blood help us to experience the salvation you won for us and the peace of the kingdom.

FIRST READING *(Deuteronomy 8.2-3, 14-16)*

Moses spoke to the people: "Remember the long way that the Lord your God has led you these forty years in the wilderness, in order to humble you, testing you to know what was in your heart, whether or not you would keep his commandments. He humbled you by letting you hunger, then by feeding you with manna, with which neither you nor your ancestors were acquainted, in order to make you understand that man does not live by bread alone, but by every word that comes from the mouth of the Lord."

"Do not exalt yourself, forgetting the Lord your God, who brought you out of the land of Egypt, out of the house of slavery, who led you through the great and terrible wilderness, an arid wasteland with poisonous snakes and scorpions. He made water flow for you from flint rock, and fed you in the wilderness with manna that your ancestors did not know, to humble you and to test you, and in the end to do you good."

The word of the Lord. **Thanks be to God.**

RESPONSORIAL PSALM *(Psalm 147)*

R̬ **Praise the Lord, Jerusalem.**

or **Alleluia!**

Praise the Lord, O Je· -**rusalem!**
Praise your God, O · **Zion!**
For he strengthens the bars of your · **gates;**
he blesses your children with·-**in_you.** R̬

He grants peace within your · **borders;**
he fills you with the finest of · **wheat.**
He sends out his command to the · **earth;**
his word runs · **swiftly.** R̬

He declares his word to · **Jacob,**
his statutes and ordinances to · **Israel.**
He has not dealt thus with any other · **nation;**
they do not know his · **ordinances.** R̬

©2010 Gordon Johnston/Novalis

SECOND READING *(1 Corinthians 10.16-17)*

Brothers and sisters: The cup of blessing that we
bless, is it not a sharing in the Blood of Christ?
The bread that we break, is it not a sharing in the
Body of Christ?

Because there is one bread, we who are many are
one body, for we all partake of the one bread.

The word of the Lord. **Thanks be to God.**

SEQUENCE *(Optional)*

This sequence is to be sung. The shorter version begins at the asterisks (p. 395). An earlier version of this Sequence is set to music in CBW III, 693.

1. Laud, O Sion, your salvation,
   laud with hymns of exultation
   Christ, your King and Shepherd true:
   Bring him all the praise you know,
   He is more than you bestow;
   never can you reach his due.

2. Wondrous theme for glad thanksgiving
   is the living and life-giving
   Bread today before you set,
   from his hands of old partaken,
   As we know, by faith unshaken,
   where the Twelve at supper met.

3. Full and clear ring out your chanting,
   let not joy nor grace be wanting.
   From your heart let praises burst.
   For this day the Feast is holden,
   When the institution olden
   of that Supper was rehearsed.

4. Here the new law's new oblation,
   by the new King's revelation,
   Ends the forms of ancient rite.
   Now the new the old effaces,
   Substance now the shadow chases,
   light of day dispels the night.

5. What he did at supper seated,
   Christ ordained to be repeated,
   His remembrance not to cease.
   And his rule for guidance taking,
   Bread and wine we hallow, making,
   thus, our sacrifice of peace.

➜

6. This the truth each Christian learns:
   bread into his own flesh Christ turns,
   To his precious Blood the wine.
   Sight must fail, no thought conceives,
   But a steadfast faith believes,
   resting on a power divine.

7. Here beneath these signs are hidden
   priceless things to sense forbidden.
   Signs alone, not things, we see:
   Blood and flesh as wine, bread broken;
   Yet beneath each wondrous token,
   Christ entire we know to be.

8. All who of this great food partake,
   they sever not the Lord, nor break:
   Christ is whole to all that taste.
   Be one or be a thousand fed
   They eat alike that living Bread,
   eat of him who cannot waste.

9. Good and guilty likewise sharing,
   though their different ends preparing:
   timeless death, or blessed life.
   Life to these, to those damnation,
   Even like participation
   is with unlike outcomes rife.

10. When the sacrament is broken,
    doubt not, but believe as spoken,
    That each severed outward token
    does the very whole contain.
    None that precious gift divides,
    breaking but the sign betides.
    Jesus still the same abides,
    still unbroken he remains.

* * *

11. Hail, the food of Angels given
    to the pilgrim who has striven,
    to the child as bread from heaven,
    food alone for spirit meant:
    Now the former types fulfilling —
    Isaac bound, a victim willing,
    Paschal Lamb, its life-blood spilling,
    manna to the ancients sent.

12. Bread yourself, good Shepherd, tend us;
    Jesus, with your love befriend us.
    You refresh us and defend us;
    to your lasting goodness send us
    That the land of life we see.
    Lord, who all things both rule and know,
    who on this earth such food bestow,
    Grant that with your saints we follow
    to that banquet ever hallow,
    With them heirs and guests to be.

Text: translation ©2009 Concacan Inc. All rights reserved.

GOSPEL ACCLAMATION *(John 6.51-52)*

Alleluia. Alleluia. I am the living bread that came down from heaven, says the Lord; whoever eats of this bread will live forever. **Alleluia.**

GOSPEL *(John 6.51-59)*

A reading from the holy Gospel according to John.
Glory to you, Lord.

Jesus said to the people: "I am the living bread that came down from heaven. Whoever eats of this bread will live forever; and the bread that I will give for the life of the world is my flesh."

The people then disputed among themselves, saying, "How can this man give us his flesh to eat?"

So Jesus said to them, "Very truly, I tell you, unless you eat the flesh of the Son of Man and drink his blood, you have no life in you. Whoever eats my flesh and drinks my blood has eternal life, and I will raise them up on the last day; for my flesh is true food and my blood is true drink. Whoever eats my flesh and drinks my blood abides in me, and I in them.

"Just as the living Father sent me, and I live because of the Father, so whoever eats me will live because of me. This is the bread that came down from heaven, not like that which your ancestors ate, and they died. But the one who eats this bread will live forever."

Jesus said these things while he was teaching in the synagogue at Capernaum.

The Gospel of the Lord. **Praise to you, Lord Jesus Christ.**

PROFESSION OF FAITH *(p. 13-14)*

PRAYER OF THE FAITHFUL

The following intentions are suggestions only.

R̠ **Lord, hear our prayer.**

For the Church, the people of God, nourished by the real presence of Christ in the community, the word and the eucharist we share, we pray to the Lord: R̠

For governments searching for ways to ensure fair and equitable distribution of food and other resources at home and abroad, we pray to the Lord: R.

For the children in our own country who live in poverty, and for all the world's children whose parents and guardians lack the means to nourish them, we pray to the Lord: R.

For the young people of our parish, in whose lives God is working, often unrecognized, we pray to the Lord: R.

PREPARATION OF THE GIFTS *(p. 15)*

PRAYER OVER THE GIFTS

Lord, may the bread and cup we offer bring your Church the unity and peace they signify.

PREFACE *(Holy Eucharist I-II, p. 31)*

COMMUNION ANTIPHON *(John 6.57)*

Whoever eats my flesh and drinks my blood will live in me and I in him, says the Lord.

PRAYER AFTER COMMUNION

Lord Jesus Christ, you give us your body and blood in the eucharist as a sign that even now we share your life. May we come to possess it completely in the kingdom where you live for ever and ever.

BLESSING AND DISMISSAL *(p. 67)*

Pause for a minute. Make a mental list of the different burdens that you (and the people you know) carry each day. Don't rush... give yourself time to really think about this.

Burdens come in all shapes and sizes, and most of us carry a few. Burdens can be small but annoying things that are eventually resolved by personal effort or some change in circumstance. They can be big, all-consuming issues that drag on for years and leave scars on our emotional or financial well-being. Burdens can also be ongoing, systemic challenges due to poverty or illness or discrimination — situations that can't be altered without significant social change. In any event, carrying a burden — big, small, everyday or unusual — has a tremendous effect on our personal well-being and how we relate to each other.

Today's gospel reminds us that a faithful, reflective life can ease whatever load we carry. But it also presents a challenge to us. If putting our faith in Jesus is important, then as followers of Jesus, we have a responsibility to connect with the people around us, to get to know the burdens that they are carrying, and to find ways to ease their load in whatever way we can. While each of us finds support in God, we also need to demonstrate our faith by supporting others. It is the gentle, humble-hearted thing to do.

Susan Eaton, Antigonish, NS

ENTRANCE ANTIPHON *(Psalm 48.9-10)*

Within your temple, we ponder your loving kind-ness, O God. As your name, so also your praise reaches to the ends of the earth; your right hand is filled with justice.

INTRODUCTORY RITES *(p. 7)*

OPENING PRAYER

Father, through the obedience of Jesus, your servant and your Son, you raised a fallen world. Free us from sin and bring us the joy that lasts for ever.

FIRST READING *(Zechariah 9.9-10)*

Thus says the Lord:
Rejoice greatly, O daughter Zion!
Shout aloud, O daughter Jerusalem!
Lo, your king comes to you;
triumphant and victorious is he,
humble and riding on a donkey,
on a colt, the foal of a donkey.

He will cut off the chariot from Ephraim
and the war horse from Jerusalem;
and the warrior's bow shall be cut off,
and he shall command peace to the nations;
his dominion shall be from sea to sea,
and from the River to the ends of the earth.

The word of the Lord. **Thanks be to God.**

RESPONSORIAL PSALM *(Psalm 145)*

I will bless your name for ev - er,

my King and my God.

℞. **I will bless your name for ever,**
my King and my God.

or **Alleluia!**

I will extol you, my God and · King,
and bless your name forever and · **ever.**
Every day I will · **bless_you,**
and praise your name forever · **and** ever. ℞.

The Lord is gracious and · **merciful,**
slow to anger and abounding in steadfast · **love.**
The Lord is good to · **all,**
and his compassion is over all
    that he · **has** made. ℞.

All your works shall give thanks to you, O · **Lord,**
and all your faithful shall · **bless_you.**
They shall speak of the glory
    of your · **kingdom,**
and tell of · **your** power. ℞.

The Lord is faithful in all his · **words,**
and gracious in all his · **deeds.**
The Lord upholds all who are · **falling,**
and raises up all who are · **bowed** down. ℞.

SECOND READING *(Romans 8.9, 11-13)*

Brothers and sisters: You are not in the flesh; you are in the Spirit, since the Spirit of God dwells in you. Anyone who does not have the Spirit of Christ does not belong to him.

If the Spirit of God who raised Jesus from the dead dwells in you, he who raised Christ from the dead will give life to your mortal bodies also through his Spirit that dwells in you.

So then, brothers and sisters, we are debtors, not to the flesh, to live according to the flesh — for if you live according to the flesh, you will die; but if by the Spirit you put to death the deeds of the body, you will live.

The word of the Lord. **Thanks be to God.**

GOSPEL ACCLAMATION *(See Matthew 11.25)*

Alleluia. Alleluia. Blessed are you, Father, Lord of heaven and earth; you have revealed to little ones the mysteries of the kingdom. **Alleluia.**

GOSPEL *(Matthew 11.25-30)*

A reading from the holy Gospel according to Matthew. **Glory to you, Lord.**

At that time Jesus said, "I thank you, Father, Lord of heaven and earth, because you have hidden these things from the wise and the intelligent and have revealed them to infants; yes, Father, for such was your gracious will."

He continued: "All things have been handed over to me by my Father; and no one knows the Son except the Father, and no one knows the Father except the Son and anyone to whom the Son chooses to reveal him.

"Come to me, all you that are weary and are carrying heavy burdens, and I will give you rest. Take my yoke upon you, and learn from me; for I am gentle and humble in heart, and you will find rest for your souls. For my yoke is easy, and my burden is light."

The Gospel of the Lord. **Praise to you, Lord Jesus Christ.**

PROFESSION OF FAITH *(p. 13-14)*

PRAYER OF THE FAITHFUL

The following intentions are suggestions only.

R. **Lord, hear our prayer.**

For all in the Church who lead in the ways of simplicity and peace, we pray to the Lord: R.

For leaders of nations, from whom their people expect words and deeds of peace, we pray to the Lord: R.

For those whose lives lack peace, and for those who reach out to them, we pray to the Lord: R.

For us, God's people gathered here, called to bring peace to the lives of others, we pray to the Lord: R.

PREPARATION OF THE GIFTS *(p. 15)*

PRAYER OVER THE GIFTS

Lord, let this offering to the glory of your name purify us and bring us closer to eternal life.

PREFACE *(Sundays in Ordinary Time, p. 20)*

COMMUNION ANTIPHON *(Matthew 11.28)*

Come to me, all you that labour and are burdened, and I will give you rest, says the Lord.

PRAYER AFTER COMMUNION

Lord, may we never fail to praise you for the fullness of life and salvation you give us in this eucharist.

BLESSING AND DISMISSAL *(p. 67)*

15th Sunday in Ordinary Time

Today, the Word of God is compared to seed, the source that goes out to bring forth new life. All of our life, all of creation, is groaning in anticipation of being all we can become. Every springtime, when working in my back yard, I'm not completely sure of the hue of the flowers from the seed I'm planting, nor do I exactly know the taste of the tomatoes. I do know that I must prepare the soil, fertilize, weed and water. By the same token, we have to activate the seed of faith we've been given, and care for it, in order to see it grow. The passage in Matthew's gospel for next Sunday promises that a massive mustard tree can grow from even the tiniest of seeds.

If we allow ourselves to become like the Pharisees, however, the opportunity for God's grace to really touch our hearts is about as likely as the chance for seed to grow on paths, on rocky ground or among thorns. With very firm language, Jesus continually warns his followers against refusing to value the Word of God and to act upon it after they have received it.

Rather, when we prepare and cultivate our hearts, we can listen and hear the Word. We can respond as does a fertile field, allowing the source of life to grow within us.

How might we encourage our faith to grow?

Joseph Gunn, Ottawa, ON

ENTRANCE ANTIPHON *(Psalm 17.15)*

In my justice I shall see your face, O Lord; when your glory appears, my joy will be full.

INTRODUCTORY RITES *(p. 7)*

OPENING PRAYER

God our Father, your light of truth guides us to the way of Christ. May all who follow him reject what is contrary to the gospel.

FIRST READING *(Isaiah 55.10-11)*

Thus says the Lord: "As the rain and the snow come down from heaven, and do not return there until they have watered the earth, making it bring forth and sprout, giving seed to the sower and bread to the one who eats, so shall my word be that goes out from my mouth; it shall not return to me empty, but it shall accomplish that which I purpose, and succeed in the thing for which I sent it."

The word of the Lord. **Thanks be to God.**

RESPONSORIAL PSALM *(Psalm 65)*

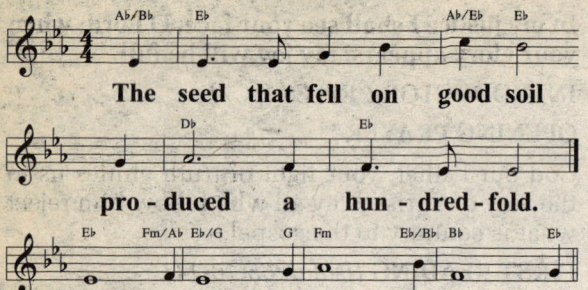

℟. **The seed that fell on good soil
produced a hundredfold.**

You visit the earth and · **water_it,**
you greatly en--**rich_it;**
the river of God is full of · **water;**
you provide the people with · **grain.** ℟.

For so you have prepared the · **earth:**
you water its furrows a--**bundantly,**
settling its ridges, softening it with · **showers,**
and blessing its · **growth.** ℟.

You crown the year with your · **bounty;**
your pathways overflow with · **richness.**
The pastures of the wilderness over--**flow,**
the hills gird themselves with · **joy.** ℟.

1- The meadows clothe themselves with · **flocks,**
3- the valleys deck themselves with · **grain,**
4- they shout and sing together for · **joy.** ℟.

SECOND READING *(Romans 8.18-23)*

Brothers and sisters: I consider that the sufferings of this present time are not worth comparing with the glory about to be revealed to us. For the creation waits with eager longing for the revealing of the children of God; for the creation was subjected to futility, not of its own will but by the will of the one who subjected it, in hope that the creation itself will be set free from its bondage to decay and will obtain the freedom of the glory of the children of God.

We know that the whole creation has been groaning in labour pains until now; and not only the creation, but we ourselves, who have the first fruits of the Spirit, groan inwardly while we wait for adoption to sonship, the redemption of our bodies.

The word of the Lord. **Thanks be to God.**

GOSPEL ACCLAMATION *(See Luke 8.11)*

Alleluia. Alleluia. The seed is the word of God, Christ is the sower; all who come to him will live for ever. **Alleluia.**

GOSPEL *(Matthew 13.1-23)*

The shorter reading ends at the asterisks.

A reading from the holy Gospel according to Matthew. **Glory to you, Lord.**

Jesus went out of the house and sat beside the sea. Such great crowds gathered around him that he got into a boat and sat there, while the whole crowd stood on the beach. And he told them many things in parables.

"Listen! A sower went out to sow. And as he sowed, some seeds fell on the path, and the birds came and ate them up. Other seeds fell on rocky ground, where they did not have much soil, and they sprang up quickly, since they had no depth of soil. But when the sun rose, they were scorched; and since they had no root, they withered away. Other seeds fell among thorns, and the thorns grew up and choked them. Other seeds 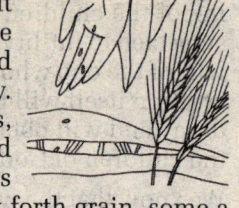 fell on good soil and brought forth grain, some a hundredfold, some sixty, some thirty. Let anyone with ears listen!"

* * *

Then the disciples came and asked Jesus, "Why do you speak to them in parables?" He answered, "To you it has been given to know the secrets of the kingdom of heaven, but to them it has not been given. For to those who have, more will be given, and they will have an abundance; but from those who have nothing, even what they have will be taken away.

"The reason I speak to them in parables is that 'seeing they do not perceive, and hearing they do not listen, nor do they understand.' With them indeed is fulfilled the prophecy of Isaiah that says: 'You will indeed listen, but never understand, and you will indeed look, but never perceive. For this people's heart has grown dull, and their ears are hard of hearing, and they have shut their eyes; so that they might not look with their eyes, and listen with their ears, and understand with their heart and turn — and I would heal them.'

"But blessed are your eyes, for they see, and your ears, for they hear. Truly I tell you, many Prophets and righteous people longed to see what you see, but did not see it, and to hear what you hear, but did not hear it.

"Hear then the parable of the sower. When anyone hears the word of the kingdom and does not understand it, the evil one comes and snatches away what is sown in the heart; this is what was sown on the path. As for what was sown on rocky ground, this is the one who hears the word and immediately receives it with joy; yet such a person has no root, but endures only for a while, and when trouble or persecution arises on account of the word, that person immediately falls away. As for what was sown among thorns, this is the one who hears the word, but the cares of the world and the lure of wealth choke the word, and it yields nothing.

"But as for what was sown on good soil, this is the one who hears the word and understands it, who indeed bears fruit and yields, in one case a hundredfold, in another sixty, and in another thirty."

The Gospel of the Lord. **Praise to you, Lord Jesus Christ.**

PROFESSION OF FAITH (*p. 13-14*)

PRAYER OF THE FAITHFUL

The following intentions are suggestions only.

R. **Lord, hear our prayer.**

For the Church, healer and refuge as Jesus was, we pray to the Lord: R.

For leaders of nations who try to respond to cries for help, locally and globally, we pray to the Lord: R.

For the wounded, the alienated, the hungry who turn to us for help, we pray to the Lord: R.

For us, God's people, needy and wounded, looking to each other for sustenance, we pray to the Lord: R.

PREPARATION OF THE GIFTS *(p. 15)*

PRAYER OVER THE GIFTS

Lord, accept the gifts of your Church. May this eucharist help us grow in holiness and faith.

PREFACE *(Sundays in Ordinary Time, p. 20)*

COMMUNION ANTIPHON *(Psalm 84.3-4)*

The sparrow even finds a home, the swallow finds a nest wherein to place her young, near to your altars, Lord of hosts, my King, my God! How happy they who dwell in your house! For ever they are praising you.

PRAYER AFTER COMMUNION

Lord, by our sharing in the mystery of this eucharist, let your saving love grow within us.

BLESSING AND DISMISSAL *(p. 67)*

I remember the first time I saw her. Long nails, flashy jewellery, dyed hair and dressed to kill. "Shallow," whispered that judgmental little voice in my brain. Who would ever have imagined that she would turn out to be one of the deepest, most spiritual people I know.

How easy it is for us to judge others, only to find out later how wrong we really were. That's exactly what Jesus is trying to get across to us today with the parable of the weeds and the wheat. At first glance, it seems to make no sense. What farmer wants weeds to take over his crop? But if we dig a little deeper, we see that's not the point Jesus is trying to make. He's not denying that the weeds are there, or saying that they don't need to be separated from the wheat. What he is saying is that it's not up to us to do the weeding. Only God can separate the weeds from the wheat, the bad from the good.

Instead of trying to be the one doing the weeding, perhaps we should try a little harder to be the wheat. Instead of judging who is good and holy and who is not, we could try to *be* good and holy and leave it at that. For my part, I'm glad the rest is up to God.

Teresa Whalen Lux, Regina, SK

ENTRANCE ANTIPHON *(Psalm 54.4, 6)*

God himself is my help. The Lord upholds my life. I will offer you a willing sacrifice; I will praise your name, O Lord, for its goodness.

INTRODUCTORY RITES *(p. 7)*

OPENING PRAYER

Lord, be merciful to your people. Fill us with your gifts and make us always eager to serve you in faith, hope and love.

FIRST READING *(Wisdom 12.13, 16-19)*

There is no god besides you, Lord,
whose care is for all people,
to whom you should prove that you have not
    judged unjustly.

For your strength is the source of righteousness,
and your sovereignty over all
    causes you to spare all.
For you show your strength
when people doubt the completeness
    of your power,
and you rebuke any insolence among those
    who know it.
Although you are sovereign in strength,
you judge with mildness,
and with great forbearance you govern us;
for you have power to act whenever you choose.

Through such works you have taught your people
that the righteous must be kind,
and you have filled your children with good hope,
because you give repentance for sins.

The word of the Lord. **Thanks be to God.**

RESPONSORIAL PSALM *(Psalm 86)*

Lord, you are good and for-giv-ing.

℟ **Lord, you are good and forgiving.**

You, O Lord, are good and for·**giving,**
abounding in steadfast love to all
who call · **on** you.
Give ear, O Lord, to my · **prayer;**
listen to my cry of · **suppli**-cation. ℟

All the nations you have made shall come
and bow down before you, O · **Lord,**
and shall glorify · **your** name.
For you are great and do wondrous · **things;**
you alone · **are** God. ℟

But you, O Lord, are a God merciful
and · **gracious,**
slow to anger and abounding in steadfast love
· **and** faithfulness.
Turn to me and be · **gracious_to_me.**
Give your strength to · **your** servant. ℟

SECOND READING *(Romans 8.26-27)*

Brothers and sisters: The Spirit helps us in our weakness; for we do not know how to pray as we ought, but that very Spirit intercedes with sighs too deep for words.

And God, who searches the heart, knows what is the mind of the Spirit, because the Spirit intercedes for the saints according to the will of God.

The word of the Lord. **Thanks be to God.**

GOSPEL ACCLAMATION *(See Matthew 11.25)*

Alleluia. Alleluia. Blessed are you, Father, Lord of heaven and earth; you have revealed to little ones the mysteries of the kingdom. **Alleluia.**

GOSPEL *(Matthew 13.24-43)*

The shorter version ends at the asterisks.

A reading from the holy Gospel according to Matthew. **Glory to you, Lord.**

Jesus put before the crowds a parable: "The kingdom of heaven may be compared to someone who sowed good seed in his field; but while everybody was asleep, an enemy came and sowed weeds among the wheat, and then went away.

"So when the plants came up and bore grain, then the weeds appeared as well. And the slaves of the householder came and said to him, 'Master, did you not sow good seed in your field? Where, then, did these weeds come from?' He answered, 'An enemy has done this.' The slaves said to him, 'Then do you want us to go and gather them?' But he replied, 'No; for in gathering the weeds you would uproot the wheat along with them.

Let both of them grow together until the harvest; and at harvest time I will tell the reapers, Collect the weeds first and bind them in bundles to be burned, but gather the wheat into my barn.'"

Jesus put before them another parable: "The kingdom of heaven is like a mustard seed that someone took and sowed in his field; it is the smallest of all the seeds, but when it has grown it is the greatest of shrubs and becomes a tree, so that the birds of the air come and make nests in its branches."

He told them another parable: "The kingdom of heaven is like yeast that a woman took and mixed in with three measures of flour until all of it was leavened."

* * *

Jesus told the crowds all these things in parables; without a parable he told them nothing. This was to fulfill what had been spoken through the Prophet: "I will open my mouth to speak in parables; I will proclaim what has been hidden from the foundation of the world."

Then Jesus left the crowds and went into the house. And his disciples approached him, saying, "Explain to us the parable of the weeds of the field." He answered, "The one who sows the good seed is the Son of Man; the field is the world, and the good seed are the children of the kingdom; the weeds are the children of the evil one, and the enemy who sowed them is the devil;

the harvest is the end of the age, and the reapers are Angels.

"Just as the weeds are collected and burned up with fire, so will it be at the end of the age. The Son of Man will send his Angels, and they will collect out of his kingdom all causes of sin and all evildoers, and they will throw them into the furnace of fire, where there will be weeping and gnashing of teeth. Then the righteous will shine like the sun in the kingdom of their Father. Let anyone with ears listen!"

The Gospel of the Lord. **Praise to you, Lord Jesus Christ.**

PROFESSION OF FAITH *(p. 13-14)*

PRAYER OF THE FAITHFUL

The following intentions are suggestions only.

R. **Lord, hear our prayer.**

For the Church, striving to live in openness to God's word revealed in our day, we pray to the Lord: R.

For our world that cries out for structures that welcome and respect the stranger, we pray to the Lord: R.

For busy people seeking stillness to listen to God and their own hearts, we pray to the Lord: R.

For this Christian community, called to put God's word of love into action every day, we pray to the Lord: R.

PREPARATION OF THE GIFTS *(p. 15)*

PRAYER OVER THE GIFTS

Lord, bring us closer to salvation through these gifts which we bring in your honour. Accept the perfect sacrifice you have given us, bless it as you blessed the gifts of Abel.

PREFACE *(Sundays in Ordinary Time, p. 20)*

COMMUNION ANTIPHON *(Psalm 111.4-5)*

The Lord keeps in our minds the wonderful things he has done. He is compassion and love; he always provides for his faithful.

PRAYER AFTER COMMUNION

Merciful Father, may these mysteries give us new purpose and bring us to a new life in you.

BLESSING AND DISMISSAL *(p. 67)*

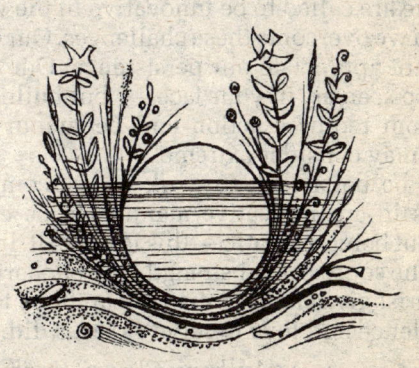

While today's gospel presents us with images of the kingdom, reading between the lines we see that the focus of the parables isn't hidden treasure, pearls or fish. It is the actions of the people in the parables.

What does the gospel tell us about these people? They are relentless in their search for the prize. They are persistent in the face of challenges and they become innovative in looking for ways to overcome the obstacles they face. At times these people may be very much 'in your face' and hence not appreciated by others.

If we are going to build the kingdom, we must also be relentless. We are called to face obstacles and we are called to be innovative in the ways in which we overcome these challenges. Our culture may not appreciate our persistence. Our actions may be seen as 'in your face' — but building the kingdom requires action and behaviour which some may consider extreme.

To be persistent, to work to overcome challenges in an innovative manner, to be extreme without being a fanatic — this is our call, in union with the source of our strength, the eucharist. The eucharist gives faith to dispel fear, hope to build confidence and love to serve as Jesus did.

Anthony Chezzi, Sudbury, ON

ENTRANCE ANTIPHON *(Psalm 68.5-6, 35)*

God is in his holy dwelling; he will give a home to the lonely, he gives power and strength to his people.

INTRODUCTORY RITES *(p. 7)*

OPENING PRAYER

God our Father and protector, without you nothing is holy, nothing has value. Guide us to everlasting life by helping us to use wisely the blessings you have given to the world.

FIRST READING *(1 Kings 3.5-12)*

At Gibeon the Lord appeared to Solomon in a dream by night; and God said, "Ask what I should give you." And Solomon said, "You have shown great and steadfast love to your servant my father David, because he walked before you in faithfulness, in righteousness, and in uprightness of heart toward you; and you have kept for him this great and steadfast love, and have given him a son to sit on his throne today.

"And now, O Lord my God, you have made your servant king in place of my father David, although I am only a little child; I do not know how to go out or come in. And your servant is in the midst of the people whom you have chosen, a great people, so numerous they cannot be numbered or counted. Give your servant therefore an understanding mind to govern your people, able to discern between good and evil; for who can govern this, your great people?"

It pleased the Lord that Solomon had asked this. God said to him, "Because you have asked this, and have not asked for yourself long life or riches, or for the life of your enemies, but have asked for yourself understanding to discern what is right, I now do according to your word. Indeed I give you a wise and discerning mind; no one like you has been before you and no one like you shall arise after you."

The word of the Lord. **Thanks be to God.**

RESPONSORIAL PSALM *(Psalm 119)*

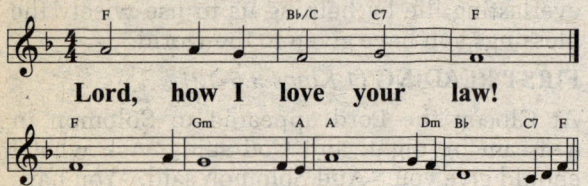

R. **Lord, how I love your law!**

The Lord is my · **portion;**
I promise to keep · **your** words.
The law of your mouth is better · **to** me
than thousands of gold and · **sil-**ver pieces. R.

Let your steadfast love become my · **comfort**
according to your promise · **to_your** servant.
Let your mercy come to me, that I · **may** live;
for your law is · **my** de-light. R.

Truly I love your commandments
    more than · **gold,**
more than · **fine** gold.
Truly I direct my steps by all · **your** precepts;
I hate · **every** false way. R.

Your decrees are · **wonderful;**
therefore my · **soul** keeps_them.
The unfolding of your words · **gives** light;
it imparts understanding · **to** the simple. R.

SECOND READING *(Romans 8.28-30)*

Brothers and sisters: We know that all things work together for good for those who love God, who are called according to his purpose.

For those whom God foreknew he also predestined to be conformed to the image of his Son, in order that he might be the firstborn among many brothers and sisters.

And those whom God predestined he also called; and those whom he called he also justified; and those whom he justified he also glorified.

The word of the Lord. **Thanks be to God.**

GOSPEL ACCLAMATION *(See Matthew 11.25)*

Alleluia. Alleluia. Blessed are you, Father, Lord of heaven and earth; you have revealed to little ones the mysteries of the kingdom. **Alleluia.**

GOSPEL *(Matthew 13.44-52)*

The shorter version ends at the asterisks.

A reading from the holy Gospel according to Matthew. **Glory to you, Lord.**

Jesus spoke to the crowds: "The kingdom of heaven is like treasure hidden in a field, which someone found and hid; then in his joy he goes and sells all that he has and buys that field.

"Again, the kingdom of heaven is like a merchant in search of fine pearls; on finding one pearl of great value, he went and sold all that he had and bought it.

"Again, the kingdom of heaven is like a net that was thrown into the sea and caught fish of every kind; when it was full, they drew it ashore, sat down, and put the good into baskets but threw out the bad."

* * *

"So it will be at the end of the age. The Angels will come out and separate the evil from the righteous and throw them into the furnace of fire, where there will be weeping and gnashing of teeth.

"Have you understood all this?" They answered, "Yes." And he said to them, "Therefore every scribe who has been trained for the kingdom of heaven is like the master of a household who brings out of his treasure what is new and what is old."

The Gospel of the Lord. **Praise to you, Lord Jesus Christ.**

PROFESSION OF FAITH (*p. 13-14*)

PRAYER OF THE FAITHFUL

The following intentions are suggestions only.

℟. **Lord, hear our prayer.**

For the Church, people of prayer and praise, we pray to the Lord: ℟.

For the healing of nations, and for the dawning of peace and justice in lands torn by strife, we pray to the Lord: ℟.

For the poor and the suffering, and for those who are hurt and wounded, we pray to the Lord: R̥.

For us, God's people, seeking strength in our common prayer and our desire to do God's will, we pray to the Lord: R̥.

PREPARATION OF THE GIFTS *(p. 15)*

PRAYER OVER THE GIFTS

Lord, receive these offerings chosen from your many gifts. May these mysteries make us holy and lead us to eternal joy.

PREFACE *(Sundays in Ordinary Time, p. 20)*

COMMUNION ANTIPHON *(Psalm 103.2)*

O, bless the Lord, my soul, and remember all his kindness.

PRAYER AFTER COMMUNION

Lord, we receive the sacrament which celebrates the memory of the death and resurrection of Christ your Son. May this gift bring us closer to our eternal salvation.

BLESSING AND DISMISSAL *(p. 67)*

It's barbecue season, time for good food and refreshing drink. If we're sharing a meal with friends, we make sure that there's plenty to go around: if we don't have leftovers, then maybe someone didn't get enough to eat! And if it's a scorcher, we need a steady supply of cool beverages to keep pace with everyone's thirst.

Do you ever think of the miracle of the loaves and fish when preparing for a party? Do you think of the eucharist when you have unexpected guests? Food and drink are the core elements of our eucharistic gathering, and Jesus' miracle in today's gospel offers a key insight into the mystery of sharing what we have with others.

The disciples saw disaster looming, but they were relying on what little they could find themselves. Jesus brings the crowd together with a blessing, and there is miraculous abundance. Generosity, open giving, true community ensure that there will be plenty.

When we gather for the eucharist, we bring our gifts: bread, wine, monetary offerings. We might also bring our voices in song, our leadership in ministry. And we bring our pain, our need, our brokenness. Isaiah writes, "Come to me; listen, so that you may live." Our eucharist — our life — is complete when we share all we have and are, making sure that everyone can eat and be filled — with leftovers to spare!

Nancy Keyes, Ottawa, ON

ENTRANCE ANTIPHON *(Psalm 70.1, 5)*

God, come to my help. Lord, quickly give me assistance. You are the one who helps me and sets me free: Lord, do not be long in coming.

INTRODUCTORY RITES *(p. 7)*

OPENING PRAYER

Father of everlasting goodness, our origin and guide, be close to us and hear the prayers of all who praise you. Forgive our sins and restore us to life. Keep us safe in your love.

FIRST READING *(Isaiah 55.1-3)*

Thus says the Lord:
"Everyone who thirsts,
come to the waters;
and you that have no money,
come, buy and eat!
Come, buy wine and milk
without money and without price.

"Why do you spend your money
    for that which is not bread,
and your labour for that which does not satisfy?
Listen carefully to me, and eat what is good,
and delight yourselves in rich food.

"Incline your ear, and come to me;
listen, so that you may live.
I will make with you an everlasting covenant,
my steadfast, sure love for David."

The word of the Lord. **Thanks be to God.**

RESPONSORIAL PSALM *(Psalm 145)*

You o - pen your hand to feed us, Lord,

and sat - is - fy our needs.

R. **You open your hand to feed us, Lord,
and satisfy our needs.**

The Lord is gracious and · **merciful,**
slow to anger and abounding in steadfast · **love.**
The Lord is good to · **all,**
and his compassion is over all
    that · **he_has** made. R.

The eyes of all look to · **you,**
and you give them their food in due · **season.**
You open your · **hand,**
satisfying the desire of every · **living** thing. R.

The Lord is just in all his · **ways,**
and kind in all his · **doings.**
The Lord is near to all who · **call_on_him,**
to all who call on him · **in** truth. R.

SECOND READING *(Romans 8.35, 37-39)*

Brothers and sisters: Who will separate us from the love of Christ? Will hardship, or distress, or persecution, or famine, or nakedness, or peril, or sword? No, in all these things we are more than conquerors through him who loved us.

For I am convinced that neither death, nor life, nor Angels, nor rulers, nor things present, nor things to come, nor powers, nor height, nor depth, nor anything else in all creation, will be able to separate us from the love of God in Christ Jesus our Lord.

The word of the Lord. **Thanks be to God.**

GOSPEL ACCLAMATION *(Matthew 4.4)*

Alleluia. Alleluia. Man does not live by bread alone, but by every word that comes from the mouth of God. **Alleluia.**

GOSPEL *(Matthew 14.13-21)*

A reading from the holy Gospel according to Matthew. **Glory to you, Lord.**

When Jesus heard that Herod had beheaded John the Baptist, he withdrew in a boat to a deserted place by himself. But when the crowds heard it, they followed him on foot from the towns. When he went ashore, Jesus saw a great crowd; and he had compassion for them and cured their sick.

When it was evening, the disciples came to him and said, "This is a deserted place, and the hour is now late; send the crowds away so that they may go into the villages and buy food for themselves." Jesus said to them, "They need not go away; you give them something to eat." They replied, "We have nothing here but five loaves and two fish." And he said, "Bring them here to me."

Then Jesus ordered the crowds to sit down on the grass. Taking the five loaves and the two fish, he looked up to heaven, and blessed and broke the loaves, and gave them to the disciples, and the disciples gave them to the crowds.

And all ate and were filled; and they took up what was left over of the broken pieces, twelve baskets full. And those who ate were about five thousand men, besides women and children.

The Gospel of the Lord. **Praise to you, Lord Jesus Christ.**

PROFESSION OF FAITH *(p. 13-14)*

PRAYER OF THE FAITHFUL

The following intentions are suggestions only.

R̠ **Lord, hear our prayer.**

For the Church, embodying Christ's ministry of sharing and service, we pray to the Lord: R̠

For civic leaders, called to ensure that everyone has enough to eat, we pray to the Lord: R̠

For those who minister to the poor, the lonely, the vulnerable, we pray to the Lord: R̠

For our community, called to share our time, treasure and talent, we pray to the Lord: R̠

PREPARATION OF THE GIFTS *(p. 15)*

PRAYER OVER THE GIFTS

Merciful Lord, make these gifts holy , and let our spiritual sacrifice make us an everlasting gift to you.

PREFACE *(Sundays in Ordinary Time, p. 20)*

COMMUNION ANTIPHON *(Wisdom 16.20)*

You gave us bread from heaven, Lord: a sweet-tasting bread that was very good to eat.

PRAYER AFTER COMMUNION

Lord, you give us the strength of new life by the gift of the eucharist. Protect us with your love and prepare us for eternal redemption.

BLESSING AND DISMISSAL *(p. 67)*

A narrow gravel road climbs steadily up the north side of Elk Creek Canyon towards Bethlehem Cave. Ponderosa pine dominate the dark road-side forests that give South Dakota's Black Hills their name. The Lakota people saw these hills as sacred.

From the mouth of Bethlehem Cave only silence speaks. There the constant din of daily life seems far away. Is it only in places like this that we hear in the sheer silence the voice of God as Elijah did at entrance of the cave on Mount Horeb?

In great anguish Paul in our second reading laments the sad reality that many do not hear the truth of "the Christ, who is over all." When confronted with this fundamental rejection, Paul wishes he was accursed if only this would save his people. What deafens us to the Word?

Holiness, though, surrounds us wherever we are. Miracles abound in our time. God is here and now. Why do we doubt? Even the disciples who had just witnessed the miracle of the loaves and fish were gripped, as the gospel tells us, by fear. Early in the morning in a boat battered by waves and far from shore, they were terrified.

Jesus tells them as he tells us "Take heart, it is I; do not be afraid." When our faith flags, let us, as did Peter, turn to the Lord to save us.

Michael Dougherty, Whitehorse, YT

ENTRANCE ANTIPHON *(Psalm 74.19-23)*

Lord, be true to your covenant, forget not the life of your poor ones for ever. Rise up, O God, and defend your cause; do not ignore the shouts of your enemies.

INTRODUCTORY RITES *(p. 7)*

OPENING PRAYER

Almighty and ever-living God, your Spirit made us your children, confident to call you Father. Increase your Spirit within us and bring to our promised inheritance.

FIRST READING *(1 Kings 19.9, 11-13)*

When Elijah reached Horeb, the mountain of God, he came to a cave, and spent the night there. Then the word of the Lord came to him, saying, "Go out and stand on the mountain before the Lord, for the Lord is about to pass by."

Now there was a great wind, so strong that it was splitting mountains and breaking rocks in pieces before the Lord, but the Lord was not in the wind; and after the wind an earthquake, but the Lord was not in the earthquake; and after the earthquake a fire, but the Lord was not in the fire; and after the fire a sound of sheer silence.

When Elijah heard it, he wrapped his face in his mantle and went out and stood at the entrance of the cave.

The word of the Lord. **Thanks be to God.**

RESPONSORIAL PSALM *(Psalm 85)*

Show us your stead-fast love, O Lord,

and grant us your sal - va - tion.

℟ **Show us your steadfast love, O Lord,
and grant us your salvation.**

Let me hear what God the Lord will · **speak,**
for he will speak peace to his · **people.**
Surely his salvation is at hand
    for those who · **fear_him,**
that his glory may dwell · **in_our** land. ℟

Steadfast love and faithfulness will · **meet;**
righteousness and peace
    will · **kiss_each_other.**
Faithfulness will spring up from the · **ground,**
and righteousness will look down
    · **from_the** sky. ℟

The Lord will give what is · **good,**
and our land will yield its · **increase.**
Righteousness will go be-·**fore_him,**
and will make a path · **for_his** steps. ℟

©2010 Gordon Johnston/Novalis

SECOND READING *(Romans 9.1-5)*

Brothers and sisters: I am speaking the truth in Christ. I am not lying; my conscience confirms it by the Holy Spirit. I have great sorrow and unceasing anguish in my heart.

For I could wish that I myself were accursed and cut off from Christ for the sake of my own people, my kindred according to the flesh. They are children of Israel, and to them belong the adoption, the glory, the covenants, the giving of the law, the worship, and the promises; to them belong the patriarchs, and from them, according to the flesh, comes the Christ, who is over all, God be blessed forever. Amen.

The word of the Lord. **Thanks be to God.**

GOSPEL ACCLAMATION *(Psalm 130.5)*

Alleluia. Alleluia. I wait for the Lord; I hope in his word. **Alleluia.**

GOSPEL *(Matthew 14.22-33)*

A reading from the holy Gospel according to Matthew. **Glory to you, Lord.**

Immediately after feeding the crowd with the five loaves and two fish, Jesus made the disciples get into the boat and go on ahead to the other side, while he dismissed the crowds. And after he had dismissed the crowds, he went up the mountain by himself to pray.

When evening came, he was there alone, but by this time the boat, battered by the waves, was far from the land, for the wind was against them.

And early in the morning Jesus came walking toward them on the sea. But when the disciples saw him walking on the sea, they were terrified, saying, "It is a ghost!" And they cried out in fear. But immediately Jesus spoke to them and said, "Take heart, it is I; do not be afraid."

Peter answered him, "Lord, if it is you, command me to come to you on the water." Jesus said, "Come." So Peter got out of the boat, started walking on the water, and came toward Jesus. But when he noticed the strong wind, he became frightened, and beginning to sink, he cried out, "Lord, save me!"

Jesus immediately reached out his hand and caught him, saying to him, "You of little faith, why did you doubt?" When they got into the boat, the wind ceased. And those in the boat worshipped him, saying, "Truly you are the Son of God."

The Gospel of the Lord. **Praise to you, Lord Jesus Christ.**

PROFESSION OF FAITH *(p. 13-14)*

PRAYER OF THE FAITHFUL

The following intentions are suggestions only.

R. **Lord, hear our prayer.**

For the Church, faithful and steadfast sign of the love and trust between God and humanity, we pray to the Lord: R.

For world leaders, called to be just and caring stewards of the world's material wealth, we pray to the Lord: R̶

For the poor, and all who search in hope for relief from their troubles, we pray to the Lord: R̶

For this parish community, striving to live as God's holy people, we pray to the Lord: R̶

PREPARATION OF THE GIFTS *(p. 15)*

PRAYER OVER THE GIFTS

God of power, giver of the gifts we bring, accept the offering of your Church and make it the sacrament of our salvation.

PREFACE *(Sundays in Ordinary Time, p. 20)*

COMMUNION ANTIPHON *(Psalm 147.12, 14)*

Praise the Lord, Jerusalem; he feeds you with the finest wheat.

PRAYER AFTER COMMUNION

Lord, may the eucharist you give us bring us to salvation and keep us faithful to the light of your truth.

BLESSING AND DISMISSAL *(p. 67)*

Our world is constantly being shaken by divisions and conflicts that spring from religious intolerance. A quick scan of the news headlines reveals examples from across the globe: hate-filled graffiti on the walls of a mosque; the bombing of a synagogue; attacks on Christians.

The message we hear in today's scriptures is startlingly relevant for our world in 2011. Over and over, the readings look beyond division and mistrust, revealing a world where the kingdom of God is big enough to welcome everyone. Wherever hatred and narrow-mindedness and prejudice come from, they clearly do not come from God, who embraces all people.

Each of us has a role to play in making God's kingdom come, in allowing God's will to be done. Every time we reach out with understanding and compassion to a neighbour who is of a different faith, every time we pray for peace among nations and religions, every time we stand up for those who are persecuted because of their beliefs in God, we help to reverse the tide of religious discrimination and prejudice. When we take responsibility and refuse to accept division in God's name, God's kingdom becomes one step closer. Isaiah states it simply, "Do what is right."

As kingdom people, we pray together, "May God continue to bless us; let all the ends of the earth revere him."

A. L. Mahoney, Ottawa, ON

ENTRANCE ANTIPHON *(Psalm 84.10-11)*

God, our protector, keep us in mind; always give strength to your people. For if we can be with you even one day, it is better than a thousand without you.

INTRODUCTORY RITES *(p. 7)*

OPENING PRAYER

God our Father, may we love you in all things and above all things and reach the joy you have prepared for us beyond all our imagining.

FIRST READING *(Isaiah 56.1, 6-7)*

Thus says the Lord: "Maintain justice, and do what is right, for soon my salvation will come, and my deliverance be revealed.

"And the foreigners who join themselves to the Lord, to minister to him, to love the name of the Lord, and to be his servants, all who keep the Sabbath, and do not profane it, and hold fast my covenant — these I will bring to my holy mountain, and make them joyful in my house of prayer; their burnt offerings and their sacrifices will be accepted on my altar; for my house shall be called a house of prayer for all peoples."

The word of the Lord. **Thanks be to God.**

RESPONSORIAL PSALM *(Psalm 67)*

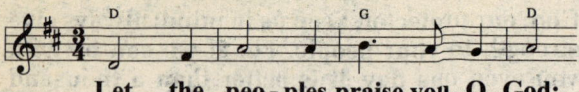

Let the peo - ples praise you, O God;

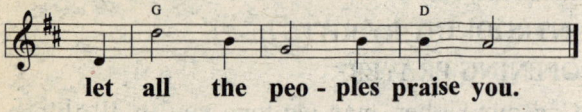

let all the peo - ples praise you.

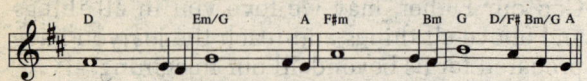

℟. **Let the peoples praise you, O God,
let all the peoples praise you!**

May God be gracious to us · **and** bless_us
and make his face to shine · **up**-on_us,
that your way may be known up--**on** earth,
your saving power a--**mong** all nations. ℟.

Let the nations be glad and sing · **for** joy,
for you judge the peoples with equity
    and guide the nations · **upon** earth.
Let the peoples praise you, · **O** God;
let all the · **peo**-ples praise_you. ℟.

The earth has yielded · **its** increase;
God, our God, · **has** blessed_us.
May God continue · **to** bless_us;
let all the ends of the · **earth** re-vere_him. ℟.

©2010 Gordon Johnston/Novalis

SECOND READING *(Romans 11.13-15, 29-32)*

Brothers and sisters: Now I am speaking to you Gentiles. Inasmuch then as I am an Apostle to the Gentiles, I glorify my ministry in order to make my own flesh and blood jealous, and thus save some of them. For if their rejection is the reconciliation of the world, what will their acceptance be but life from the dead!

The gifts and the calling of God are irrevocable. Just as you were once disobedient to God but have now received mercy because of their disobedience, so they have now been disobedient in order that, by the mercy shown to you, they too may now receive mercy. For God has imprisoned all in disobedience so that he may be merciful to all.

The word of the Lord. **Thanks be to God.**

GOSPEL ACCLAMATION *(See Matthew 4.23)*

Alleluia. Alleluia. Jesus proclaimed the good news of the kingdom and cured every sickness. **Alleluia.**

GOSPEL *(Matthew 15.21-28)*

A reading from the holy Gospel according to Matthew. **Glory to you, Lord.**

Jesus went away to the district of Tyre and Sidon. A Canaanite woman from that region came out, and started shouting, "Have mercy on me, Lord, Son of David; my daughter is tormented by a demon." But he did not answer her at all.

And his disciples came and urged him, saying, "Send her away, for she keeps shouting after us." He answered, "I was sent only to the lost sheep of the house of Israel."

But the woman came and knelt before him, saying, "Lord, help me." He answered, "It is not fair to take the children's food and throw it to the dogs." She said, "Yes, Lord, yet even the dogs eat the crumbs that fall from their masters' table."

Then Jesus answered her, "Woman, great is your faith! Let it be done for you as you wish." And her daughter was healed instantly.

The Gospel of the Lord. **Praise to you, Lord Jesus Christ.**

PROFESSION OF FAITH *(p. 13-14)*

PRAYER OF THE FAITHFUL

The following intentions are suggestions only.

R̲. **Lord, hear our prayer.**

For the Church and its leaders, called to hear and to proclaim the words of the prophets, we pray to the Lord: R̲.

For leaders of nations willing to risk the prophetic task of establishing peace and justice, we pray to the Lord: R̲.

For those among us who are poor, sick and persecuted, and for all who minister to them, we pray
to the Lord: ℟

For travellers, especially young people on their
way to World Youth Days in Madrid, Spain, we
pray to the Lord: ℟

For us, called in baptism to be a people of prophetic words and actions, we pray to the Lord: ℟

PREPARATION OF THE GIFTS *(p. 15)*

PRAYER OVER THE GIFTS

Lord, accept our sacrifice as a holy exchange of
gifts. By offering what you have given us may we
receive the gift of yourself.

PREFACE *(Sundays in Ordinary Time, p. 20)*

COMMUNION ANTIPHON *(Psalm 130.7)*

**With the Lord there is mercy, and fullness of
redemption.**

PRAYER AFTER COMMUNION

God of mercy, by this sacrament you make us one
with Christ. By becoming more like him on earth,
may we come to share his glory in heaven.

BLESSING AND DISMISSAL *(p. 67)*

This is not the first time in Matthew's Gospel that Jesus is acknowledged as the "Son of God." Earlier, after Jesus rescued Peter from the waters, quieted the sea, and the wind had ceased at his command, those on board the boat recognized who Jesus really is. However, in today's passage there is a pivotal dramatic moment in the relationship between Jesus and his closest friends.

Jesus first asks: Who do people say that I am? Those around Jesus reach back into the history of the Jewish people and respond: John the Baptist, Elijah, Jeremiah and other prophets. Jesus then asks those whom he has lovingly invited into his community, patiently taught — those on whom the future of the mission depend: Who do you say that I am? It is at this critical moment, the time in between the question and the answer, that Jesus must wonder if all that he has shared with them has taken root. And then from Peter, the solemn answer: "You are the Christ, the Son of the living God."

Today, Jesus continues to look to each and every one of us to respond as Peter did, to proclaim to the entire world that Jesus Christ is Lord, the Son of the living God. It is our time to make our solemn response to this crucial question for the life of the world.

Connie Paré, London, ON

ENTRANCE ANTIPHON *(Psalm 86.1-3)*

Listen, Lord, and answer me. Save your servant who trusts in you. I call to you all day long, have mercy on me, O Lord.

INTRODUCTORY RITES *(p. 7)*

OPENING PRAYER

Father, help us to seek the values that will bring us enduring joy in this changing world. In our desire for what you promise make us one in mind and heart.

FIRST READING *(Isaiah 22.15, 19-23)*

Thus says the Lord God of hosts: Go to the steward, to Shebna, who is master of the household, and say to him:

"I will thrust you from your office, and you will be pulled down from your post. On that day I will call my servant Eliakim son of Hilkiah, and will clothe him with your robe and bind your sash on him. I will commit your authority to his hand, and he shall be a father to the inhabitants of Jerusalem and to the house of Judah.

"I will place on his shoulder the key of the house of David; he shall open, and no one shall shut; he shall shut, and no one shall open. I will fasten him like a peg in a secure place, and he will become a throne of honour to the house of his ancestors."

The word of the Lord. **Thanks be to God.**

RESPONSORIAL PSALM *(Psalm 138)*

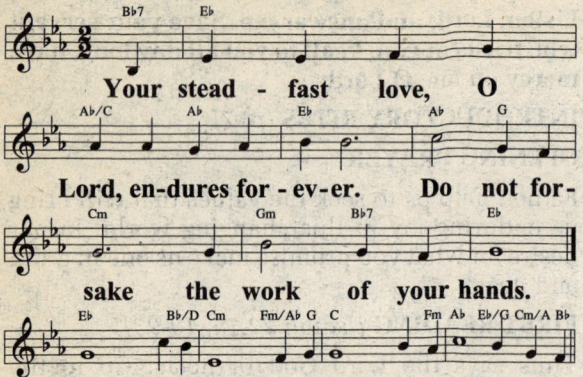

℟. **Your steadfast love, O Lord, endures forever.
Do not forsake the work of your hands.**

I give you thanks, O Lord,
   with my · **whole** heart;
before the Angels I sing · **your** praise;
I bow down toward your holy temple,
   and give thanks to · **your** name
for your steadfast · **love_and** your
   faithfulness. ℟.

For you have exalted · **your** name
and your word a-·**bove** everything.
On the day I called, · **you** answered_me,
you increased my · **strength** of soul. ℟.

For though the Lord is high,
  he regards · **the** lowly;
but the haughty he perceives
  from · **far_a**-way.
Your steadfast love, O Lord,
  endures · **for**-ever.
Do not forsake the · **work_of** your hands. R.

©2010 Gordon Johnston/Novalis

SECOND READING *(Romans 11.33-36)*

O the depth of the riches and wisdom and knowledge of God! How unsearchable are his judgments and how inscrutable his ways! "For who has known the mind of the Lord? Or who has been his counsellor?" "Or who has given a gift to him, to receive a gift in return?" For from him and through him and to him are all things. To him be the glory forever. Amen.

The word of the Lord. **Thanks be to God.**

GOSPEL ACCLAMATION *(Matthew 16.18)*

Alleluia. Alleluia. You are Peter, and on this rock I will build my Church; the gates of Hades will not prevail against it. **Alleluia.**

GOSPEL *(Matthew 16.13-20)*

A reading from the holy Gospel according to Matthew. **Glory to you, Lord.**

When Jesus came into the district of Caesarea Philippi, he asked his disciples, "Who do people say that the Son of Man is?" And they said, "Some say John the Baptist, but others Elijah, and still others Jeremiah or one of the Prophets."

He said to them, "But who do you say that I am?" Simon Peter answered, "You are the Christ, the Son of the living God."

And Jesus answered him, "Blessed are you, Simon son of Jonah! For flesh and blood has not revealed this to you, but my Father in heaven. And I tell you, you are Peter, and on this rock I will build my Church, and the gates of Hades will not prevail against it. I will give you the keys of the kingdom of heaven, and whatever you bind on earth will be bound in heaven, and whatever you loose on earth will be loosed in heaven."

Then Jesus sternly ordered the disciples not to tell anyone that he was the Christ.

The Gospel of the Lord. **Praise to you, Lord Jesus Christ.**

PROFESSION OF FAITH *(p. 13-14)*

PRAYER OF THE FAITHFUL

The following intentions are suggestions only.

R̫ **Lord, hear our prayer.**

For all Christians, and all people of faith, sharing in the work of building up the reign of God, we pray to the Lord: R̫

For those who work, publicly and privately, to end unjust structures that oppress the poor and the powerless, we pray to the Lord: R̫

For those who feel excluded or unwelcome in our communities, we pray to the Lord: R̫

For continuing life in the Spirit for all World Youth Day participants who are returning home from Madrid, we pray to the Lord: R̫

For us, called in baptism to welcome all in God's name, we pray to the Lord: R̲

PREPARATION OF THE GIFTS *(p. 15)*

PRAYER OVER THE GIFTS

Merciful God, the perfect sacrifice of Jesus Christ made us your people. In your love, grant peace and unity to your Church.

PREFACE *(Sundays in Ordinary Time, p. 20)*

COMMUNION ANTIPHON *(Psalm 104.13-15)*

Lord, the earth is filled with your gift from heaven; man grows bread from earth, and wine to cheer his heart.

PRAYER AFTER COMMUNION

Lord, may this eucharist increase within us the healing power of your love. May it guide and direct our efforts to please you in all things.

BLESSING AND DISMISSAL *(p. 67)*

Peter and Jeremiah, in today's readings, feel mis-led, steered in the wrong direction. They've ended up some place they had no intention of going.

Peter had just got the right answer. In last Sunday's gospel, Jesus asked: "Who do you say that I am?" Peter answered, "the Christ, the Son of the Living God," and was praised. But now: "Get behind me, Satan!" His idea of what it means to be the Christ was not the same as God's.

Jeremiah complains that he's been "enticed." He's been chosen to be a prophet, to proclaim God's word... but he's wishing that privilege had gone to someone else. All he gets to talk about is "violence and destruction." He can't stop, though: God's word burns within him.

What happened to Jeremiah and Peter happens to all of us, albeit less dramatically. To be a Christian, to be on the journey of discipleship, is to have our life changed, to be led in unexpected ways. Sometimes, it's in ways we'd rather not go: taking up our cross. However we encounter God, it means change: in a vision, or through Scripture; in a favourite hymn or a sunset; in the words of a friend. We are moved along the unpredictable path of discipleship through all of our encounters with God. In fact, all encounters with God should come with a warning label: "will lead to conversion."

Dinah Simmons, Halifax, NS

ENTRANCE ANTIPHON *(Psalm 86.3, 5)*

I call to you all day long, have mercy on me, O Lord. You are good and forgiving, full of love for all who call to you.

INTRODUCTORY RITES *(p. 7)*

OPENING PRAYER

Almighty God, every good thing comes from you. Fill our hearts with love for you, increase our faith, and by your constant care protect the good you have given us.

FIRST READING *(Jeremiah 20.7-9)*

O Lord, you have enticed me, and I was enticed; you have overpowered me, and you have prevailed. I have become a laughingstock all day long; everyone mocks me. For whenever I speak, I must cry out, I must shout, "Violence and destruction!" For the word of the Lord has become for me a reproach and derision all day long.

If I say, "I will not mention him, or speak any more in his name," then within me there is something like a burning fire shut up in my bones; I am weary with holding it in, and I cannot.

The word of the Lord. **Thanks be to God.**

RESPONSORIAL PSALM *(Psalm 63)*

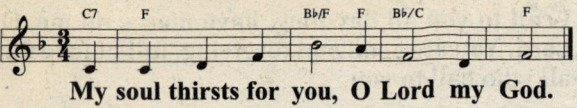

My soul thirsts for you, O Lord my God.

R. **My soul thirsts for you, O Lord my God.**

O God, you are my God, I · **seek_you,**
my soul · **thirsts_for_you;**
my flesh · **faints_for_you,**
as in a dry and weary land
    where there · **is** no water. R.

So I have looked upon you in the · **sanctuary,**
beholding your power and · **glory.**
Because your steadfast love is better than · **life,**
my · **lips** will praise_you. R.

So I will bless you as long as I · **live;**
I will lift up my hands and call on your · **name.**
My soul is satisfied as with a rich · **feast,**
and my mouth praises you
    with · **joy**-ful lips. R.

For you have been my · **help,**
and in the shadow of your wings I sing for · **joy.**
My soul · **clings_to_you;**
your right · **hand** up-holds_me. R.

©2009 Gordon Johnston/Novalis

SECOND READING *(Romans 12.1-2)*

I appeal to you, brothers and sisters, by the mercies of God, to present your bodies as a living sacrifice, holy and acceptable to God, which is your spiritual worship. Do not be conformed to this world, but be transformed by the renewing of your minds, so that you may discern what is the will of God — what is good and acceptable and perfect.

The word of the Lord. **Thanks be to God.**

GOSPEL ACCLAMATION *(See Eph 1.17-18)*

Alleluia. Alleluia. May the Father of our Lord Jesus Christ enlighten the eyes of our heart, that we might know the hope to which we are called. **Alleluia.**

GOSPEL *(Matthew 16.21-27)*

A reading from the holy Gospel according to Matthew. **Glory to you, Lord.**

Jesus began to show his disciples that he must go to Jerusalem and undergo great suffering at the hands of the elders and chief priests and scribes, and be killed, and on the third day be raised.

And Peter took Jesus aside and began to rebuke him, saying, "God forbid it, Lord! This must never happen to you." But he turned and said to Peter, "Get behind me, Satan! You are a stumbling block to me; for you are thinking not as God does, but as humans do."

Then Jesus told his disciples, "If anyone wants to become my follower, let him deny himself and take up his cross and follow me. For whoever wants to save their life will lose it, and whoever loses their life for my sake will find it. For what will it profit anyone to gain the whole world but forfeit their life? Or what will anyone give in return for their life?

• "For the Son of Man is to come with his Angels in the glory of his Father, and then he will repay each according to their work."

The Gospel of the Lord. **Praise to you, Lord Jesus Christ.**

PROFESSION OF FAITH *(p. 13-14)*

PRAYER OF THE FAITHFUL

The following intentions are suggestions only.

R. **Lord, hear our prayer.**

For the Church, witness in Christ's name to the dignity and equality of all people, we pray to the Lord: R.

For leaders of countries who work together to protect the environment, fragile gift of God's creation, we pray to the Lord: R.

For those among us excluded from society for whatever reason, we pray to the Lord: R.

For us, called in baptism to make room at God's table for all people, we pray to the Lord: R.

PREPARATION OF THE GIFTS *(p. 15)*

PRAYER OVER THE GIFTS

Lord, may this holy offering bring us your blessing and accomplish within us its promise of salvation.

PREFACE *(Sundays in Ordinary Time, p. 20)*

COMMUNION ANTIPHON *(Psalm 31.19)*

O Lord, how great is the depth of the kindness which you have shown to those who love you.

PRAYER AFTER COMMUNION

Lord, you renew us at your table with the bread of life. May this food strengthen us in love and help us to serve you in each other.

BLESSING AND DISMISSAL *(p. 67)*

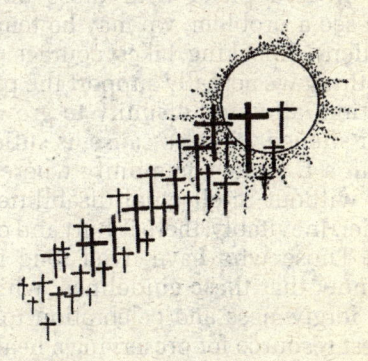

When was the last time you heard someone say, "I'm not talking to that person any more"? This may be a natural response to being hurt, but it is not usually a fruitful one. Today's readings offer the most helpful guidelines to be found anywhere for handling conflict and restoring unity.

In the gospel, Jesus gives simple, respectful directives for talking with the person who is offending. Paul, in Romans, reminds us of the commandments by which we live, and the spirit in which we are to speak: "love does no harm to a neighbour." The psalmist urges us not to harden our hearts, but to remain open, grateful. And in the reading from Ezekiel, God warns the prophet to speak up and plead with those offending. When we see a problem, we may be tempted to remain silent. Speaking takes courage, but by saying nothing we actually support the problematic situation, allowing disunity to grow. Eventually, our silence will also cause us suffering.

I live in a L'Arche community where people with and without intellectual disabilities share life together. Inevitably, there is hurt and disunity by times. Those who have lived long in community know that these guidelines, which give space for forgiveness and celebration to return, are our best resource for preserving a healthy life together.

Beth Porter, Richmond Hill, ON

ENTRANCE ANTIPHON *(Psalm 119.137, 124)*

Lord, you are just, and the judgments you make are right. Show mercy when you judge me, your servant.

INTRODUCTORY RITES *(p. 7)*

OPENING PRAYER

God our Father, you redeem us and make us your children in Christ. Look upon us, give us true freedom and bring us to the inheritance you promised.

FIRST READING *(Ezekiel 33.7-9)*

Thus says the Lord: "So you, O son of man, I have made a watchman for the house of Israel; whenever you hear a word from my mouth, you shall give them warning from me.

"If I say to the wicked, 'O wicked one, you shall surely die,' and you do not speak to warn the wicked to turn from their ways, the wicked person shall die in their iniquity, but their blood I will require at your hand.

"But if you warn the wicked person to turn from their ways, and they do not turn from their ways, they shall die in their iniquity, but you will have saved your life."

The word of the Lord. **Thanks be to God.**

RESPONSORIAL PSALM *(Psalm 95)*

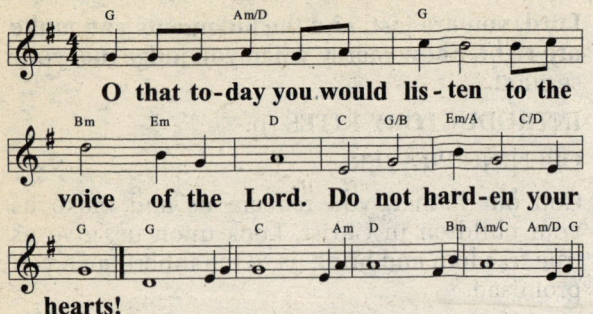

O that to-day you would lis-ten to the voice of the Lord. Do not hard-en your hearts!

R. **O that today you would listen to the voice of the Lord. Do not harden your hearts!**

O come, let us sing to · **the** Lord;
let us make a joyful noise to the rock of
our · **sal**-vation!
Let us come into his presence
with · **thanks**-giving;
let us make a joyful noise to him
with songs · **of** praise! R.

O come, let us worship and · **bow** down,
let us kneel before the Lord, · **our** Maker!
For he is our God, and we are the people
of · **his** pasture,
and the sheep of · **his** hand. R.

O that today you would listen to · **his** voice!
Do not harden your hearts, as at Meribah,
as on the day at Massah in · **the** wilderness,
when your ancestors tested me,
and put me to · **the** proof,
though they had seen · **my** work. R.

SECOND READING *(Romans 13.8-10)*

Brothers and sisters: Owe no one anything, except to love one another; for the one who loves another has fulfilled the law.

The commandments, "You shall not commit adultery; You shall not murder; You shall not steal; You shall not covet"; and any other commandment, are summed up in this word, "Love your neighbour as yourself."

Love does no wrong to a neighbour; therefore, love is the fulfilling of the law.

The word of the Lord. **Thanks be to God.**

GOSPEL ACCLAMATION *(See 2 Cor 5.19)*

Alleluia. Alleluia. In Christ, God was reconciling the world to himself, and entrusting the message of reconciliation to us. **Alleluia.**

GOSPEL *(Matthew 18.15-20)*

A reading from the holy Gospel according to Matthew. **Glory to you, Lord.**

Jesus spoke to his disciples. "If your brother or sister sins against you, go and point out the fault when the two of you are alone. If he or she listens to you, you have regained your brother or sister. But if the person does not listen, take one or two others along with you, so that every word may be confirmed by the evidence of two or three witnesses. If the person refuses to listen to them, tell it to the Church; and if that person refuses to listen even to the Church, let such a one be to you as a Gentile and a tax collector.

"Truly I tell you, whatever you bind on earth will be bound in heaven, and whatever you loose on earth will be loosed in heaven. Again, truly I tell you, if two of you agree on earth about anything you ask, it will be done for you by my Father in heaven. For where two or three are gathered in my name, I am there among them."

The Gospel of the Lord. **Praise to you, Lord Jesus Christ.**

PROFESSION OF FAITH *(p. 13-14)*

PRAYER OF THE FAITHFUL

The following intentions are suggestions only.

R. **Lord, hear our prayer.**

For the Church and all its ministers, on whom the Spirit pours out the gift of wisdom, we pray to the Lord: R.

For world leaders, standing in need of wisdom, prudence and a passion for justice and compassion as they respond to our world's problems, we pray to the Lord: R.

For the needy and suffering, reaching out for God's healing strength, peace and joy, we pray to the Lord: R.

For us, God's people gathered here, on whom God pours out wisdom and love, we pray to the Lord: R.

PREPARATION OF THE GIFTS *(p. 15)*

PRAYER OVER THE GIFTS

God of peace and love, may our offering bring you true worship and make us one with you.

PREFACE *(Sundays in Ordinary Time, p. 20)*

COMMUNION ANTIPHON *(Psalm 42.1-2)*

Like a deer that longs for running streams, my soul longs for you, my God. My soul is thirsting for the living God.

PRAYER AFTER COMMUNION

Lord, your word and your sacrament give us food and life. May this gift of your Son lead us to share his life for ever.

BLESSING AND DISMISSAL *(p. 67)*

What a puzzle a human being is! Take that slave in today's gospel passage. His debt was enormous. The king was entitled to balance his books by selling the slave, his few possessions and even his wife and children — possibly to different owners. But the slave asked for patience on the part of the king and was granted mercy in abundance. The king erased his entire debt! This was beyond what the slave had hoped or asked for. His money problems were gone in an instant.

You'd think this slave would be overflowing with 'the milk of human kindness.' But no! He had his neighbour thrown into debtors' prison. Truly, this slave's behaviour does not make sense. Sin seldom makes sense. We're led to ask, "What were you thinking?!" When we take time to reflect on our own misdeeds, we realize that we should have known better; we do know better. This is the mystery of sin.

The king's behaviour doesn't make sense either. Who in their right mind would simply erase such a large debt? Who could be so gracious? Who but God, the true king! God's grace is also a mystery. As we leave the liturgy today, we are sent forth in the peace of Christ, carrying within us God's mercy and forgiveness which are meant to be passed on to those we meet this week.

Margaret Bick, Toronto, ON

ENTRANCE ANTIPHON *(See Sirach 36.21-22)*

Give peace, Lord, to those who wait for you and your prophets will proclaim you as you deserve. Hear the prayers of your servant and of your people Israel.

INTRODUCTORY RITES *(p. 7)*

OPENING PRAYER

Almighty God, our creator and guide, may we serve you with all our heart and know your forgiveness in our lives.

FIRST READING *(Sirach 27.30 – 28.7)*

Anger and wrath, these are abominations, yet a sinner holds on to them. The vengeful person will face the Lord's vengeance, for he keeps a strict account of their sins. Forgive your neighbour the wrong that is done, and then your sins will be pardoned when you pray.

Does anyone harbour anger against another, and expect healing from the Lord? If one has no mercy toward another like oneself, can one then seek pardon for one's own sins? If one who is but flesh harbours wrath, who will make an atoning sacrifice for that person's sins?

Remember the end of your life, and set enmity aside; remember corruption and death, and be true to the commandments. Remember the commandments, and do not be angry with your neighbour; remember the covenant of the Most High, and overlook faults.

The word of the Lord. **Thanks be to God.**

RESPONSORIAL PSALM *(Psalm 103)*

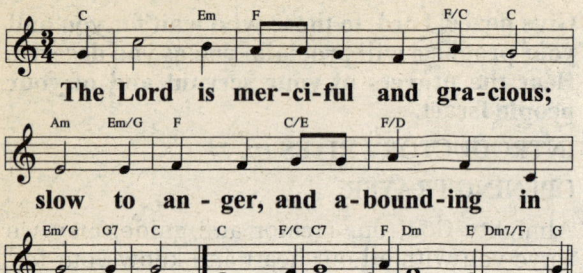

The Lord is mer-ci-ful and gra-cious;
slow to an - ger, and a-bound-ing in
stead-fast love.

R̶ **The Lord is merciful and gracious;**
slow to anger,
and abounding in steadfast love.

Bless the Lord, O my · **soul,**
and all that is within me,
   bless his · **holy** name.
Bless the Lord, O my · **soul,**
and do not forget all · **his** benefits. R̶

It is the Lord who forgives all your in-·**iquity,**
who heals all your · **dis**-eases,
who redeems your life from the · **Pit,**
·who crowns you with steadfast love
   · **and** mercy. R̶

He will not always ac-·**cuse,**
nor will he keep his anger · **for**-ever.
He does not deal with us according
   to our · **sins,**
nor repay us according to our · **in**-iquities. R̶

For as the heavens are high above the · **earth,**
so great is his steadfast love
    toward those · **who** fear_him;
as far as the east is from the · **west,**
· so far he removes our transgressions
    · **from** us. R.

©2010 Gordon Johnston/Novalis

SECOND READING *(Romans 14.7-9)*

Brothers and sisters: We do not live to ourselves, and we do not die to ourselves. If we live, we live to the Lord, and if we die, we die to the Lord; so then, whether we live or whether we die, we are the Lord's. For to this end Christ died and lived again, so that he might be Lord of both the dead and the living.

The word of the Lord. **Thanks be to God.**

GOSPEL ACCLAMATION *(John 13.34)*

Alleluia. Alleluia. I give you a new commandment: love one another just as I have loved you. **Alleluia.**

GOSPEL *(Matthew 18.21-35)*

A reading from the holy Gospel according to Matthew. **Glory to you, Lord.**

Peter came and said to Jesus, "Lord, how often should I forgive my brother or sister if they sin against me? As many as seven times?" Jesus said to him, "Not seven times, but, I tell you, seventy-seven times.

"For this reason the kingdom of heaven may be compared to a king who wished to settle accounts with his slaves. When he began the reckoning, one who owed him ten thousand talents was brought to him; and, as he could not pay, his lord ordered him to be sold, together with his wife and children and all his possessions, and payment to be made. So the slave fell on his knees before him, saying, 'Have patience with me, and I will pay you everything.' The lord of that slave released him and forgave him the debt.

"But that same slave, as he went out, came upon one of his fellow slaves who owed him a hundred denarii; and seizing him by the throat, he said, 'Pay what you owe.' Then his fellow slave fell down and pleaded with him, 'Have patience with me, and I will pay you.' But he refused; then he went and threw him into prison until he would pay the debt.

"When his fellow slaves saw what had happened, they were greatly distressed, and they went and reported to their lord all that had taken place. Then his lord summoned him and said to him, 'You wicked slave! I forgave you all that debt because you pleaded with me. Should you not have had mercy on your fellow slave, as I had mercy on you?' And in anger his lord handed him over to be tortured until he would pay his entire debt.

"So my heavenly Father will also do to every one of you, if you do not forgive your brother or sister from your heart."

The Gospel of the Lord. **Praise to you, Lord Jesus Christ.**

PROFESSION OF FAITH *(p. 13-14)*

PRAYER OF THE FAITHFUL

The following intentions are suggestions only.

R. **Lord, hear our prayer.**

For the reconciliation of all Christians, called to be sacraments of God's unconditional love and infinite compassion, we pray to the Lord: R.

For the leaders of all nations and their peoples, entrusted as stewards of God's creation, we pray to the Lord: R.

For those whose anger, resentment and bitterness have caused them to withdraw, and for those who await their return, we pray to the Lord: R.

For us, God's people, called to stretch out our arms to all, we pray to the Lord: R.

PREPARATION OF THE GIFTS *(p. 15)*

PRAYER OVER THE GIFTS

Lord, hear the prayers of your people and receive our gifts. May the worship of each one here bring salvation to all.

PREFACE *(Sundays in Ordinary Time, p. 20)*

COMMUNION ANTIPHON *(See 1 Cor 10.16)*

When we break the bread, we share in the body of the Lord; when we bless the cup, we share in the blood of Christ.

PRAYER AFTER COMMUNION

Lord, may the eucharist you have given us influence our thoughts and actions. May your Spirit guide and direct us in your way.

BLESSING AND DISMISSAL *(p. 67)*

An amazingly generous landowner in today's gospel stretches our idea about what is fair and just. As we listen to the story of the vineyard labourers being hired at various times throughout the day for the same wage, we sympathize with those who, after bearing the heat of the day, expected a better wage than the latecomers. Here Jesus invites us to go deeper.

The generous landowner's hiring practice was not based on performance, hours worked, or production quotas, but on the ideal that each labourer would take home an adequate wage to feed their families. In his day-long search for workers for the vineyard, the landowner shows a striking compassion for all labourers and a deep sense of inclusive justice.

Generosity and justice, mercy and compassion, are key qualities in the kingdom of God. They enable just relationships to flourish, broken ones to heal, the weak to share in God's bounty along with those who have fared better in life.

To what does this parable invite us today? Is it not about living generously as signs and witnesses to the reign of God? God's passion is to invite all peoples to discover how valued they are and to live in the joy and goodness of the kingdom. Let us pray for our own generosity to be stretched and our compassion to grow in the spirit of our amazing God.

Michael Traher, Scarborough, ON

ENTRANCE ANTIPHON

I am the Saviour of all people, says the Lord. Whatever their troubles, I will answer their cry, and l will always be their Lord.

INTRODUCTORY RITES *(p. 7)*

OPENING PRAYER

Father, guide us as you guide creation according to your law of love. May we love one another and come to perfection in the eternal life prepared for us.

FIRST READING *(Isaiah 55.6-9)*

Seek the Lord while he may be found,
call upon him while he is near;
let the wicked person forsake their way,
and the unrighteous person their thoughts;
let that person return to the Lord
  that he may have mercy on them,
and to our God, for he will abundantly pardon.

For my thoughts are not your thoughts,
nor are your ways my ways, says the Lord.
For as the heavens are higher than the earth,
so are my ways higher than your ways
and my thoughts than your thoughts.

The word of the Lord. **Thanks be to God.**

RESPONSORIAL PSALM *(Psalm 145)*

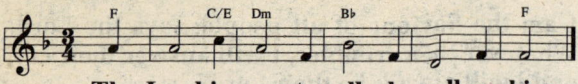

The Lord is near to all who call on him.

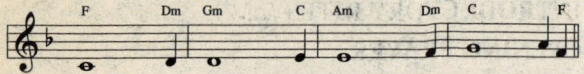

R̰. **The Lord is near to all who call on him.**

Every day I will · **bless_you,**
and praise your name forever and · **ever.**
Great is the Lord, and greatly to be · **praised;**
his greatness is · **un**-searchable. R̰.

The Lord is gracious and · **merciful,**
slow to anger and abounding
  in steadfast · **love.**
The Lord is good to · **all,**
and his compassion is over all
  that he · **has** made. R̰.

The Lord is just in all his · **ways,**
and kind in all his · **doings.**
The Lord is near to all who · **call_on_him,**
to all who call on him · **in** truth. R̰.

SECOND READING *(Philippians 1.20-24, 27)*

Brothers and sisters: Christ will be exalted now as
always in my body, whether by life or by death.
For to me, living is Christ and dying is gain. If I
am to live in the flesh, that means fruitful labour
for me; and I do not know which I prefer. I am
hard pressed between the two: my desire is to
depart and be with Christ, for that is far better; but

to remain in the flesh is more necessary for you. Live your life in a manner worthy of the Gospel of Christ.

The word of the Lord. **Thanks be to God.**

GOSPEL ACCLAMATION *(See Acts 16.14)*

Alleluia. Alleluia. Open our hearts, O Lord, to listen to the words of your Son. **Alleluia.**

GOSPEL *(Matthew 20.1-16)*

A reading from the holy Gospel according to Matthew. **Glory to you, Lord.**

Jesus spoke this parable to his disciples. "The kingdom of heaven is like a landowner who went out early in the morning to hire labourers for his vineyard. After agreeing with the labourers for the usual daily wage, he sent them into his vineyard. When he went out about nine o'clock, he saw others standing idle in the marketplace; and he said to them, 'You also go into the vineyard, and I will pay you whatever is right.' So they went.

"When he went out again about noon and about three o'clock, he did the same. And about five o'clock he went out and found others standing around; and he said to them, 'Why are you standing here idle all day?' They said to him, 'Because no one has hired us.' He said to them, 'You also go into the vineyard.'

"When evening came, the owner of the vineyard said to his manager, 'Call the labourers and give them their pay, beginning with the last and then going to the first.' When those hired about five o'clock came, each of them received the usual daily wage.

"Now when the first came, they thought they would receive more; but each of them also received the usual daily wage. And when they received it, they grumbled against the landowner, saying, 'These last  worked only one hour, and you have made them equal to us who have borne the burden of the day and the scorching heat.' But he replied to one of them, 'Friend, I am doing you no wrong; did you not agree with me for the usual daily wage? Take what belongs to you and go; I choose to give to this last the same as I give to you. Am I not allowed to do what I choose with what belongs to me? Or are you envious because I am generous?'

"So the last will be first, and the first will be last."

The Gospel of the Lord. **Praise to you, Lord Jesus Christ.**

PROFESSION OF FAITH *(p. 13-14)*

PRAYER OF THE FAITHFUL

The following intentions are suggestions only.

℟ **Lord, hear our prayer.**

For the Church, entrusted with the riches of the Gospel of life, we pray to the Lord: ℟

For those who govern nations and hold offices of authority, called to serve their people and the common good, we pray to the Lord: ℟

For the poor and needy of our world, defenceless against those who oppress them, we pray to the Lord: ℟

For us, God's people gathered here today, called to nurture true justice and resist the temptation to exploit the disadvantaged, we pray to the Lord: ℟.

PREPARATION OF THE GIFTS *(p. 15)*

PRAYER OVER THE GIFTS

Lord, may these gifts which we now offer to show our belief and our love be pleasing to you. May they become for us the eucharist of Jesus Christ your Son.

PREFACE *(Sundays in Ordinary Time, p. 20)*

COMMUNION ANTIPHON *(Psalm 119.4-5)*

You have laid down your precepts to be faithfully kept. May my footsteps be firm in keeping your commands.

PRAYER AFTER COMMUNION

Lord, help us with your kindness. Make us strong through the eucharist. May we put into action the saving mystery we celebrate.

BLESSING AND DISMISSAL *(p. 67)*

At a recent meeting we were naming the personal qualities we were looking for in a search to fill an important position. The first quality mentioned was "follow-through... she has to have follow-through." All of us appreciate those people who actually do what they say they are going to do. We can trust them and depend on them.

In today's gospel Jesus describes two kinds of people — those who say "no" at first but then do it anyhow, and those who say "yes" and don't follow through. In the end, it is those who do God's will who will be judged as righteous. Jesus reminds us that we might be surprised at those we meet in God's kingdom. Tax collectors and prostitutes don't seem like likely candidates. What about drug dealers and crooked politicians in our day? How do they line up against the more religious, law-abiding citizens?

As we celebrate the eucharist, we are a gathering of all kinds of people who are here for all kinds of reasons. It is not for us to judge each other's motivation. What is essential is that all of us are embraced by the unconditional love and mercy of the Creator and by Jesus whose eternal "yes" liberates us to live in the Spirit.

Mary Ellen Green, Sinsinawa, WI

National Collection for the Church in Canada

ENTRANCE ANTIPHON *(Daniel 3)*

O Lord, you had just cause to judge us as you did: because we sinned against you and disobeyed your will. But now show us your greatness of heart, and treat us with your unbounded kindness.

INTRODUCTORY RITES *(p. 7)*

OPENING PRAYER

Father, you show your almighty power in your mercy and forgiveness. Continue to fill us with your gifts of love. Help us to hurry toward the eternal life you promise and come to share in the joys of your kingdom.

FIRST READING *(Ezekiel 18.25-28)*

Thus says the Lord: "You object, O House of Israel! You say, 'The way of the Lord is unfair.' Hear now, O house of Israel: Is my way unfair? Is it not your ways that are unfair?

"When the righteous person turns away from their righteousness and commits iniquity, they shall die for it; for the iniquity that they have committed they shall die.

"Again, when the wicked person turns away from the wickedness they have committed and does what is lawful and right, they shall save their life. Because that person considered and turned away from all the transgressions that they had committed, they shall surely live; they shall not die."

The word of the Lord. **Thanks be to God.**

RESPONSORIAL PSALM *(Psalm 25)*

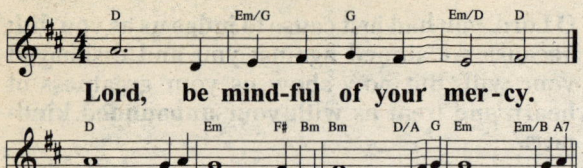

Lord, be mind-ful of your mer-cy.

R. **Lord, be mindful of your mercy.**

Make me to know your ways, · **O** Lord;
teach · **me** your paths.
Lead me in your · **truth,** and teach_me,
for you are the God of · **my** sal-vation. R.

Be mindful of your mercy, O Lord,
 and of your stead-·**fast** love,
for they have been · **from** of old.
According to your steadfast · **love**
 re-member_me,
for the sake of your · **goodness,** O Lord! R.

Good and upright · **is_the** Lord;
therefore he instructs sinners · **in** the way.
He leads the humble in · **what** is right,
and teaches the · **humble** his way. R.

SECOND READING *(Philippians 2.1-11)*

The shorter version ends at the asterisks.

Brothers and sisters: If there is any encouragement in Christ, any consolation from love, any sharing in the Spirit, any compassion and sympathy, then make my joy complete: be of the same mind, having the same love, being in full accord and of one mind. Do nothing from selfish ambition or conceit, but in humility regard others as better than yourselves. Let each of you look not to your own interests, but to the interests of others.

Let the same mind be in you that was in Christ Jesus.

* * *

who, though he was in the form of God,
did not regard equality with God
    as something to be exploited,
but emptied himself, taking the form of a slave,
being born in human likeness.
And being found in human form,
he humbled himself
and became obedient to the point of death —
even death on a cross.

Therefore God highly exalted him
and gave him the name that is above
    every name,
so that at the name of Jesus
    every knee should bend,
in heaven and on earth and under the earth,
and every tongue should confess
    that Jesus Christ is Lord,
to the glory of God the Father.

The word of the Lord. **Thanks be to God.**

GOSPEL ACCLAMATION *(See John 10.27)*

Alleluia. Alleluia. My sheep hear my voice, says the Lord; I know them, and they follow me. **Alleluia.**

GOSPEL *(Matthew 21.28-32)*

A reading from the holy Gospel according to Matthew. **Glory to you, Lord.**

Jesus said to the chief priests and the elders of the people: "What do you think? A man had two sons; he went to the first and said, 'Son, go and work in the vineyard today.' He answered, 'I will not'; but later he changed his mind and went. The father went to the second and said the same; and he answered, 'I am going, sir'; but he did not go. Which of the two did the will of his father?" They said, "The first."

Jesus said to them, "Truly I tell you, the tax collectors and the prostitutes are going into the kingdom of God ahead of you. For John came to you in the way of righteousness and you did not believe him, but the tax collectors and the prostitutes believed him; and even after you saw it, you did not change your minds and believe him."

The Gospel of the Lord. **Praise to you, Lord Jesus Christ.**

PROFESSION OF FAITH *(p. 13-14)*

PRAYER OF THE FAITHFUL

The following intentions are suggestions only.

℟. **Lord, hear our prayer.**

For the Church, called to give up everything that separates us from each other, we pray to the Lord: ℟.

For leaders in Church and society, as they struggle to heal our world so in need of compassion, we pray to the Lord: ℟.

For those among us whom we have rejected, we pray to the Lord: ℟.

For young people everywhere who seek our support in building a world of justice and peace, we pray to the Lord: ℟.

PREPARATION OF THE GIFTS *(p. 15)*

PRAYER OVER THE GIFTS

God of mercy, accept our offering and make it a source of blessing for us.

PREFACE *(Sundays in Ordinary Time, p. 20)*

COMMUNION ANTIPHON *(Psalm 119.49-50)*

O Lord, remember the words you spoke to me, your servant, which made me live in hope and consoled me when I was downcast.

PRAYER AFTER COMMUNION

Lord, may this eucharist in which we proclaim the death of Christ bring us salvation and make us one with him in glory.

BLESSING AND DISMISSAL *(p. 67)*

In today's gospel, Jesus tells a harsh and bloody story that makes a direct and uncompromising point. It must have sent a chill down the spines of his unhappy listeners. After all, who would like being compared to thieves and murderers? Who would like to be told they are going to lose everything?

Almost 2000 years later, we can still feel that uncomfortable chill. And that shouldn't be surprising, for Jesus is speaking just as much to us now as he was to those standing right in front of him in the Temple then. When he says, "the kingdom of God will be taken away from you," he is looking at us, too.

Jesus' message might be painfully clear, but he also never shuts the door. In the very same sentence, he adds that God's kingdom will be "given to a people that produces the fruits of the kingdom."

But what are the fruits of the kingdom and how can we become the kind of people who produce them? Luckily, Paul offers some help today in his letter to the Christians of Philippi. He tells them: Don't worry; pray and ask God for help; then act honourably, justly and with a pure heart.

And if we plant and tend these fruits of the kingdom, we will taste their sweetness at harvest time — "the peace of God, which surpasses all understanding."

Patrick Gallagher, Toronto, ON

ENTRANCE ANTIPHON *(Esther 13.9, 10-11)*

O Lord, you have given everything its place in the world, and no one can make it otherwise. For it is your creation, the heavens and the earth and the stars: You are the Lord of all.

INTRODUCTORY RITES *(p. 7)*

OPENING PRAYER

Father, your love for us surpasses all our hopes and desires. Forgive our failings, keep us in your peace and lead us in the way of salvation.

FIRST READING *(Isaiah 5.1-7)*

Let me sing for my beloved my love song concerning his vineyard:

"My beloved had a vineyard on a very fertile hill. He dug it and cleared it of stones, and planted it with choice vines; he built a watchtower in the midst of it, and hewed out a wine vat in it; he expected it to yield grapes, but it yielded wild grapes.

"And now, inhabitants of Jerusalem and people of Judah, judge between me and my vineyard. What more was there to do for my vineyard that I have not done in it? When I expected it to yield grapes, why did it yield wild grapes?

"And now I will tell you what I will do to my vineyard. I will remove its hedge, and it shall be devoured; I will break down its wall, and it shall be trampled down. I will make it a waste; it shall not be pruned or hoed, and it shall be overgrown with briers and thorns; I will also command the clouds that they rain no rain upon it. For the vineyard of the Lord of hosts is the house of

Israel, and the people of Judah are his pleasant planting; he expected justice, but saw bloodshed; righteousness, but heard a cry!"

The word of the Lord. **Thanks be to God.**

RESPONSORIAL PSALM *(Psalm 80)*

The vine-yard of the Lord is the house of Is-ra-el.

℟. **The vineyard of the Lord is the house of Israel.**

You brought a vine out of · **Egypt;**
you drove out the nations and · **planted_it.**
It sent out its branches to the · **sea,**
and its shoots to · **the** River. ℟.

Why then have you broken down its · **walls,**
so that all who pass along the way
    pluck its · **fruit?**
The boar from the forest · **ravages_it,**
and all that move in the · **field** feed_on_it. ℟.

Turn again, O God of · **hosts;**
look down from heaven, and · **see;**
have regard for this · **vine,**
the stock that your right · **hand** planted. ℟.

Then we will never turn back from · **you;**
give us life, and we will call on your · **name.**
Restore us, O Lord God of · **hosts;**
let your face shine, that we may · **be** saved. ℟.

SECOND READING *(Philippians 4.6-9)*

Brothers and sisters: Do not worry about anything, but in everything by prayer and supplication with thanksgiving let your requests be made known to God. And the peace of God, which surpasses all understanding, will guard your hearts and your minds in Christ Jesus.

Finally, brothers and sisters, whatever is true, whatever is honourable, whatever is just, whatever is pure, whatever is pleasing, whatever is commendable, if there is any excellence and if there is anything worthy of praise, think about these things. Keep on doing the things that you have learned and received and heard and seen in me, and the God of peace will be with you.

The word of the Lord. **Thanks be to God.**

GOSPEL ACCLAMATION *(See John 15.16)*

Alleluia. Alleluia. I have chosen you from the world, says the Lord, to go and bear fruit that will last. **Alleluia.**

GOSPEL *(Matthew 21.33-43)*

A reading from the holy Gospel according to Matthew. **Glory to you, Lord.**

Jesus said to the chief priests and the elders of the people: "Listen to another parable. There was a landowner who planted a vineyard, put a fence around it, dug a wine press in it, and built a watchtower. Then he leased it to tenants and went to another country.

"When the harvest time had come, he sent his slaves to the tenants to collect his produce. But the tenants seized his slaves and beat one, killed another, and stoned another. Again he sent other slaves, more than the first; and they treated them in the same way.

"Finally he sent his son to them, saying, 'They will respect my son.' But when the tenants saw the son, they said to themselves, 'This is the heir; come, let us kill him and get his inheritance.' So they seized him, threw him out of the vineyard, and killed him.

"Now when the owner of the vineyard comes, what will he do to those tenants?" They said to him, "He will put those wretches to a miserable death, and lease the vineyard to other tenants who will give him the produce at the harvest time."

Jesus said to them, "Have you never read in the Scriptures: 'The stone that the builders rejected has become the cornerstone; this was the Lord's doing, and it is amazing in our eyes'?

"Therefore I tell you, the kingdom of God will be taken away from you and given to a people that produces the fruits of the kingdom."

The Gospel of the Lord. **Praise to you, Lord Jesus Christ.**

PROFESSION OF FAITH *(p. 13-14)*

PRAYER OF THE FAITHFUL

The following intentions are suggestions only.

℟. **Lord, hear our prayer.**

For the Church, people of God, entrusted with offering the gift of faith to the world, we pray to the Lord: ℟.

For leaders of the world's peoples, called to help their people grow to the fullness of their human dignity, we pray to the Lord: ℟.

For those who struggle for a share in the bounty of God's creation, we pray to the Lord: ℟.

For us, God's people gathered here, community of faith called to recognize the power entrusted to us, we pray to the Lord: ℟.

PREPARATION OF THE GIFTS *(p. 15)*

PRAYER OVER THE GIFTS

Father, receive these gifts which our Lord Jesus Christ has asked us to offer in his memory. May our obedient service bring us to the fullness of your redemption.

PREFACE *(Sundays in Ordinary Time, p. 20)*

COMMUNION ANTIPHON *(Lamentations 3.25)*

The Lord is good to those who hope in him, to those who are searching for his love.

PRAYER AFTER COMMUNION

Almighty God, let the eucharist we share fill us with your life. May the love of Christ which we celebrate here touch our lives and lead us to you.

BLESSING AND DISMISSAL *(p. 67)*

October 9

28th Sunday
in Ordinary Time

Today's readings speak of abundance: Isaiah of a feast, the psalmist of an overflowing cup, and Paul of a God who satisfies every need. Matthew tells the story of a lavish wedding banquet, of the many who refuse to attend, and then of the one who is mysteriously thrown outside. We search for understanding.

Jesus is a practical teacher: we can relate to his examples. If the kingdom of God is like a wedding feast, we can imagine invitations, good company and good food. We know the usual reply is an immediate and eager *yes*. Yet this is a story of both repeated refusal and consistent determination that this kingdom feast will be filled.

As the celebration finally begins, we are speechless as one of the guests is cast out for improper attire. Perhaps he was not invited to be a mere guest. Perhaps he was invited to join the wedding party: a symbol of his deep, faithful and lasting relationship with the Son of the Father. Of course he would need a wedding robe: a special and beautiful garment made of such qualities as kindness, justice, humility, love and compassion.

We are all invited to share in the banquet and to wear the wedding robe. Simple? Yes. Easy? Not always. We are all called and chosen. Today, we accept the treasured invitation and celebrate this feast with joy.

Brenda Merk Hildebrand, Campbell River, BC

ENTRANCE ANTIPHON *(Psalm 130.3-4)*

If you, O Lord, laid bare our guilt, who could endure it? But you are forgiving, God of Israel.

INTRODUCTORY RITES *(p. 7)*

OPENING PRAYER

Lord, our help and guide, make your love the foundation of our lives. May our love for you express itself in our eagerness to do good for others.

FIRST READING *(Isaiah 25.6-10)*

On this mountain the Lord of hosts will make for all peoples a feast of rich food, a feast of well-aged wines, of rich food filled with marrow, of well-aged wines strained clear.

And he will destroy on this mountain the shroud that is cast over all peoples, the sheet that is spread over all nations; he will swallow up death forever. Then the Lord God will wipe away the tears from all faces, and the disgrace of his people he will take away from all the earth, for the Lord has spoken.

It will be said on that day, "Lo, this is our God; we have waited for him, so that he might save us. This is the Lord for whom we have waited; let us be glad and rejoice in his salvation. For the hand of the Lord will rest on this mountain."

The word of the Lord. **Thanks be to God.**

RESPONSORIAL PSALM *(Psalm 23)*

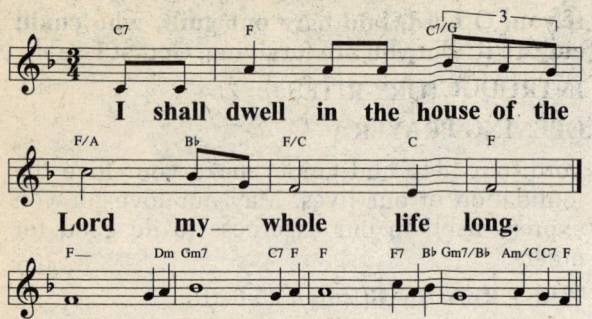

R. **I shall dwell in the house of the Lord
my whole life long.**

The Lord is my shepherd, I shall · **not** want.
He makes me lie down in · **green** pastures;
he leads me be--**side** still waters;
he re--**stores** my soul. R.

He leads me in right paths
    for his · **name's** sake.
Even though I walk through
    the darkest valley, I fear · **no** evil;
for · **you** are with_me;
your rod and your · **staff**—they comfort_me. R.

You prepare a table · **be**-fore_me
in the presence · **of_my** enemies;
you anoint my · **head** with oil;
my · **cup** over-flows. R.

Surely goodness and mercy · **shall** follow_me
all the days of · **my** life,
and I shall dwell in the · **house_of** the Lord
my · **whole** life long. R.

©2010 Gordon Johnston/Novalis

SECOND READING *(Philippians 4.12-14, 19-20)*

Brothers and sisters: I know what it is to have little, and I know what it is to have plenty. In any and all circumstances I have learned the secret of being well-fed and of going hungry, of having plenty and of being in need. I can do all things through him who strengthens me. In any case, it was kind of you to share my distress.

My God will fully satisfy every need of yours according to his riches in glory in Christ Jesus. To our God and Father be glory forever and ever. Amen.

The word of the Lord. **Thanks be to God.**

GOSPEL ACCLAMATION *(See Eph 1.17-18)*

Alleluia. Alleluia. May the Father of our Lord Jesus Christ enlighten the eyes of our heart, that we might know the hope to which we are called. **Alleluia.**

GOSPEL *(Matthew 22.1-14)*

The shorter version ends at the asterisks.

A reading from the holy Gospel according to Matthew. **Glory to you, Lord.**

Once more Jesus spoke to the chief priests and Pharisees in parables: "The kingdom of heaven may be compared to a king who gave a wedding banquet for his son. He sent his slaves to call those who had been invited to the wedding banquet, but they would not come.

"Again he sent other slaves, saying, 'Tell those who have been invited: "Look, I have prepared my dinner, my oxen and my fat calves have been slaughtered, and everything is ready; come to the wedding banquet.'" But they made light of it and went away, one to his farm, another to his business, while the rest seized his slaves, mistreated them, and killed them. The king was enraged. He sent his troops, destroyed those murderers, and burned their city.

"Then he said to his slaves, 'The wedding is ready, but those invited were not worthy. Go therefore into the main streets, and invite everyone you find to the wedding banquet.' Those slaves went out into the streets and gathered all whom they found, both good and bad; so the wedding hall was filled with guests.

* * *

"But when the king came in to see the guests, he noticed a man there who was not wearing a wedding robe, and he said to him, 'Friend, how did you get in here without a wedding robe?' And he was speechless. Then the king said to the attendants, 'Bind him hand and foot, and throw him into the outer darkness, where there will be weeping and gnashing of teeth.' For many are called, but few are chosen."

The Gospel of the Lord. **Praise to you, Lord Jesus Christ.**

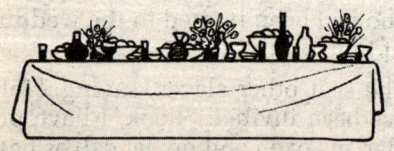

PROFESSION OF FAITH *(p. 13-14)*

PRAYER OF THE FAITHFUL

The following intentions are suggestions only.

R. **Lord, hear our prayer.**

For the Church, a community committed to faith and justice, we pray to the Lord: R.

For the leaders of nations, called to effective action on behalf of the poor, we pray to the Lord: R.

For those whom our society casts out: addicts, refugees, the jobless, the homeless, we pray to the Lord: R.

For us, God's people gathered here, called as a parish to act justly and lovingly, we pray to the Lord: R.

PREPARATION OF THE GIFTS *(p. 15)*

PRAYER OVER THE GIFTS

Lord, accept the prayers and gifts we offer in faith and love. May this eucharist bring us to your glory.

PREFACE *(Sundays in Ordinary Time, p. 20)*

COMMUNION ANTIPHON *(Psalm 34.10)*

The rich suffer want and go hungry, but nothing shall be lacking to those who fear the Lord.

PRAYER AFTER COMMUNION

Almighty Father, may the body and blood of your Son give us a share in his life.

BLESSING AND DISMISSAL *(p. 67)*

In today's first reading, God tells Cyrus, "I call you by your name." I once walked into a church just after Easter and saw a huge banner bearing the words, "Barbara, I have called you by name." My heart skipped a beat! I later learned that "Barbara" was that year's sole RCIA candidate, but for a brief moment the message was mine. God had singled *me* out! What would he ask of me?

In today's gospel, Matthew tells a story which had political implications in Jesus' time. In an attempt to trap Jesus, the Pharisees questioned whether or not the Jews should be paying taxes to their Roman conquerors. Surely whatever he replied would offend someone However, Jesus calmly told them: Give God what is *God's* due and give Caesar what is *his* due. Jesus' message could be similarly interpreted for our time. We are called to love, honour and obey God, our Creator. We are also meant to have our feet firmly planted in the world we live in, gifting others with our love, care and compassion.

God does not call to us with messages splashed across banners. God speaks to us in the silence of our hearts, inviting us to be God's presence in our families, parishes and communities. If we listen, we will *often* hear God call us by our name.

Barbara d'Artois, Pierrefonds, QC

ENTRANCE ANTIPHON *(Psalm 17.6, 8)*

I call upon you, God, for you will answer me; bend your ear and hear my prayer. Guard me as the pupil of your eye; hide me in the shade of your wings.

INTRODUCTORY RITES *(p. 7)*

OPENING PRAYER

Almighty and ever-living God, our source of power and inspiration, give us strength and joy in serving you as followers of Christ.

FIRST READING *(Isaiah 45.1, 4-6)*

Thus says the Lord to his anointed, to Cyrus, whose right hand I have grasped to subdue nations before him and strip kings of their robes, to open doors before him — and the gates shall not be closed:

"For the sake of my servant Jacob, and Israel my chosen, I call you by your name, I surname you, though you do not know me. I am the Lord, and there is no other; besides me there is no god. I arm you, though you do not know me, so that all may know, from the rising of the sun and from the west, that there is no one besides me; I am the Lord, and there is no other."

The word of the Lord. **Thanks be to God.**

RESPONSORIAL PSALM *(Psalm 96)*

As-cribe to the Lord glo-ry and strength.

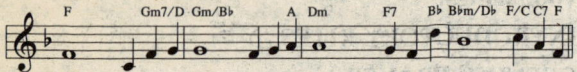

℟. **Ascribe to the Lord glory and strength.**

O sing to the Lord · **a** new song;
sing to the Lord, · **all** the earth.
Declare his glory a·-**mong** the nations,
his marvellous works a·-**mong_all**
   the peoples. ℟.

For great is the Lord, and greatly · **to** be praised;
he is to be revered a·-**bove** all gods.
For all the gods of the · **peoples** are idols,
but the **Lord_made** the heavens. ℟.

Ascribe to the Lord, O families · **of** the peoples,
ascribe to the Lord · **glory** and strength.
Ascribe to the Lord the glory · **due** his name;
bring an offering, and come · **into** his courts. ℟.

Worship the Lord in · **ho**-ly splendour;
tremble before him, · **all** the earth.
Say among the nations, "The · **Lord** is king!
He will judge the · **peoples** with equity," ℟.

©2010 Gordon Johnston/Novalis

SECOND READING *(1 Thessalonians 1.1-5)*

From Paul, Silvanus, and Timothy, to the Church of the Thessalonians in God the Father and the Lord Jesus Christ: Grace to you and peace.

We always give thanks to God for all of you and mention you in our prayers, constantly remembering before our God and Father your work of faith and labour of love and steadfastness of hope in our Lord Jesus Christ. For we know, brothers and sisters beloved by God, that he has chosen you, because our message of the Gospel came to you not in word only, but also in power and in the Holy Spirit and with full conviction.

The word of the Lord. **Thanks be to God.**

GOSPEL ACCLAMATION *(See Phil 2.15-16)*

Alleluia. Alleluia. Shine like stars in the world, holding fast to the word of life. **Alleluia.**

GOSPEL *(Matthew 22.15-21)*

A reading from the holy Gospel according to Matthew. **Glory to you, Lord.**

The Pharisees went and plotted to entrap Jesus in what he said. So they sent their disciples to him, along with the Herodians, saying, "Teacher, we know that you are sincere, and teach the way of God in accordance with truth, and show deference to no one; for you do not regard people with partiality. Tell us, then, what you think. Is it lawful to pay taxes to the emperor, or not?"

But Jesus, aware of their malice, said, "Why are you putting me to the test, you hypocrites? Show me the coin used for the tax." And they brought him a denarius.

Then he said to them, "Whose head is this, and whose title?" They answered, "Caesar's." Then he said to them, "Give therefore to Caesar the things that are Caesar's, and to God the things that are God's."

The Gospel of the Lord. **Praise to you, Lord Jesus Christ.**

PROFESSION OF FAITH *(p. 13-14)*

PRAYER OF THE FAITHFUL

The following intentions are suggestions only.

R̲ **Lord, hear our prayer.**

For the Church and its leaders, called to proclaim Jesus Christ in today's world, we pray to the Lord: R̲

For all who seek God by whatever path, enriching our human community by their spiritual values, we pray to the Lord: R̲

For those who seek meaning in their lives and those who search for hope, we pray to the Lord: R̲

For us, community of faith, entrusted by our baptism to witness to Jesus Christ, we pray to the Lord: R̲

PREPARATION OF THE GIFTS *(p. 15)*

PRAYER OVER THE GIFTS

Lord God, may the gifts we offer bring us your love and forgiveness and give us freedom to serve you with our lives.

PREFACE *(Sundays in Ordinary Time, p. 20)*

COMMUNION ANTIPHON *(Psalm 33.18-19)*

See how the eyes of the Lord are on those who fear him, on those who hope in his love that he may rescue them from death and feed them in time of famine.

PRAYER AFTER COMMUNION

Lord, may this eucharist help us to remain faithful. May it teach us the way to eternal life.

BLESSING AND DISMISSAL *(p. 67)*

As we approach the end of the Church year, we see Jesus teaching us how to live. The message is simple: love. Love of God, neighbour and self go hand in hand; one doesn't exist without the others.

Jesus understood how difficult this way of living could be, but he did not compromise. Those who want to follow him must make love their whole life — not just a part, but to love with one's whole heart (compassion), soul (desire) and mind (decision). Love is a decision to give of ourselves and our resources — personal and material — and Jesus expects that our love of God and neighbour will be the centre and sum of our lives.

Recently I witnessed a person who was begging on the street receive a coin from a passer-by. As they exchanged a greeting, he seemed to pray and give thanks for this gift. Was this a small gift given and received in love? It made me pause and reflect. We all want to be loved and loving.

The daily news shows us how challenging this singular message is. In a world where the word 'love' is used to impress, to sell and even to exert power, Jesus challenges us to see a different way — God's way of love. 'I will listen, for I am compassionate' is a great way to sum it all up.

Carmen Diston, Rome, Italy

ENTRANCE ANTIPHON *(Psalm 105.3-4)*

Let hearts rejoice who search for the Lord. Seek the Lord and his strength, seek always the face of the Lord.

INTRODUCTORY RITES *(p. 7)*

OPENING PRAYER

Almighty and ever-living God, strengthen our faith, hope, and love. May we do with loving hearts what you ask of us and come to share the life you promise.

FIRST READING *(Exodus 22.21-27)*

Thus says the Lord: "You shall not wrong or oppress a resident alien, for you were aliens in the land of Egypt. You shall not abuse any widow or orphan. If you do abuse them, when they cry out to me, I will surely heed their cry; my wrath will burn, and I will kill you with the sword, and your wives shall become widows and your children orphans.

"If you lend money to my people, to the poor one among you, you shall not deal with them as a creditor; you shall not exact interest from them. If you take your neighbour's cloak in pawn, you shall restore it to that person before the sun goes down; for it may be their only clothing to use as cover; in what else shall that person sleep? And if that person cries out to me, I will listen, for I am compassionate."

The word of the Lord. **Thanks be to God.**

RESPONSORIAL PSALM *(Psalm 18)*

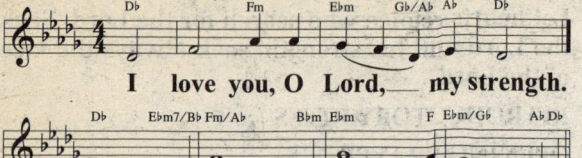

R. **I love you, O Lord, my strength.**

I love you, O Lord, my · **strength.**
The Lord is my rock, my fortress,
   and my de-·**liverer.**
My God, my rock in whom I take · **refuge,**
my shield, and the source
   of my salvation, · **my** stronghold. R.

I call upon the Lord, who is worthy
   to be · **praised,**
so I shall be saved from my · **enemies.**
From his temple he heard my · **voice,**
and my cry to him reached · **his** ears. R.

The Lord lives! Blessed be my · **rock,**
and exalted be the God of my sal-·**vation,**
Great triumphs he gives to his · **king,**
and shows steadfast love to · **his_a**-nointed. R.

SECOND READING *(1 Thessalonians 1.5-10)*

Brothers and sisters: You know what kind of
persons we proved to be among you for your
sake. And you became imitators of us and of the
Lord, for in spite of persecution you received
the word with joy inspired by the Holy Spirit, so
that you became an example to all the believers
in Macedonia and in Achaia. For the word of

the Lord has sounded forth from you not only in Macedonia and Achaia, but in every place your faith in God has become known, so that we have no need to speak about it. For the people of those regions report about us what kind of welcome we had among you, and how you turned to God from idols, to serve a living and true God, and to wait for his Son from heaven, whom he raised from the dead — Jesus, who rescues us from the wrath that is coming.

The word of the Lord. **Thanks be to God.**

GOSPEL ACCLAMATION *(John 14.23)*

Alleluia. Alleluia. The one who loves me will keep my word and my Father will love him and we will come to him. **Alleluia.**

GOSPEL *(Matthew 22.34-40)*

A reading from the holy Gospel according to Matthew. **Glory to you, Lord.**

When the Pharisees heard that Jesus had silenced the Sadducees, they gathered together, and one of them, a lawyer, asked him a question to test him. "Teacher, which commandment in the Law is the greatest?"

Jesus said to him, "'You shall love the Lord your God with all your heart, and with all your soul, and with all your mind.' This is the greatest and first commandment.

"And a second is like it: 'You shall love your neighbour as yourself.' On these two commandments hang all the Law and the Prophets."

The Gospel of the Lord. **Praise to you, Lord Jesus Christ.**

PROFESSION OF FAITH *(p. 13-14)*

PRAYER OF THE FAITHFUL

The following intentions are suggestions only.

R. **Lord, hear our prayer.**

For the Church, sacrament of God's forgiveness in word and action, we pray to the Lord: R.

For leaders, entrusted with the protection and promotion of the common good, we pray to the Lord: R.

For all who search for forgiveness and for those who reach out to them, we pray to the Lord: R.

For us, God's holy people, called to offer each other God's mercy and forgiveness in our local community, we pray to the Lord: R.

PREPARATION OF THE GIFTS *(p. 15)*

PRAYER OVER THE GIFTS

Lord God of power and might, receive the gifts we offer and let our service give you glory.

PREFACE *(Sundays in Ordinary Time, p. 20)*

COMMUNION ANTIPHON *(Ephesians 5.2)*

Christ loved us and gave himself up for us as a fragrant offering to God.

PRAYER AFTER COMMUNION

Lord, bring to perfection within us the communion we share in this sacrament. May our celebration have an effect in our lives.

BLESSING AND DISMISSAL *(p. 67)*

As autumn moves to winter and the days get shorter, we seek ways to bring light into our lives. Everyone recognizes the contrast between the glow of one candle and complete darkness, for a single candle can make a difference in how and what we see.

In today's readings, we cannot fail to note the contrast between Paul's attitude in the second reading and that of the scribes and Pharisees of the gospel.

The scribes and Pharisees of whom Jesus speaks are focused entirely on themselves: how they might be honoured and recognized. Yet they do nothing to earn this, but only lay burdens on the people. Their focus on themselves is in stark contrast to Paul's attitude toward the Thessalonians. Paul made no demands on the community. He was gentle with them and so reflected the light and warmth of God. We can imagine that the community responded not only to what Paul said but to how he lived, and so recognized Paul's words as the words of God.

These readings lead us to ponder our own lives, to see whether how we live reflects the attitude of the priests, scribes and Pharisees or that of Paul. As eucharistic people we, like Paul, are invited to proclaim, by the light and warmth of our lives, God's presence to all we meet.

Barbara Bozak Windsor, CT

ENTRANCE ANTIPHON *(Psalm 38.21-22)*

Do not abandon me, Lord. My God, do not go away from me! Hurry to help me, Lord, my Saviour.

INTRODUCTORY RITES *(p. 7)*

OPENING PRAYER

God of power and mercy, only with your help can we offer you fitting service and praise. May we live the faith we profess and trust your promise of eternal life.

FIRST READING (*Malachi 1.14 – 2.2, 8-10)*

"I am a great King," says the Lord of hosts, "and my name is reverenced among the nations.

"And now, O priests, this command is for you. If you will not listen, if you will not lay it to heart to give glory to my name," says the Lord of hosts, "then I will send the curse on you and I will curse your blessings; indeed I have already cursed them, because you do not lay it to heart.

"You have turned aside from the way; you have caused many to stumble by your instruction; you have corrupted the covenant of Levi," says the Lord of hosts, "and so I make you despised and abased before all the people, inasmuch as you have not kept my ways but have shown partiality in your instruction."

Have we not all one father? Has not one God created us? Why then are we faithless to one another, profaning the covenant of our ancestors?

The word of the Lord. **Thanks be to God.**

RESPONSORIAL PSALM *(Psalm 131)*

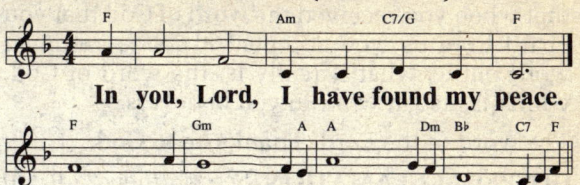

In you, Lord, I have found my peace.

℟. **In you, Lord, I have found my peace.**

O Lord, my heart is not lifted · **up,**
my eyes are not raised · **too** high;
I do not occupy myself · **with** things
too great and too · **marvellous** for me. ℟.

But I have calmed and quieted my · **soul,**
like a weaned child with · **its** mother;
my soul is like the · **weaned** child
that · **is** with me. ℟.

1- O Israel, hope in the · **Lord**
4- from this time on and for-·**ev**-er-more. ℟.

©2010 Gordon Johnston/Novalis

SECOND READING *(1 Thessalonians 2.7-9, 13)*

Brothers and sisters: Though we might have made demands as Apostles of Christ, we were gentle among you, like a nurse tenderly caring for her own children. So deeply do we care for you that we are determined to share with you not only the Gospel of God but also our own selves, because you have become very dear to us. You remember our labour and toil, brothers and sisters; we worked night and day, so that we might not burden any of you while we proclaimed to you the Gospel of God.

We also constantly give thanks to God for this, that when you received the word of God that you heard from us, you accepted it not as a human word but as what it really is, the word of God, which is also at work in you believers.

The word of the Lord. **Thanks be to God.**

GOSPEL ACCLAMATION *(See Matthew 23.9, 10)*

Alleluia. Alleluia. You have one Father, your Father in heaven; you have one teacher, the Lord Jesus Christ! **Alleluia.**

GOSPEL *(Matthew 23.1-12)*

A reading from the holy Gospel according to Matthew. **Glory to you, Lord.**

Then Jesus said to the crowds and to his disciples, "The scribes and the Pharisees sit in Moses' chair; therefore, do whatever they teach you and follow it; but do not do as they do, for they do not practise what they teach. They tie up heavy burdens, hard to bear, and lay them on the shoulders of others; but they themselves are unwilling to lift a finger to move them. They do all their deeds to be seen by others; for they make their phylacteries broad and their fringes long.  They love to have the place of honour at banquets and the best seats in the synagogues, and to be greeted with respect in the marketplaces, and to have people call them rabbi.

"But you are not to be called rabbi, for you have one teacher, and you are all brothers and sisters.

And call no one your father on earth, for you have one Father — the one in heaven. Nor are you to be called instructors, for you have one instructor, the Christ. The greatest among you will be your servant. Whoever exalts himself will be humbled, and whoever humbles himself will be exalted."

The Gospel of the Lord. **Praise to you, Lord Jesus Christ.**

PROFESSION OF FAITH *(p. 13-14)*

PRAYER OF THE FAITHFUL

The following intentions are suggestions only.

℟. **Lord, hear our prayer.**

For the Church, sacrament of Christ's salvation offered to all, we pray to the Lord: ℟.

For all leaders, called to serve others through their leadership, we pray to the Lord: ℟.

For the sick and the elderly who struggle to maintain dignity, and for those who care for them, we pray to the Lord: ℟.

For us, God's priestly people gathered here, called to pray daily, we pray to the Lord: ℟.

PREPARATION OF THE GIFTS *(p. 15)*

PRAYER OVER THE GIFTS

God of mercy, may we offer a pure sacrifice for the forgiveness of our sins.

PREFACE *(Sundays in Ordinary Time, p. 20)*

COMMUNION ANTIPHON *(Psalm 16.11)*

Lord, you will show me the path of life and fill me with joy in your presence.

PRAYER AFTER COMMUNION

Lord, you give us new hope in this eucharist. May the power of your love continue its saving work among us and bring us to the joy you promise.

BLESSING AND DISMISSAL *(p. 67)*

"No fair!" Anyone who has spent time with young children is probably familiar with that cry of protest. Some of the parables in Scripture can, at first glance, provoke a similar reaction in us. Stories like the Prodigal Son, for example, or the workers in the vineyard who are all paid the same wage, can seem 'unfair' to our limited human understanding. Today's gospel is, I think, another such story.

Why are the five 'wise' bridesmaids so unhelpful to their ill-prepared companions? Why is the bridegroom so inflexible, shutting the door without even acknowledging them? Is this 'fair'?

Such stories are difficult for us to grasp with our limited human perceptions of justice. If God's love is comprehensive and unconditional, what are we to make of the unfortunate bridesmaids?

Yes, God's love is unconditional and all-embracing. However, that gift of love calls forth a response in us: the response of being ready and open to receive it. All of the bridesmaids fall asleep; but when they hear the call to meet the bridegroom, only the wise ones are prepared to answer that call.

The God of surprises beckons to us in the most unexpected circumstances. Let us pray that we may always keep the lamp of our heart lit so as to recognize and welcome the divine presence wherever it may be found.

Krystyna Higgins, Fredericton, NB

ENTRANCE ANTIPHON *(Psalm 88.2)*

Let my prayer come before you, Lord; listen, and answer me.

INTRODUCTORY RITES *(p. 7)*

OPENING PRAYER

God of power and mercy, protect us from all harm. Give us freedom of spirit and health in mind and body to do your work on earth.

FIRST READING *(Wisdom 6.12-16)*

Wisdom is radiant and unfading,
and she is easily discerned by those who love her,
and is found by those who seek her.
She hastens to make herself known
    to those who desire her.
One who rises early to seek her
    will have no difficulty,
for she will be found sitting at the gate.

To fix one's thought on her is perfect
    understanding,
and one who is vigilant on her account
    will soon be free from care,
because she goes about seeking
    those worthy of her,
and she graciously appears to them
    in their paths,
and meets them in every thought.

The word of the Lord. **Thanks be to God.**

RESPONSORIAL PSALM *(Psalm 63)*

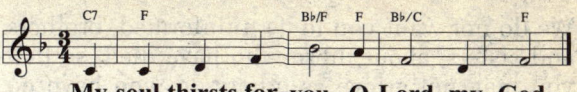

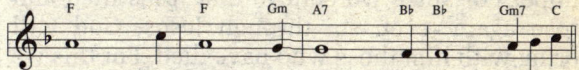

R̸. **My soul thirsts for you, O Lord my God.**

O God, you are my God, I · **seek_you**,
my soul · **thirsts_for_you**;
my flesh · **faints_for_you**,
as in a dry and weary land where there · **is**
 no water. R̸.

So I have looked upon you in the · **sanctuary**,
beholding your power and · **glory**.
Because your steadfast love is better than · **life**,
my · **lips** will praise_you. R̸.

So I will bless you as long as I · **live**;
I will lift up my hands and call
 on your · **name**.
My soul is satisfied as with a rich · **feast**,
and my mouth praises you with · **joy**-ful lips. R̸.

I think of you on my · **bed**,
and meditate on you in the watches
 of the · **night**;
for you have been my · **help**,
and in the shadow of your wings
 I · **sing** for joy. R̸.

©2010 Gordon Johnston/Novalis

SECOND READING *(1 Thessalonians 4.13-18)*

We do not want you to be uninformed, brothers and sisters, about those who have died, so that you may not grieve as others do who have no hope. For since we believe that Jesus died and rose again, even so, through Jesus, God will bring with him those who have died. For this we declare to you by the word of the Lord, that we who are alive, who are left until the coming of the Lord, will by no means precede those who have died.

For the Lord himself, with a cry of command, with the Archangel's call and with the sound of God's trumpet, will descend from heaven, and the dead in Christ will rise first. Then we who are alive, who are left, will be caught up in the clouds together with them to meet the Lord in the air; and so we will be with the Lord forever. Therefore encourage one another with these words.

The word of the Lord. **Thanks be to God.**

GOSPEL ACCLAMATION *(See Mt 24.42, 44)*

Alleluia. Alleluia. Keep awake and be ready: you do not know when the Son of Man is coming. **Alleluia.**

GOSPEL *(Matthew 25.1-13)*

A reading from the holy Gospel according to Matthew. **Glory to you, Lord.**

Jesus spoke this parable to the disciples: "The kingdom of heaven will be like this. Ten bridesmaids took their lamps and went to meet the bridegroom. Five of them were foolish, and five were wise. When the foolish took their lamps, they took no oil with them; but the wise took flasks of oil with their lamps. As the bridegroom was delayed, all of them became drowsy and slept.

"But at midnight there was a shout, 'Look! Here is the bridegroom! Come out to meet him.' Then all those bridesmaids got up and trimmed their lamps. The foolish said to the wise, 'Give us some of your oil, for  our lamps are going out.' But the wise replied, 'No! There will not be enough for you and for us; you had better go to the dealers and buy some for yourselves.' And while they went to buy it, the bridegroom came, and those who were ready went with him into the wedding banquet; and the door was shut.

"Later the other bridesmaids came also, saying, 'Lord, lord, open to us.' But he replied, 'Truly I tell you, I do not know you.' Keep awake therefore, for you know neither the day nor the hour."

The Gospel of the Lord. **Praise to you, Lord Jesus Christ.**

PROFESSION OF FAITH *(p. 13-14)*

PRAYER OF THE FAITHFUL

The following intentions are suggestions only.

℟ **Lord, hear our prayer.**

For the Church, called to follow Jesus boldly, secure in the promise of the resurrection, we pray to the Lord: ℟

For all those who clamour for justice in the world, we pray to the Lord: R̰.

For the needs of the forgotten in our midst, we pray to the Lord: R̰.

For us, God's people, called as a parish community to recognize and respond to local issues of injustice, we pray to the Lord: R̰.

PREPARATION OF THE GIFTS *(p. 15)*

PRAYER OVER THE GIFTS

God of mercy, in this eucharist we proclaim the death of the Lord. Accept the gifts we present and help us follow him with love.

PREFACE *(Sundays in Ordinary Time, p. 20)*

COMMUNION ANTIPHON *(Psalm 23.1-2)*

The Lord is my shepherd; there is nothing l shall want. In green pastures he gives me rest, he leads me beside the waters of peace.

PRAYER AFTER COMMUNION

Lord, we thank you for the nourishment you give us through your holy gift. Pour out your Spirit upon us and in the strength of this food from heaven keep us single-minded in your service.

BLESSING AND DISMISSAL *(p. 67)*

Within us is a unique heart-song placed there by God. Our vocation is to respond to this gift by singing the song and leaving a voiceprint for others to hear. We might not be the first violin or the loudest trumpet, but without that one note from a simple triangle a symphony is incomplete.

We may think we are civilized, yet we are often confronted by evil wrought by human hands. This may be because we do not choose to develop our talents and so make the world a better place. Have we became tone-deaf to God's heart-song? Have we buried our talent? Gifts grow with use but wither with neglect. If we risk nothing, we gain nothing. If we risk even a little and deposit just one talent, eternal reward can be ours.

Whenever time runs out, we typically muse about what might have been and regret what we have squandered or wasted. As this liturgical year draws to a close, let us not rue the past. Instead, let us rediscover our heart-song and help others discover theirs. Let us reach out with the power of that song and sing it loud and clear. Then, let us listen for the voice of the Master calling us home: "Well done." Our vocation is simply to receive from God the gift of who we are and return that gift to God through an authentic response.

Wanda Conway, Winnipeg, MB

ENTRANCE ANTIPHON *(Jeremiah 29.11, 12, 14)*

The Lord says: my plans for you are peace and not disaster; when you call to me, I will listen to you, and I will bring you back to the place from which I exiled you.

INTRODUCTORY RITES *(p. 7)*

OPENING PRAYER

Father of all that is good, keep us faithful in serving you, for to serve you is lasting joy.

FIRST READING
(Proverbs 31.10-13, 16-18, 20, 26, 28-31)

A capable wife, who can find her?
She is far more precious than jewels.
The heart of her husband trusts in her,
and he will have no lack of gain.
She does him good, and not harm,
all the days of her life.
She seeks wool and flax,
and works with willing hands.

She considers a field and buys it;
with the fruit of her hands
    she plants a vineyard.
She girds herself with strength,
and makes her arms strong.
She perceives that her merchandise
    is profitable.
Her lamp does not go out at night.

She opens her hand to the poor,
and reaches out her hands to the needy.
She opens her mouth with wisdom,
and the teaching of kindness is on her tongue.

Her children rise up and call her happy;
her husband too, and he praises her:
"Many women have done excellently,
but you surpass them all."
Charm is deceitful, and beauty is vain,
but a woman who fears the Lord
    is to be praised.
Give her a share in the fruit of her hands,
and let her works praise her in the city gates.

The word of the Lord. **Thanks be to God.**

RESPONSORIAL PSALM *(Psalm 128)*

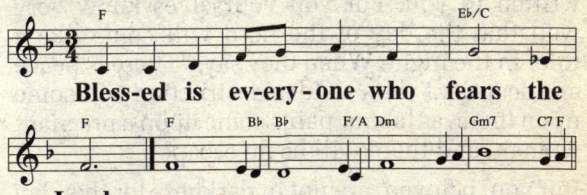

Bless-ed is ev-ery-one who fears the Lord.

R. **Blessed is everyone who fears the Lord.**

    Blessed is everyone who fears · **the** Lord,
who walks in · **his** ways.
You shall eat the fruit of the labour
    of · **your** hands;
you shall be happy,
    and it shall go well · **with** you. R.

    Your wife will be like a fruit-·**ful** vine
within · **your** house;
your children will be · **like** olive_shoots
around · **your** table. R.

→

Thus shall the man be blessed
    who fears · **the** Lord.
The Lord bless you · **from** Zion.
May you see the prosperity of · **Je**-rusalem
all the days of · **your** life. ℟

℟ **Blessed is everyone who fears the Lord.**

©2010 Gordon Johnston/Novalis

SECOND READING *(1 Thessalonians 5.1-6)*

Now concerning the times and the seasons, brothers and sisters, you do not need to have anything written to you. For you yourselves know very well that the day of the Lord will come like a thief in the night. When they say, "There is peace and security," then sudden destruction will come upon them, as labour pains come upon a pregnant woman, and there will be no escape!

But you, beloved, are not in darkness for that day to surprise you like a thief. You are all children of light and children of the day; we are not of the night or of darkness. So then let us not fall asleep as others do, but let us keep awake and be sober.

The word of the Lord. **Thanks be to God.**

GOSPEL ACCLAMATION *(See John 15.4, 5)*

Alleluia. Alleluia. Abide in me as I in you, says the Lord; my branches bear much fruit. **Alleluia.**

GOSPEL *(Matthew 25.14-30)*

For the shorter version, omit the indented parts.

A reading from the holy Gospel according to Matthew. **Glory to you, Lord.**

Jesus spoke this parable to his disciples: "For it is as if a man, going on a journey, summoned his slaves and entrusted his property to them; to one he gave five talents, to another two, to another one, to each according to his ability. Then he went away.

> "The one who had received the five talents went off at once and traded with them, and made five more talents. In the same way, the one who had the two talents made two more talents. But the one who had received the one talent went off and dug a hole in the ground and hid his master's money.

"After a long time the master of those slaves came and settled accounts with them. Then the one who had received the five talents came forward, bringing five more talents, saying, 'Master, you handed over to me five talents; see, I have made five more talents.' His master said to him, 'Well done, good and trustworthy slave; you  have been trustworthy in a few things, I will put you in charge of many things; enter into the joy of your master.'

> "And the one with the two talents also came forward, saying, 'Master, you handed over to me two talents; see, I have made two more

talents. His master said to him, 'Well done, good and trustworthy slave; you have been trustworthy in a few things, I will put you in charge of many things; enter into the joy of your master.'

"Then the one who had received the one talent also came forward, saying, 'Master, I knew that you were a harsh man, reaping where you did not sow, and gathering where you did not scatter seed; so I was afraid, and I went and hid your talent in the ground. Here you have what is yours.'

"But his master replied, 'You wicked and lazy slave! You knew, did you, that I reap where I did not sow, and gather where I did not scatter? Then you ought to have invested my money with the bankers, and on my return I would have received what was my own with interest. So take the talent from him, and give it to the one with the ten talents. For to all those who have, more will be given, and they will have an abundance; but from those who have nothing, even what they have will be taken away. As for this worthless slave, throw him into the outer darkness, where there will be weeping and gnashing of teeth.'"

The Gospel of the Lord. **Praise to you, Lord Jesus Christ.**

PROFESSION OF FAITH *(p. 13-14)*

PRAYER OF THE FAITHFUL

The following intentions are suggestions only.

R̞. **Lord, hear our prayer.**

For the Church, working to establish peace and justice as we pray for the coming of God's kingdom, we pray to the Lord: R̞.

For world leaders inspired to work together to make peace a reality in our world, we pray to the Lord: R̞.

For those among us who suffer from depression and despair, we pray to the Lord: R̞.

For us, called as God's holy people to witness to God's presence in our daily lives, we pray to the Lord: R̞.

PREPARATION OF THE GIFTS *(p. 15)*

PRAYER OVER THE GIFTS

Lord God, may the gifts we offer increase our love for you and bring us to eternal life.

PREFACE *(Sundays in Ordinary Time, p. 20)*

COMMUNION ANTIPHON *(Psalm 73.28)*

It is good for me to be with the Lord and to put my hope in him.

PRAYER AFTER COMMUNION

Father, may we grow in love by the eucharist we have celebrated in memory of the Lord Jesus.

BLESSING AND DISMISSAL *(p. 67)*

People living in democratic societies tend to be suspicious of absolute rule. Citizens of representative governments prefer consensus and dialogue. The idea of one-person rule is too close to the experience of dictatorship. Jesus opposes political power founded on oppression and violence. What, then, is this feast of Christ the King about?

The scripture readings portray a different kind of authority. The prophet Ezekiel speaks of God as a shepherd who guides the scattered sheep with tender care. One might rewrite the image to say that the shepherd also leaves the one sheep and searches for the 99! Paul uses strong language to evoke Christ's coming as one that abolishes "every ruler and every authority and power." The gospel portrays Jesus as Ruler of the End-Time. Like a shepherd he separates the sheep from the goats. "Just as you did not do it to one of the least of these..." This is indeed a new mandate.

Christ appears as the divine governor of the City of God. As citizens of 'the City,' Christians are called to challenge the many forms of violence in the world today with the charter of the Beatitudes, service and self-giving love, especially to the needy and marginalized in society. May today's eucharist give us the strength to do our part in building the City of God.

Robert Dueweke, El Paso, TX

ENTRANCE ANTIPHON *(Revelation 5.12; 1.6)*

The Lamb who was slain is worthy to receive strength and divinity, wisdom and power and honour: to him be glory and power for ever.

INTRODUCTORY RITES *(p. 7)*

OPENING PRAYER

Almighty and merciful God, you break the power of evil and make all things new in your Son Jesus Christ, the King of the universe. May all in heaven and earth acclaim your glory and never cease to praise you.

FIRST READING *(Ezekiel 34.11-12, 15-17)*

Thus says the Lord God:
"I myself will search for my sheep,
and will seek them out.
As a shepherd seeks out his flock
when he is among his scattered sheep,
so I will seek out my sheep.
I will rescue them from all the places
to which they have been scattered
on a day of clouds and thick darkness.

"I myself will be the shepherd of my sheep, and
I will make them lie down," says the Lord God.
"I will seek the lost,
and I will bring back the strayed,
and I will bind up the injured,
and I will strengthen the weak,
but the fat and the strong I will destroy.
I will feed my sheep with justice.

"As for you, my flock," thus says the Lord God:
"I shall judge between one sheep and another,
between rams and goats."

The word of the Lord. **Thanks be to God.**

RESPONSORIAL PSALM *(Psalm 23)*

The Lord is my shep - herd;

I shall not want.

℟. **The Lord is my shepherd; I shall not want.**

The Lord is my shepherd, I shall · **not** want.
He makes me lie down in · **green** pastures;
he leads me be··**side** still waters;
he re··**stores** my soul. ℟.

He leads me in right paths for his · **name's** sake.
Even though I walk through
    the darkest valley, I fear · **no** evil;
for · **you** are with_me;
your rod and your · **staff** — they comfort_me. ℟.

You prepare a table · **be**-fore_me
in the presence · **of_my** enemies;
you anoint my · **head** with oil;
my · **cup** over-flows. ℟.

Surely goodness and mercy · **shall** follow_me
all the days of · **my** life,
and I shall dwell in the · **house_of** the Lord
my · **whole** life long. ℟.

©2009 Gordon Johnston/Novalis

SECOND READING *(1 Corinthians 15.20-26, 28)*

Brothers and sisters: Christ has been raised from the dead, the first fruits of those who have fallen asleep. For since death came through a man, the resurrection of the dead has also come through a man; for as all die in Adam, so all will be made alive in Christ. But each in his own order: Christ the first fruits, then at his coming those who belong to Christ.

Then comes the end, when he hands over the kingdom to God the Father, after he has destroyed every ruler and every authority and power. For he must reign until he has put all his enemies under his feet. The last enemy to be destroyed is death.

When all things are subjected to him, then the Son himself will also be subjected to the one who put all things in subjection under him, so that God may be all in all.

The word of the Lord. **Thanks be to God.**

GOSPEL ACCLAMATION *(Mark 11.9-10)*

Alleluia. Alleluia. Blessed is the one who comes in the name of the Lord. Blessed is the coming kingdom of our father David. **Alleluia.**

GOSPEL *(Matthew 25.31-46)*

A reading from the holy Gospel according to Matthew. **Glory to you, Lord.**

Jesus said to his disciples: "When the Son of Man comes in his glory, and all the Angels with him, then he will sit on the throne of his glory. All the nations will be gathered before him, and he will separate people one from another as a shepherd separates the sheep from the goats, and he will put the sheep at his right hand and the goats at the left.

"Then the king will say to those at his right hand, 'Come, you that are blessed by my Father, inherit the kingdom prepared for you from the foundation of the world; for I was hungry and you gave me food, I was thirsty and you gave me something to drink, I was a stranger and you welcomed me, I was naked and you gave me clothing, I was sick and you took care of me, I was in prison and you visited me.'

"Then the righteous will answer him, 'Lord, when was it that we saw you hungry and gave you food, or thirsty and gave you something to drink? And when was it that we saw you a stranger and welcomed you, or naked and gave you clothing? And when was it that we saw you sick or in prison and visited you?' And the king will answer them, 'Truly I tell you, just as you did it to one of the least of these brothers and sisters of mine, you did it to me.'

"Then he will say to those at his left hand, 'You that are accursed, depart from me into the eternal fire prepared for the devil and his angels; for I was hungry and you gave me no food, I was thirsty and you gave me nothing to drink, I was a stranger and you did not welcome me, naked and you did not give me clothing, sick and in prison and you did not visit me.'

"Then they also will answer, 'Lord, when was it that we saw you hungry or thirsty or a stranger or naked or sick or in prison, and did not take care of you?' Then he will answer them, 'Truly I tell you, just as you did not do it to one of the least of these, you did not do it to me.' And these will go away into eternal punishment, but the righteous into eternal life."

The Gospel of the Lord. **Praise to you, Lord Jesus Christ.**

PROFESSION OF FAITH *(Nicene Creed, p. 14)*

PRAYER OF THE FAITHFUL

The following intentions are suggestions only.

R. **Lord, hear our prayer.**

For the Church, instrument of unity and salvation, we pray to the Lord: R.

For the triumph of peace, harmony and hope in our world community, we pray to the Lord: R.

For those among us who are poor, persecuted or alone, we pray to the Lord: R.

For us, God's people, called as a parish to witness to Christ and his salvation, we pray to the Lord: R.

PREPARATION OF THE GIFTS *(p. 15)*

PRAYER OVER THE GIFTS

Lord, we offer you the sacrifice by which your Son reconciles the human family. May it bring unity and peace to the world.

PREFACE *(Christ the King, p. 32)*

COMMUNION ANTIPHON *(Psalm 29.10-11)*

The Lord will reign for ever and will give his people the gift of peace.

PRAYER AFTER COMMUNION

Lord, you give us Christ, the King of all creation, as food for everlasting life. Help us to live by his gospel and bring us to the joy of his kingdom.

BLESSING AND DISMISSAL *(p. 67)*

LITURGY NOTES

The Liturgical Calendar

For historical reasons, the civil and liturgical calendars are not identical. The civil calendar always begins on January 1st, while the liturgical calendar always begins on the First Sunday of Advent. *Living with Christ Sunday Missal* follows the liturgical calendar and so spans two civil years: 2010-2011.

Every year, the liturgical seasons follow the same pattern: Advent, Christmas, Ordinary Time, Lent, Easter, and back to Ordinary Time. Within each season, the readings reflect suitable themes. There are many readings available on certain liturgical themes and the Church seeks to broaden our experience of the Bible by varying the readings from one year to the next.

The treasures of the Bible are to be opened up more lavishly, so that richer fare may be provided for the faithful at the table of God's Word. In this way a more representative portion of the holy Scriptures will be read to the people over a set cycle of years (Vatican II, *Constitution on the Sacred Liturgy*, §51).

The Bible is a 'library' of 73 books from which readings have been selected for pastoral purposes and arranged in a book called the *Lectionary*. These readings are "aimed at giving the faithful an ever-deepening perception of the faith they profess and of the history of salvation" (*Introduction to the Lectionary for Mass*, §60).

The preparation of a lectionary takes years of study, consultation, and revision. In 1992 the Canadian Church inaugurated a new Sunday Lectionary based on the New Revised Standard Version of the Bible (NRSV).

The lectionary features a different Synoptic Gospel each year over a three-year cycle. The first year of the cycle, Year A, is the year for the reading of the Gospel of Matthew; in the second and third years, the readings are from the Gospel of Mark (Year B) and the Gospel of Luke (Year C). John's Gospel is featured at other liturgical times, for instance during Lent and the Easter Season. This liturgical year is Year A. Therefore, Matthew's Gospel will be emphasized all year.

All this has been planned to develop among the faithful a greater hunger for the word of God... We are fully confident on this account that both priests and faithful will prepare their minds and hearts more devoutly for the Lord's Supper and that, meditating on the Scriptures, they will be nourished more each day by the words of the Lord. In accord with the hopes of Vatican Council II, all will thus regard sacred Scripture as the abiding source of spiritual life, the foundation for Christian instruction, and the core of all theological study (Paul VI, *Apostolic Constitution on the Roman Missal*).

Composing the Prayer of the Faithful

When you are composing intercessions for the Prayer of the Faithful for Eucharist or for the Liturgy of the Hours, keep in mind that liturgy is communal action. This is not the time for personal prayer for individual needs. Rather this is the moment when God's priestly people, united to Jesus their High Priest, intercede with God for the needs of the world—the whole world.

The General Instruction of the Roman Missal provides a specific pattern to follow to ensure that the universal nature of this prayer is maintained. It invites us to pray: a) for the needs of the universal Church; b) for public authorities and the salvation of the world; c) for those oppressed by any need; d) for the local community.

Because this prayer is a litany, it is best to maintain a fixed response, such as "Lord, hear our prayer," so that people can respond easily. A fixed response also allows the possibility of singing the prayer if the community desires.

The Prayer of the Faithful does not have to be thematic or linked to the readings of the day. The true needs of the world for this week may not be specifically linked to the readings. What the readings do is inspire our confidence that God will hear our prayer, for they have just shown us how God has acted towards us; the homily helps us recognize that God still saves us today.

Composing this prayer, either spontaneously or in writing, is not without certain pitfalls. One is the 'we/they split.' The unity of the assembly is fundamental: language must not divide the people. For example, to pray for "those who do not follow God's law" implies that sinfulness is not part of our experience or that sinners are not in church. This approach forgets that the liturgical assembly is always made up of saved sinners.

Another common pitfall is 'duelling intentions,' where one ideological group prays for the conversion of another. Sweeping generalizations judge groups or people. To avoid this, pray *for* persons or *for* something that applies to persons or groups: healing, peace, reconciliation, etc. Avoid constructing petitions around 'that' or 'may' which prescribe the outcome and virtually tell God what to do. Remember that we are asking God to watch over people; we are not giving our orders for the week. For example, rather than say "For persons with AIDS, that they may..." say "For persons with AIDS, their families and those who assist them." Thus God decides how best to save those for whom we are praying.

Feel free to repeat some of the same intentions from week to week. The basic quality of this prayer is not its novelty, but its universality.

The intercessions provided in *Living with Christ* are simply suggestions. Communities are encouraged to compose their own Prayer of the Faithful.

Bernadette Gasslein

For weekly suggested intentions for the Prayer of the Faithful, consult www.livingwithchrist.ca

MORNING AND EVENING PRAYERS

See also p. 573 and p. 577.

Morning Offering

Lord Jesus,
I give you my hands to do your work.
I give you my feet to go your way.
I give you my eyes to see as you do.
I give you my tongue to speak your words.
I give you my mind that you may think in me.
I give you my spirit that you may pray in me.
Above all, I give you my heart that you may love
in me your Father and all humanity.
I give you my whole self that you may grow in me,
so that it is you, Lord Jesus, who live and work
and pray in me.

Grail Prayer

Dedication

Father, I dedicate this new day to you; as I go
about my work, I ask you to bless those with
whom I come in contact.

Lord, I pray for all men and women who work to
earn their living; give them satisfaction in what
they do.

Spirit of God, comfort the unemployed and their
families; they are your children and my brothers
and sisters. I ask you to help them find work soon.

St. Ignatius Loyola, 1491-1556

Morning Hymn

Breathe on me, breath of God, fill me with life anew, that I may love the things you love, and do what you would do.

Breathe on me, breath of God, until my heart is pure, until with you I have one will to live and to endure.

Breathe on me, breath of God, my soul with grace refine, until this earthly part of me glows with your fire divine.

Breathe on me, breath of God, so I shall never die, but live with you the perfect life in your eternity.

Edwin Hatch, 1835-1889

Each New Day

Let me pause as I begin this new day to give it to you, Lord. Before the tumult of activities breaks in; before breakfast plates crash through my still sleepy mind; for this last moment in my bed, thank you, Lord.

Let me hold your promise of new life. Keep me from slipping back for I know that what is forgiven is as if it never were. Each new day, your grace gives me a fresh start to walk in your light again.

May the Lord support us all the day long, till the shades lengthen and the evening comes, and the busy world is hushed, and the fever of life is over, and our work is done. Then in his mercy may he give us a safe lodging, and a holy rest, and peace at the last. Amen.

John Henry Cardinal Newman, 1801-1890

Evening Praise

All praise to you, O God, this night
For all the blessings of the light;
Keep us, we pray, O King of kings,
Beneath your own almighty wings.

Forgive us, Lord, through Christ your Son,
Whatever wrong this day we've done;
Your peace give to the world, O Lord,
That we might live in one accord.

Enlighten us, O blessed Light,
and give us rest throughout this night.
O strengthen us, that for your sake,
We all may serve you when we wake.

Thomas Ken, 1673-1711

At Eventide

O radiant Light, O Sun divine
Of God the Father's deathless face,
O image of the light sublime
That fills the heav'nly dwelling place.

Son of God, source of life,
Praise is yours both day and night;
Our happy voice must raise the strain
Of your proclaimed and splendid name.

Lord Jesus Christ, as daylight fades,
As shine the lights of eventide,
We praise the Father with the Son,
The Spirit blest and with them one.

Third-century Greek hymn

TRADITIONAL PRAYERS

The Lord's Prayer I

Our Father, who art in heaven, hallowed be thy name; thy kingdom come; thy will be done on earth as it is in heaven.

Give us this day our daily bread; and forgive us our trespasses as we forgive those who trespass against us; and lead us not into temptation, but deliver us from evil. Amen.

The Lord's Prayer II

Our Father in heaven, hallowed be your name, your kingdom come, your will be done, on earth as in heaven.

Give us today our daily bread. Forgive us our sins as we forgive those who sin against us. Save us from the time of trial and deliver us from evil.

For the kingdom, the power, and the glory are yours, now and for ever. Amen.

© English Language Liturgical Consultation

Hail Mary

Hail Mary, full of grace, the Lord is with thee. Blessed art thou among women and blessed is the fruit of thy womb, Jesus.

Holy Mary, Mother of God, pray for us sinners, now and at the hour of our death. Amen.

Glory Be to the Father

Glory be to the Father, and to the Son, and to the Holy Spirit. As it was in the beginning, is now, and ever shall be, world without end. Amen.

Act of Contrition

My God, I am sorry for my sins with all my heart. In choosing to do wrong and failing to do good, I have sinned against you whom I should love above all things. I firmly intend, with your help, to do penance, to sin no more, and to avoid whatever leads me to sin.

Our Saviour Jesus Christ suffered and died for us. In his name, my God, have mercy.

Act of Faith

O my God, I firmly believe that you are one God in three divine Persons, Father, Son, and Holy Spirit. I believe that your divine Son became man, died for our sins, and that he will come to judge the living and the dead. I believe these and all the truths which the holy Catholic Church teaches, because you have revealed them, who can neither deceive nor be deceived.

Act of Hope

O my God, relying on your almighty power and infinite mercy and promises, I hope to obtain pardon of my sins, the help of your grace, and life everlasting through the merits of Jesus Christ, my Lord and Redeemer.

Act of Love

O my God, I love you above all things, with my whole heart and soul, because you are all good and worthy of all love. I love my neighbour as myself for the love of you. I forgive all who have injured me, and ask pardon of all whom I have injured. Amen.

The Rosary

In the Rosary we focus on 20 events or mysteries in the life and death of Jesus and meditate on how we share with Mary in the redemptive work of Christ. Reading a pertinent passage from the Bible helps to deepen meditation on a particular mystery. The scriptural references given here are not exhaustive. In many instances, other biblical texts are equally suitable for meditation.

~ Begin the Rosary at the crucifix by praying the *Apostles' Creed (p. 13)*
~ At each large bead, pray the *Lord's Prayer*
~ At each small bead, pray the *Hail Mary*
~ At the first three beads it is customary to pray a *Hail Mary* for each of the gifts of faith, hope, and love
~ For each mystery, begin with the *Lord's Prayer*, then recite the *Hail Mary* ten times, and end with *Glory Be to the Father*.

The Five Joyful Mysteries:

The Annunciation (Luke 1.26-38)
The Visitation (Luke 1.39-56)
The Nativity (Luke 2.1-20)
The Presentation (Luke 2.22-38)
The Finding in the Temple (Luke 2.41-52)

The Five Mysteries of Light:

The Baptism in the Jordan (Matthew 3.13-17)
The Wedding at Cana (John 2.1-12)
The Proclamation of the Kingdom (Mark 1.15)
The Transfiguration (Luke 9.28-36)
The First Eucharist (Matthew 26.26-29)

The Five Sorrowful Mysteries:

The Agony in the Garden (Matthew 26.36-56)
The Scourging at the Pillar (Matthew 27.20-26)
The Crowning with Thorns (Matthew 27.27-30)
The Carrying of the Cross (Matthew 27.31-33)
The Crucifixion (Matthew 27.34-60)

The Five Glorious Mysteries:

The Resurrection (John 20.1-18)
The Ascension (Acts 1.9-11)
The Descent of the Holy Spirit (John 20.19-23)
The Assumption of Mary (John 11.26)
The Crowning of Mary (Philippians 2.1-11)

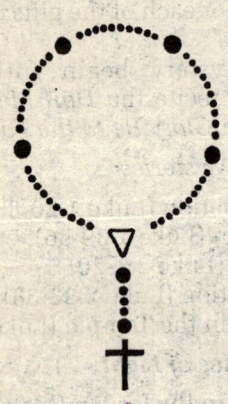

Come, Holy Spirit

Come, Holy Spirit, fill the hearts of your faithful and kindle in them the fire of your love. Send forth your Spirit, O Lord, and renew the face of the earth.

O God, on the first Pentecost you instructed the hearts of those who believed in you by the light of the Holy Spirit: under the inspiration of the same Spirit, give us a taste for what is right and true and a continuing sense of his presence and power, through Jesus Christ our Lord. Amen.

Anima Christi

Soul of Christ, make me holy.
Body of Christ, save me.
Blood of Christ, inebriate me.
Water from the side of Christ, wash me clean.
Passion of Christ, strengthen me.
Kind Jesus, hear me.
Hide me within your wounds.
Let me never be separated from you.
Defend me from evil.
In the hour of my death call me to yourself,
that with your saints I may praise you
in everlasting life. Amen.

Jesus Prayer

(The Jesus Prayer, a favourite especially in the Eastern Churches of the Slavic tradition, is repeated as a litany until it becomes part of one's heart.)

Lord Jesus Christ,
Son of the living God,
have mercy on me, a sinner.

Angelus

The angel of the Lord declared unto Mary, and she conceived of the Holy Spirit. *Hail Mary...*

Behold, the handmaid of the Lord; be it done to me according to your word. *Hail Mary...*

And the word was made flesh, and dwelt among us. *Hail Mary...*

Pray for us, O holy Mother of God; that we may be made worthy of the promises of Christ.

Pour forth, we beseech you, O Lord, your grace into our hearts that we, to whom the incarnation of your Son was made known by the message of an angel, may by his passion and cross be brought to the glory of his resurrection. We ask this through the same Christ, our Lord. Amen.

Regina Caeli

O Queen of heaven, rejoice, alleluia!
For he whom you chose to bear, alleluia!
Is risen as he said, alleluia!
Pray for us to God, alleluia!
Rejoice and be glad, O Virgin Mary, alleluia!
For the Lord is truly risen, alleluia!

O God, by the resurrection of your Son, our Lord, you were pleased to make glad the whole world. Grant, we beseech you, that through the intercession of the Virgin Mary, his mother, we may attain the joys of everlasting life, through the same Christ our Lord. Amen.

Divine Praises

Blessed be God.
Blessed be his holy name.

Blessed be Jesus Christ, true God and true man.
Blessed be the name of Jesus.
Blessed be his most sacred heart.
Blessed be his most precious blood.
Blessed be Jesus in the sacrament of the altar.

Blessed be the Holy Spirit, the Paraclete.

Blessed be the Mother of God, Mary most holy.
Blessed be her holy and immaculate conception.
Blessed be her glorious assumption.
Blessed be the name of Mary, virgin and mother.
Blessed be Saint Joseph, her most chaste spouse.
Blessed be God in his angels and in his saints.

Hail, Holy Queen

Hail, holy Queen, mother of mercy, our life, our
sweetness and our hope. To you do we cry, poor
banished children of Eve. To you we send up our
sighs, mourning and weeping in this valley of
tears. Turn then, most gracious advocate, your
eyes of mercy upon us, and after this, our exile,
show unto us the blessed fruit of your womb,
Jesus. O clement, O loving, O kind Virgin Mary.

Magnificat: see p. 578

Canticle of Zechariah: see p. 575

The Stations of the Cross

(Traditional version)

Prayer before each station:

> We adore you, O Christ, and we praise you, because by your holy cross you have redeemed the world.

1. Jesus is condemned to death

Consider how Jesus, having been scourged and crowned with thorns, is unjustly condemned by Pilate to death on a cross.

2. Jesus takes up his cross

Consider how Jesus, bearing this cross on his shoulders, offers his suffering to the Father for us.

3. Jesus falls for the first time

Consider this first fall. Jesus, bleeding, crowned with thorns, so weak he can hardly walk, yet forced to carry this heavy burden. The soldiers strike him and he falls.

4. Jesus meets his mother

Consider this meeting between mother and son... their tender love for one another, their hearts torn asunder.

5. Simon helps Jesus carry the cross

Consider how the torturers force the bystander Simon to carry Jesus' cross. They want Jesus to stay alive long enough to die crucified.

6. Veronica wipes Jesus' face

Consider how Veronica recognizes Jesus' pain and attempts to lessen his suffering.

7. Jesus falls for the second time

Consider this second fall. It reopens his wounds, hurts his head, pains his whole body.

8. The women of Jerusalem weep for Jesus

Consider how these compassionate women wept at the sight of the tortured Jesus.

9. Jesus falls for the third time

Consider this third fall. Though extremely weak, Jesus is urged on by the soldiers.

10. Jesus is stripped of his garments

Consider the violence with which the soldiers tear off the bloody garments which cling to his broken skin and start the wounds bleeding again.

11. Jesus is nailed to the cross

Consider how Jesus, arms extended on the cross, offers to his Father the ultimate sacrifice for our salvation.

12. Jesus dies on the cross

Consider how Jesus, after hours of agony and anguish on the cross, abandons himself to the Father and dies.

13. Jesus is removed from the cross

Consider how two disciples take the broken body down from the cross and place Jesus in his grieving mother's arms.

14. Jesus is placed in the tomb

Consider how the disciples, filled with grief, carry the body to the burial place. They close the tomb and come away confused and sorrowful.

The Way of the Cross

(Revised version: The Sacred Congregation for Divine Worship recommends that the traditional Stations be revised to emphasize that the sufferings and resurrection of Christ are one redemptive mystery.)

Opening Prayer

Lord Jesus, all of your life led up to the Way of the Cross. In this final journey you lay down your life for your friends.

Jesus, you consider us your friends. You walk side by side with us on the journey of life. You know its joys and hopes, its suffering and pain. Today we want to walk side by side with you on your way to the Cross. Your suffering, your death, your rising from the dead give meaning to our lives. The way of the Cross is the way of life.

Lord, as you took the bread, your body, take us, bless us, break us, give us to others, so that in you we may be instruments of salvation for the world. Amen.

1. The Last Supper

Jesus said to them, "I have wanted so much to eat this Passover meal with you before I suffer! For I tell you, I will never eat it until it is given its full meaning in the Kingdom of God."

Then Jesus took a cup, gave thanks to God, and said, "Take this and share it among yourselves. I tell you that from now on I will not drink this wine until the Kingdom of God comes."

Then he took a loaf of bread, gave thanks to God, broke it, and gave it to them, saying, "This is my body, which is given for you. Do this in memory of me." In the same way, he gave them the cup after supper, saying, "This cup is God's new covenant sealed with my blood, which is poured out for you."

(Luke 22.15-20)

Jesus, you love us. Make us realize we are a covenant people, make our eucharists moments when we feel your friendship, so that we may live this out for all humankind.

2. In the Garden of Gethsemane

Then Jesus went with his disciples to a place called Gethsemane, and said to them, "Sit here while I go over there and pray." He took with him Peter and the two sons of Zebedee. Grief and anguish came over him, and he said to them, "The sorrow in my heart is so great that it almost crushes me. Stay here and keep watch with me."

(Matthew 26.36-38)

Jesus, you love us. Comfort us in times of distress. Help us to see beyond ourselves; help us to overcome the feeling of senseless chaos; help us to see the joy and hope of those who truly suffer and who truly believe. Remind us of your covenant of friendship with us.

3. Before the Sanhedrin

Jesus was taken to the High Priest's house, where the chief priests, the elders, and the teachers of the Law were gathering. Peter followed at a distance and went into the courtyard, where he sat down with the guards, keeping himself warm by the fire. The chief priests and the whole Council tried to find some evidence against Jesus in order to put him to death, but they could not find any.

(Mark 14.53-55)

Jesus, you love us. Help us live out your covenant of friendship; give us strength to stand against authorities who exercise power for evil. Make us nonviolent, but strong in this struggle for humankind. Jesus, strengthen us.

4. Before Pontius Pilate

Early in the morning Jesus was taken from Caiaphas' house to the governor's palace. The Jewish authorities did not go inside the palace, for they wanted to keep themselves ritually clean in order to be able to eat the Passover meal. So Pilate went outside to them and asked, "What do you accuse this man of?" Their answer was, "We would not have brought him to you if he had not committed a crime." *(John 18.28-30)*

Jesus, you love us. You stand with the victims in this world. Is that one meaning of the covenant for us: that we too should side with the oppressed against the oppressor? Lord, this is hard for us, teach us how to side with the oppressed, with the victims.

5. The whipping and crowning with thorns

Then Pilate took Jesus and had him whipped. The soldiers made a crown of thorny branches, put it on his head, then put a purple robe on him. They came to him and said, "Long live the King of the Jews!" and slapped him. *(John 19.1-3)*

Jesus, you love us. Turn our sympathies to the poor victims of desperate soldiers all over the world. Empower us to stop the sale of arms to ruthless armies. Show us the way to curb senseless attacks by states against their own people. Jesus, teach us how to resist evil.

6. The carrying of the cross

So they took charge of Jesus. He went out, carrying his cross, and came to the 'Place of the Skull,' as it is called. (In Hebrew it is called 'Golgotha.')

(John 19.16-17)

> Jesus, you love us. Your love for us affirms the goodness of our humanity. We are the friends for whom you suffered. Teach us to respect others, not to dismiss or diminish them as less human.

7. Simon of Cyrene

On the way they met a man named Simon, who was coming into the city from the country. The soldiers forced him to carry Jesus' cross.

(Mark 15.21)

> Jesus, you love us. We don't like carrying crosses, but many times our cross is of our own making. It is a self-centred cross. Help us find the true cross in the lives of the poor. Help us to help carry their burden. Jesus, help us!

8. The women of Jerusalem

A large crowd of people followed him; among them were some women who were weeping and wailing for him. Jesus turned to them and said, "Women of Jerusalem! Do not cry for me, but for yourselves and your children. For the days are coming when people will say, 'How lucky are the women who never had children, who never bore babies, who never nursed them!' "

(Luke 23.27-31)

Jesus, you love us. Allow us to comfort the grieving women of our time. But even more, enable us to prevent their grief, which so often could be avoided. Help us to break down the human systems which starve and kill. Jesus, make us angry about this unnecessary grief and suffering. Teach us to weep, knowing all the time that tears are never enough.

9. The stripping and crucifixion

They came to a place called Golgotha, which means 'Place of the Skull.' There they offered Jesus wine mixed with a bitter substance; but after tasting it, he would not drink it.

They crucified him and then divided his clothes among them by throwing dice.

(Matthew 27.33-35)

Jesus, you love us. Stripped naked, nailed to the cross, you have given your all for us. Jesus, help us break the bonds of our selfishness and materialism. Show us how we can give our life for others, in your covenant.

10. The second thief

One of the criminals hanging there hurled insults at him: "Aren't you the Messiah? Save yourself and us!"

The other one, however, rebuked him, saying, "Don't you fear God? You received the same sentence he did. Ours, however, is only right because we are getting what we deserve; but he has done no wrong." And he said to Jesus, "Remember me, Jesus, when you come as King!"

Jesus said to him, "I promise you that today you will be in Paradise with me."

(Luke 23.39-43)

Jesus, you love us. Impress on us that the lives we live, the work we do, have consequences for others. Awaken our awareness to real evil and real faith. Help us honour your covenant of friendship in our lives.

11. Mary and John

Standing close to Jesus' cross were his mother, his mother's sister, Mary the wife of Clopas, and Mary Magdalene. Jesus saw his mother and the disciple he loved standing there; so he said to his mother, "He is your son."

Then he said to the disciple, "She is your mother." From that time the disciple took her to live in his home.

(John 19.25-27)

Jesus, you love us. You gave us your mother Mary as our own mother. Touch our hearts with her sorrow at your death. Lift our eyes so we may see in her the beauty of your covenant; the beauty of her gift of herself to you and to us.

12. Death on the cross

But when they came to Jesus, they saw that he was already dead, so they did not break his legs. One of the soldiers, however, plunged his spear into Jesus' side, and at once blood and water poured out. *(John 19.33-34)*

Jesus, you love us. Teach us your way. Give us the wisdom to recognize evil. Give us the courage to confront it, to struggle against it, so that we may truly be your friends.

13. The new sepulchre

When it was evening, a rich man from Arimathea arrived; his name was Joseph, and he also was a disciple of Jesus. He went to Pilate and asked for the body of Jesus. Pilate gave orders for the body to be given to Joseph. So Joseph took it, wrapped it in a new linen sheet, and placed it in his own tomb which he had just recently dug out of solid rock. Then he rolled a large stone across the entrance to the tomb and went away.

(Matthew 27.57-60)

Jesus, you love us. Help us to distinguish justice and charity. Sometimes it is easier to do charity than to do justice. Let us know which should be our response and when, in our lives. Give us the grace to act charitably and justly.

14. The resurrection

Very early on Sunday morning the women went to the tomb, carrying the spices they had prepared. They found the stone rolled away from the entrance to the tomb, so they went in; but they did not find the body of the Lord Jesus.

(Luke 24.1-3)

Jesus, you love us. You have returned from the dead to be with us. Be our promise, our hope that all evil will be overcome. Bless us with full life for all humankind, under your covenant.

Final Prayer

We know that Christ has been raised from death and will never die again—death will no longer rule over him. And so, because he died, sin has no power over him; and now he lives his life in fellowship with God. In the same way, you are to think of yourselves as dead, so far as sin is concerned, but living in fellowship with God through Christ Jesus.

(Romans 6.9-11)

Father, your only Son gave up his life for us, his friends. Help us understand the meaning of that friendship. Help us grow in that friendship.

We are a weak and distracted people. Often we neglect you, but you never abandon us. You love us. Make us a less selfish and a more caring people. Help us to share the crosses of others, as Simon did. Show us how to live your covenant of friendship day by day with the victims and the poor of this world. Father, we depend on you.

We pray this through Jesus, the Christ, your Son who has risen from the dead. Amen.

PRAYERS AND MEDITATIONS FROM THE SAINTS

Memorare

Remember, most gracious Virgin Mary, that never was it known that anyone who fled to your protection, implored your help, and sought your intercession, was left unaided.

Inspired with this confidence, I fly to you, O Virgin of virgins, my mother. To you I come; before you I stand, sinful and sorrowful. Mother of the Word Incarnate, despise not my petitions but in your mercy hear and answer me.

St. Bernard of Clairvaux, 1090-1153

Prayer for Trust

O Christ Jesus, when all is darkness and we feel our weakness and helplessness, give us the sense of your presence, your love, and your strength. Help us to have perfect trust in your protecting love and strengthening power, so that nothing may frighten or worry us, for, living close to you, we shall see your hand, your purpose, your will through all things.

St. Ignatius of Loyola, 1491-1556

Love and Do What You Will

Therefore once for all this short command is given to you: "Love and do what you will." If you keep silent, keep silent by love; if you speak, speak by love; if you correct, correct by love; if you pardon, pardon by love: let love be rooted in you, and from the root nothing but good can grow.

St. Augustine of Hippo, 354-430

Lines Written in Her Breviary

Let nothing disturb you, nothing frighten you;
All things are passing, God never changes;
Patient endurance attains to all things;
She whom God possesses wants for nothing.
God alone suffices.

St. Teresa of Avila, 1515-1582

Patrick's Breastplate

Christ be with me, Christ within me
Christ behind me, Christ before me
Christ beside me, Christ to win me
Christ to comfort and restore me.
Christ beneath me, Christ above me
Christ in quiet, Christ in danger
Christ in hearts of all that love me
Christ in mouth of friend or stranger.

Attributed to St. Patrick, ca. 390-461

556

Almsgiving

Let us now speak of the *manner* of bestowing alms, for that is necessary more than any other thing, that we may virtuously live and die most happily. First, it is necessary that we give alms with a most *sincere intention* of pleasing God and not for seeking popular praise...

Again, our alms is to be given *readily*, and with facility, that it may not seem to be wrung out by entreaty, nor delayed from day to day when it may presently be dispatched...

Thirdly, it is requisite that our alms be given *cheerfully*, and not with grudging...

Fourthly, it is necessary that our alms be given with *humility*, in such manner as the giver may know himself to receive more than he gives...

Fifthly, it is necessary that we give *abundantly*, according to the proportion or measure of our ability.

St. Robert Bellarmine, 1542-1621
The Art of Dying Well

Service

Lord Jesus, teach me to be generous;
teach me to serve you as you deserve,
to give and not to count the cost,
to fight and not to heed the wounds,
to toil and not to seek for rest,
to labour and not to seek reward,
except that of knowing that I do your will.

St. Ignatius Loyola, 1491-1556

Nothing great was ever done without much enduring.

St. Catherine of Siena, 1347-1380

God be in my head, and in my understanding;
God be in my eyes, and in my looking;
God be in my mouth, and in my speaking;
God be in my heart, and in my thinking;
God be at my end, and at my departing.

Sarum Breviary (1085)

Cling now to nothing save to God alone.

St. Vincent de Paul, ca. 1580-1660

Perfect prayer is achieved not with many words but with loving desire.

St. Catherine of Siena, 1347-1380, The Dialogue

You can do nothing about avoiding death, but you can do something about living well.

St. Augustine of Hippo, 354-430

Day by day, O dear Lord, three things I pray: to see thee more clearly, love thee more dearly, follow thee more nearly, day by day.

St. Richard of Chichester, ca. 1197-1253

Flood the Path with Light

God of our life, there are days when the burdens we carry chafe our shoulders and weigh us down; when the road seems dreary and endless, the skies grey and threatening; when our lives have no music in them, and our hearts are lonely, and our souls have lost their courage.

Flood the path with light, turn our eyes to where the skies are full of promise; tune our hearts to brave music; give us the sense of comradeship with heroes and saints of every age; and so quicken our spirits that we may be able to encourage the souls of all who journey with us on the road of life, to your honour and glory.

Attributed to St. Augustine of Hippo, 354-430

On Scripture

Can there be a more fitting pursuit in youth or a more valuable possession in old age than a knowledge of sacred scripture? In the midst of storms it will preserve you from the dangers of shipwreck and guide you to the shore of an enchanting paradise and the everlasting bliss of the angels... "Wisdom overcomes evil: it stretches from end to end mightily and disposes all things sweetly. Her have I loved from my youth" (Wis 8:1).

St. Boniface
Letter to St. Nithard

A Spirit to Know You

Gracious and holy Father, please give me:
intellect to understand you,
reason to discern you,
diligence to seek you,
wisdom to find you,
a spirit to know you,
a heart to meditate upon you,
ears to hear you,
eyes to see you,
a tongue to proclaim you,
a way of life pleasing to you,
patience to wait for you
and perseverance to look for you.
Grant me a perfect end,
your holy presence,
a blessed resurrection
and life everlasting.

St. Benedict of Nursia, ca. 480-547

On Prayer

My blessed daughter, know now that prayer is more perfect when it is made in the essence of the soul—when the soul prays in the Spirit of God. This is a most profound language, but when God wants to, he can make even stones speak. Allow then this great Good, this immense Good to repose in your spirit. This is a reciprocal rest: God in you, you in God. Oh, what a sweet work! What a divine work!...

Lucy, my daughter in Christ, God wants you to be a saint; he wants you to be holy. So be humble of heart, persevering in the prayer God gives you...

Enter more deeply into that holy desert, into that divine solitude within you, in the very essence of your soul, and there you will be reborn in the divine Word to a new life of love. God rests in you: God fills you and you are all in God. God is transforming you completely in his love.

St. Paul of the Cross, 1694-1775
Letter to Lucy Berlini

Prayer of Saint Thomas Aquinas

Grant me, O Lord my God, a mind to know you, a heart to seek you, wisdom to find you, conduct pleasing to you, faithful perseverance in waiting for you, and a hope of finally embracing you. Amen.

St. Thomas Aquinas, 1225-1274

PRAYERS AND MEDITATIONS FOR YOUTH

Quiet Time

Lighting the candle this morning
I sit quietly before it.
This is time set aside for God and me
to be together.

I wait...
In stillness...
I listen. God listens...
God is never too busy to listen.

My heart is open.
I come empty,
I come in hope,
I come in need to be made new.

Come Lord, your presence is creative, life-giving.
Cleanse and refresh me.
Encourage and strengthen me for the day ahead.
Thank you for our time together. Amen.

J. Bourgeau
North Bay ON

If we really want to pray,
we must first learn to listen,
for in the silence of the heart,
God speaks.

Blessed Teresa of Calcutta, 1910–1997

On Vocation

God calls all the souls he has created to love him with their whole being, here and hereafter, which means that he calls all of them to holiness, to perfection, to a close following of him and obedience to his will. But he does not ask all souls to show their love by the same works, to climb to heaven by the same ladder, to achieve goodness in the same way of life. What sort of work, then, must *I* do? Which is *my* road to heaven? In what kind of life am *I* to sanctify myself?...

This question: "What kind of life am I going to undertake?" is the question of *vocation*...

There is therefore a very grave duty for each one of us when we reach a certain age to take the most careful trouble to find out what vocation we have to follow. This vocation is God's call to undertake such-and-such a sort of holy life in preference to all others, his urgent call to each individual soul to sanctify itself in this particular way. There can never be any question of *choosing* a vocation: the word 'choice' is excluded by the word 'vocation,' which means 'calling,' a call from God.

Charles de Foucauld, 1858-1916
Sermons in the Sahara (1938)

Blessed Trinity

Blessed Trinity,
    loving and caring God of youth.
    The world we're in is both
    wonderful and dangerous.
    We can be with you or away from you!

Make us, Ever powerful Father,
    candles of light
        in places of darkness,
    oceans of generosity
        in places of need.

Make us, Ever gentle Jesus,
    pillars of faith
        in moments of godlessness,
    highways of truth
        in moments of illusion.

Make us, Ever kind Holy Spirit,
    icons of hope
        in times of despair,
    rivers of forgiveness
        in times of hatred,
    songs of peace
        in places of war.

These we ask as a gift through Mary. Amen.

P. A. Lucero
Quezon City, Philippines

Dear God,

Grant me the strength to be who I must be,
to do what I must do.
Give me the courage to stand strong
    against my fears
and have the will to express my feelings
    and needs.
Help me realize I have the power to change
—no matter what anyone tells me—
because of you.
Give me the faith I need to believe in you always
    —even when it seems you are not there.
I ask this in Jesus' name. Amen.

L. Bird
Charters Settlement, NB

Into Your Hands

Father, I abandon myself into your hands; do with me what you will. Whatever you may do, I thank you: I am ready for all, I accept all. Let only your will be done in me, and in all your creatures—I wish no more than this, O Lord.

Into your hands I commend my soul; I offer it to you with all the love of my heart, for I love you, Lord, and so need to give myself, to surrender myself into your hands, without reserve, and with boundless confidence, for you are my Father.

Charles de Foucauld, 1858-1916

PRAYERS AND MEDITATIONS
FROM MODERN TIMES

Christmas Prayer

Moonless darkness stands between.
Past, the Past, no more be seen!
But the Bethlehem star may lead me
To the sight of Him Who freed me
From the self that I have been.
Make me pure, Lord: Thou art Holy;
Make me meek, Lord: Thou wert lowly;
Now beginning, and alway:
Now begin, on Christmas day.

Gerard Manley Hopkins, 1844-1889

Irish Blessing

Deep peace of the running wave to you.
Deep peace of the flowing air to you.
Deep peace of the quiet earth to you.
Deep peace of the shining stars to you.
Deep peace of the Son of Peace to you.

The Desert

We must have no illusions. We shall not walk
on roses. People will not throng to hear us and
applaud; we shall not always be aware of divine
protection. If we are to be pilgrims for justice and
peace, we must expect the desert.

Dom Helder Camara, 1909-1999
Me llaman el obispo rojo

To Keep a True Lent

Is this a Fast, to keep
    The larder lean
      And clean
From fat of veals and sheep?

Is it to quit the dish
    Of flesh, yet still
      To fill
The platter high with fish?

Is it to fast an hour,
    Or ragg'd to go,
      Or show
A down-cast look and sour?

No: 'tis a Fast to dole
    Thy sheaf of wheat
      And meat
Unto the hungry soul.

It is to fast from strife
    And old debate,
      And hate;
To circumcise thy life.

To show a heart grief-rent;
    To starve thy sin,
      Not bin;
And that's to keep thy Lent.

Robert Herrick, 1591-1674

The Peace Prayer of St. Francis

Lord, make me an instrument of your peace.
Where there is hatred, let me sow love;
where there is injury, pardon;
where there is doubt, faith;
where there is despair, hope;
where there is darkness, light;
and where there is sadness, joy.

Divine Master,
grant that I may not so much seek
to be consoled as to console,
to be understood as to understand,
to be loved as to love.

For it is in giving that we receive,
in pardoning that we are pardoned,
and in dying that we are born to eternal life.

Unknown, ca. 1915

The Serenity Prayer

O God, grant me the serenity
to accept the things I cannot change,
the courage to change the things I can,
and the wisdom to know the difference.

Living one day at a time, enjoying one moment
at a time. Accepting hardships as the pathway to
peace. Taking, as he did, this sinful world as it is,
not as I would have it. Trusting that he will make
all things right if I surrender to his will; that I may
be reasonably happy in this life, and supremely
happy with him forever.

Reinhold Niebuhr, 1892-1971

Abide with Me

Abide with me; fast falls the eventide;
The darkness deepens; Lord, with me abide;
When other helpers fail, and comforts flee,
Help of the helpless, O abide with me.

Swift to its close ebbs out life's little day;
Earth's joys grow dim, its glories pass away;
Change and decay in all around I see;
O thou who changest not, abide with me.

Hold thou thy Cross before my closing eyes;
Shine through the gloom, and point me
    to the skies;
Heaven's morning breaks,
    and earth's vain shadows flee;
In life, in death, O Lord, abide with me.

Henry Francis Lyte (1847)

Solidarity

Solidarity is not a feeling of vague compassion
or shallow distress at the misfortunes of so many
people, both near and far. On the contrary, it is
a firm and persevering determination to commit
oneself to the common good: that is to say, to the
good of all and of each individual, because we are
all really responsible for all.

Pope John Paul II, 1920-2005
Concern for the Social Order (1987)

Prayer for Peace

Almighty and eternal God, may your grace enkindle in all of us a love for the many unfortunate people whom poverty and misery reduce to a condition of life unworthy of human beings.

Arouse in the hearts of those who call you Father a hunger and thirst for justice and peace and for fraternal charity in deeds and in truth.

Grant, O Lord, peace in our days, peace to souls, peace to families, peace to our country, and peace among nations. Amen.

Pope Pius XII, 1876-1958

Character of Mind

It is difficult and rare virtue to mean what we say, to love without dissimulation, to think no evil, to bear no grudge, to be free from selfishness, to be innocent and straightforward. This character of mind... is one of the surest marks of Christ's elect.

Cardinal Newman, 1801-1890
Parochial and Plain Sermons

The best prayers often have more groans than words.

John Bunyan, 1628-1688

LITURGY OF THE HOURS

Prayer of the Whole People of God

In the Apostolic Letter *Novo Millennio Ineunte,* I expressed the hope that the Church would become more and more distinguished in the "art of prayer," learning it ever anew from the lips of the Divine Master. This effort must be expressed above all in the liturgy, the source and summit of ecclesial life. Consequently, it is important to devote greater pastoral care to promoting the Liturgy of the Hours as a prayer of the whole People of God. [...]

By praying the Psalms as a community, the Christian mind [remembers and understands] that it is impossible to turn to the Father who dwells in heaven without an authentic communion of life with one's brothers and sisters who live on earth. Moreover, by being vitally immersed in the Hebrew tradition of prayer, Christians [learn] to pray by recounting the great marvels worked by God both in the creation of the world and humanity, and in the history of Israel and the Church. This form of prayer drawn from Scripture does not exclude certain freer expressions, which will continue not only to characterize personal prayer, but also to enrich liturgical prayer itself [...] But the Book of Psalms remains the ideal source of Christian prayer and will continue to inspire the Church in the new millennium. [...]

[In] singing the Psalms, the Christian feels a sort of harmony between the Spirit present in the Scriptures and the Spirit who dwells within him through the grace of Baptism. [...]

In addition to the presence of the Holy Spirit, another important dimension is that of the priestly action which Christ carries out in this prayer, associating with himself the Church, his Bride. In this regard, referring to the Liturgy of the Hours, the Second Vatican Council teaches: "Jesus Christ... attaches to himself the entire community of mankind and has them join him in singing his divine song of praise. For he continues his priestly work through his Church. The Church, by celebrating the Eucharist and by other means, especially the celebration of the Divine Office, is ceaselessly engaged in praising the Lord and interceding for the salvation of the entire world" (*Sacrosanctum Concilium*, n. 83). [...]

Christian prayer is born, nourished and develops around the event of faith par excellence: Christ's paschal mystery. Thus Easter, the Lord's passing from death to life, is commemorated in the morning, in the evening, at sunrise and at sunset. [...]

Giving their prayer this rhythm, Christians respond to the Lord's command "to pray always" but without forgetting that their whole life must, in a certain way, become a prayer.

Pope John Paul II
excerpts from General Audiences
March 28 and April 4, 2001

PRAYER IN THE MORNING

Invitation to Prayer

Lord, open our lips.
And we shall proclaim your praise.

Glory to God in the highest.
And peace to God's people on earth.

PRAISE

Hymn of Praise *(Optional)*

Psalm of Praise

Psalm 63 and/or another psalm of praise (see psalms, p. 603), followed by a moment of silence.

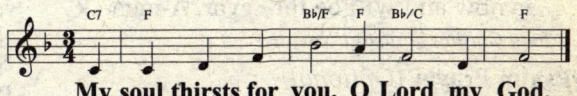

My soul thirsts for you, O Lord my God.

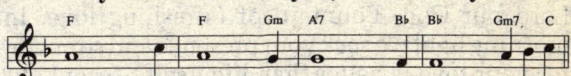

R. **My soul thirsts for you, O Lord my God.**

O God, you are my God, I · **seek_you,**
my soul · **thirsts_for_you;**
my flesh · **faints_for_you,**
as in a dry and weary land
   where there · **is** no water. R.

So I have looked upon you in the · **sanctuary,**
beholding your power and · **glory.**
Because your steadfast love is better than · **life,**
my · **lips** will praise_you. R.

→

So I will bless you as long as I · **live;**
I will lift up my hands and call on your · **name.**
My soul is satisfied as with a rich · **feast,**
and my mouth praises you
  with · **joy**-ful lips. R.

R. **My soul thirsts for you, O Lord my God.**

For you have been my · **help,**
and in the shadow of your wings I sing for · **joy.**
My soul · **clings_to_you;**
your right · **hand** up-holds_me. R.

Glory to the Father, and to the · **Son,**
and to the Holy · **Spirit.**
As it was in the be-·**ginning,**
is now and will be for · **ever.** A-men. R.

Psalm Prayer *(Optional)*

Lord our God, Fountain of refreshing love, in
morning light we seek your presence and strength,
for your love is better than life itself. Accept our
prayers with uplifted hands as we proclaim your
praise in songs of joy. Satisfy our longing hearts
and renew our thirsting spirits that our worship
may give you glory and our lives be poured out
in loving service.

Glory and praise to you, loving God, through our
Lord Jesus Christ, your Son, who lives and reigns
with you in the unity of the Holy Spirit, God for
ever and ever. **Amen.**

Word of God

*Appropriate verse(s) selected beforehand from the
readings of the day, followed by a moment of silence.*

Canticle of Zechariah

1. Blessed be the God of Israel,
   Who comes to set us free,
   Who visits and redeems us,
   And grants us liberty.
   The prophets spoke of mercy,
   Of freedom and release;
   God shall fulfill the promise
   To bring our people peace.

2. Now from the house of David
   A child of grace is giv'n;
   A Saviour comes among us
   To raise us up to heaven.
   Before him goes the herald,
   Forerunner in the way:
   The prophet of salvation,
   The messenger of Day.

3. Where once were fear and darkness
   The sun begins to rise,
   The dawning of forgiveness
   Upon the sinners' eyes,
   To guide the feet of pilgrims
   Along the paths of peace:
   O bless our God and Saviour
   With songs that never cease!

Text: Michael Perry, ©1973 Hope Publishing Co.
Tune: MERLE'S TUNE, 76.76.D.; ©1983 Hope Publishing
Co. Used by permission. All rights reserved.
Music: CBW III 13E

INTERCESSION

Petitions

These reflect the needs of the Church, the world, the suffering, and the local community. Weekly suggestions are available at www.livingwithchrist.ca

Our Father...

Concluding Prayer

God of glory and compassion, at your touch the wilderness blossoms, broken lives are made whole, and fearful hearts grow strong in faith. Open our eyes to your presence and awaken our hearts to sing your praise. To all who long for your Son's return grant perseverance and patience, that we may announce in word and deed the good news of the kingdom.

We ask this through our Lord Jesus Christ, your Son, who lives and reigns with you in the unity of the Holy Spirit, God for ever and ever. **Amen.**

Blessing

May the Lord almighty order our days and our deeds in lasting peace. **Amen.**

Let us offer each other a sign of Christ's peace.

The celebration ends with the exchange of peace.

***

For a fuller version of the Liturgy of the Hours, consult the Living with Christ *missalette, regular or large-print edition.*

PRAYER IN THE EVENING

The paschal candle is lit and carried in procession. During Advent, the Advent wreath may be lit instead. If you plan to use Psalm 141, prepare the thurible beforehand so that incense may be burned during the singing of the psalm.

Invitation to Prayer

God, come to our assistance.
Lord, make haste to help us.

Glory to the Father, and to the Son, and to the Holy Spirit.
As it was in the beginning, is now, and will be forever. Amen.

PRAISE

Hymn of Praise *(Optional)*

Psalm of Praise

Psalm 141 and/or another psalm of praise (see psalms, p. 603), followed by a moment of silence.

Let my prayer a-rise like in-cense be-fore you.

R̷ **Let my prayer arise like incense before you.**

I call upon you, O Lord: come quickly to · **me;**
give ear to my voice when I call to · **you.**
Let my prayer be counted as incense
be-**fore_you.**
and the lifting up of my hands as
an eve-**ning** sacrifice. R̷ →

Set a guard over my mouth, O · **Lord;**
keep watch over the door of my · **lips.**
But my eyes are turned toward you,
  O God, my · **Lord;**
in you I seek refuge; do not leave me
  · **de**-fenceless. ℟

℟ **Let my prayer arise like incense before you.**

Glory to the Father, and to the · **Son,**
and to the Holy · **Spirit.**
As it was in the be-·-**ginning,**
is now and will be for ever. · **A**-men. ℟

©2008 Gordon Johnston/Novalis

Psalm Prayer *(Optional)*

Loving God, creator of light and life, may our prayers ascend to you like the fragrance of incense. Purify our hearts to sing your praise in the company of your saints in glory.

We ask this through Christ our Lord. **Amen.**

Word of God

Appropriate verse(s) selected beforehand from the readings of the day, followed by a moment of silence.

Canticle of Mary

1. My soul proclaims the Lord my God.
    My spirit sings God's praise,
    Who looks on me and lifts me up,
    That gladness fill my days.

2. All nations now will share my joy,
    For gifts God has outpoured.
    This lowly one has been made great
    I magnify the Lord.

3. For those who fear the Holy One,
   God's mercy will not die,
   Whose strong right arm puts down the proud,
   And lifts the lowly high.

4. God fills the hungry with good things,
   And sends the rich away.
   The promise made to Abraham,
   Is filled to endless day.

5. Then let all nations praise our God,
   The Father and the Son,
   The Spirit blest who lives in us,
   While endless ages run.

Text: Anne Carter, ©1988 Religious of the Sacred Heart.
Tune: HEATHER DEW
Music: *CBW III* 592, 617; *CBW II* 74, 589

INTERCESSION

Petitions

These reflect the needs of the Church, the world, the suffering, and the local community. Weekly suggestions are available at www.livingwithchrist.ca

Our Father...

Concluding Prayer

Creator of the universe, watch over us and keep us in the light of your presence. May our praise continually blend with that of all creation, until we come together to the eternal joys which you promise in your love.

We ask this through our Lord Jesus Christ, your Son, who lives and reigns with you in the unity of the Holy Spirit, God for ever and ever. **Amen.**

Blessing

May God the Father almighty bless and keep us. **Amen.**

May Jesus Christ, his only Son, our Lord, graciously smile upon us. **Amen.**

May the Holy Spirit, the Lord and giver of life, grant us peace. **Amen.**

Let us offer each other a sign of Christ's peace.

The celebration ends with the exchange of peace.

***

For a fuller version of the Liturgy of the Hours, consult the Living with Christ *missalette, regular or large-print edition.*

EUCHARISTIC ADORATION

Entrance Procession

An appropriate song may accompany the procession. At the altar, the presider places the lunula in the monstrance and invites the assembly to kneel in adoration for several minutes.

Welcome

The presider invites the assembly to stand and welcomes them in these or other words.

We are gathered today to adore the Lord and to witness to each other our faith in Jesus present in the eucharist.

United in prayer, we have come to meet Jesus, our Lord, to learn from him how to worship in spirit and in truth.

The Lord remains with us and his presence in the eucharist always goes before us. This is why we call on the Holy Spirit to open our hearts and our spirits to help us to grasp the depth of the eucharistic mystery and its continuation in our lives.

A moment of silence or a brief refrain invoking the Holy Spirit may follow. Suggestions: Veni, Sancte Spiritus (Taizé); Christopher Walker setting, 419; Come Holy Spirit, 416.

This outline is adapted from In Christ's Presence: Leader's Guide (Ottawa: Novalis, 2007). For detailed suggestions, please consult p. 6-9. All hymn suggestions refer to CBW III, unless otherwise specified.

Word of God *(Luke 11.1-4)*

Lectionary for Weekdays, vol. B, # 463, p. 1657-58. The presider invites the assembly to be seated. Following the reading and a brief period of silence, the presider may comment in these or similar words:

"Jesus was praying in a certain place" says the evangelist Luke. Today Jesus is still praying in a certain place. He is here with us in his eucharistic presence. Let us dare to ask the Lord to teach us to adore. Jesus' response to his disciples allows us to grasp one aspect of his interior life. We can see the adoration and praise that well up in his heart when he is at prayer, "When you pray, say 'Father...'." To pray with Jesus, to pray as he does, is to turn to the Father.

Litany

A reader proclaims slowly and reflectively:

For the eternal love out of which you have created us, Lord, we adore you. With Jesus, through him and in him, we bless you, Father, Lord of heaven and earth.

R. **We bless you, Father,
Lord of heaven and earth.**

For the gift of creation which speaks to us of your beauty: Lord, we adore you. With Jesus, through him and in him, we bless you, Father, Lord of heaven and earth. R.

For the gift of your Son who has revealed to us your loving face: Lord, we adore you. With Jesus, through him and in him, we bless you, Father, Lord of heaven and earth. R.

For your solicitude and your goodness towards your children: Lord we adore you. With Jesus, through him and in him, we bless you, Father, Lord of heaven and earth. ℟.

Song of Adoration

Hymn suggestions: Joyful, Joyful, We Adore You, *511;* Let All Things Now Living, *534;* O God Beyond All Praising, *561;* Celtic Alleluia, *549A;* Strong Is God's Love for Us, *546;* Holy God, *558;* How Great Thou Art, *554;* Holy God, We Praise Your Name, *555.*

First Incensation

A designated person raises a pot of burning incense before the blessed sacrament and then places it on the table or stand prepared for it before the altar. After people have prayed in silence for a few moments, the reader says slowly:

"When you pray, say, 'Father, hallowed be your name'."

The presider may comment in these or similar words:

These words of Jesus reveal the deepest desire of his heart: that his Father's name be made holy. In the Bible, speaking of someone's name refers to more than a simple 'name tag' that designates someone. The name evokes the person's identity and deepest nature. Thus, when Jesus prays that his Father's name be made holy, he expresses his deepest desire that the whole universe recognize that God is holy. In the same breath, he prays that all God's children may share his holiness. To adore Jesus present in the eucharist is to make this desire of Jesus at prayer our own.

Litany

A reader reads the petitions slowly and reflectively:

In the heart of all the baptized who were plunged into the death and resurrection of your Son, with Jesus, through him and in him, Father, hallowed be your name.

R. **Father, hallowed be your name.**

In the priests who have received the mission of prolonging the eucharistic presence of your Son, with Jesus, through him and in him, Father, hallowed be your name. R.

In the spirit of all persons who, without knowing you, are looking for meaning in their lives, with Jesus, through him and in him, Father, hallowed be your name. R.

In people who are hungry, alone and sick, with Jesus, through him and in him, Father, hallowed be your name. R.

In the children of the whole world who each day struggle against death and sickness, with Jesus, through him and in him, Father, hallowed be your name. R.

In the missionaries and messengers of the Gospel, with Jesus, through him and in him, Father, hallowed be your name. R.

In the heart of all the members of our families whom we love so dearly, with Jesus, through him and in him, Father, hallowed be your name. R.

In all the young people who are looking for happiness, with Jesus, through him and in him, Father, hallowed be your name. R.

In our hearts open to the gift of your love, with Jesus, through him and in him, Father, hallowed be your name. R.

Song of Adoration

Sing the same song as before.

Second Incensation

A designated person raises a second pot of burning incense and proceeds as for the previous incensation. After people have prayed in silence for a few moments, the reader says slowly:

"When you pray, say, 'Father, may your kingdom come'."

The presider may comment in these or similar words:

With these words, Jesus expresses another secret of his inner life. He came into the world to reveal the Father's love. His heart burns with desire to see this love consuming the earth. The Father's reign is a reign of love – but not just any kind of love. It is the reign of the love that is presence. Jesus himself is God's reign among us. We are in his presence. In the eucharist, the reign of God encounters us in our own daily lives to enable us to pass from this world to the Father. Jesus has opened to us the path that leads to eternal life, the Father's path. In the eucharist we are united, incorporated into Jesus. In this time of adoration, let us allow ourselves to be filled by the love that springs without end from the heart of Jesus and draws us to the Father.

Litany

A reader reads the petitions slowly and reflectively:

In this world that you made to show forth your glory, with Jesus, through him and in him, Father, may your kingdom come.

R. **Father, may your kingdom come.**

That all people who are hungry for love may find you, with Jesus, through him and in him, Father, may your kingdom come. R.

That your holiness shine forth in the Church, with Jesus, through him and in him, Father, may your kingdom come. R.

In the heart of our pastors who show forth your concern and your goodness, with Jesus, through him and in him, Father, may your kingdom come. R.

In the hidden life of people who suffer, with Jesus, through him and in him, Father, may your kingdom come. R.

That we might live in love, with Jesus, through him and in him, Father, may your kingdom come. R.

That our lives might be adoration and praise, with Jesus, through him and in him, Father, may your kingdom come. R.

That our hearts be open and generous, with Jesus, through him and in him, Father, may your kingdom come. R.

Song of Adoration

Sing the same song as before.

Third Incensation

A designated person raises a third pot of burning incense and proceeds as for the previous incensation. After people have prayed in silence for a few moments, the reader says slowly:

"When you pray, say, 'Father, may your will be done'."

The presider may comment in these or similar words:

The Father's will nourishes Jesus, that is, it gives him life. Jesus is turned towards the Father in a posture of inner openness and self-giving. For Jesus, doing the will of the Father is the totality of love. It means remaining in a stance of giving and of offering even unto death. Neither suffering, nor agony, nor fear of death turned Jesus away from his Father. When we participate in the eucharist, Jesus transforms us in our depths so that we might become, with him, through him and in him, a living offering of praise and love.

Litany

A reader reads the petitions slowly and reflectively:

That we may become living sacrifices, holy and pleasing to God, with Jesus, through him and in him, Father, may your will be done.

R. **Father, may your will be done.**

That we might offer spiritual worship in proclaiming the Gospel, with Jesus, through him and in him, Father, may your will be done.

That our lives might be truly transformed by our participation in the eucharist, with Jesus, through him and in him, Father, may your will be done. R.

That we might allow ourselves to be caught up in the eucharistic sacrifice, with Jesus, through him and in him, Father, may your will be done. R̰

R̰ **Father, may your will be done.**

That we might grow in true worship through the gift of ourselves in love, with Jesus, through him and in him, Father, may your will be done. R̰

That our adoration continue by daily fulfilling your will, with Jesus, through him and in him, Father, may your will be done. R̰

That an inner posture of adoration might always be pre-eminent in the Church and in the hearts of your faithful people, with Jesus, through him and in him, Father, may your will be done. R̰

Incensation

The presider incenses the blessed sacrament.

Benediction and Dismissal

If a priest or deacon is presiding at this celebration, he takes the monstrance and blesses the people. Then he dismisses the assembly.

May the spiritual fruits of this hour of adoration keep you faithful to God and to a life of self-giving. Go and remain in the peace of Christ. **Thanks be to God.**

If a layperson is presiding, he or she does not bless the people with the monstrance, but dismisses them in the following manner:

May the spiritual fruits of this hour of adoration keep us faithful to God and to a life of self-giving. Let us go and remain in the peace of Christ. **Thanks be to God.**

An appropriate song may be sung as the assembly leaves.

PAPAL PRAYER INTENTIONS 2011

November 2010

That, with the support of the Christian community, victims of drugs or of other dependencies find in the power of our Saving God strength for a radical life-change.

That the Churches of Latin America move ahead with the continent-wide mission proposed by their bishops, making it part of the universal missionary task of the People of God.

December 2010

That our personal experience of suffering be an occasion for better understanding the situation of unease and pain which is the lot of many people who are alone, sick or elderly, and stir us all to give them generous help.

That the peoples of the earth open their doors to Christ and to his Gospel of peace, brotherhood and justice.

January 2011

That the riches of the created world be preserved, valued, and made available as God's precious gift to all.

That Christians attain full unity, witnessing to all the universal fatherhood of God.

February 2011

That all respect the family and recognize it for its unmatched contribution to the advancement of society.

That Christian communities witness to the presence of Christ in serving those who suffer from disease in those mission territories where the fight against disease is most urgent.

March 2011

That the nations of Latin America walk in fidelity to the Gospel and progress in justice and peace.

That the Holy Spirit give light and strength to those in many regions of the world who are persecuted and discriminated against because of the Gospel.

April 2011

That through its compelling preaching of the Gospel, the Church give young people new reasons for life and hope.

That by proclamation of the Gospel and the witness of their lives, missionaries bring Christ to those who do not yet know him.

May 2011

That those working in communications media respect the truth, solidarity, and dignity of all people.

That the Lord help the Church in China persevere in fidelity to the Gospel and grow in unity.

June 2011

That priests, united to the Heart of Christ, always be true witnesses to the caring and merciful love of God.

That the Holy Spirit bring forth from our communities many missionaries who are ready to be fully consecrated to spreading the Kingdom of God.

July 2011

That Christ ease the physical and spiritual sufferings of those who are sick with AIDS, especially in the poorest countries.

That religious women in mission territories be witnesses of the joy of the Gospel and living signs of the love of Christ.

August 2011

That World Youth Day in Madrid encourage young people throughout the world to have their lives rooted and built up in Christ.

That Western Christians be open to the action of the Holy Spirit and rediscover the freshness and enthusiasm of their faith.

September 2011

That all teachers know how to communicate love of the truth and instill authentic moral and spiritual values.

That the Christian communities of Asia proclaim the Gospel with fervour, witnessing to its beauty with the joy of faith.

October 2011

That the terminally ill be supported by their faith in God and the love of their brothers and sisters.

That the celebration of World Mission Sunday foster in the People of God a passion for evangelization with the willingness to support the missions with prayer and economic aid for the poorest Churches.

November 2011

That the Eastern Catholic Churches and their venerable traditions be known and esteemed as a spiritual treasure for the whole Church.

That the African continent find strength in Christ to pursue justice and reconciliation as set forth by the second Synod of African Bishops.

December 2011

That all peoples grow in harmony and peace through mutual understanding and respect.

That children and young people be messengers of the Gospel and that they be respected and preserved from all violence and exploitation.

MUSIC

These hymns, psalms and acclamations offer a limited selection of music for the liturgical seasons. Familiarize yourself with all the selections offered, since they may be suitable for other celebrations as well. The seasonal psalms from the *Lectionary, Sundays and Solemnities* are also included *(p. 603)*.

For many of the metred hymns, you will find words only, along with the metre of the tune (indicated by the numbers following the name of the hymn tune) and a recommendation for a hymn tune (indicated by the name of the tune in block capitals). In this way, a number of different texts may be used with the same melody. You may find, however, that one tune seems to 'fit' a text better than others. Using this simple system, you can match the text provided with a tune that is familiar to your congregation. Most standard hymnals, such as the *Catholic Book of Worship (CBW)*, index their contents both by tune and by metre. We refer to numbers in *CBW II* and *CBW III*.

To hear a recording of the Sunday psalm, go to www.livingwithchrist.ca and choose Music. The complete accompaniment for the psalms may be purchased at www.novalis.ca or telephone 1(800) 387-7164.

Reborn of Water and the Spirit

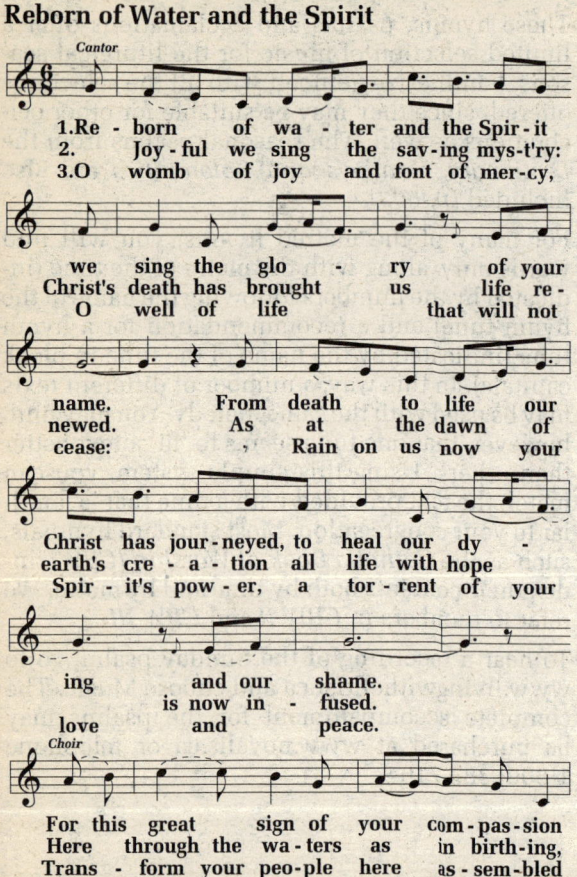

Cantor

1. Re - born of wa - ter and the Spir - it
2. Joy - ful we sing the sav - ing mys - t'ry:
3. O womb of joy and font of mer - cy,

we sing the glo - ry of your
Christ's death has brought us life re -
O well of life that will not

name. From death to life our
newed. As at the dawn of
cease: Rain on us now your

Christ has jour - neyed, to heal our dy -
earth's cre - a - tion all life with hope
Spir - it's pow - er, a tor - rent of your

ing and our shame.
is now in - fused.
love and peace.

Choir

For this great sign of your com - pas - sion
Here through the wa - ters as in birth - ing,
Trans - form your peo - ple here as - sem - bled

we sing, one bo - dy, in one Lord:
your peo - ple pass through death to life.
in - to a sign of your great love: A

clothed in the Spir - it, now com - mis - sioned to
Here, too, you feed us at your ban - quet with
ho - ly, priest - ly, roy - al peo - ple, a

bring good news to all your world.
bread and cup that end all strife.
seed on earth of heav'n a - bove.

Refrain (Assembly)

Al - le - lu - ia, al - le - lu - ia!

Al - le - lu - ia, al - le - lu - ia!

Re - born of wa - ter and the Spir - it we

cel - e - brate! Al - le - lu - ia!

Text: ©1994 Bernadette Gasslein, b. 1952
Music: ©2004 Geoffrey S. Angeles, b. 1977

TE DEUM EUCHARISTIC ACCLAMATIONS

Keyboard accompaniment is available from Novalis, Bayard Press Canada Inc., 223 Main St., Ottawa, ON K1S1C4.

Preface Dialogue

Priest: The Lord be with you.

All: And al - so with you.

Priest: Lift up your hearts.

All: We lift them up to the Lord.

Priest: Let us give thanks to the Lord our God.

All: It is right to give him thanks and praise.

Tune: M. A. Charpentier, adapt. R. J. Lahey. ©2000 Raymond J. Lahey, b. 1940. All rights reserved.

Holy, Holy

Ho-ly, ho-ly, ho-ly Lord, God of pow er, God of might, heav-en and earth are full of your great glo - ry. Ho - san-na in the high - est, Ho - san - na in the high - est. Bless'd is he who comes in the name of the Lord. Ho - san - na in the high - est, Ho - san-na in the high - est.

Tune: M. A. Charpentier, adapt. R. J. Lahey. ©2000 Raymond J. Lahey, b. 1940. All rights reserved.

Memorial Acclamation 1

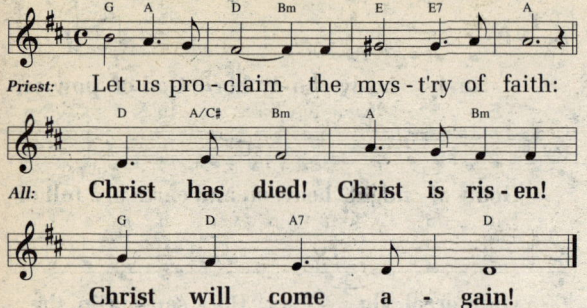

Priest: Let us pro-claim the mys-t'ry of faith:

All: Christ has died! Christ is ris-en!

Christ will come a - gain!

Tune: M. A. Charpentier, adapt. R. J. Lahey. ©2000 Raymond
J. Lahey, b. 1940. All rights reserved.

Memorial Acclamation 2

Priest: Praise to you, Lord Jesus, first-born from the dead!

All: Dy-ing you de-stroyed our death, ris-ing you re-stored our life. Lord Je-sus, come in glo-ry, come in glo-ry.

Memorial Acclamation 3

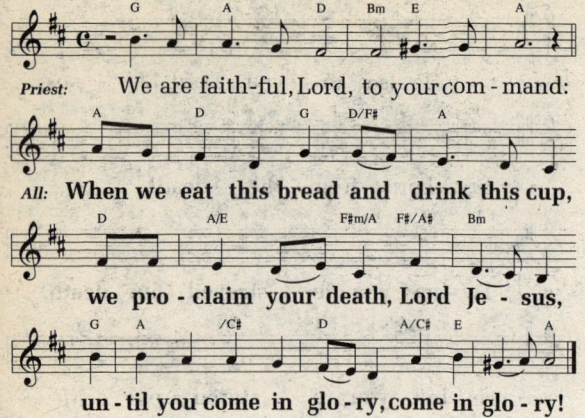

Priest: We are faith-ful, Lord, to your com-mand:

All: When we eat this bread and drink this cup,

we pro-claim your death, Lord Je-sus,

un-til you come in glo-ry, come in glo-ry!

Tune: M. A. Charpentier, adapt. R. J. Lahey.

Memorial Acclamation 4

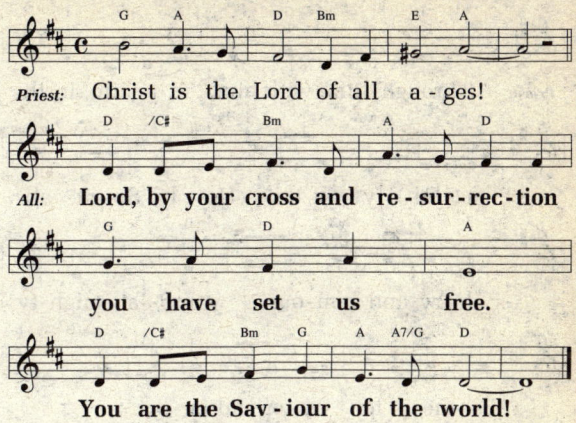

Priest: Christ is the Lord of all a-ges!

All: Lord, by your cross and re-sur-rec-tion

you have set us free.

You are the Sav-iour of the world!

Tune: M. A. Charpentier, adapt. R. J. Lahey. ©2000 Raymond J. Lahey, b. 1940. All rights reserved.

Doxology

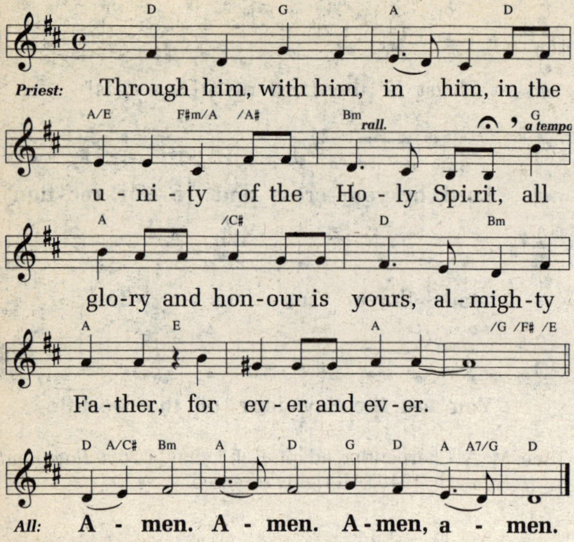

Priest: Through him, with him, in him, in the u‑ni‑ty of the Ho‑ly Spi‑rit, all glo‑ry and hon‑our is yours, al‑migh‑ty Fa‑ther, for ev‑er and ev‑er.

All: A‑men. A‑men. A‑men, a‑men.

Tune: M. A. Charpentier, adapt. R. J. Lahey.

SEASONAL PSALMS

Using Seasonal Psalms

In your parish, do you rarely sing the psalm? Perhaps it is too daunting to learn a new psalm to sing each week. If this is the case, take time to discover the seasonal psalms, one of the Sunday lectionary's best-kept secrets. These psalms are designed "to make the sung response easier for the people" (*Lectionary, Sundays and Solemnities* [*LS*]).

At the end of each season (Advent, Christmas, Lent, Easter and Ordinary Time), the Sunday lectionary lists the common psalms for that particular season. A real option is to choose a psalm different from the one for the Mass of the day.

How do you choose a seasonal psalm? "Care should be taken that the alternate text be similar in meaning to [the psalm of the Sunday]," advises *LS*. While this may be easier during the high seasons than during Ordinary Time, here are a few ways to simplify the process.

1. Divide Ordinary Time (OT) into various parts: winter OT (between Christmas and Ash Wednesday); spring OT (between Pentecost and the end of June); summer OT (July to Labour Day); autumn OT (September and October); and finally, November OT, known liturgically as the "Last Weeks of Ordinary Time." Each division is long enough for people to learn a refrain and yet not get tired of it. This means you might use five seasonal psalms in a year. The assembly will more easily pray

these psalms, and the responses will become part of them. During the other seasons, using a single psalm can bring a sense of unity to the season.

2. Check the psalms for the weeks in question to see if there is a seasonal psalm. For example, in Year B, Psalm 34 is the appointed psalm for three consecutive weeks in summer OT. It is also a seasonal psalm for Ordinary Time. Therefore, it could be used during the summer months.

3. Remember that the psalm is a response to the first reading (selected in relationship with the gospel). In choosing a seasonal psalm, look for "similar meaning" in a broad sense, reading the first reading, the psalm of the day and the gospel. For instance, replace a psalm of praise in a Sunday's liturgy with a seasonal psalm of praise.

4. You can use a seasonal psalm on a single Sunday or on consecutive weeks, using a psalm that is well-known and appropriate to the liturgy.

5. Many communities that celebrate (or would like to celebrate) Morning and Evening Prayer find the psalm singing challenging. Consider using a single seasonal psalm throughout the celebration of Morning and Evening Prayer during a particular season.

Singing the psalms roots these ancient prayers deep in our consciousness. Whatever we can do to promote psalm singing within our communities will be important for the ongoing spiritual formation of the people of God.

Bernadette Gasslein

Full accompaniment for the psalms is available at www.novalis.ca *or telephone* 1(800) 387-7164.

ADVENT SEASONAL PSALM *(Psalm 25)*

To you, O Lord, I lift my soul.

℟. **To you, O Lord, I lift my soul.**

Make me to know your ways, O · **Lord,**
teach me your · **paths.**
Lead me in your truth and · **teach_me,**
for you are the God of my · **sal**-vation. ℟.

Good and upright is the · **Lord,**
therefore he instructs sinners in the · **way.**
He leads the humble in what is · **right,**
and teaches the humble · **his** way. ℟.

All the paths of the Lord are steadfast love
    and · **faithfulness,**
for those who keep his covenant and his de-·-**crees.**
The friendship of the Lord is for those
    who · **fear_him,**
and he makes his covenant known · **to** them. ℟.

For the Liturgy of the Hours, add:

Glory to the Father, and to the · **Son,**
and to the Holy · **Spirit.**
As it was in the be-·-**ginning,**
is now and will be for ever. · **A**-men. ℟.

ADVENT SEASONAL PSALM *(Psalm 85)*

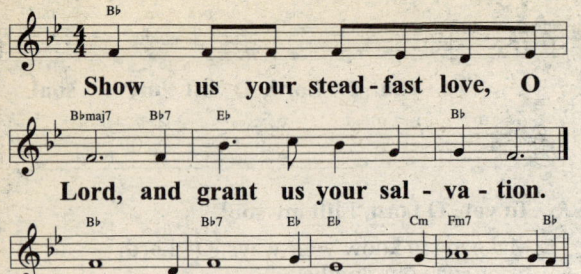

R. **Show us your steadfast love, O Lord,**
and grant us your salvation.

Let me hear what God the Lord will · **speak,**
for he will speak peace to his · **people.**
Surely his salvation is at hand for those
    who · **fear_him,**
that his glory may dwell · **in_our** land. R.

Steadfast love and faithfulness will · **meet;**
righteousness and peace will · **kiss_each_other.**
Faithfulness will spring up from the · **ground,**
and righteousness will look down · **from_the** sky. R.

The Lord will give what is · **good,**
and our land will yield its · **increase.**
Righteousness will go be-·**fore_him,**
and will make a path · **for_his** steps. R.

For the Liturgy of the Hours, add:

Glory to the Father, and to the · **Son,**
and to the Holy · **Spirit.**
As it was in the be-·ginning,
is now and will be for ever. · **A-men.** R.

©2009 Gordon Johnston/Novalis

ADVENT SEASONAL PSALM *(Psalm 146)*

Lord, come and save us.

R̷ **Lord, come and save us.**

It is the Lord who keeps faith for-·**ever,**
who executes justice for the op-·**pressed;**
who gives food to the · **hungry.**
The Lord sets the · **prisoners** free. R̷

The Lord opens the eyes of the · **blind**
and lifts up those who are bowed · **down;**
the Lord loves the · **righteous**
and watches over · **the** strangers. R̷

The Lord upholds the orphan and the · **widow,**
but the way of the wicked he brings to · **ruin.**
The Lord will reign for-·**ever,**
your God, O Zion, for all · **gener-**ations. R̷

For the Liturgy of the Hours, add:

Glory to the Father, and to the · **Son,**
and to the Holy · **Spirit.**
As it was in the be-·**ginning,**
is now and will be for ever. · **A-men.** R̷

©2009 Gordon Johnston/Novalis

CHRISTMAS SEASONAL PSALM *(Psalm 34)*

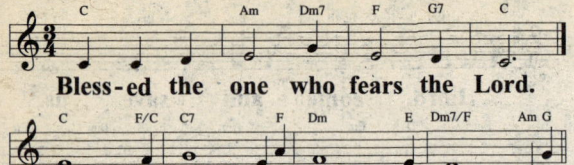

Bless-ed the one who fears the Lord.

℟. **Blessed the one who fears the Lord.**

I will bless the Lord at all · **times;**
his praise shall continually be in · **my** mouth.
My soul makes its boast in the · **Lord;**
let the humble hear and · **be** glad. ℟.

O fear the Lord, you his · **holy_ones,**
for those who fear him have · **no** want.
The young lions suffer want and · **hunger,**
but those who seek the Lord lack no · **good** thing. ℟.

Come, O children, · **listen_to_me;**
I will teach you the fear of · **the** Lord.
Which of you desires · **life,**
and covets many days to en-·**joy** good? ℟.

Keep your tongue from · **evil,**
and your lips from speaking · **de**-ceit.
Depart from evil, and do · **good;**
seek peace, and · **pur**-sue_it. ℟.

For the Liturgy of the Hours, add:

Glory to the Father, and to the · **Son,**
and to the Ho-·**ly** Spirit.
As it was in the be-·**ginning,**
is now and will be for ever. ·**A**-men. ℟.

CHRISTMAS SEASONAL PSALM *(Psalm 72)*

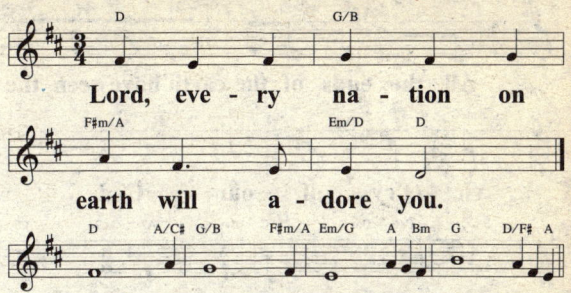

Lord, eve-ry na-tion on earth will a-dore you.

R. **Lord, every nation on earth will adore you.**

Give the king your justice, O · **God,**
and your righteousness to a king's · **son.**
May he judge your · **people** with righteousness,
and your · **poor** with justice. **R.**

In his days may righteousness · **flourish**
and peace abound, until the moon is no · **more.**
May he have dominion from · **sea** to sea,
and from the River to the · **ends_of** the earth. **R.**

May the kings of Tarshish and of the isles
render him · **tribute,**
may the kings of Sheba and Seba bring · **gifts.**
May all kings fall · **down** be-fore_him,
all nations · **give** him service. **R.**

For he delivers the needy one who · **calls,**
the poor and the one who has no · **helper.**
He has pity on the · **weak_and** the needy,
and saves the · **lives_of** the needy. **R.**

For the Liturgy of the Hours, add:

Glory to the Father, and to the · **Son,**
and to the Holy · **Spirit.**
As it was in · **the** be-ginning,
is now and will be for · **ever.** A-men. **R.**

©2009 Gordon Johnston/Novalis

CHRISTMAS SEASONAL PSALM *(Psalm 98)*

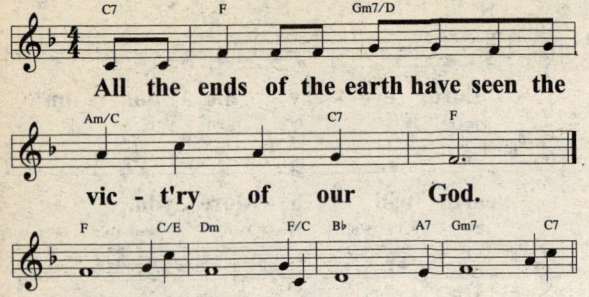

All the ends of the earth have seen the
vic - t'ry of our God.

R. **All the ends of the earth have seen
the victory of our God.**

O sing to the Lord a · **new** song,
for he has done · **marvellous** things.
His right hand and his holy · **arm**
have brought · **him** victory. **R.**

The Lord has made known · **his** victory;
he has revealed his vindication in the sight
of · **the** nations.
He has remembered his steadfast love
and · **faithfulness**
to the house · **of** Israel. **R.**

All the ends of the earth · **have** seen
the victory of · **our** God.
Make a joyful noise to the Lord, all the · **earth;**
break forth into joyous song and · **sing** praises. **R.**

Sing praises to the Lord with · **the** lyre,
with the lyre and the sound · **of** melody.
With trumpets and the sound of the · **horn**
make a joyful noise before the King, · **the** Lord. **R.**

For Liturgy of the Hours, add:

Glory to the Father, and to · **the** Son,
and to the Ho-**ly** Spirit.
As it was in the be-**ginning,**
is now and will be for ever. · **A-men.** **R.**

LENT SEASONAL PSALM *(Psalm 22)*

My God, my God,
why have you for - sak - en me?

R. **My God, my God, why have you forsaken me?**

All who see me · **mock_at_me;**
they make mouths at me, they shake · **their** heads;
"Commit your cause to the Lord; let him de-·-**liver;**
let him rescue the one in whom he · **de-**lights!" R.

For dogs are all a-·-**round_me;**
a company of evildoers · **en-**circles_me.
My hands and feet have · **shrivelled;**
I can count all · **my** bones. R.

They divide my clothes a-·-**mong_themselves,**
and for my clothing they · **cast** lots.
But you, O Lord, do not be far a-·-**way!**
O my help, come quickly · **to_my** aid! R.

I will tell of your name to my brothers and sisters; in
the midst of the congregation I will · **praise_you:**
You who fear the · **Lord,** praise_him!
All you offspring of Jacob, · **glorify_him;**
stand in awe of him, all you offspring · **of** Israel! R.

For Liturgy of the Hours, add:

Glory to the Father, and to the · **Son,**
and to the Ho-·-**ly** Spirit.
As it was in the be-·-**ginning,**
is now and will be for ever. · **A-**men. R.

©2009 Gordon Johnston/Novalis

LENT SEASONAL PSALM *(Psalm 51)*

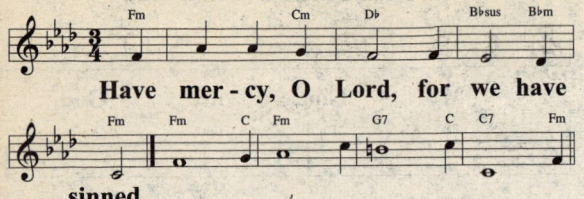

Have mer - cy, O Lord, for we have sinned.

R. **Have mercy, O Lord, for we have sinned.**

Have mercy on me, O God, according
    to your steadfast · **love;**
according to your abundant mercy
    blot out my trans--**gressions.**
Wash me thoroughly from my in--**iquity,**
and cleanse me from my · **sin.** R.

For I know my trans--**gressions,**
and my sin is ever be--**fore_me.**
Against you, you alone, have I · **sinned,**
and done what is evil in your · **sight.** R.

Create in me a clean heart, O · **God,**
and put a new and right spirit with--**in_me.**
Do not cast me away from your · **presence,**
and do not take your holy spirit from · **me.** R.

Restore to me the joy of your sal--**vation,**
and sustain in me a willing · **spirit.**
O Lord, open my · **lips,**
and my mouth will declare your · **praise.** R.

For Liturgy of the Hours, add:

Glory to the Father, and to the · **Son,**
and to the Holy · **Spirit.**
As it was in the be--**ginning,**
is now and will be for ever. · **Amen.** R.

LENT SEASONAL PSALM *(Psalm 91)*

Be with me, Lord, when I am in trou-ble.

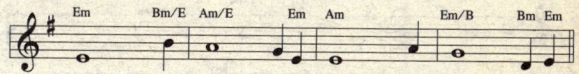

℟. **Be with me, Lord, when I am in trouble.**

You who live in the shelter of the Most · **High,**
who abide in the shadow of the · **Al**-mighty,
will say to the Lord, "My refuge and my · **fortress;**
my God, in whom · **I** trust." ℟.

No evil shall be·-**fall_you,**
no scourge come near · **your** tent.
For he will command his Angels con-·**cerning_you**
to guard you in all · **your** ways. ℟.

On their hands they will bear you · **up,**
so that you will not dash your foot against · **a** stone.
You will tread on the lion and the · **adder,**
the young lion and the serpent
    you will trample · **under** foot. ℟.

The one who loves me, I will de-·**liver;**
I will protect the one who knows · **my** name.
When he calls to me, I will · **answer_him;**
I will be with him in trouble,
    I will rescue him · **and** honour_him. ℟.

For Liturgy of the Hours, add:

Glory to the Father, and to the · **Son,**
and to the Ho·-**ly** Spirit.
As it was in the be·-**ginning,**
is now and will be for ever. · **A**-men. ℟.

LENT SEASONAL PSALM *(Psalm 130)*

With the Lord there is stead - fast
love and great pow'r to re - deem.

R. **With the Lord there is steadfast love,
and great power to redeem.**

Out of the depths I cry to you, O · **Lord.**
Lord, hear · **my** voice!
Let your ears be at-·**tentive**
to the voice of my sup-·**pli**-cations! R.

If you, O Lord, should mark in-·**iquities,**
Lord, who · **could** stand?
But there is forgiveness with · **you,**
so that you may be · **re**-vered. R.

I wait for the · **Lord,**
my soul waits, and in his word · **I** hope;
my soul waits for the · **Lord**
more than watchmen for · **the** morning. R.

For with the Lord there is steadfast · **love,**
and with him is great power to · **re**-deem.
It is he who will redeem · **Israel**
from all its · **in**-iquities. R.

For Liturgy of the Hours, add:

Glory to the Father, and to the · **Son,**
and to the Ho-·**ly** Spirit.
As it was in the be-·**ginning,**
is now and will be for ever. · **A**-men. R.

EASTER SEASONAL PSALM *(Psalm 47)*

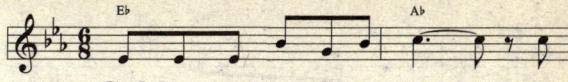

God has gone up with a shout, the

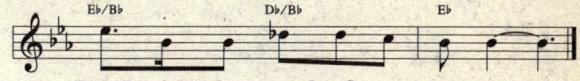

Lord with the sound of a trum - pet.

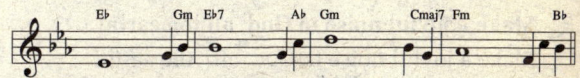

R̶. **God has gone up with a shout,**
the Lord with the sound of a trumpet.

Clap your hands, all · **you** peoples;
shout to God with loud songs · **of** joy.
For the Lord, the Most High, · **is** awesome,
a great king over · **all** the earth. R̶.

God has gone up · **with_a** shout,
the Lord with the sound of · **a** trumpet.
Sing praises to God, · **sing** praises;
sing praises to our · **King,** sing praises. R̶.

For God is the king of all · **the** earth;
sing praises · **with_a** Psalm.
God is king over · **the** nations;
God sits on his · **ho**-ly throne. R̶.

For Liturgy of the Hours, add:

Glory to the Father, and to · **the** Son,
and to the Ho··**ly** Spirit.
As it was in the · **be**-ginning,
is now and will be for · **ever.** A-men. R̶.

©2009 Gordon Johnston/Novalis

EASTER SEASONAL PSALM *(Psalm 66)*

R. **Make a joyful noise to God, all the earth!**

Make a joyful noise to God, all · **the** earth;
sing the glory · **of_his** name;
give to him · **glorious** praise.
Say to God, "How awesome are your · **deeds!**" **R.**

"All the earth · **worships** you;
they sing praises to you,
    sing praises · **to_your** name."
Come and see what God · **has** done:
he is awesome in his deeds among
    the children of · **Adam. R.**

He turned the sea into · **dry** land;
they passed through the river · **on** foot.
There we rejoiced · **in** him,
who rules by his might for--**ever. R.**

Come and hear, all you who · **fear** God,
and I will tell what he · **has** done_for_me.
Blessed be God, because he has not
    rejected · **my** prayer
or removed his steadfast love from · **me. R.**

For Liturgy of the Hours, add:
Glory to the Father, and to · **the** Son,
and to the Ho--**ly** Spirit.
As it was in the · **be**-ginning,
is now and will be for ever. · **Amen. R.**

©2009 Gordon Johnston/Novalis

616

EASTER SEASONAL PSALM *(Psalm 104)*

Lord, send forth your Spir-it,

and re-new the face of the earth.

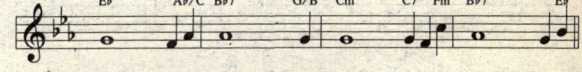

R. **Lord, send forth your Spirit,**
   and renew the face of the earth.

Bless the Lord, O · **my** soul.
O Lord my God, you are very · **great.**
O Lord, how manifold · **are** your works!
The earth is full of · **your** creatures. R.

When you take away · **their** breath,
they die and return to their · **dust.**
When you send forth your spirit, they · **are** cre-ated;
and you renew the face of · **the** earth. R.

May the glory of the Lord endure · **for**-ever;
may the Lord rejoice in his · **works.**
May my meditation be · **pleasing** to him,
for I rejoice in · **the** Lord. R.

For Liturgy of the Hours, add:

Glory to the Father, and to · **the** Son,
and to the Holy · **Spirit.**
As it was in · **the** be-ginning,
is now and will be for ever. · **A-men.** R.

EASTER SEASONAL PSALM *(Psalm 118)*

This is the day the Lord has made;
let us re - joice and be glad.

R̷. **This is the day the Lord has made;**
let us rejoice and be glad.

O give thanks to the Lord, for · **he** is good;
his steadfast love en--**dures** for-ever.
Let Is--**rael** say,
"His steadfast love en--**dures** for-ever." R̷.

"The right hand of the Lord · **is** ex-alted;
the right hand of the · **Lord** does valiantly."
I shall not die, but · **I_shall** live,
and recount the · **deeds_of** the Lord. R̷.

The stone that the · **builders** re-jected
has become · **the** chief cornerstone.
This is the · **Lord's** doing;
it is marvellous · **in** our eyes. R̷.

For Liturgy of the Hours, add:

Glory to the Father, and · **to** the Son,
and to the · **Ho**-ly Spirit.
As it was in · **the_be**-ginning,
is now and will be for · **ever.** A-men. R̷.

©2009 Gordon Johnston/Novalis

ORDINARY TIME
SEASONAL PSALM *(Psalm 19)*

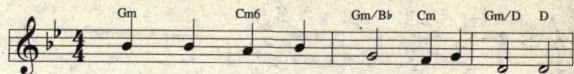

Lord, you have the words of e - ter - nal

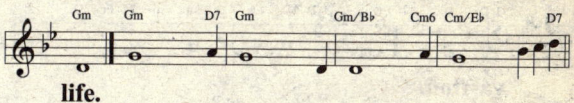

life.

℟. **Lord, you have the words of eternal life.**

The law of the Lord is · **perfect,**
reviving the · **soul;**
the decrees of the Lord are · **sure,**
making · **wise** the simple. ℟.

The precepts of the Lord are · **right,**
rejoicing the · **heart;**
the commandment of the Lord is · **clear,**
en-·**lightening** the eyes. ℟.

The fear of the Lord is · **pure,**
enduring for-·**ever;**
the ordinances of the Lord are · **true**
and righteous · **al**-to-gether. ℟.

More to be desired are they than · **gold,**
even much fine · **gold;**
sweeter also than · **honey,**
and drippings · **of** the honeycomb. ℟.

For Liturgy of the Hours, add:

Glory to the Father, and to the · **Son,**
and to the Holy · **Spirit.**
As it was in the be-·**ginning,**
is now and will be for · **ever.** A-men. ℟.

©2009 Gordon Johnston/Novalis

ORDINARY TIME
SEASONAL PSALM *(Psalm 27)*

The Lord is my light and my sal -

va - tion.

R. **The Lord is my light and my salvation.**

The Lord is my light and my sal-·**vation**;
whom shall · **I** fear?
The Lord is the stronghold of my · **life**;
of whom shall I be · **a**-fraid? R.

One thing I asked of the Lord, that will **I** · **seek_after:**
to live in the house of the Lord
   all the days of · **my** life,
to behold the beauty of the · **Lord,**
and to inquire in · **his** temple. R.

I believe that I shall see the goodness of the · **Lord**
in the land of · **the** living.
Wait for the Lord; be · **strong,**
and let your heart take courage;
   wait · **for_the** Lord! R.

For Liturgy of the Hours, add:

Glory to the Father, and to the · **Son,**
and to the Ho-·**ly** Spirit.
As it was in the be-·**ginning,**
is now and will be for ever. · **A-**men. R.

©2009 Gordon Johnston/Novalis

ORDINARY TIME
SEASONAL PSALM *(Psalm 34)*

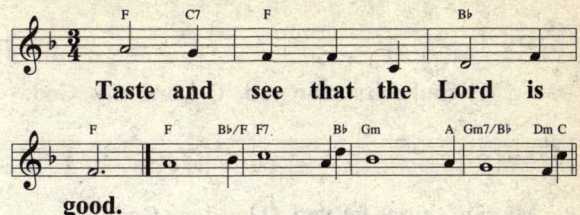

Taste and see that the Lord is

good.

R̥. **Taste and see that the Lord is good.**

I will bless the Lord at all · **times;**
his praise shall continually be in · **my** mouth.
My soul makes its boast in the · **Lord;**
let the humble hear and · **be** glad. R̥.

O magnify the Lord with · **me,**
and let us exalt his name · **to**-gether.
I sought the Lord, and he · **answered_me,**
and delivered me from all · **my** fears. R̥.

Look to him, and be · **radiant;**
so your faces shall never · **be_a**-shamed.
The poor one called, and the Lord · **heard,**
and saved that person from ev--**ery** trouble. R̥.

The Angel of the Lord en--**camps**
around those who fear him, and · **de**-livers_them.
O taste and see that the Lord is · **good;**
blessed is the one who takes refuge · **in** him. R̥.

For Liturgy of the Hours, add:

Glory to the Father, and to the · **Son,**
and to the Ho--**ly** Spirit.
As it was in the be--**ginning,**
is now and will be for ever. · **A**-men. R̥.

©2009 Gordon Johnston/Novalis

ORDINARY TIME
SEASONAL PSALM *(Psalm 63)*

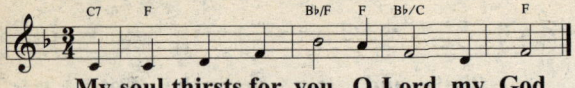

My soul thirsts for you, O Lord my God.

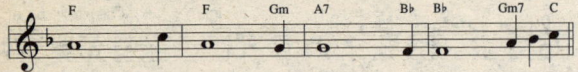

℟. **My soul thirsts for you, O Lord my God.**

O God, you are my God, I · **seek_you,**
my soul · **thirsts_for_you;**
my flesh · **faints_for_you,**
as in a dry and weary land
    where there · **is** no water. ℟.

So I have looked upon you in the · **sanctuary,**
beholding your power and · **glory.**
Because your steadfast love is better than · **life,**
my · **lips** will praise_you. ℟.

So I will bless you as long as I · **live;**
I will lift up my hands and call on your · **name.**
My soul is satisfied as with a rich · **feast,**
and my mouth praises you with · **joy**-ful lips. ℟.

For you have been my · **help,**
and in the shadow of your wings I sing for · **joy.**
My soul · **clings_to_you;**
your right · **hand** up-holds_me. ℟.

For Liturgy of the Hours, add:

Glory to the Father, and to the · **Son,**
and to the Holy · **Spirit.**
As it was in the be-·**ginning,**
is now and will be for · **ever.** A-men. ℟.

ORDINARY TIME
SEASONAL PSALM *(Psalm 95)*

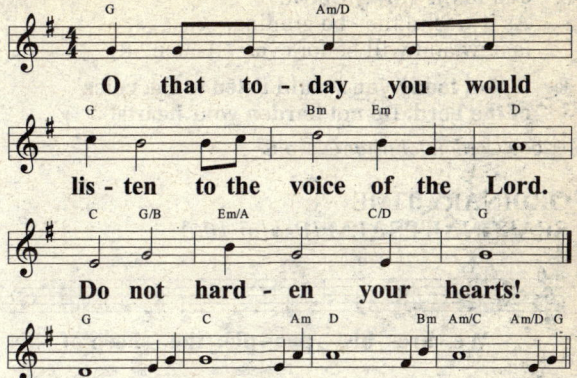

O that to-day you would lis-ten to the voice of the Lord. Do not hard-en your hearts!

R̸. **O that today you would listen to the voice
of the Lord. Do not harden your hearts!**

O come, let us sing to · **the** Lord;
let us make a joyful noise to the rock
   of our · **sal**-vation!
Let us come into his presence with · **thanks**-giving;
let us make a joyful noise to him
   with songs · **of** praise! R̸.

O come, let us worship and · **bow** down,
let us kneel before the Lord, · **our** Maker!
For he is our God, and we are the people
   of · **his** pasture,
and the sheep of · **his** hand. R̸.

O that today you would listen to · **his** voice!
Do not harden your hearts, as at Meribah,
   as on the day at Massah in · **the** wilderness,
when your ancestors tested me,
   and put me to · **the** proof,
though they had seen · **my** work. R̸.   →

For Liturgy of the Hours, add:

> Glory to the Father, and to · **the** Son,
> and to the Ho-·**ly** Spirit.
> As it was in the · **be**-ginning,
> is now and will be for ever. · **A**-men. ℟

℟ **O that today you would listen to the voice of the Lord. Do not harden your hearts!**

ORDINARY TIME
SEASONAL PSALM *(Psalm 100)*

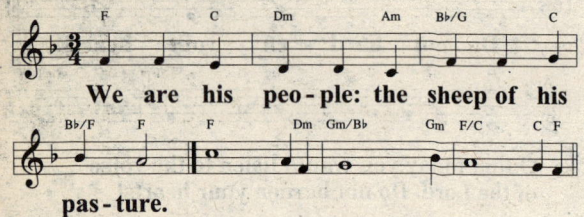

We are his peo-ple: the sheep of his pas-ture.

℟ **We are his people: the sheep of his pasture.**

> Make a joyful noise to the Lord, all · **the** earth.
> Worship the Lord with · **gladness;**
> come into his presence · **with** singing. ℟

> Know that the Lord · **is** God.
> It is he that made us, and we are · **his;**
> we are his people, and the sheep of · **his** pasture. ℟

> For the Lord · **is** good;
> his steadfast love endures for-**ever,**
> and his faithfulness to all · **gener**-ations. ℟

For Liturgy of the Hours, add:

> Glory to the Father, and to the Son, and to
> the Ho-·**ly** Spirit.
> As it was in the be-·**ginning,**
> is now and will be for ever. · **A**-men. ℟

ORDINARY TIME
SEASONAL PSALM *(Psalm 103)*

The Lord is mer-ci-ful and gra-cious.

R. **The Lord is merciful and gracious.**

Bless the Lord, O my · **soul,**
and all that is within me, bless his · **holy** name.
Bless the Lord, O my · **soul,**
and do not forget all · **his** benefits. **R.**

It is the Lord who forgives all your in-**iquity,**
who heals all your · **dis**-eases,
who redeems your life from the · **Pit,**
who crowns you with steadfast love · **and** mercy. **R.**

The Lord is merciful and · **gracious,**
slow to anger and abounding in stead--**fast** love.
He does not deal with us according to our · **sins,**
nor repay us according to our · **in**-iquities. **R.**

As far as the east is from the · **west,**
so far he removes our transgressions · **from** us.
As a father has compassion for his · **children,**
so the Lord has compassion
for those · **who** fear_him. **R.**

For Liturgy of the Hours, add:

Glory to the Father, and to the · **Son,**
and to the Ho--**ly** Spirit.
As it was in the be--**ginning,**
is now and will be for ever. · **A**-men. **R.**

©2009 Gordon Johnston/Novalis

ORDINARY TIME
SEASONAL PSALM *(Psalm 122)*

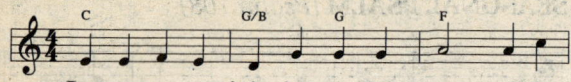

Let us go re-joic-ing to the house of the

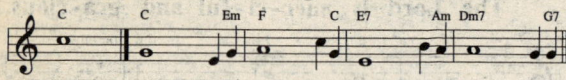

Lord.

R̥ **Let us go rejoicing to the house of the Lord.**

I was glad when they said · **to** me,
"Let us go to the house of · **the** Lord!"
Our feet · **are** standing
within your gates, O · **Je**-rusalem. R̥

Jerusalem—built as · **a** city
that is bound firmly · **to**-gether.
To it the tribes · **go** up,
the tribes · **of the** Lord. R̥

As was decreed · **for** Israel,
to give thanks to the name of · **the** Lord.
For there the thrones for judgment · **were set** up,
the thrones of the · **house of** David. R̥

Pray for the peace of · **Je**-rusalem:
"May they prosper · **who** love you.
Peace be within · **your** walls,
and security within · **your** towers." R̥

For the sake of my relatives · **and** friends
I will say, "Peace be · **with**-in you."
For the sake of the house of the Lord · **our** God, ·
I will seek · **your** good. R̥

For Liturgy of the Hours, add:

Glory to the Father, and to · **the** Son,
and to the Ho·-**ly** Spirit.
As it was in the · **be**-ginning,
is now and will be for ever. · **A**-men. R̥

©2009 Gordon Johnston/Novalis

626

ORDINARY TIME
SEASONAL PSALM (Psalm 145)

I will bless your name for ev – er,

my King and my God.

R. **I will bless your name for ever,
my King and my God.**

I will extol you, my God and · **King,**
and bless your name forever and · **ever.**
Every day I will · **bless_you,**
and praise your name forever · **and** ever. R.

The Lord is gracious and · **merciful,**
slow to anger and abounding in steadfast · **love.**
The Lord is good to · **all,**
and his compassion is over all
that he · **has** made. R.

All your works shall give thanks to you, O · **Lord,**
and all your faithful shall · **bless_you.**
They shall speak of the glory of your · **kingdom,**
and tell of · **your** power. R.

The Lord is faithful in all his · **words,**
and gracious in all his · **deeds.**
The Lord upholds all who are · **falling,**
and raises up all who are · **bowed** down. R.

For Liturgy of the Hours, add:

Glory to the Father, and to the · **Son,**
and to the Holy · **Spirit.**
As it was in the be··**ginning,**
is now and will be for ever. · **A-men.** R.

HYMNS

O Come, O Come Emmanuel

1. O come, o come Emmanuel,
   And ransom captive Israel,
   That mourns in lowly exile here,
   Until the son of God appear.

Ref: Rejoice! Rejoice! Emmanuel
   Shall come to you, O Israel.

2. O come, O come, great Lord of might,
   Who to your tribes on Sinai's height,
   In ancient times once gave the law
   In cloud, and majesty and awe.

3. O come, O Rod of Jesse's stem,
   From ev'ry foe deliver them
   That trust your mighty pow'r to save
   And give them vict'ry o'er the grave.

4. O come, O Key of David, come
   And open wide our heav'nly home;
   Make safe the way that leads on high,
   And close the path to misery.

5. O come, O Dayspring from on high
   And cheer us by your drawing nigh;
   Disperse the gloomy clouds of night
   And death's dark shadows put to flight.

Text: 9th century; tr. John Mason Neale, 1818-66 and others
Tune: VENI, VENI EMMANUEL, 88.88.88.
Music: *CBW II* 440; *CBW III* 312

O Come, Divine Messiah

1. O come, divine Messiah!
   The world in silence waits the day
   When hope shall sing its triumph,
   And sadness flee away.

Ref: Sweet Saviour, haste;
      Come, come to earth:
      Dispel the night, and show thy face,
      And bid us hail the dawn of grace.
      O come, divine Messiah!
      The world in silence waits the day
      When hope shall sing its triumph,
      And sadness flee away.

2. O thou, whom nations sighed for,
   Whom priests and prophets long foretold,
   Wilt break the captive fetters,
   Redeem the long-lost fold.

3. Shalt come in peace and meekness,
   And lowly will thy cradle be:
   All clothed in human weakness
   Shall we thy Godhead see.

Text: Abbé Pellegrin, 1663-1745; tr. Sr. Mary of St. Philip
Tune: VENEZ DIVIN MESSIE, 78.76.888
Music: *CBW II* 441; *CBW III* 310

Listen, My People

Lis-ten, my peo-ple, your hopes are an-swered. Lis-ten, and hear my voice, your hopes are an - swered, your hopes are an - swered.

1. God waits for his peo-ple to throw
2. God waits for his peo-ple to
3. God waits for his peo-ple to cast

off the dark of night and to
o - pen wide their eyes, and to
off their cloak of fear, and to

wel - come the new day,
mar - vel at the sight
walk up - on this earth:

where all is light,
of the sun - rise.
God is so near.

Text and Music: © Paul-André Durocher
Full accompaniment: CBW III 309

O Come, All Ye Faithful

1. O come, all ye faithful, joyful and triumphant,
   O come ye, o come ye to Bethlehem;
   Come and behold him, born the King of angels.

Ref: O come, let us adore him,
         O come, let us adore him,
         O come, let us adore him,
         Christ, the Lord.

2. Sing, choirs of angels, sing in exultation,
   Sing, all ye citizens of heav'n above.
   Glory to God in the highest.

3. Yea, Lord, we greet thee,
      born this happy morning,
   Jesus, to thee be glory giv'n;
   Word of the Father, now in flesh appearing.

Text: 18th century, tr. Frederick Oakely (1802-80) and others
Tune: ADESTE FIDELES; Irregular
Music: *CBW II* 458; *CBW III* 329

O First-Born Daughter

1. O first-born daugh-ter of God's grace,
2. O true dis-ci-ple of the Lord,
3. O wo-man, bear-er of our God,

You lead the vast ar - ray
You call us to de - clare
Now mid-wife at the birth

Of all who sing God's ho - ly name
The deep com-pas-sion of your Son,
Of God's own just-ice, God's great day:

Through time to end-less day.
God's peace be - yond com - pare.
The hope of all the earth.

Refrain

Might-y God! a-cross the spans of time

Your mer-cy still we sing;

With Ma-ry we re-call your deeds

And joy-filled praise now bring.

Text: ©*1993 Bernadette Gasslein,* b. 1952. Tune: FOREST GREEN
or KINGSFOLD. Music: *CBW II* 730; *CBW III* 502, 425

On Jordan's Bank

1. On Jordan's bank the Baptist's cry
   Announces that the Lord is nigh;
   Awake and hearken, for he brings
   Glad tidings of the King of kings.

2. Then cleansed be ev'ry heart from sin,
   Make straight the way for God within,
   And let each heart prepare a home
   Where such a mighty guest may come.

3. For you are our salvation, Lord,
   Our refuge and our great reward;
   Without your grace we waste away,
   Like flow'rs that wither and decay.

4. To heal the sick, stretch out your hand,
   And bid the fallen sinner stand;
   Shine forth, and let your light restore
   Earth's own true loveliness once more.

5. To God the Son all glory be
   Whose advent sets your people free;
   Whom with the Father we adore
   And Holy Spirit evermore.

Text: Charles Coffin, 1676-1749; tr. John Chandler, 1806-76
Tune: WINCHESTER NEW, LM
Music: *CBW II* 443; *CBW III* 350

Jesus, Word of God, Kyrie!

Suitable as a processional during Lent. The refrain is a fitting response to the Penitential Rite or to the Prayer of the Faithful throughout Lent and Easter seasons.

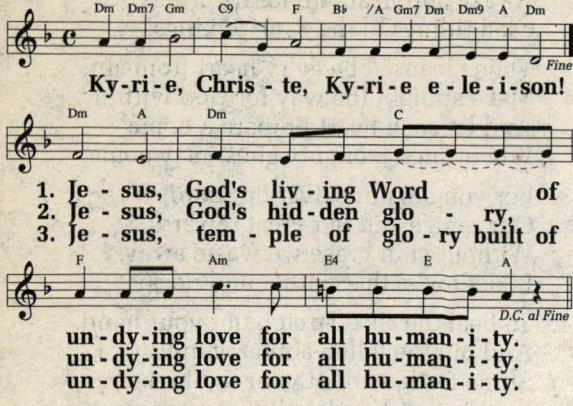

Ky-ri-e, Chris-te, Ky-ri-e e-le-i-son!

1. Je-sus, God's liv-ing Word of
2. Je-sus, God's hid-den glo-ry,
3. Je-sus, tem-ple of glo-ry built of

un-dy-ing love for all hu-man-i-ty.
un-dy-ing love for all hu-man-i-ty.
un-dy-ing love for all hu-man-i-ty.

4. Jesus, raised on the tree of
   undying love for all humanity.

5. Jesus, harvest of new life,
   sown in undying love for all humanity.

6. Jesus, God crucified
   out of undying love for all humanity.

7. Jesus, Servant and Lord,
   you are undying love for all humanity.

8. Jesus, bread born of wheat,
   food of undying love for all humanity.

9. Jesus, wine from the grape,
   cup of undying love for all humanity.

10. Jesus, abandoned on the tree
    in your undying love for all humanity.

Verses for Sundays of Lent, Year A:

3rd Sunday of Lent:

Jesus, fountain of life,
source of undying love for all humanity.

4th Sunday of Lent:

Jesus, light for the blind and
undying love for all humanity.

5th Sunday of Lent:

Jesus, Lord of all life
in your undying love for all humanity.

Text: Didier Rimaud, © CNPL; tr., adapt. ©1993 Bernadette
    Gasslein
Source: "Jésus, Verbe de Dieu, Kyrie," ©Éditions Musicales
    Studio SM, 060794-2
Music: Jacques Berthier

Kyrie

Suitable as a response to the Penitential Rite or to the Prayer of the Faithful.

Ky - ri - e e - lei - son.

Ky - ri - e e - lei - son.

Ky - ri - e e - lei - son.

Tune: Orthodox chant

O Sacred Head Surrounded

1. O sacred head surrounded
   By crown of piercing thorn.
   O bleeding head, so wounded,
   Reviled and put to scorn!
   Death's pallid hue comes o'er you,
   The glow of life decays.
   Yet angel hosts adore you
   And tremble as they gaze.

2. In this your bitter passion,
   Good Shepherd, think of me
   With your most sweet compassion,
   Unworthy though I be:
   Beneath your cross abiding
   For ever would I rest,
   In your dear love confiding,
   And with your presence blest.

3. Christ Jesus, we adore you,
   Our thorn-crowned Lord and King.
   We bow our heads before you
   And to your cross we cling.
   Lord, give us strength to bear it
   With patience and with love,
   That we may truly merit
   A glorious crown above.

Text: Bernard of Clairvaux, v. 1 tr. Henry W. Baker, 1821-77;
vv. 2 and 3 tr. Arthur Tozer Russell, 1806-74
Tune: PASSION CHORALE; 76.76.D., Hans Leo Hassler, 1564-1612
Music: *CBW II* 491; *CBW III* 377

Hail Our Saviour's Glorious Body (Pange Lingua)

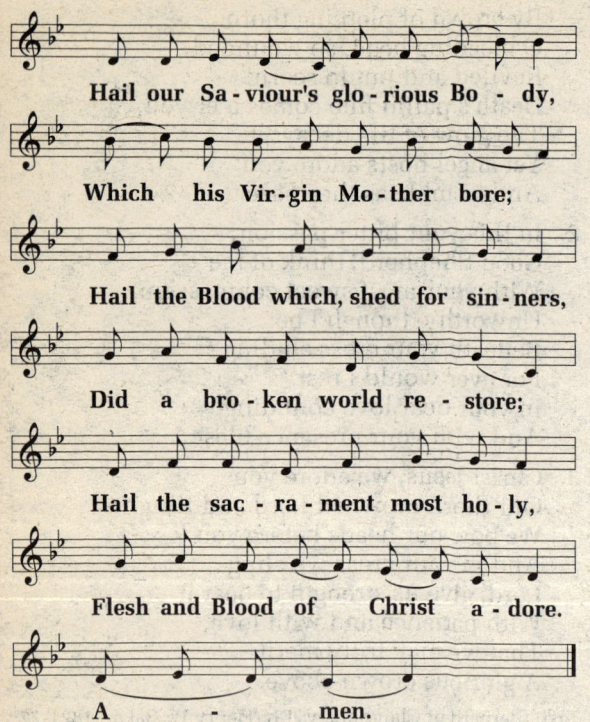

Hail our Sa-viour's glo-rious Bo - dy,

Which his Vir-gin Mo-ther bore;

Hail the Blood which, shed for sin-ners,

Did a bro-ken world re - store;

Hail the sac-ra-ment most ho-ly,

Flesh and Blood of Christ a-dore.

A - men.

2. To the Virgin, for our healing,
   His own Son the Father sends;
   From the Father's love proceeding
   Sower, seed and word descends;
   Wondrous life of Word incarnate
   With his greatest wonder ends.

3. On that paschal evening see him
   With the chosen twelve recline,
   To the old law still obedient
   In its feast of love divine;
   Love divine, the new law giving,
   Gives himself as Bread and Wine.

4. By his word the Word almighty
   Makes of bread his flesh indeed;
   Wine becomes his very life-blood;
   Faith God's living Word must heed!
   Faith alone may safely guide us
   Where the senses cannot lead!

At the incensing of the Blessed Sacrament:

5. Come, adore this wondrous presence;
   Bow to Christ, the source of grace!
   Here is kept the ancient promise
   Of God's earthly dwelling place!
   Sight is blind before God's glory,
   Faith alone may see God's face.

6. Glory be to God the Father,
   Praise to his co-equal Son,
   Adoration to the Spirit,
   Bond of love in God-head one!
   Blest be God by all creation
   Joyously while ages run! Amen.

Text: *Pange Lingua*, Thomas Aquinas, 1227-74; tr. James Quinn, SJ (1919-2010). Used by permission of Geoffrey Chapman. A division of Cassell PLC, London, England.
Tune: PANGE LINGUA, 87.87.87.
Music: *CBW II* 583; *CBW III* 381

Sing My Tongue the Ageless Story

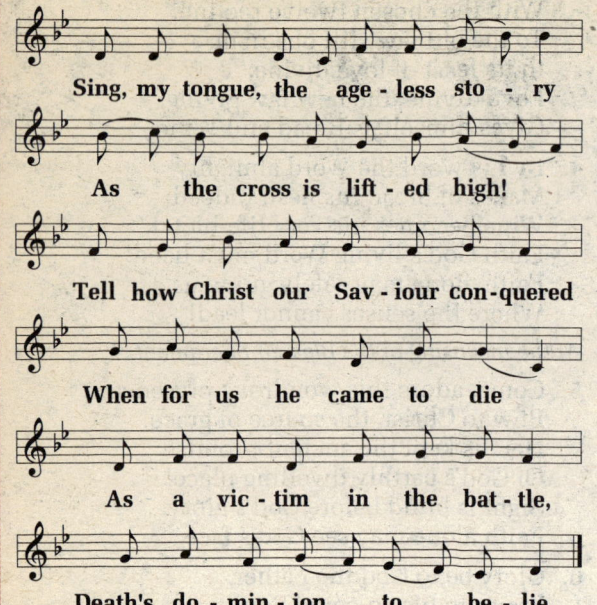

Sing, my tongue, the age-less sto-ry

As the cross is lift-ed high!

Tell how Christ our Sav-iour con-quered

When for us he came to die

As a vic-tim in the bat-tle,

Death's do-min-ion to be-lie.

2. Adam tasted sin and sorrow,
   Eating of the fearful tree;
   All undoing our enchainment,
   By the tree Christ sets us free,
   Crushing hell's own tool of bondage,
   By his great humility.

3. Silence cloaked the earth and heavens
   Round the hill of Calvary;
   Nailed upon the tree of glory,
   Christ endured his agony.
   In his royal blood descending
   Comes our peace, our liberty.

4. Cross triumphant! Cross transforming!
   Ensign of humanity!
   Faithful cross, above all others,
   One and only noble tree:
   Gracious wood and gracious iron,
   Gracious burden borne on thee!

Text: © *Dominican Friars of Toronto.* Used by permission.
Tune: PANGE LINGUA, REGENT SQUARE, PICARDY, 87.87.87.
Music: *CBW II* 583, 528, 571; *CBW III* 381, 456, 596

When I Behold the Wondrous Cross

1. When I behold the wondrous cross
   On which the prince of glory died,
   My richest gain I count but loss
   And pour contempt on all my pride.

2. Forbid it, Lord, that I should boast
   Save in the death of Christ, my God;
   The vain things that attract me most,
   I sacrifice them to his blood.

3. See, from his head, his hands, his feet,
   Sorrow and love flow mingled down.
   Did e'er such love and sorrow meet,
   Or thorns compose so rich a crown?

4. Were all the realms of nature mine,
   It would be off'ring far too small;
   Love so amazing, so divine,
   Demands my soul, my life, my all!

Text: Isaac Watts, 1674-1748, alt.
Tune: ROCKINGHAM, LM
Music: *CBW II* 489; *CBW III* 382

Ye Sons and Daughters

Refrain: Alleluia, alleluia, alleluia!

1. Ye sons and daughters, let us sing!
   The King of heav'n, our glorious King,
   From death today rose triumphing. Alleluia!

2. That Easter morn, at break of day,
   The faithful women went their way
   To seek the tomb where Jesus lay. Alleluia!

3. An angel clothed in white they see,
   Who sat and spoke unto the three,
   "Your Lord has gone to Galilee." Alleluia!

4. That night th'apostles met in fear;
   And Christ did in their midst appear,
   And said, "My peace be with you here."
      Alleluia!

5. How blest are they who have not seen,
   And yet whose faith has constant been,
   For they eternal life shall win. Alleluia!

6. On this most holy day of days,
   To God your hearts and voices raise,
   In laud, and jubilee, and praise. Alleluia!

Text: Jean Tisserand, †1494; tr.: John Mason Neale,
   1818-66, alt.
Tune: O FILII ET FILIAE or VICTORY
Music: *CBW II* 506, 503; *CBW III* 404, 395

Be Joyful, Mary, Heav'nly Queen

1. Be joyful, Mary, heav'nly queen,
   Gaude Maria:
   Your Son who died was living seen,
   Alleluia! Laetare, O Maria.

2. The Son you bore by heaven's grace,
   Gaude Maria:
   Did all our guilt and sin efface,
   Alleluia! Laetare, O Maria.

3. The Lord has risen from the dead,
   Gaude Maria:
   He rose with might as he had said,
   Alleluia! Laetare, O Maria.

4. O pray to God, O virgin fair,
   Gaude Maria:
   That he our souls to heaven bear,
   Alleluia! Laetare, O Maria.

Text: Anon., 17th century
Tune: REGINA CAELI, 8.8. with refrains
Music: *CBW II* 497; *CBW III* 460

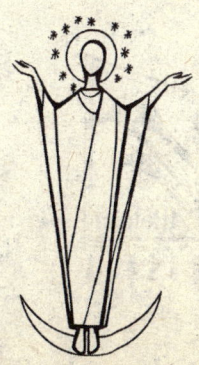

Jesus Christ Is Ris'n Today

1. Jesus Christ is ris'n today, Alleluia!
   Our triumphant holy day, Alleluia!
   Who did once upon the cross, Alleluia!
   Suffer to redeem our loss. Alleluia!

2. Hymns of praise then let us sing, Alleluia!
   Unto Christ our heav'nly king, Alleluia!
   Who endured the cross and grave, Alleluia!
   Sinners to redeem and save. Alleluia!

3. But the pains which he endured, Alleluia!
   Our salvation have procured; Alleluia!
   Now above the sky he's king, Alleluia!
   Where the angels ever sing. Alleluia!

4. Sing we to our God above, Alleluia!
   Praise eternal as his love, Alleluia!
   Praise him, now his might confess, Alleluia!
   Father, Son and Spirit bless. Alleluia!

Text: *Lyra Davidica*, 1708 and others
Tune: EASTER HYMN; 77.77. with alleluias
Music: *CBW II* 500; *CBW III* 389

O Holy Spirit, Lord of Grace

1. O Holy Spirit, Lord of grace,
   Eternal fount of love,
   Inflame, we pray, our inmost hearts
   With fire from heaven above.

2. As you in bond of love do join
   The Father and the Son,
   So fill us all with mutual love,
   And knit our hearts in one.

3. All glory to the Father be,
   All glory to the Son,
   All glory, Spirit blest, to you,
   While endless ages run.

Text: Chas. Coffin, 1679-1749; tr., alt. John Chandler,
1808-76
Tune: ST. ANNE, C.M.
Music: *CBW II* 640; *CBW III* 420

O God of Love, O King of Peace

1. O God of love, O King of peace,
   Make wars throughout the world to cease;
   Our violent ways help us contain;
   Give peace, O God, give peace again!

2. Whom shall we trust but you, O Lord?
   Where rest but on your faithful word?
   None ever called on you in vain;
   Give peace, O God, give peace again!

3. Where saints and angels dwell above,
   All hearts are joined in holy love;
   O bind us in that heav'nly chain;
   Give peace, O God, give peace again!

Text: Sir Henry Williams Baker, 1821-77, alt.
Tune: ROCKINGHAM
Music: *CBW II* 489; *CBW III* 382

Your Very Life

Life-giv-ing bread, blessed and shared,
life-sav-ing cup poured out for all,
feast of the earth, feast of heav'n:
we be-come your ve-ry life.

Fine

1. Je-sus, bread of all our hun-gers;
2. Je-sus, bread of all our long-ings;

Je-sus, bread of all our hopes,
Je-sus, bread of all our needs,

bro-ken and blessed for all to share.
bread of your life so free-ly giv'n.

Je-sus, wine of all our thirsts;
Je-sus, wine of all our sor-rows,

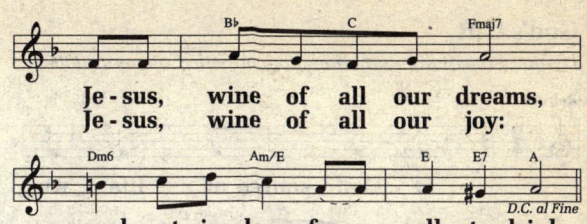

Je - sus, wine of all our dreams,
Je - sus, wine of all our joy:

poured out in love for all to drink.
Come to the feast of the Lamb of God.

D.C. al Fine

Text and music: ©1993 Michel Guimont

God's Gift

Hymn of the 49th International Eucharistic Congress 2008

Refrain

O God source of life, we thank you for your gift: this bread and wine for the life of the world. U-ni-ted in praise, we come to the feast to take in our hands God's gift for life. For this we praise you, Lord. For this we praise you, Lord.

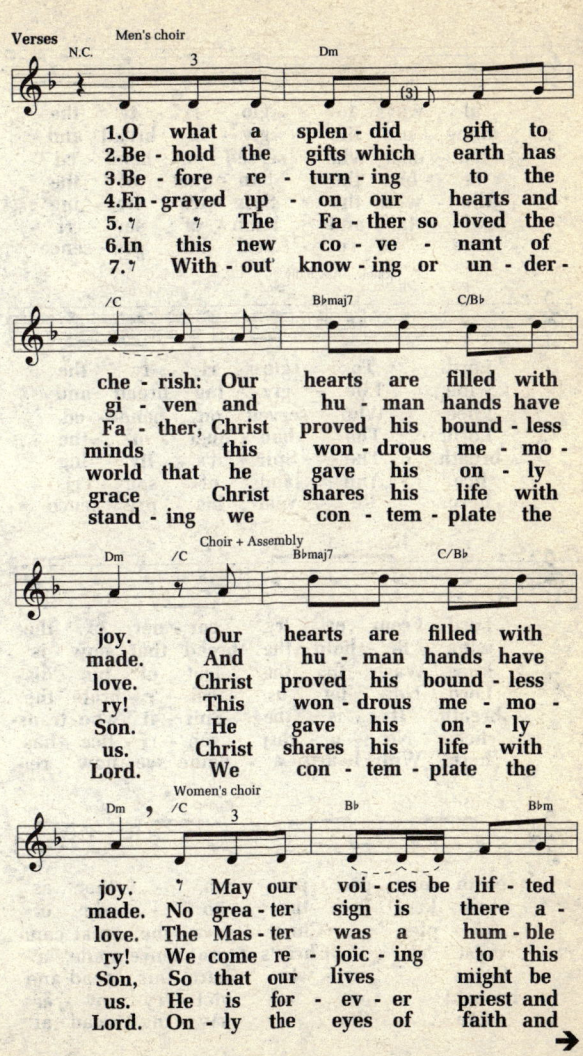

Verses

Men's choir

1. O what a splen-did gift to
2. Be-hold the gifts which earth has
3. Be-fore re-turn-ing to the
4. En-graved up-on our hearts and
5. The Fa-ther so loved the
6. In this new co-ve-nant of
7. With-out know-ing or un-der-

che-rish: Our hearts are filled with
gi-ven and hu-man hands have
Fa-ther, Christ proved his bound-less
minds this won-drous me-mo-
world that he gave his on-ly
grace Christ shares his life with
stand-ing we con-tem-plate the

Choir + Assembly

joy. Our hearts are filled with
made. And hu-man hands have
love. Christ proved his bound-less
ry! This won-drous me-mo-
Son. He gave his on-ly
us. Christ shares his life with
Lord. We con-tem-plate the

Women's choir

joy. May our voi-ces be lif-ted
made. No grea-ter sign is there a-
love. The Mas-ter was a hum-ble
ry! We come re-joic-ing to this
Son, So that our lives might be
us. He is for-ev-er priest and
Lord. On-ly the eyes of faith and

→

649

al - ways to glo - ri - fy the
mong us: life - giv - ing bread and
tea - cher, who served on bend - ed
ta - ble, the ban - quet of the
filled with the Spir - it's liv - ing
al - tar and lamb of sac - ri -
love re - veal his pre - sence

Choir + Assembly
F   /E   Dm   C/E

Lord. To glo - ri - fy the
wine. Life - giv - ing bread and
knee. Who served on bend - ed
Lord. The ban - quet of the
breath. The Spir - it's liv - ing
fice. And lamb of sac - ri -
here. Re - veal his pre - sence

Choir
F   F#dim7   3   Gm   /F

Lord. From ev - 'ry cor - ner of the
wine. Be - hold the bread that now is
knee. Wash - ing the feet of his dis -
Lord. Now let us cel - e - brate the
breath. It is the Spir - it who trans -
fice. No o - ther sac - ri - fice has
here. With hearts a - flame we now re -

Em7(♭5)   B♭/D   C#dim7   Dm

earth may peo - ple ga - ther as
bro - ken; See the bo - dy of
ci - ples, Christ gave the great com-
myst - 'ry, Christ's pre - sence made a -
forms us who share this bread and
brought us vict - 'ry ov - er
ceive the sav - ing bread of

one. U - ni - ted with them in thanks-
Christ. See in the cup of our sal -
mand: What I have done you must do
new; Do not our hearts burn when we
cup in - to the bo - dy of
death. Once and for all his bo - dy
life. This is the One who is our

giv - ing, we cel - e - brate the
va - tion the blood of Christ out -
al - so, now serve with love and
hear him and when we break the
Christ: A sac - ri - fice of
giv - en the world is now made
hope and our com - fort all our

Choir + Assembly

Lord. We cel - e - brate the Lord. O
poured. The blood of Christ out - poured. O
care. Now serve with love and care. O
bread? And when we break the bread? O
praise. A sac - ri - fice of praise. O
new. The world is now made new. O
days. Our com - fort all our days. O

Text: R. Lebel; tr.: B. Gasslein, J. Hibbard, M. Kroetsch
Music: M. Jacques

Feed Us, O Lord

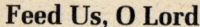

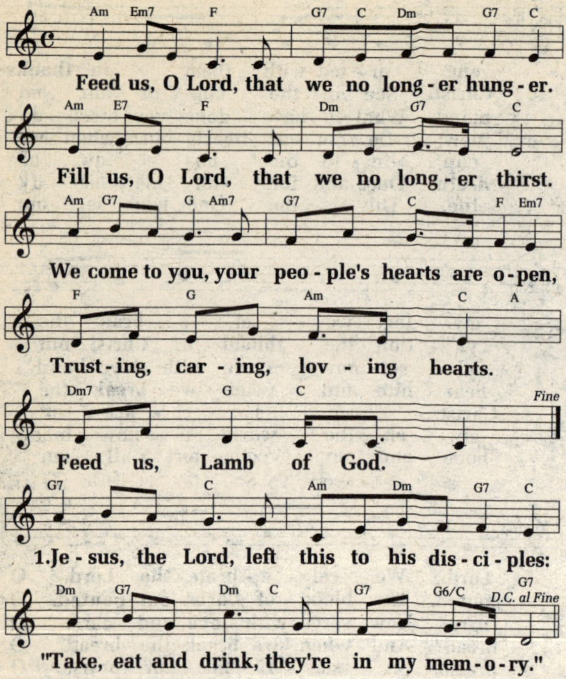

Feed us, O Lord, that we no long-er hung-er.
Fill us, O Lord, that we no long-er thirst.
We come to you, your peo-ple's hearts are o-pen,
Trust-ing, car-ing, lov-ing hearts.
Feed us, Lamb of God.
Fine
1.Je-sus, the Lord, left this to his dis-ci-ples:
"Take, eat and drink, they're in my mem-o-ry."
D.C. al Fine

2. Hear then our prayers,
like those lost in the desert.
Send manna down,
so we, too, know your love.

3. Give us that bread,
so we no longer hunger.
Food for our lives,
no more than this we need.

4. And, as we leave,
   the Christ abides within us.
   We share that Lord,
   that Love with all we meet.

Text and music: ©1992 William J. Turner and the Archdiocese
   of Edmonton

God, Who Gives to Life Its Goodness

1. God, who gives to life its goodness,
   God, Creator of all joy,
   God who gives to all their freedom,
   God who blesses tool and toy:
   Teach us now to laugh and praise you,
   Deep within your praises sing,
   Till the whole creation dances
   God's love filling everything.

2. God, who fills the earth with beauty,
   God, who binds each friend to friend,
   God who names us co-creators,
   God who wills that chaos end:
   Grant us now creative spirits,
   Minds responsive to your mind,
   Hearts and wills your rule extending,
   All our acts by love refined.

Text: © W.H. Farquharson, b. 1936. Used by permission.
Tune: ABBOT'S LEIGH
Music: CBW II 643, 536; CBW III 560, 691

Praise Is Yours, O God, Forever

1. Praise is yours, O God, for - ev - er;
yours all hom - age, Lord, a - lone.
Earth it - self, e - ter - nal Fa - ther,
bows in awe be - fore your throne.
An - gel pow - ers sound your glo - ry:
Ho - ly, Ho - ly God of hosts!
Ho - ly, Ho - ly God of hosts!

2. Glory-crowned apostles praise you,
   white-robed martyrs shout your name.
   Prophet voices give you honour,
   earthly church joins loud acclaim.
   Praise is yours, almighty Father,
   with the Son and Spirit one,
   with the Son and Spirit one.

3. You, O Christ, enthroned triumphant,
   God the Father's only Son,
   scorning not our human nature,
   death defeated, vict'ry won.
   By your blood you brought redemption:
   Grant us glory with your saints.
   Grant us glory with your saints.

4. Come now, Lord, to save your people,
   bless the flock you call your own.
   Day by day we sound your praises,
   evermore your name make known.
   Keep us in your mercy always:
   Lord, in you our hope is sure.
   Lord, in you our hope is sure.

Text: *Te Deum*, tr. ©1996 Raymond J. Lahey, b. 1940
Tune: CWM RHONDDA 87.87.8 and repeat
Music: John Hughes, 1873-1932

O Day of Rest and Gladness

1. O day of rest and glad-ness, O day of joy and light, dis-spell-ing care and sad-ness, most beau-ti-ful, most bright! A count-less host of voi-ces, this no-ble day of days, sings "Ho-ly, Ho-ly, Ho-ly," in joy-ful thanks and praise.

2. This day from life's beginning
   became a day of rest.
   His wondrous triumph winning,
   Christ made this day twice blest:
   the day of re-creation,
   the feast of life and love,
   the day of resurrection,
   when earth joins heav'n above.

3. Today, on all creation,
   God first brought light to birth.
   This day, when dawned salvation,
   Christ rose from depths of earth.
   Today, in blazing splendour,
   came down the Spirit bright,
   each Sunday making glorious,
   with heaven's triple light.

4. Now here in God's own dwelling,
   a grateful church gives praise,
   Christ's glorious deeds retelling
   this day above all days.
   To joyful acclamation,
   his living Word is read;
   in thankful celebration,
   his banquet table spread.

5. By gospel truth enlightened,
   renewed by prayer and praise,
   today, our vision brightened,
   we look to future days.
   Alert and forward facing,
   with awe and wonder filled,
   our daily world embracing,
   God's Sunday world we build.

6. Christ's light in us increasing
   through worship and repose,
   we reach the day unceasing
   that night will never close.
   To Spirit blest sing praises,
   to Father and to Son:
   the church its prayer now raises
   to God, great Three in One.

Text: Vv. 1 and 3: Christopher Wordsworth (1807-1885), alt.
Raymond J. Lahey; vv. 2, 4 and 5: ©1999 Raymond J.
Lahey, b. 1940
Tune: MORNING LIGHT (WEBB), 76.76.D., George James Webb,
1803-87

Praise the Lord

1. Praise the Lord with jub - i - la - tion,
2. Praise the Lord, the God al - migh - ty,
3. Praise the Lord, the God of pow - er,
4. Praise the Lord, the God of won - der,
5. Praise the Lord, the God life - giv - ing,

All God's works, God's whole cre - a - tion.
Daz - zling stars, suns glow - ing bright - ly.
Rush - ing wind and gen - tle show - er;
All on earth, a - bove and un - der.
Ev - 'ry hu - man per - son liv - ing;

Shout a - loud in ex - ul - ta - tion,
Rad - iant light, dis - play God's glo - ry.
Na - ture's for - ces, great and hum - ble,
Bound - less land, blue sky, broad o - cean,
You that car - ry God's own i - mage,

1-5 Bless the Lord, your God!

Bless God, vast hosts of an - gels!
Bless God, swift speed - ing com - ets!
Bless God, strong heat of sum - mer!
Bless God, earth's wond - rous crea - tures!
Bless God, all men and wo - men!

Give praise, all heav-'nly crea-tures!
Give praise, slow moons in or - bit!
Give praise, soft win - ter slow-fall!
Give praise, plants low and loft - ty!
Give praise, both youth and chil-dren!

Round God's throne your wor - ship bring-ing,
Deep - est space, God's ways con - ceal-ing,
Strik - ing hours, God's pres - ence toll-ing,
May your beau - ty al - ways mir - ror
In your lives that like - ness nour-ish;

From the heights, your voic - es ring-ing.
Plan - ets close, God's hand re - veal-ing.
Night and day, God's care un - fold-ing.
God's own splen - dour, ev - en fair - er.
Let God's spark with - in you flour-ish.

1-4 Glo - ri - fy the one who made you.
5 Glo - ri - fy the one who made us.

1-4 Ev - er praise your God!
5 Ev - er praise our God!

Text: ©1997 Raymond J. Lahey, b. 1940; based on Daniel
3.57-82.

Tune: HARLECH, 88.85.77.88.85, traditional Welsh air, adapta-
tion ©1997 Raymond J. Lahey

Jesus Christ Is Lord!

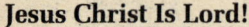

1. Praise Je - sus Christ the Lord! All
2. All praise the Word made flesh, who

praise his ho - ly name: one with the God of
did not claim as right his e - qual stat - us

ma - jes - ty, his form the same. From
as our God nor strength, nor might. With

bend - ed knee, let ev - 'ry voice pro -
grate - ful heart, let ev - 'ry voice pro -

claim that Je - sus Christ is Lord!
claim that Je - sus Christ is Lord!

3. All praise the Son of Man,
   who walked our earthly ways,
   and shared each human's life and toil
   and end of days.
   With blessed hope,
   let every voice proclaim
       that Jesus Christ is Lord!

4. All praise the suffering Christ,
   obedient unto death,
   his lasting trust in God's great love
   his dying breath.
   With humble thanks,
   let every voice proclaim
      that Jesus Christ is Lord!

5. All praise the Crucified,
   now lifted up on high,
   exalted by the pow'r of God,
   no more to die.
   With joyful song,
   let every voice proclaim
      that Jesus Christ is Lord!

6. Praise him at God's right hand,
   his marvellous name make known,
   who pleads for us unceasingly
   before God's throne.
   God's glory sound
   as every voice proclaims
      that Jesus Christ is Lord!

Tune: DARWELL'S 148TH

Peace Be With You!

1. "Peace be with you!" Christ an-noun-ces,

For my wounds will make you whole.

Peace for bo-dy, mind and spir-it,

Peace to heal your wea-ry soul.

Peace, Christ's greet-ing, peace his pro-mise,

Peace, his Eas-ter breath of life,

That the world might know his ris-ing

In the death of all its strife.

2. "Peace be with you!" Christ announces,
   Peace to those both near and far,
   Peace to ocean depths and mountains,
   Peace on furthest newborn star.
   Peace and justice, mercy, freedom,
   Now shall know a second birth,
   As creation's Lord and lover
   Breathes his Spirit on the earth.

3. "Peace be with you!" Christ announces,
   One with him, we sing God's praise,
   Shouts of jubilation sounding
   for the gifts that fill our days.
   For the warmth of love and friendship,
   For the hope of things unseen,
   For the peace beyond all dreaming
   Where God's love will reign supreme.

Text: ©1999 Bernadette Gasslein (b. 1952)
Tune: BLAENWERN 87.87.D.
Music: Wm. P. Rowlands (1860-1937) ca. 1905, © G.A. Gabe

The Beatitudes

1.Blest are they, the poor in spir-it,

theirs in-deed will be the king-dom.

They have wealth be-yond all mea-sure:

Rich in God's own love.

Ev-er blest are those who mourn now,

who must live with grief and sad-ness.

They will have their con-so-la-tion:

God will dry their tears.

2. They are blest, the meek and gentle,
   like the lowly and the humble.
   God will share with them dominion
   over all the earth.
   Those who thirst for right and goodness,
   they must surely know God's blessing.
   All whose hunger is for justice,
   they will have their fill.

3. Those who show a tender mercy,
   that same mercy will be shown them.
   With the pure in heart beside them,
   they will see their God.
   Blest are they who heal division,
   planting peace where there is discord.
   They will be God's sons and daughters,
   close to God's own heart.

4. Blest are those who suffer greatly
   for the service of the Gospel.
   In the kingdom of the righteous,
   glory will be theirs.
   Blest are you if others scorn you
   when you live as my disciples.
   Your reward will be unending:
   truly blest are you.

Text: Based on Matthew 5.13-12, ©1998 Raymond J. Lahey,
     b. 1940
Music: Scots air, adapted.

Love Divine, All Loves Excelling

1. Love divine, all loves excelling,
   Joy of heaven, to earth come down.
   Fix in us thy humble dwelling,
   All thy faithful mercies crown.
   Jesus, thou art all compassion,
   Pure, unbounded love thou art;
   Visit us with thy salvation,
   Enter every trembling heart.

2. Come, Almighty to deliver,
   Let us all thy grace receive;
   Suddenly return, and never
   Nevermore thy temples leave.
   Thee we would be always blessing,
   Serve thee as thy hosts above,
   Pray, and praise thee, without ceasing,
   Glory in thy perfect love.

3. Finish then thy new creation,
   Pure and spotless let us be;
   Let us see thy great salvation,
   Perfectly restored in thee;
   Changed from glory into glory,
   Till in heaven we take our place,
   Till we cast our crowns before thee,
   Lost in wonder, love and praise.

Text: Charles Wesley, 1707-88
Tune: HYFRYDOL, 87.87.D.
Music: *CBW II* 536; *CBW III* 426

For the Beauty of the Earth

1. For the beauty of the earth,
   For the glory of the skies,
   For the love which from our birth
   Over and around us lies,
   Lord of all to you we raise
   This our hymn of grateful praise.

2. For the beauty of each hour,
   Of the day and of the night,
   Hill and vale and tree and flow'r,
   Sun and moon and stars of light.
   Lord of all to you we raise
   This our hymn of grateful praise.

3. For the joy of ear and eye,
   For the heart and mind's delight,
   For the mystic harmony
   Linking sense to sound and sight,
   Lord of all to you we raise
   This our hymn of grateful praise.

4. For the joy of human love,
   Brother, sister, parent, child,
   Friends on earth and friends above,
   For all gentle thoughts and mild.
   Lord of all to you we raise
   This our hymn of grateful praise.

Text: Folliot Sandford Pierpont, 1835-1917, alt.
Tune: DIX, 77.77.77.
Music: *CBW II* 624; *CBW III* 531

This Day God Gives Me

1. This day God gives me
   Strength of high heaven,
   Sun and moon shining,
   Flame in my hearth,
   Flashing of lightning,
   Wind in its swiftness,
   Deeps of the ocean,
   Firmness of earth.

2. This day God gives me
   Strength to sustain me,
   Might to uphold me,
   Wisdom as guide.
   Your eyes are watchful,
   Your ears are list'ning,
   Your lips are speaking,
   Friend at my side.

3. God's way is my way,
   God's shield is round me,
   God's host defends me,
   Saving from ill.
   Angels of heaven,
   Drive from me always
   All that would harm me,
   Stand by me still.

4. Rising I thank you,
   Mighty and strong one,
   King of creation,
   Giver of rest,
   Firmly confessing
   Threeness of Persons,
   Oneness of Godhead,
   Trinity blest.

Text: Ascribed to St. Patrick; adapted by James Quinn, SJ
(1919-2010). Used by permission of Geoffrey Chapman.
A division of Cassell PLC, London, England.
Tune: BUNESSAN, 55.54.D
Music: *CBW II* 724; *CBW III* 650

Lord Jesus Christ, Abide with Us

1. Lord Jesus Christ, abide with us,
   Now that the sun has run its course;
   Let hope not be obscured by night,
   But may faith's darkness be as light.

2. Lord Jesus Christ, grant us your peace,
   And when the trials of earth shall cease,
   Grant us the morning light of grace,
   The radiant splendour of your face.

3. Immortal, Holy, Threefold Light,
   Yours be the kingdom, pow'r, and might;
   All glory be eternally
   To you, lifegiving Trinity.

Text: *Mane nobiscum, Domine; Ach bleib bei uns;* para-
phrased by St. Joseph's Abbey, 1967, 1968; Jerome Leaman
Tune: OLD HUNDREDTH or JESU DULCIS MEMORIA or FULDA
Music: *CBW II* 577, 724; *CBW III* 434, 578, 653

Breathe on Me, Breath of God

1. Breathe on me, breath of God,
   fill me with life anew,
   that I may love the things you love,
   and do what you would do.

2. Breathe on me, breath of God,
   until my heart is pure,
   until with you I have one will
   to live and to endure.

3. Breathe on me, breath of God,
   my soul with grace refine,
   until this earthly part of me
   glows with your fire divine.

4. Breathe on me, breath of God,
   so I shall never die,
   but live with you the perfect life
   in your eternity.

Text: Edwin Hatch, 1835-1889, alt.
Tune: YATTENDON 46
Music: *CBW II* 519

Music Index

Sprinkling Rite